T0276273

CARE *and* MANAGEMENT *of* HORSES

Also available from Eclipse Press

Believe: A Horseman's Journey, Revised Edition

Faraway Horses: The Adventures and Wisdom of One of America's Most Renowned Horsemen, Revised Edition

The Book of Donkeys: A Guide to Selecting, Caring, and Training

The Book of Miniature Horses: A Guide to Selecting, Caring, and Training

The Greatest Horse Stories Ever Told: Thirty Unforgettable Horse Tales

Horsewatching: Why Does a Horse Whinny and Everything Else You Ever Wanted to Know

Understanding Basic Horse Care

Understanding the Broodmare

Understanding Equine Business Basics

Understanding the Foal

Understanding the Pony

Understanding the Stallion

Understanding Your Horse's Behavior

CARE *and* MANAGEMENT *of* HORSES

A PRACTICAL GUIDE for the HORSE OWNER

UPDATED EDITION

Heather Smith Thomas

ECLIPSE
PRESS

Essex, Connecticut

**ECLIPSE
PRESS**

An imprint of Globe Pequot, the trade division of
The Rowman & Littlefield Publishing Group, Inc.
4501 Forbes Blvd., Ste. 200
Lanham, MD 20706
www.rowman.com

Distributed by NATIONAL BOOK NETWORK

Copyright © 2004, 2024 by Blood-Horse Publications
First edition published 2004 by The Blood-Horse, Inc.
Updated edition published 2024 by Eclipse Press

All rights reserved. No part of this book may be reproduced in any form or by any
electronic or mechanical means, including information storage and retrieval systems,
without written permission from the publisher, except by a reviewer who may quote
passages in a review.

British Library Cataloguing in Publication Information available

Library of Congress Cataloging-in-Publication Data

Names: Thomas, Heather Smith, 1944– author.
Title: Care and management of horses : a practical guide for the horse owner /
  Heather Smith Thomas
Description: Updated edition | Essex, Connecticut : Eclipse Press, 2024 | Includes
  index
Identifiers: LCCN 2024020402 (print) | LCCN 2024020403 (ebook) | ISBN
  9781493080816 (paperback) | ISBN 9781493085170 (epub)
Subjects: LCSH: Horses. | Handbooks and manuals.
Classification: LCC SF285.3 .T486 2024 (print) | LCC SF285.3 (ebook) | DDC
  636.1—dc23/eng/20240517
LC record available at https://lccn.loc.gov/2024020402
LC ebook record available at https://lccn.loc.gov/2024020403

♾™ The paper used in this publication meets the minimum requirements of
American National Standard for Information Sciences—Permanence of Paper for
Printed Library Materials, ANSI/NISO Z39.48-1992.

Contents

THIS BOOK IS DEDICATED
to my family:
To my parents, Don and Betty Smith,
who tolerated with good humor
my fanatic love of horses when I was a young child,
and who enabled me to start upon a lifelong journey with horses;
To my husband, Lynn, for his support and patience.
Without his help and partnership
I could not have centered my life on horses;
To my children, Michael and Andrea,
who as youngsters rode long hours with me, riding range,
and who continue an interest in horses;
To their spouses, who are also very much a part
of this horse-loving family;
To my grandchildren, who eagerly started
on the path to good horsemanship,
riding with Grandma to help take care of the cattle,
and to several great-grandchildren
who are expressing an interest in horses at a very young age.

Preface

MY PURPOSE IN WRITING THIS BOOK is to provide a comprehensive handbook for the serious horseperson — novice and professional alike — who is committed to caring for horses. The book discusses conscientious management of horses and givies common-sense advice, including numerous tips and management ideas gleaned from my more than sixty years of studying and working with horses.

While a whole library would be needed for a complete guide to horse care, I have tried to gather as much useful information as possible here to augment the horse owner's ever-growing knowledge of how to keep a horse healthy, sound, comfortable, and happy in the various roles we ask of him. The essence of good horsemanship is working with a horse to bend him to our purpose while interfering least with his natural "horsiness." He is more able to do a good job for us (with less stress, illness, injury, or problem behavior spawned by the frustration of trying to cope with unnatural conditions) if we center our horsekeeping around his needs rather than our desires.

Many horse care books deal with traditional ways of caring for horses. Much of the traditional wisdom, however, centers on making horsekeeping convenient for horseman rather than taking the horse's nature and actual needs into consideration. Much of traditional horse lore addresses how to deal with the problems and vices created by unnatural horsekeeping. This book also addresses how to deal with vices and behavior issues, but my emphasis is on how to avoid these problems as much as possible.

My purpose here is on care and management that encompass the whole horse, mental and physical, with wise use of this animal as we strive to keep him healthy and happy. This focus and priority in dealing with horses will take the horseperson further toward any goal, whether breeding good horses, training for various disciplines, or just using horses for pleasure.

Care & Management of Horses is slanted toward helping the horse owner more fully understand these animals, and the hows and whys of good care. This book provides horse owners with a handy reference for "good horsekeeping" as they develop their own philosophy of horse handling and deal with the day-to-day problems and challenges of horse ownership.

1

An Introduction to Good Horsekeeping:
The Horse in Nature

TO CARE FOR HORSES and handle them intelligently, we need to understand the basic nature of these once-wild yet highly adaptable animals. Even though a horse can adjust to a wide variety of unnatural conditions, many health problems, "stable vices," and handling/training problems stem from artificial conditions in which horses are kept and the unthinking ways we train or handle them. We need to be aware of the physical needs and nature of this large herbivore that evolved roaming vast grasslands. We must understand the emotional and social makeup of this prey animal that depended upon keen senses, athletic ability, and herd life for survival. Physical and emotional stresses due to domestication (which include rich feed, poor conditions for hoof health such as inactivity or standing in mud or manure, emotional stresses due to isolation from other horses, or the boredom of confinement) can contribute to problems the horse owner must try to minimize or contend with.

This book examines the problems of domestication and how the horseman can prevent or deal with them. It discusses practical and safe ways to handle horses, taking into consideration their natural instincts and social structure. The chapter on facilities looks at ways to maintain horses safely — in pastures, paddocks, or barns — with least adverse impact on physical and mental health. Nutritional needs, foot care, and special health considerations that may vary with the seasons are also addressed, giving the horseman a comprehensive guide for total care.

If we never forget the horse's basic nature — physical and emotional — we will do a better job of handling and caring for him.

Understanding how the horse evolved and adapted to his natural environment and social order can help us better understand (and minimize) behavioral and metabolic problems often encountered in horses that live in the artificial environment we provide.

Physical Evolution

The horse's early ancestors were far different from equines today in size, appearance, and interaction with their environment. A vastly changing habitat (from sixty million years ago until the present) created selective pressures that continually shaped and reshaped equine anatomy and behavior. As prey animals, they had to escape carnivorous predators. Of all domestic herbivorous animals, only the horse is descended from an ancestor that depended on flight as its primary survival tactic. Cattle, sheep, and goats had horns as their first line of defense.

The earliest recognized ancestor of the modern horse was a small creature called *Eohippus*, a Greek word meaning "dawn horse." *Eohippus* lived about sixty million years ago at the beginning of a tropical period known as the Eocene epoch. At some earlier point he may have shared a common ancestor with the dog.

An adult *Eohippus* was the size of a small fox, about ten inches tall, with an arched back, long tail, small brain case, egg-shaped head like a sheep, and a slightly tapered muzzle. He had four toes on the front feet and three on the hind, with pads of heavy cuticle on which to walk. *Eohippus* was not built for speed. His teeth were changing from the sharp canine teeth of early meat-eating ancestors to a front set for biting off foliage and a rear set for grinding it up.

The habitat of the dawn horse was swampy and lush with vegetation. *Eohippus* was well suited to this environment, with splayed toes that did not sink into the mud and short teeth for munching soft leaves of shrubs and swamp plants. He scuttled around the forest floor or fed on plants in lowlands bordering the underbrush of forests. He resembled his modern-day relative, the tapir, with splayed toes and pads to rest the toes on, like a dog. His tail was long and held in a curve like a cat's. He was not as fleet as his modern descendants and had to stay constantly alert to avoid large predatory birds. When frightened, he scurried to cover, much like a rabbit.

His backbone was arched; joints between individual vertebrae (especially in the lumbar region between the last rib and the point of the hip) were quite mobile. He could make bending and twisting movements that a modern horse cannot make. When running, he was more flexible than most dogs but not as supple as a cat. He could accelerate rapidly and change direction quickly since his hind legs were longer than his forelegs, similar in posture to a rabbit. His flexible backbone and ground-gripping toes enabled him to dodge at speed around trees and brush.

By contrast, the modern horse is programmed for swift flight in straight lines since his recent ancestors had to adapt to terrain with open spaces. About forty million years ago, when open spaces in the forests first began to appear, several types of animals began to venture out of the woods. Camels were the first to develop the teeth and gut for chewing and digesting grasses, and they preceded the horse in losing the arched spine and its flexibility. Horses and camels developed withers as a firm anchor for the neck, and their lumbar span of vertebrae shortened and strengthened to stabilize the coupling between hind legs and backbone. All these adaptations were needed for straight-line running — a necessary skill for survival in wide-open spaces. After the horse's backbone became less arched and more stable, his legs became longer, enabling him to run faster.

The early horse changed from a browser to a grazer, making changes in teeth and digestion. Evolutionary changes created *Orohippus* and *Epihippus*, and then *Mesohippus* — an animal that was as large as a collie dog. *Mesohippus* was followed by *Miohippus*, who was taller, with a narrow and weak-jawed version of the modern horse's head, a tapered muzzle, and six grinding cheek teeth. As grass became more abundant, many browsing animals were unable to adapt to this new food (grass is tougher and more fibrous than leaves) and became extinct. But the horse's ancestor thrived, assuming a new role as a traveling grazer instead of a small browsing, hiding-in-the-bushes swamp animal. He was the size of a small donkey, with longer cannon bones that enabled him to run faster and survive better in open prairies.

Now called *Merychippus*, he adapted to his new environment by developing long, harder-layered teeth capable of uninterrupted growth (continually moving upward through the gum line in the jawbone). He could graze coarse grasses without wearing out his teeth over a long life span. His tooth pattern altered to permit grinding, and he could eat almost any kind of vegetable matter, including harsh grasses.

As his teeth, backbone, and legs changed, so did his vision. His eyes became larger and wider spaced so he

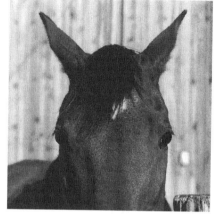

The horse's eye placement evolved.

could see danger on the vast horizons of the plains. This gave him excellent peripheral vision and explains why the horse often startles at things we cannot see. His side-vision (a different picture with each eye) interferes with straight-ahead focus, however, and he has poor depth perception. As a prey animal dependent upon quick reflexes and swift flight, he did not need good depth perception as much as he needed the ability to become instantly aware of any movement around him. A change in head position was a quicker way to focus on something in the distance than a change in pupil shape. This type of vision makes it harder for a horse to focus on something straight ahead, however, and he may raise or lower his head or turn it a bit to get a better look.

As these changes took place in his teeth and eyes, the feet of *Merychippus* became more suited to hard, dry ground. He still had three toes on each foot, but only the enlarged middle toe reached the ground and carried his weight. Eventually all external signs of the outer toes disappeared except for vestigial splint bones on each side of the cannon and the ergots (small round horny growths) at the back of the fetlock.

Seven million years ago the horse's ancestors split into smaller subgroups, and only one of these continued the line that eventually became the modern horse. *Pliohippus* lost his side toes, which, along with an earlier adaptation that limited side-to-side rotation of the foot, enabled him to run more swiftly. The pastern became more upright, and the central toe became a hoof.

The once-large toe pad (shock absorber and ground gripper) became the frog. In the horse's relatives — rhinoceros and tapir — the three-toed frogless foot remained; these animals stayed on the soft footing of river bottoms and jungles. But in the horse line, feet adapted to running on harder ground as the terrain underfoot became drier. The original soft foot pad was likely to be cut or bruised in this terrain and receded to become the frog.

In the modern equine, frog size and shape vary from horse to horse and from species to species (the frog of a zebra, kiang, ass, or donkey is much different from that of a horse), depending on hoof shape and bone structure. In all equines, however, the frog is composed of modified hair-skin material like the rest of the hoof — with the addition of oil glands responsible for the rubbery texture and individual scent. The frog, chestnut, and ergot of the horse exude a scent that makes each individual identifiable and trackable, as when one horse follows the trail of another.

Sometime between one million and 2.5 million years ago, *Pliohippus* became *Equus* — the genus of today — and resembled a zebra. The modern horse descended from ancestors in north central Asia. He perfected sprinting as his best defense in a grassland habitat, where large predatory cats preyed upon him. He had to be able to run far enough and fast enough to outdistance the more short-winded cat.

As the horse's legs and body adapted to faster sprints on the open prairie, his head and muzzle lengthened to accommodate a long row of grinding teeth to make use of abundant grass. The longer nose enabled the horse to develop a sharp sense of smell (with the ability to sort a variety of olfactory signals and decipher pheromones) and to warm and filter the air he breathed before it reached the lungs — an important adaptation for running hard in cold weather. Increased head size also allowed for a larger brain. His body grew larger, with stronger bones and larger muscle mass for strength and speed.

The horse's physical evolution led to important behavioral adaptations that helped him survive. He developed keen senses and quick reactions that enabled him to take advantage of his physical abilities. His mental and emotional makeup would be considered "flighty" — quick to react to any stimuli. His first interaction with humans was as a prey animal; our ancestors were eating horses long before they tried to domesticate them.

Domestic horses came from at least three types of wild horse, which helps explain differences in breeds. In 1949 Swedish zoologist Bengt Lundholm became convinced that modern horses did not spring from just one type of early horse, as people had supposed. He studied skulls of horses dug up in southern Sweden and other fossil remains in western Europe, and found that early horses could be divided into two groups, the main difference being in the relative size of the second and third molars. The eastern group included the Tarpan, Przewalski's horse, and today's Exmoor pony and Polish konik pony (a descendant of the forest Tarpan).

The western group had second and third molars equal in size and could be further divided into two types — a large Germanic type and a much smaller type Lundholm called the *Microhippus* group. The large Germanic horse became the forerunner of the big "forest horse," the heavy draft horses, and some of the Swedish and Gotland horses. The smaller type was the forerunner of Celtic ponies, Fjord ponies, and the Arabian horse. This group diversified, as some stayed north (the ponies) and some migrated south, becoming ancestors of the Arabian.

Lundholm's study provided the first fossil evidence that several types of wild prehistoric horses inhabited Eurasia, and that these gave rise to different domestic types. Early man domesticated local horses and later traded them and selectively bred them for various purposes (some for draft; others for riding, racing, packing, etc.). With selective breeding and interbreeding of different types, domestic breeds became even more diversified.

Horses were probably domesticated about the same time in many places; early remains of horses found with human artifacts have been discovered in China, Turkistan, Mesopotamia, Persia, and the Ukraine. It is impossible to tell from those early remains whether the horse was being used as a beast of burden or a meat animal, or how man captured the first horses. We don't know when humans stopped eating the horse and started using him for transportation, but it was much later than domestication of the dog and cow. He was used in harness long before he was ridden. The horse revolutionized the lives of his human masters, enabling them to become more nomadic, better hunters, or more successful warriors.

The Horse Is Well Adapted To Survive and Cope With His Environment

Even though humans have selectively bred the horse for several thousand years, we haven't changed his basic nature or function. He is still a creature shaped by evolution to live on grassy plains, outrunning predators. His defining characteristics and unique aspects helped him survive and cope with his environment.

Much of the horse's development during the past several million years took place in regions with cold winters, so he is well adapted to cold weather. As days get shorter in the fall, he grows a thick winter coat. His skin thickens, and the capillaries do not bring blood as close to the surface as they do in summer for cooling the blood and for fluid release as sweat; his metabolism is more programmed for conserving body heat than in dissipating it.

He has thicker skin and denser hair along his back and rump, where rain and

Horses adapt well to cold weather.

snow first strike, and he instinctively turns his back to wind and rain. The pattern and lay of the hair on his body channel dripping water to the backs of his legs and to a single drip spot under his belly, to minimize the body area that gets wet.

When a storm hits, horses drift ahead of it to seek shelter behind brush or a contour in the land. They get out of the wind or wait out the storm with their backs to it and heads lowered — using the body as a windbreak for their heads; their well-padded hindquarters take the brunt of the storm. With tail clamped down for protection of their underparts, horses facing away from the wind can withstand a lot of bad weather and conserve body heat. A group of horses stands in a tight bunch, protecting each other from the wind and benefiting from the group's body heat.

A horse can exert strenuously on a cold day, breathing deeply without injuring delicate lung tissues with cold air, thanks to a large empty pocket inside his nose that warms the air. This pocket also helps him communicate with herd members, snorting or whistling to warn them of danger. When he snorts, air blows through this empty pouch, making it vibrate with a loud hollow sound.

During hot weather or exertion, he cools himself by sweating, and his skin dissipates body heat. The hair lies down flatter than normal and loses much of its insulating quality, allowing more heat to escape. The small capillaries bring overheated blood closer to the surface for cooling; the sweat glands open and allow fluid from the bloodstream to escape to the body surface for evaporation, which produces a cooling effect.

Some animals (such as dogs, sheep, and cattle) have few sweat glands and must rely on air exchange through the lungs for cooling. They pant open mouthed for faster air exchange. The horse has more sweat glands than other domestic animals or humans and only rarely has to pant to cool himself. Horses forced to acclimate to strenuous exercise in hot, humid climates will often learn to pant. Generally, however, a horse cools himself adequately by sweating.

Summer brings insects that feed on blood or eye secretions, and the horse developed weapons against these irritating parasites. He has accurate aim with his tail and can swat flies off most areas of his body. A shake of his head and mane usually brushes flies off his face and head. On shoulders, back, and chest (where he cannot reach with the tail), he has a thin sheet of "fly-shaker" muscle; the panniculus muscle can make rippling movements, wiggling the skin to dislodge flies that land there. He cannot vibrate skin on his head and neck so he needs his mane for swishing flies off these areas. He also stomps to dislodge flies on his legs or uses a hind leg to brush flies off his belly or underparts. Horses often stand together fighting flies; a pair of horses will stand head to tail, swishing the flies from each other's head. The horse's long flexible neck enables him to bend around and nose at flies on his sides, udder, or sheath if he cannot dislodge them any other way.

His large head and long neck also help him balance at all gaits and when making sudden changes in direction. By raising or lowering his head, he can counterbalance whatever movements are being made by other parts of his body. And his large head enables him to have wide nostrils and large airways for maximum airflow when running from predators.

His wide-spaced eyes at the outer edges of his face would seem vulnerable to injury, but the bony orbit around them protects them well. So does the dent above his eye (between eye and ear) that goes in and out when he chews. It is part of a fat-filled cavity that lies behind the eye as a cushion. If the eye is bumped, it is pushed back into this cavity and can "give" instead of bursting. If a fly or piece of dirt touches the surface of the eye, it can draw back into the fatty cavity and a third eyelid membrane quickly wipes over the front of the eyeball.

His thin-skinned ears help dissipate heat in summer, and their nervous mobility can tune into sounds from any direction. His ears are full of soft hairs **Horses engage in mutual grooming.** to help keep out flies and dirt. His nose and lips are soft, sensitive, and flexible, the equivalent of the human hand for tactile perceptions. He can wiggle his upper lip when he grazes, sorting grass from weeds or foreign objects. His lips are amazingly adept at sorting out even the tiniest particles of medication you might mix with his grain. His prehensile upper lip is also useful for scratching his back or rubbing an itchy leg, or grooming and communicating with another horse. The long, stiff whiskers on chin and muzzle serve as feelers because he cannot see the end of his nose. Muzzle, lips, and whiskers are his fingertips for gathering information. Whiskers feel the ground (or stall wall) and protect his chin or detect an obstacle in the dark.

For such a large, heavy animal the horse is quite agile and swift, able to travel at speed over firm ground without suffering much concussion because of how his legs and body are constructed for counteracting and dissipating the impact. His body is also designed for spending most of his time on his feet, even when sleeping. Horses can doze standing up, a characteristic developed as a way to escape predators. With his long legs and heavy body, it is a gymnastic feat to get up and down, so adult horses do most of their sleeping standing up — ready to run in an instant. Young horses often sleep stretched out on the ground, since they have ever-watchful adults and the communal alertness of the herd to protect them, but adult horses lie down for only short snatches of deep sleep.

In a band of wild horses, at least one horse is on sentry duty. Even domestic horses rarely sleep all at the same time; most horses in groups take turns standing guard while their pasture mates rest or sleep. Even with his buddies covering for him, the average adult horse sleeps only two and a half to three hours in a twen-

ty-four-hour period — in small snatches — and most of that sleep time is standing; he may spend only forty-five minutes of his total sleep time lying down. The actual amount of sleep will depend on the individual horse and whether he is confined and bored or free to roam. A confined horse will usually spend more hours sleeping per day than an unconfined horse.

While resting or drowsing in light sleep, the horse remains standing, with eyes closed and head drooping, resting a hind leg. He can relax completely while standing, due to strong muscles

Mares guard their sleeping foals.

and neck ligaments that support his head, and the leg joints locking to keep the legs from giving way.

When he is in deep sleep, he must lie down, for at this level of sleep all of his muscles are totally relaxed. Deep sleep is crucial to good health. If deprived of chances for deep sleep (on a long trailer trip, tied in a stall where he can't lie down, or any other unnatural situation), he will make up for it later. Most horses spend about two hours daily (four or five short periods) in intermediate sleep, standing or lying down.

Horses at pasture or in the wild usually nap during the hottest part of the day when things are quiet and there's not much predator activity. In the wild, the horse is nocturnal, grazing when it's cool, staying alert in case of predator threat. The domestic horse, by contrast, may spend some time at night sleeping if he's in a paddock or barn with not much going on. His human-influenced activities all occur during the day, so he may adapt to taking more of his relaxation time at night.

A horse with a leg injury, extreme muscle soreness, or any problem that makes it hard for him to get up and down may not lie down as much as he should (and become short on deep sleep) or may spend too much time lying down. It isn't healthy for the adult horse to spend much time on the ground. Due to the way his body is constructed, it functions best when standing. Changes take place in his respiratory patterns when lying on his side, with pressure and strain on the bottom lung. A horse that is down for a long time due to injury or some other problem becomes susceptible to pneumonia because the lungs can't work properly. A horse in the wild that spends much time lying down generally doesn't last long enough to develop pneumonia since he is slow to get going when the herd takes off and the most vulnerable to predators.

The horse's keen senses aid him in survival and in communication with the rest of the herd. Smell is the most important social sense — for identifying individuals. Sense of smell is crucial in the bond between mare and foal; they identify each other by smell more than by sight or sound. At a distance a horse cannot identify an individual by sight except by body language and way of moving, but the smell test is always accurate. Horses smell manure to identify each other (stallions mark their territories with piles of manure) and can detect the smell of an individual's track (from oil secretions of the frog).

Horses can smell fear and other emotions of another horse by the hormone-like secretions (in sweat and urine) called pheromones. Pheromones are also sexual signals; a stallion can distinguish a mare in heat from other mares and can detect a mare in heat as far away as two hundred feet (farther if the wind currents are coming his way) without seeing her. He can tell the difference between a mare in true estrus and one that has been injected with estrogen to create an artificial heat, by smelling her urine. He can also "read" postures and body language, which give clues to a mare's status.

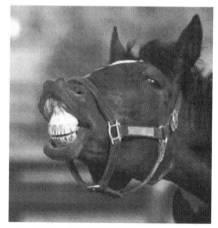

The flehmen posture.

When checking a mare's sexual status, the stallion smells her urine and then sticks his nose in the air, curls back his upper lip, and closes his nostrils to a slit as he draws air into a special organ inside the nasal passage. This organ captures and sorts the chemical odors for thorough molecular analysis. This lip-curled, nostril-clamped facial expression is called the flehmen posture, and it enables the horse to interpret olfactory information better. The stallion expresses this behavior the most, but any horse encountering an unusual smell (cigarette smoke, a certain dewormer, etc.) may do it to help sort out the strange odor and try to identify it. A horse may occasionally exhibit this facial posture when meeting and "checking out" a strange horse or smelling another horse's urine.

Sense of smell is also important to a horse in finding his way, whether following the trail of other horses or determining where he is on his home range. Horses can track other horses or retrace their own steps, mainly because of odors left in their wake. Domestic horses can unerringly find their way home even when hauled a long distance, and they generally pick the most direct route. Their homing abilities are best when the wind is blowing at them from the home direction, indicating that they are using scents (getting a smell of something familiar) to guide them. Even in a strange place, a horse is more likely to head into the wind (except when waiting out a storm with his back to it) because he feels safer being able to smell what might be ahead of him.

The horse also uses his nose to select what he eats. He smells the grass that grows up around horse manure and refuses to eat it unless there is nothing else to eat (thus protecting himself from infestation by parasites whose larvae crawl onto the forage plants) and also refuses feeds with an unusual smell. He may still eat a poisonous plant (his smell and taste test is not always enough to protect him from certain toxins) but usually is hesitant to eat something totally different from what he is accustomed to eating; the domestic horse may refuse a new feed or a medication in feed just because it is different. This may be part of an instinct to stick to the "safe" things he is accustomed to eating.

All of a horse's senses — sight, sound, smell, taste, and touch — are more acute than ours, partly because of his priorities in learning all he can about his surroundings and storing information crucial to survival in the wild. Horses know their world far more intimately than we do, and every day of their lives they collect smells and listen to the sounds of their environment, storing memories of sight, sound, smell, and taste. The horse is constantly sorting and storing information and never forgets it.

The horse also has a "sixth sense," a combination of ground sense and radar. Horses read the ground underfoot with more than just their eyes and can traverse difficult terrain at great speed with agility and balance — partly because of their proprioceptive abilities (unconscious sense of where the body and limbs are at any given moment) and partly because of ability to feel their footing.

The hind feet automatically follow the steps of the front feet over difficult obstacles, but the horse's ground sense goes beyond that. He can sense vibrations and changes underfoot that tell him whether ground is solid or soft, smooth or rough, or hard or crumbling. This foot sense can alert a horse to the distant vibrations of an oncoming herd or things such as earthquakes before humans can sense them.

The horse's heightened senses and intuitive abilities to judge space and body relationships are similar to that of flocking birds that can fly in large groups and never run into one another. A mare and foal can gallop madly around a pasture, or a group of horses dash over the range at full speed (as when chased — traveling too fast to consider unfamiliar and precarious terrain), and they never run into one another, stumble or fall, or trample the young ones underfoot. They flow as a unit, keeping ideal body spacing between them like birds in flight — banking and turning, wheeling and flowing as one. This kind of instinctive herd intelligence is something the horse must have developed as he became a fleet gregarious plains animal that depended upon herd life for survival.

Horses have a sense of space.

The horse today is a product of millions of years of shaping. A few thousand years of human intervention and selective breeding have made him more refined, graceful, and finer boned (we've increased his size and lung capacity without increasing the circumference and strength of his leg bones) and possibly made him less hardy and durable (with smaller, weaker feet and less toughness against the elements), but we haven't changed his basic body systems. His digestive tract still functions better when processing natural feeds such as grasses than it does grain, molasses, alfalfa, or other foods that humans have introduced into his diet. His teeth are best adapted for chewing grasses rather than grains, and his gut best handles continual small amounts (grazing through the day and night).

Because he is a grazer, moving continually as he eats, his feet and legs are designed for constant travel and are healthiest when he is active. The hooves of feral equines that travel many miles a day are harder, tougher, and stronger than those of most confined horses and have proper foot angle from natural wear. Hoof and circulatory problems arise when a horse is confined and inactive (stocked up legs, inefficient blood supply to the navicular bone, etc.). His physical and mental health are both at risk when he is put into an unnatural environment.

Psychological Evolution

As a prey animal, the horse developed a finely tuned nervous system to keep him constantly aware of danger. While highly adaptable, enabling him to be trained by humans, the horse is still a creature mentally and emotionally programmed for flight, happiest in a herd, and ready to flee from any real or perceived danger at the slightest hint of trouble.

It is this flightiness that makes horses prone to many types of injury in an artificial environment. It is also the reason that horses can be hard to handle and even dangerous, requiring a certain amount of "horse sense" and skill in handling and training them. People who do not understand a horse's basic nature are apt to think him stupid because he causes injury to himself or humans in situations we consider safe and logical. Nothing in his development, however, prepared him for fences, barriers, noise, confined spaces like horse trailers, or crowds of people. He has a distrust of dark or enclosed places or deep woods with low-hanging tree branches since predators could be lurking there.

It is amazing that this flighty, timid creature has been able to adapt to the demands of humans — pulling carts, chasing cattle, charging into battle, living in barns, riding in trailers, jumping obstacles, participating in horse shows, races, and parades where multitudes of people create an abundance of noise. Some horses adapt better and learn alternative behaviors rather than fight or flight. These individual differences greatly affect whether a certain horse is suitable for a particular career, owner, or circumstance.

The horse's basic instincts include the will to survive (self-preservation being the strongest motivator of equine behavior) and the desire to eat, be comfortable and avoid pain, reproduce, protect offspring, and communicate and interact with other horses. The will to survive dictates almost all his actions and reactions. To him, the safest response to anything unusual is flight. When faced with an unfamiliar situation, creature, or object, he relies on herdmates' responses to help guide his reaction. If one horse in a group jumps or bolts because of a perceived threat (a noise in the grass, a bit of movement behind him), they all bolt, and the action is nearly simultaneous. Group flight was the best defense against a predator attack; any horse that was slow was the one most likely to be caught and eaten.

If the perceived threat does not materialize (the rustle in the grass was just a

As prey animals, horses are programmed for flight.

gust of wind or the movement was only a bird), a jumpy horse goes back to grazing and his herdmates do the same. A horse is highly influenced by what the other horses are doing. If the rest of the herd is calm, he gains assurance from their lack of fear and holds his ground while he gathers more information (trying to get a better look, listen, or smell of the unfamiliar object of his attention). He may freeze, directing his focus on determining whether the strange thing is dangerous. His motionlessness not only minimizes his own visibility to a predator (since most animals perceive movement before recognizing a stationary object), but also helps him direct his senses.

His first response to sudden noise or movement is to whirl and run or leap away from the threat. This "startle response" or shying, is part of his instinct for self-preservation. If a threat is too close for comfort and he feels trapped or is startled by something that comes upon him before he is aware, his instinct is to defend himself — striking or kicking. His desire to avoid pain or discomfort is another manifestation of this self-preservation instinct and may make him resent or fight medical treatments or other things we humans try to do to him.

A mare's instinct to protect her new foal may come to the fore rather sharply; sometimes a human owner is surprised to find an old dependable mare suddenly aggressive and threatening. Though horses adapt to human handling (and may trust and respect their owners), a mare's instinct to protect her foal should not be taken lightly.

The basic instinct for nourishment keeps the horse eating or nibbling more or less constantly, since his digestive system is adapted to nearly continuous grazing. In the wild, availability of adequate grass depended on the season, weather conditions, and the number of grazing animals using a region. As a survival tactic the horse is programmed to eat at every opportunity, spending up to 70 percent of his time grazing. The domestic horse can get by on less frequent, more concentrated meals, leaving more of his day free for human use, but he still prefers to eat continuously.

The horse's dependence upon herd life was part of his survival strategy in the wild, and he keeps that instinct in domestication. Many horses are reluctant to leave pasture mates or stablemates and refuse to leave home or become frustrating to their riders because of their hurry to return to their buddies. The horse is merely following his instinct that tells him he is safer and better off as part of a group; it is unnatural for him to be alone.

To survive in group society, horses — like other herd species — develop a hierarchy among the group to establish who leads and who follows, who bosses and who is bossed. The social order and interdependence within the herd were crucial for survival and also the reason humans could readily domesticate and train horses. The horse handler assumes dominance in the relationship, taking on the role of the lead mare in the herd.

The leader of a group of horses, wielding the most authority, is generally an "alpha" mare — an older, aggressive individual who has established her role as boss. She determines when the herd flees, which direction it goes, and when it stops to rest, graze, or go to water. She makes the decisions, drinks first, rests in the best shade, eats the best feed (and sometimes drives off younger mares in heat until she has been bred and settled). Since she has already established dominance she rarely asserts herself to keep her top spot; a mere threatening gesture with ears back, tail swishing, or raised hind foot is enough to keep lower-ranking herd members in place. She leads the herd, and even the stallion defers to her, bringing up the rear to keep stragglers moving.

Each member of the herd has a place in the social order; the second highest-ranking individual can threaten any horse but the alpha mare. Each horse has certain individuals it can boss and those it is bossed by, down to the horse that is bossed by everyone else and threatens none. Immature horses are submissive to adults, but as they grow up, the aggressive ones challenge the ranking and find their own place in the hierarchy.

Both dominant and submissive individuals can be successfully trained, especially if proper training is begun while they are young. The point at which humans enter and influence the horse's life makes a difference in our success, especially when handling dominant individuals. A captured wild horse is easier to train as a foal or yearling than an older stallion or alpha mare. Some independent and aggressive mature horses that are not handled until late in life are more difficult to domesticate fully. Submissive individuals may train easily at any age, while a very independent animal may be a challenge even as a youngster.

Usually the younger the animal when training begins, the easier the task of gaining his trust if he's timid or instilling respect if he tries to be dominant. Until about two years of age, young horses tend to be submissive to adults in the herd and to human handlers who assume that role. The aggressive youngster, however, may be a difficult challenge to an unskilled trainer and is best put in his place by an older dominant equine. Herd life is often the best teacher for impressing upon the aggressive young horse that he's not boss.

The horse is fairly willing to shift his allegiance to humans — transferring his tendency to submit to an older member of the herd or to a dominant herd boss. Horses are very manageable if their human handlers understand this aspect of their nature and assume the proper role (not letting a horse become the dominant one in the relationship). The human trainer acquaints the horse with "threat" cues that can be very subtle — such as the pressure of a leg or a voice command such as "whoa" — reducing the need for actual physical reprimands, just as the alpha mare needs only a gesture to make a herd mate obey her. Body language is adequate communication.

2

Problems of Domestication

THE FREE-ROAMING EQUINE is perfectly adapted to his natural habitat. When natural conditions are good, he is the epitome of physical and emotional good health. By contrast, domestic horses are prone to ailments unheard of in wild horses — athletic injuries, digestive disorders, contagious diseases, hoof problems, skeletal disorders in young growing horses, etc., plus a host of emotional and behavioral problems.

When the horse was domesticated, he was forced to live in situations convenient for man but unnatural for him. He has adapted reasonably well to these artificial situations — though some horses adjust better than others — but unnatural conditions can cause problems. The incidence and degree of these problems may depend upon the nature of the individual horse, the extent to which his natural environment or experiences are altered, and his reaction to these situations. Horses kept at pasture in a herd may not develop some of the physical or psychological problems that plague horses kept in stalls or in isolation from other horses, for instance.

In some ways, horses living under human care are better off than their wild counterparts (always having food available, safe from predators, secure in their "home space," and able to relax more completely than any wild horse ever does), but every horse has a limit to how much confinement or unnatural care he can tolerate. When intensive human management crosses that line, the horse's health and mental well being suffer.

Confinement is convenient for humans but hard on horses.

"Confinement is hard on a horse's feet and disposition" as old-timers used to say. The mental stress of being confined can be devastating; confinement is totally unnatural for a horse. Most neurotic stable vices such as weaving, stall kicking, cribbing, and wood chewing result from being cooped up with nothing to do or being isolated from other horses. The greater the contact a horse has with other horses or with what is going on around him outside the stall, the less likely he will develop frustrated behavior. A horse crowded into a small area with too many other horses also may develop vices.

The horse is a creature of open spaces, wandering and grazing. He'll eat awhile — moving as he grazes — rest awhile, then graze again. His almost constant routine of eating and motion aids digestion and waste elimination (he rarely develops impaction), respiration, and circulation. His feet and legs are designed for moving; if he is stationary too long, their circulation is impaired.

Physical Consequences of Confinement

The stress of confinement may hinder a horse's immunity to diseases (prolonged stress with production of cortisol within the body interferes with proper

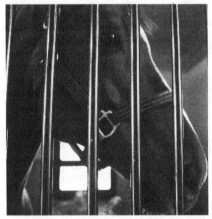

function of the immune system), making the horse more vulnerable to infectious illnesses. Respiratory problems are common in stall-bound horses, partly because of the underuse of their lungs due to inactivity and partly due to the dusty atmosphere in most enclosed areas. A stall's dust-laden air can harbor mold spores, bacteria, and other pollutants that may overwhelm the respiratory tract. Chronic cough may result or acute respiratory infections. Horses confined in stalls eating hay from a feed rack are also deprived of normal head-down grazing, a position that keeps the respiratory tract free of mucous secretions. High ammonia levels in many stalls cause respiratory problems, particularly in foals.

The immune system can suffer.

Digestive Problems

The horse's digestive tract works best when small amounts of roughage are continually passing through. He has a small stomach compared with that of a ruminant like the cow; a horse's stomach holds only about two to three gallons of chewed, liquefied feed (and accounts for only about 9 percent of the total digestive tract's capacity).

The microbes in his cecum (the large pouch that serves as a fermentation vat) help break down otherwise indigestible fibrous portions of roughage. The population of "gut bugs" stays in balance with the digestive job at hand. Colic is rare in free-roaming horses but is the number one killer of domestic horses, partly due to unnatural feeds and to confinement.

Colic occurs in domesticated horses.

Many horses are confined and fed hay and grain. The latter is an unnatural feed; the horse is best adapted to digesting forages that are low in energy and high in fiber. The bacteria population in his digestive tract changes to accommodate a high-carbohydrate diet such as grain, and this creates a greater risk for problems such as stress colic or founder. Changes in diet — even just adding a little more grain to the ration if the horse is already getting a lot — or a combination of stress (emotional or physical) and high-quality feeds can change the chemistry of digestion, altering the "gut bug" population.

Anaerobic bacteria may multiply rapidly for a while and then die off in large numbers, releasing endotoxins. This creates a potentially deadly condition called endotoxemia. This can result in serious colic or laminitis. Even just the stress of being confined in a stall, especially for a high-strung or nervous horse, may lead to indigestion and colic.

Hay is a more natural feed (unless it is rich alfalfa), but we still disrupt the horse's normal eating habits if he is confined and fed just twice a day. He eats for only a couple hours in the morning and again in the evening, instead of interspersing his eating with all his other activities through the day and night. Standing idly for an extended period without eating (if he has a placid nature) or pacing nervously in the stall between meals can interfere with the normal digestive process and microbe action in the gut. The large blocks of time in which he has nothing to do may cause boredom or anxiety, depending on the individual horse, and either condition can lead to abnormal behavior.

The mental stress of being confined, along with the unnatural feeds and feeding times, can set a horse up for colic. Athletic horses accustomed to steady exercise that are suddenly confined because of injury or some other situation often develop colic. The colic risk can be more deadly than the injury. An injured horse is usually confined in a stall because of human reasons, such as convenience for treatment, time factors, or ease of handling. Except for very serious injuries in which a horse should not move, most injured horses are better off in a pen, where they can move around a little and function more normally.

In a stall, most horsemen keep feed tubs, waterers, feed racks, or mangers up off the ground, often as high as a horse's shoulder, to avoid contamination of feed and water with manure or to keep the horse from pawing them. But eating or drinking with the head this high is unnatural for the horse. He does not exercise his neck muscles properly and increases the risk of food going "down the wrong way" into the windpipe. There is also more risk of choke (food blockage in the esophagus) due to improper eating and spilling over into the windpipe if the horse cannot lower his head to cough it out. This can be fatal if the horse is tied while eating (in a tie stall or eating from a trailer manger) and is unable to lower his head to drain off the backed-up fluid.

Feet and Leg Problems

Confinement is also hard on a horse's feet and legs. Circulation in the lower legs depends on muscle activity along with expansion and contraction of the

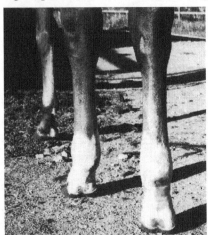

feet. It's easy for the circulatory system to supply blood to the lower leg, but getting the blood back up the leg is more difficult. The horse depends on movement for proper function; most veins are located between masses of muscle. As these muscles contract with activity, they squeeze the veins, aiding return of blood to the heart.

In the foot, the frog acts like a little pump at the end of the line. Each time the horse puts weight on a foot and the hoof walls expand, the sole flattens. When the foot is lifted, the walls spring back into place, the sole returns to normal position, and the frog push-

These legs are stocked up.

es the blood on its way. Movement keeps the circulatory system efficient and maintains the health of feet and legs.

The confined horse, eating feed he can consume while standing still, may be immobile for hours at a time. His heart is pumping blood down to his feet but getting little help in its return. In severe cases of inactivity, immobility may lead to contracted feet or navicular disease. Overweight horses, pregnant mares, or lame horses that favor a good leg are especially susceptible to foot problems from immobility. Any horse may develop temporary edema in the lower legs (called stocking up — swelling due to leaking of fluid into spaces between cells from increased capillary pressure) from prolonged inactivity. Often just hind legs are affected since circulation is poorer there to begin with.

Some horses stock up more readily than others; their legs may swell just from spending time in a stall overnight when they are accustomed to moving around a large pen or pasture. Others stock up if confined after a long ride or strenuous exercise. Confining a horse accustomed to freedom of movement is the most common cause of stocking up. The swelling can be a continuous problem for some horses in stalls or small paddocks. The less exercise you are able to give a horse, the more room he needs to provide it for himself.

Navicular disease is a common problem in confined horses, especially those with feet too small for their body weight. It has been called the man-made crippler, as it is rarely seen in free-roaming horses. One cause of navicular disease is improper foot angle, such as long toes and low heels — a problem that can occur when horses don't get enough exercise to wear their feet properly or are not trimmed or shod properly.

Many horsemen overfeed and confine their animals, making them vulnerable to problems. Feet and legs are durable when a horse is doing things he was programmed for, such as traveling long distances barefoot at moderate speeds. As the hoof continually takes and releases weight, it expands and contracts, aiding circulation. Natural hoof wear creates a normal foot angle. The demands on feet and legs by man's requirements, however, make the navicular bone's circulation system vulnerable to problems.

A horse may also develop navicular disease if he stands in a stall with sloping sides, putting his feet off level. The forces on his navicular bone as he stands on an upslope are the same as if he had long toes and low heels, putting a constant, unyielding load on leg and foot. This problem is compounded if the foot is levered up in front (with a long toe) and is low in back (low heel). If front feet are not allowed to load and unload continually by moving (as they carry two-thirds of the horse's weight), oxygen supply to the navicular bone is reduced, starving the tissues and damaging the bone. If a horse must be confined in a stall, a roomy box stall with a slight hump in the floor rather than a depression in the center is best.

Another foot problem that can occur with confinement is thrush, especially if a horse spends time in a wet, muddy pen or a stall that is not regularly cleaned. If the bottom of the hoof is packed with mud or manure and no air gets to it, infectious organisms that cause thrush may proliferate. Thrush (a foul-smelling infection of the frog) can be prevented by keeping the horse in a cleaner environment, cleaning out his hooves often, and applying iodine along the frog if the problem gets started. Exercise on dry ground, allowing the foot to dry out and air to get to it, is the best preventative.

2

Emotional Consequences of Confinement

All too often we tend to "kill our horses with kindness" or do them harm with our good intentions. We pamper them too much and don't allow them to live normal lives, thinking we are doing them a favor. We expect them to behave politely even when isolated from other horses or confined, expecting them to accept the unnatural conditions of stall life or to perform in an athletic career and live in a stall during off hours. Yet many horses cannot adjust that well to the human-controlled environment or to many hours alone. This can lead to both physical and emotional stress.

Bad weather may tempt you to put your horse in a stall, but outdoor horses have the lowest incidence of respiratory disease and colic. Many horsemen do

Confinement can lead to vices.

not realize how hardy and resilient their horses are. When given a choice of shelter or staying outdoors in bad weather, horses will stay outside unless weather is severely stormy. Horses will seek shelter from wind or rain but rarely from the cold.

Most horses would be better off if allowed to spend more time at pasture with compatible herd mates. They need to graze, exercise by running and playing, and interact with companions. The horse is an animal of action, constantly using his mouth for eating, and his feet for socializing and travel-

ing. If these activities are thwarted, he may resort to alternative behaviors in an attempt to compensate for his unnatural lifestyle. These behaviors involve frustrated attempts at traveling (weaving, stall walking) or grazing (oral vices like wood chewing or cribbing).

Weaving, in which the horse rhythmically shifts weight from one foreleg to the other, or stall walking, in which he walks or trots around his stall in a fixed pattern, may be efforts to escape confinement. Vices such as stall kicking or pawing may develop as a form of self-stimulation. A horse with a lot of nervous energy is not going to stand idly for hours at a time and will figure out some means to expend his energy and vent his frustration. Stable vices are man-made. The horse can't spend time grazing; he eats his highly concentrated, human-designed meals in a short time and has hours with nothing to do. Boredom spawns abnormal activities, as does the anxiety he may feel when confined.

The horse most likely to develop what we call a vice is usually a nervous, hyperactive, sensitive individual kept in a stall or small paddock and fed a high-energy diet. Placid draft horses and ponies rarely crib or weave; they seem to adjust to boredom and inactivity more easily. Thoroughbreds seem prone to habits spawned by frustration, but they are also the horses most likely to be locked in stalls most of the day and fed lots of carbohydrates. Isolating horses provokes a state of insecurity in which they are more likely to develop abnormal behavior. The longer a horse is bored or has no social stimulation, the more frequently he indulges in abnormal behavior.

A Closer Look at Cribbing

A cribber is usually a horse that needs something more to do. Horses that can occupy their time with grazing and normal "horse" activities usually don't turn to cribbing.

Cribbing ("crib biting") occurs when a horse grips a horizontal surface such as a fence rail or manger (in earlier times called a "crib") with his teeth. He anchors his top teeth over the object or presses them into the wood and lets his lower jaw hang slack, then flexes his neck, opens his throat, pulls back with his mouth open, and swallows air with a grunting sound. He may draw air into his mouth as he bites onto the wood surface, then swallows air into the esophagus with a backward jerk of his chin. Some horses can flex their necks and swallow air without having to grasp an object. Swallowing air is called aerophagia or "wind sucking," but the latter term is confusing as it's also used to describe mares that suck air into the vagina when trotting or galloping.

Cribbing is a stereotypic behavior, a repetitive action that an animal develops in response to stress. The action stimulates endorphins in the body, which help relieve the stress. In the 1980s a team of researchers at Tufts University School of Veterinary Medicine in Massachusetts discovered why horses crib and why the habit is so persistent. They found that horses given morphine showed an increase in stereotypic behavior. Morphine and endorphins (the body's natural "opiates") are very similar, and horses can become "addicted" to the effects of cribbing. In experiments, when cribbers were given narcotic-blocking drugs that neutralize the endorphins, they ceased cribbing.

Researchers at Tufts thought the frustration of isolation and confinement (or waiting for food), and the horse's attempts to escape it, caused cribbing. As the horse's frustration mounts, his escape attempts (which might at first consist of walking around looking for a way out, pawing at the door, or biting it) become increasingly frantic. Then he discovers his frenzied actions are rewarded by a feeling of calm brought on by release of endorphins that stimulate the brain's pleasure center. So the horse repeats the action; the behavior becomes a habit, even if his stress is alleviated.

Horsemen used to think that air gulping would cause chronic indigestion or flatulent colic due to buildup of gas in the stomach and intestine. A horse doesn't burp very readily to relieve gas pressure — the way his esophagus is constructed, it is hard for anything to come back up from the stomach.

In 1995 researchers in the United Kingdom discovered that most cribbers do not actually swallow air (as people previously thought); they gulp it into the esophagus where it comes right back up, rather than going into the stomach. Cribbers tend to have more gastrointestinal problems such as recurrent colic, gastritis, and ulcers than the average horse population, but researchers are not sure whether these problems are due to cribbing or the stress that leads to crib-

Cribbing is a man-made vice.

bing. These problems may be interrelated; ulcers and cribbing are caused by stress (ulcers are common in domestic horses, especially those in performance careers).

The cribber shows abnormal wear of the upper front teeth due to continual wood grabbing. A habitual cribber may wear the top front teeth completely away and create malocclusion (teeth become so worn they do not meet when the mouth is closed, and the horse cannot graze properly) and dental disease in the molars. Some cribbers have misshapen teeth that slant

forward more than normal due to the repeated pulling on objects. Damaged teeth and improper chewing may contribute to weight loss and colic. Cribbing can lead to unsightly extra muscle development in the lower part of the neck, which interferes with neck flexibility when the horse is ridden. In addition to the problem of damaged teeth, serious cribbers may lose weight because they become so addicted to their habit that they'd rather crib than eat. Some will crib between mouthfuls of food or stop eating to crib.

Cribbing can be detrimental to the horse in severe cases, but generally this habit is more destructive to the facility in which the horse is kept, which can frustrate the horse owner. Once the habit starts, many horses keep cribbing even if given access to pasture and grass and end up killing trees, damaging fences, and destroying stall dividers and feed boxes. The confirmed cribber continues his habit because of the stimulation. Many cribbers display other stall habits such as pacing or weaving— to occupy themselves with one compulsive behavior or another.

Once started, cribbing is a habit almost impossible to break. Cribbers are a bad influence on other horses that may mimic and pick up the habit. Young horses, especially, often imitate their elders, and a cribber in the barn may start others cribbing, or a foal may learn the habit from its mother.

Horse owners have tried many ways to halt cribbing, including surgery to remove muscles and/or nerves to the muscles involved. Prevention is much easier than a cure and mainly consists of letting the horse live a more natural life.

The confined horse has no way to channel his energy or social needs, so he tries to release his frustration through other means such as stall walking, pawing, or cribbing. These rhythmic actions invented by a confined or frustrated horse are similar to other stereotypical behaviors such as paw-licking in bored dogs, cage pacing in zoo animals, feather plucking in caged birds, etc.

In horses these repetitive actions were earlier called stall vices and include head bobbing, kicking the wall, chewing at themselves, hanging the tongue out the side of the mouth, blanket chewing, and obsessive water drinking. The term "vice" is actually not appropriate; vices are undesirable behaviors (such as bucking or biting) that can generally be corrected through proper handling and training. A stereotypy is an obsessive-compulsive behavior that is often an abnormal expression of otherwise normal behavior. The habit involves a need-related drive developed in an environment that thwarts opportunities for satisfying the need.

When a horse develops abnormal behavior, it's a clue that something is seriously wrong with his environment and his needs are not being met. Once established, a stereotypic behavior can become a need in itself, and the horse insists on continuing it. Underfeeding, restricted feeding, and insufficient roughage are triggers for oral compulsions, such as cribbing, that later become preferred pastimes regardless of how much feed the horse is given.

When dealing with a horse that performs stereotypic actions, it is important to remember that punishment is not effective and that the behavior is simply a result of the horse's attempt to cope with a stressful environment. A change in environment is the best solution but may not solve the problem if the horse is already addicted to his habit.

Allow a horse as much room and activity as possible where he has things to do and see. Feed more roughage and less grain or smaller amounts more often so the horse spends more time eating and less time inactive. He won't have so much energy to burn. Pasture time is best, but if this is impossible, devise ways to increase his eating time in stall or paddock.

Some horsemen use a double hay net (two or even three hay nets wrapped around several flakes of hay) to make the horse work harder at get-

Electric wire discourages cribbing.

31

ting the hay out, thus spending more time eating. Hang some hay in several corners of the stall to encourage the horse to move around more while he eats. If using a hay feeder, put two-inch wire mesh along the front of it (with no sharp wires protruding) so the horse can only pull out small amounts at a time, or put a bale of hay in a rack with very narrow openings. Today there are "slow feeders" commercially available that have very small openings. If he can only pull out a few wisps of hay at a time, he can spend the whole day "grazing" rather than eating his food in a short time. Make sure part of his hay ration is lower in energy and nutrition (such as late-cut grass hay) so it provides more fiber and less nutrients, giving him more eating time without providing excess energy or making him fat.

If he's in a paddock, put electric wire along the fences so he stays back from them and never grabs onto the posts or poles. If he must be in a stall, give him a window so he can see what's going on outside. Offer him toys to keep him occupied. An old tire, a big nylon or rubber ball, or something indestructible to play with may help, or give him a rubber feed tub, a partially deflated soccer ball hung from the ceiling, a string of bells, or a plastic jug with a few rocks so he can rattle it. You may have to change toys every few days to give him something new to divert his attention. Sometimes a radio playing at a moderate level can help keep a horse more interested in his surroundings, more mentally occupied.

Horses have a hard time cribbing on objects below knee level, so feed bunks can be lowered. Make sure stall walls are "slick" so the horse cannot get a toothhold on any edge or projection. You may have to cover the window edge or stall door with metal sheeting (with no protrusions that might injure his mouth) or use foul-tasting substances on some of these surfaces.

Companionship can keep a horse healthier and happier.

Provide a way he can be near or see other horses. Isolation is more frustrating to him than is confinement, since he is a gregarious animal and emotionally dependent upon his peers. Horses in rows of tie stalls (in close proximity to one another) generally do not crib as much as horses kept in roomier box stalls that allow them to move around. Horses in box stalls are happier (and less apt to crib) when stall walls are not solid, so they can see one another. Visual contact between stalls will often cut down on abnormal behavior. If the horses next to one another are compatible, partitions can allow them to touch and smell one another. A bond with a neighboring horse can satisfy the horse's social needs. A horse with no neighbors is less likely to crib if the stall has mirrors (protected with mesh wire for safety) so he can see his reflection.

A companion animal may help him feel less isolated. Having another animal in the stall often calms a nervous horse and helps keep him happy. Horse owners have used chickens, ducks, sheep, ponies, small donkeys, and dogs, but the most commonly used companion is a goat. They are inexpensive, easy to care for, and horses tend to bond with them and become content.

A daily grooming session can help the attitude of an isolated horse, partially replacing the affectionate physical contact he would otherwise get from his herd mates. Horses in groups nuzzle and scratch each other, swat each other's flies, and interact in many ways. You can help alleviate a solitary horse's loneliness and frustration (and frequent sequel of irritability, bad temper, or stable vices) by working with him as much as possible and giving him the attention he needs. Another deterrent to cribbing is to give the horse more work and exercise; hard-working horses have less interest in cribbing.

Some horse owners put electric wire around fences or stalls so the horse that is already cribbing can't get to the wood. Other alternatives include painting bad-tasting substances on the horse's favorite cribbing spots, using shock collars to train the horse not to crib, or using a cribbing strap.

The equine "shock collar" has been used successfully in a number of horses to halt cribbing (and sometimes other undesirable behavior such as stall kicking, weaving, aggression, etc.). It takes time and diligence to impress upon the horse that his undesirable action causes him instant discomfort — a form of self-punishment. The horseman carries a small remote-control transmitter that can activate the receiver on the collar. Walls or windows don't impede the signal, so the operator can stay out of sight and still activate the collar. The equine collar is not the same as a dog collar. The latter should never be used on horses because most dog collars deliver a much stronger shock.

A cheaper alternative, the cribbing strap, is a leather or leather and metal strap fastened around the throatlatch and adjusted so that it causes discomfort while the horse is cribbing by making it painful for him to tense the muscles that retract the larynx. A cribbing strap often will deter all but the most determined cribber. Most will resume cribbing, however, whenever it is removed. Many of these straps are fitted with a heart-shaped piece of metal or stiff leather that goes on the underside of the neck, pointing at the throat. When the horse arches his neck to suck in air, the strap tightens and the point of the metal piece jabs him, making him put his head forward again so he cannot swallow air.

Other collars fit over the forehead in front of the ears; some horsemen feel this type is more humane and more effective because it does not jab the horse in the throatlatch when he puts his head in the cribbing position. Another type combines two straps, with one going behind the ears and the other in front.

Adjust the cribbing strap for snugness while the horse's head is up, since it loosens when he lowers his head and thus will not interfere with normal movements while eating and drinking. With the strap on and fitted properly, most cribbers will not be able to suck air and give up trying. The habitual cribber may have to wear the strap at all times, however, except when being ridden, and it may rub out his mane, wear the hair off his throatlatch, or create sores or calluses.

Wearing a cribbing strap all the time can be just as risky as wearing a halter; it could catch on something and cause a fatal accident. This is the reason some horsemen prefer to use an old worn-out stirrup leather as a cribbing strap because it is more likely to break if snagged. A safer alternative is a stainless steel muzzle attached to a breakable halter. The muzzle prevents cribbing yet still allows the horse to eat and drink (some types allow a horse to drink but not eat; these must be removed at mealtime). Since it takes longer for the muzzled horse to eat, it keeps him busy more of the day.

Another alternative for a confirmed cribber that cannot be deterred is for the owner to find a way to live with his habit, such as installing a sturdy, rubber-covered bar in the horse's stall that he can crib on safely, without damaging his teeth or the stall.

Acupuncture has been used to treat cribbers, but the success rate varies depending upon the horse, the acupuncturist, and the choice of stimulation sites. As with many types of treatment or methods, success is highest if undertaken in the early stages of the problem rather than after the horse has a well-established cribbing habit.

Surgery to remove portions of the three major neck muscles (at the underside of the neck) used in cribbing can be performed to keep the horse from arching his neck to draw in air. Sometimes a neurectomy is done to remove a small portion of the nerve on the left side of the horse's neck that goes to the largest of those muscles. The muscle itself is not removed, so the horse is less disfigured.

Wood Chewing

Cribbing is often confused with wood chewing, but they are two separate behaviors. Under the right circumstances, wood chewing can lead to cribbing in isolated horses, and some of the tactics that help prevent cribbing also can deter a wood chewer.

Horses are browsers as well as grazers; horses at pasture will nibble on trees, eating bark, leaves, and branch tips, especially if grass becomes short or dry, or snow covers the grass. The confined horse takes his browsing to an extreme, however, chewing up and eating fence posts and rails, stall walls, feed mangers, and so on, due to boredom or nervousness. A serious wood chewer can kill trees, can destroy fences and stalls, and may swallow splinters that could puncture the digestive tract or become the core of an enterolith (stone in the digestive tract composed of mineral salts deposited around the foreign object).

Damage from wood chewing.

Horses chew wood when hungry, when the weather is cold, wet, or changing, when suffering from nutritional or mineral deficiency (such as being short on salt or having a low pH in the cecum and colon), when roughage is lacking in the diet (ground-up fiber in pellets is not enough), and when bored. Wood chewing can be a sign of ulcers; horses will nibble wood and other odd things when they have digestive tract discomfort.

Horses need adequate roughage for proper digestion and for generating body heat. The digestion and breakdown of roughage by microbes during the fermentation process of digestion create heat. In cold or wet weather, for instance, wood chewing in horses increases unless they are fed more total roughage. In some regions selenium deficiency causes wood chewing, but in most cases insufficient roughage is the culprit. Horses need a certain amount of fiber fill for proper digestion and to keep the hindgut (cecum and large intestine)

Horses need adequate roughage.

somewhat full so they don't feel hungry. Grain and high-quality, high-energy feeds may more than satisfy a horse's need for calories and nutrients but leave him short on fiber and chew time. A concentrated diet is unnatural for the horse and can make him feel hungry, creating a decrease in blood sugar for part of the day. After his quickly eaten meal, blood sugar rises, followed by a rise in insulin, which then creates a drop in blood sugar that can last several hours. He thus feels a need to eat more.

A Cornell University study in the 1970s showed that horses chew wood when no hay is available, even when fed an adequate diet. Ponies were fed a pelleted ration and no hay but had access to pine two-by-fours. Each pony chewed or consumed about three-quarters of a pound of pine per day. When hay was added to their diets, wood chewing decreased by 80 percent. More recent studies have shown that increasing the hay ration prolongs the time that horses spend eating and decreases wood chewing.

Horses also chew wood when confined without enough exercise. Wood chewing often occurs at night and early morning. A confined horse that is being ridden or exercised during the day is not as restless and bored at night; he is content to rest — unless he is shortchanged on roughage. Horses at pasture graze a lot at night, but confined horses don't have as much food to occupy their time and often do some nocturnal wood chewing. Giving the horse more exercise during the day and more grass hay in the evenings (not alfalfa, unless it is overly mature and stemmy, providing more fiber) to keep him

Chicken wire curtails chewing.

occupied longer may solve the problem. In cold weather, a horse chews wood at night because he is cold and is trying to fill his gut to increase the volatile fatty acids that can provide energy to keep him warm. He also feels hungry because of the decrease in blood sugar when he goes too long between meals.

Horses also may chew wood while on lush pasture, especially in early spring. The grass has a high water content but low fiber (and low nutrition by volume since it is mostly water). The lush grass goes through the digestive tract rapidly. Being shortchanged on both fiber and nutrients, a horse may start chewing on trees and wood. Feeding a little hay until the nutrient and fiber content of the grass increases later in the season when its growth is slower may solve the problem. In the wild, horses eat bunch grasses, which have more fiber, even when young and green, than some of the lusher tame pasture grasses that grow in a wetter environment.

As a general rule, horses that grow up with lots of room and pasture, rather than in stalls and paddocks, don't become wood chewers as readily. Many pasture-raised horses never develop the fence-chewing habit. The confined horse learns it early on, however. The bored youngster chews on anything and everything, and once a chewer, always a chewer.

This habit can be curtailed by installing electric fencing to protect paddock and pasture fences, using hardwood for stalls and paddock fences (horses chew it less than a softer wood), and covering posts and poles with chicken wire. Trees also can be protected by wrapping mesh wire around them. To halt destruction of favorite chew spots in a stall, some horse owners rub soap on windowsills or mangers, or use foul-tasting substances such as Tabasco sauce or commercial "chew stop" preparations. These require frequent application to areas horses may chew and are only partially effective. One horse may find the substance unappetizing while another may continue chewing.

Any application should be safe in case the horse continues to nibble. Check label warnings. Usually any substance that is not harmful to children is safe for horses. Do not use old motor oil on fences; it contains lead and is poisonous. Some of the wood preservatives such as creosote and pentachlorophenol are also unsafe if a horse eats the treated wood.

Horses rarely chew new oak or locust wood but readily eat pine or fir (softer woods that are easier to chew) and well-weathered woods. If you have a very determined wood eater, you can save your paddock fences by giving the horse an alternative to nibble on, such as clean straw.

Wood chewing is a bad habit but not an addiction like cribbing. It can be halted with forethought and good management. If you make it physically impossible or distasteful for the horse, he won't consume your fences. If you make sure he has enough exercise and roughage to relieve his boredom and alleviate his hunger pangs (and solve any nutritional deficiencies), he usually won't feel the need to chew wood.

Locomotor Stereotypies

Stall walking and weaving, in which a horse moves in a constant repetitive rhythm, are the most common ambulatory stereotypies. Variations include pawing and stall kicking. These latter two habits are sometimes exhibited as a stereotypy but are often just responses to certain frustrations, such as impatience to be fed — performed in reaction to certain stimuli rather than as a compulsive behavior.

The weaver remains stationary but sways back and forth in place, shifting weight from one foreleg to the other, usually standing in the same place in his stall every time he performs this ritual. He may just shift his weight, rocking from side to side on his front feet, or lift his whole forehand and swing his head, neck, and both front feet back and forth in a dancing motion, pivoting in place.

Some horses just bob their head up and down. Many horses weave by the door or gate (perhaps in anticipation of getting out) or in front of the stall partition.

Weaving is usually due to confinement, lack of interaction with other horses, or being unable to graze. The horse's instinct is to find his buddies or graze, but his escape is thwarted. He takes a step but can go nowhere, so

Fence walking.

he resigns himself to starting the movement again, refining it to a constant weight shifting as he discovers it's a way to relieve stress and frustration through endorphin release. The endorphin levels in his bloodstream rise when he performs this stereotypic behavior. When the levels become high, he seems satisfied and stops weaving. When the endorphins drop to a low level, he starts again and becomes very intense in his weaving until the endorphin levels rise.

A weaver may develop physical problems from this constant action, since he puts stress on leg joints and widens his stance as he shifts from one foot to the other. Extra stress on the inside of the leg can lead to ringbone, knee problems, and extra wear on the feet or shoes.

The stall walker constantly circles his stall (usually in the same direction, leaving a well-worn trail), or paces back and forth in a certain pattern, while a fence walker may develop a pattern of pacing back and forth in front of the gate or along one side of his paddock when he is separated from other horses. He may pace by the gate because he knows it is the way out of his "cage," or pace along the fence nearest horses he can see in the distance. A horse that paces or runs along a fence, stopping and turning always in the same direction, may develop physical problems due to strain on leg joints or abnormal wearing of the feet from this constant action that stresses one side of the leg.

The best remedy for weaving, stall walking, or fence pacing is to give the horse more room and keep him with or near other horses. Pasture turnout often solves the problem. If this is impossible, change the management of the stall-bound horse so he has company and can spend more time eating and less time idle. The same tactics to prevent cribbing will also help the weaver or stall walker.

Reducing or eliminating grain, which releases endorphins that help promote compulsive behaviors, can decrease weaving and stall walking.

Some confined horses can become obsessive kickers. A stall kicker pounds his hind feet against walls and may develop hock or tendon problems from the banging or overextension of the joint. There is also risk of injury to the hoof or leg from repeated concussion against the wall. A horse may damage his heels or coronet if he kicks through a broken board. He may fracture the coffin bone or pastern bone when kicking a solid wall.

This behavior is considered a stereotypy if a horse repeatedly strikes the wall or floor of the stall. The sound made by kicking or banging may be enough to stimulate the horse to keep doing it. When a horse exhibits this type of behavior only at feeding time or when someone is in the barn (as an attention-getting device, hoping for food), it is a ritualized pattern rather than a stereotypy, since the behavior is only associated with feeding and is not an obsessive/compulsive action. Some horses quickly learn that the noise of kicking brings someone to the stall with feed.

One way to thwart mealtime bad manners is to withhold the horse's feed until he has stopped kicking or pawing and has been standing quietly awhile. Otherwise, he is being rewarded for impatient behavior and thinks he will always be fed when he stomps, paws, or kicks the stall wall or paddock fence. A shock collar can also work for a horse that paws or kicks just at feeding time.

Some stall kickers stand with their hindquarters next to the wall and rhythmically kick with one hind foot, bobbing the head simultaneously. Others may rock forward and backward and then kick out with both hind feet, giving several hard kicks in a row. This can destroy a stall wall or door and may also damage the horse's hind legs or loosen his shoes. Kicking is natural among horses in groups, for self-defense or in play. In the stall, kicking

Pawing can become a habit.

might be an interactive game in which several horses in the barn participate or a single horse may kick to vent frustration. Kicking may occur between stalls if horses next to one another do not get along. If an incompatible neighbor triggers kicking, shifting the horse's place in the barn may halt the problem.

The best way to correct a perpetual kicker is to leave him outdoors. If this is not possible, use a tie stall when he has to be in the barn. If he must live in a box stall, place horizontal boards around the inside of a box stall at rump height to keep the horse from backing close enough to the wall to kick.

Another alternative is a kick rail around the stall, just above hock level, with a shelf above it so he cannot get a leg caught if he kicks that high. Most kicks will hit the rail, and the horse bangs the leg below the hock. This method prevents damage to the stall wall and may deter the horse from kicking; the whack on his leg is uncomfortable. The rail can be effective if the horse does not chew the rail or does not kick it hard enough to injure his legs. The portion of the kick rail and shelf at the doorway can be hinged so it can be opened for bringing the horse in and out of the stall. Kick rails work best if the stall is quite large (sixteen by sixteen feet); otherwise, they reduce the available stall space too much.

A deterrent used by some horsemen is a kicking chain, hanging from a leather strap fastened around the horse's leg above the hock. Each time he kicks, the chain slaps back and bangs him, producing a form of self-punishment. The chain, which is available commercially for this purpose, should be about a half-inch thick and eight inches long, enough to hang down to about the mid-point of the cannon bone. Risk of leg injury from the chain is generally less than the harm a horse can do to himself when constantly kicking the wall.

Confined horses often acquire a pawing habit; some will paw every time they become frustrated or impatient, whenever they want something they cannot get. In the wild a horse will paw to dig through snow to grass, to dig up roots when grass is scarce in a dry season, to stir up hard-packed ground to make a softer rolling spot, or to break ice on a water hole. This instinctive action helps him get something he wants.

In confinement he may resort to pawing whenever his needs or desires are frustrated, as when he is impatient at feeding time or if his grain tub or water bucket is empty. Horses that paw at feeding time often make it a habit because they are rewarded by food. Punishment rarely halts this behavior since most horse owners are not consistent enough in the punishment and an instinct-based behavior is also difficult to eliminate. A person determined to halt a horse's feeding-time pawing habit may have more success using a reward, giving the horse a bite of feed whenever he stops pawing for a moment, never feeding the horse when he is pawing.

A horse might also paw when he cannot move around as he wishes — when confined in a stall when he'd rather be outside, when tied, or when loaded in a trailer. He may bang at the stall door, paw a hole in the dirt, or make pawing motions in the air. A nervous horse may paw, as will a young horse that has not learned patience or an insecure horse that is unhappy at being left alone.

Continual pawing can be detrimental to the horse. He might develop carpitis (inflammation of the knee joint) if he hits his knee on the stall door, or scrape the skin off his knees and the front of his fetlock joints. He might wear off the toe of his foot or cause damage to joints. Pawing on hard ground also could cause sole bruising. The constant pounding may loosen clinches on shoes or shift the shoe; there is also risk of a shoe catching on something. If a horse paws so much that he risks damage to his feet, a form of self-punishment may deter him. As with kicking chains, using an ankle chain as a punishment is less damaging to the horse's legs than the continual concussion of pawing.

Self-Mutilation Syndrome

One of the most detrimental equine stereotypies is self-mutilation. It seems to be a displacement behavior and, in some horses, a response to stress or fear. Free-roaming horses under natural conditions do not exhibit stereotypies. Unnatural aspects of domestication, confinement, and stress do not create stereotypies in all horses, so researchers suspect that the tendency toward this type of compulsive behavior may be genetic; this seems to be especially true with self-mutilation.

Horses that suffer this problem bite at themselves, often spinning around to grab at their flanks, sometimes causing injury. The self-mutilating horse may pin his ears back, gesture toward his flank, suddenly lunging and squealing as he circles and nips at himself. Or he may make biting movements at his legs, flanks, or tail without actually taking hold. Some horses take chunks of skin out with their teeth, necessitating sutures to repair the wounds. Some look agitated and turn the head slowly to the side or down, then suddenly nip at the air or bite themselves on the flank or chest. Some will grunt or "bark" during or immediately after the nip. Some kick out with one hind leg, make repetitive kicking motions or shake their heads while turning in circles.

The problem at first may be mistaken for colic, since the animal continually bites at his sides and flanks as if they were causing discomfort, but he also may bite his chest, legs, or other parts of his body. Baffled owners check for flies, parasites, ulcers, skin disease, hormonal imbalance, or gut blockages, but the horse is healthy. This destructive activity occurs mainly in stallions, because they are most often kept isolated. This behavior is rarely seen in stallions that live with other horses. Geldings seldom display this behavior; mares, even less so.

The repetitive action may begin as displacement behavior due to stress, fear, or frustration. An aggressive stallion that is isolated and confined with no other outlet for his energies may fight himself.

Equine self-mutilation was first described as "flank biting" and thought to be a problem only in stallions. But as researchers received more input from horse owners, they found it occurs in both sexes and involves not only flank biting but also kicking out with the hind legs and squealing. The condition begins when the horse is young, generally between the ages of one and two and hardly ever after age four. Most horse owners' attempts to alter this destructive habit are fruitless, and in many cases the horse is eventually euthanized.

In some cases self-mutilation can be halted if the horse's environment or routine is changed at the first hint of strange behavior. A stallion can be put out with a group of pregnant mares, for instance. Sometimes a change in management such as giving a horse more exercise or putting him where he can see other horses can halt the problem, but in other instances change itself may cause stress. Castration resolves the problem in some stallions. In a study in which ten horses were gelded, two showed slight improvement, five showed substantial or complete improvement, while three showed no change.

Susceptibility may be inherited. Owners of fifteen horses reported that relatives of the self-mutilating horses had similar behavior. The most similar condition in another species is Tourette's syndrome in humans, which causes spasms, tics, and other involuntary movements, and uncontrollable bursts of aggression and antisocial speech. Tourette's syndrome is most common in males, with onset at an early age, and is an inherited neurological chemical imbalance.

Self-mutilation in horses seems to be a neurological condition, brought on by stress or a combination of stresses depending on how the horse is managed. The behavior can become addictive, much like cribbing. Dr. Nicholas Dodman, a Tufts University researcher, used opiate-receptor-blocker medications (which he'd found successful in treating cribbers) on self-mutilating horses and some of these medications halted the behavior.

Dodman thought that release of opioids in the body was made possible in a stress-primed system. Stress, like pain, might cause the body to release endorphins, which desensitize the horse to pain and and thus he keeps biting himself. The horse is sensitized to his body's reactions and in the complex stress process is stimulated to repeat the activity. The opioids activate the reward centers in the brain and increase the pain threshold so the horse feels little pain from self-abuse.

In all reported cases of stallions that exhibit self-mutilation, the animals have been confined, away from a natural herd and mating situation. Pasture breeding stallions are too busy to experience the frustration that might lead to self-mutilation. General frustration may be the cause in confined geldings and mares that show this behavior, such as at feeding time when impatient and angry. Horses in groups rarely show self-mutilation since they can release any extra energy, aggression, or displeasure in social interaction, playing, and chasing.

Excessive Drinking and Urination

Confinement sometimes triggers excessive water drinking. Some horses drink more water than they need, just for something to do, and urinate more than normal. There are a few serious diseases that cause thirst and above-normal water consumption and urination. If a horse starts drinking and urinating more, have a veterinarian check him to make sure the thirst is not caused by Cushing's syndrome, diabetes, kidney disease, or some other serious condition.

Cushing's syndrome affects the pituitary gland at the base of the brain. Though the disease can be treated, it is eventually fatal. Affected horses drink a lot and pass great quantities of diluted urine. As the disease progresses, the horse loses weight and his hair becomes rough and shaggy. He may not shed in the spring. Skin abscesses may develop, and wounds are slow to heal.

Another metabolic problem that causes thirst is diabetes, but it is rare in horses. Affected horses are constantly hungry as well as thirsty, but tend to lose weight. They urinate frequently, but the urine is not diluted and contains a lot of sugar. Even more rare in horses is excessive drinking and urination due to kidney disease. Horsemen used to worry about kidney problems in horses, but kidney trouble and urinary disease are less common in horses than in any other domestic animal.

Horses also drink more and urinate more frequently when fed rich alfalfa hay, because it is so high in protein. The kidney excretes the by-products of protein metabolism. If the horse is fed more protein than he needs, the excess is metabolized and excreted. More protein in the diet means more urine, since the horse drinks more water to flush metabolized protein by-products from his system (nitrogen compounds). The working horse will also need more water if fed alfalfa, since protein has a higher heat of digestion; the horse has more body heat to dissipate and will sweat more, needing more water.

Fever can dehydrate a horse. Most cases of excessive drinking and urination, however, are not due to disease or illness. Most of these horses are physically normal but drink more water than they need just from nervous habit. This situation is rarely encountered in horses at pasture. It is just one more attempt to relieve boredom or anxiety. Other confined animals such as dogs in kennels sometimes develop the excess water consumption habit also. When the horse runs out of feed, he starts chewing his stall or fences, or drinks water.

Some bored horses eat more salt than they need. Excessive salt consumption can become a habit just like wood chewing; the horse continually licks his salt block for something to do. Extra salt consumption will not harm a horse as long as he has plenty of water. The extra salt requires dilution with water to flush it out of his system, and he will be thirsty and drink more water. If he has access to plenty of fresh water, he will flush extra salt on through in the urine. If his water supply is limited, however, his salt-eating habit can be toxic.

If a horse suddenly starts drinking a lot, make sure there is no physical reason. If the horse is healthy, look to some other cause such as a protein-rich diet or just a nervous habit. The main problem with the confined horse is that extra urine makes more soiled bedding and stall clean up. The water-drinking habit creates more problems for the horseman than for the horse.

If a horse is consuming too much salt, you may want to switch from a salt block to granulated loose salt, which most horses won't overeat.

Signs of Stress

Domestication has created problems for the horse, including stomach ulcers. Stress of confinement and unnatural conditions, stress from emotional and physical aspects of athletic careers — all the stresses that go with trying to adapt to human management — can create ulcers in horses. Ulcers, once thought to be mainly a problem in confined foals, also plague adult horses. Racehorses and other performance horses have an especially high incidence.

Research reported at the 1998 American Association of Equine Practitioners (AAEP) convention in Maryland showed that gastric ulcers affect up to 90 percent of performance horses and that many of the factors associated with intensive training and conditioning contribute to ulcer formation.

Stomach ulcers occur when the lining is damaged by excessive acid or by impairment of the stomach lining's natural protection. Signs of ulcers are dullness, decreased performance, poor appetite, poor condition, rough hair coat, and poor weight gain. Often the problem is not obvious; the horse just isn't doing as well as he should be. Some horses adjust to the stress better than others, but it's hard to predict which ones will have problems.

Many common management practices used with performance horses contribute to ulcer development — high grain–low roughage diets (increased stomach acid due to infrequent high-concentrate meals, with lack of roughage in the tract to help buffer the acid); lack of continual grazing; stress of confinement combined with periods of intense exercise; use of anabolic steroids; the steroid-like plant substances in some feeds; and use of non-steroidal anti-inflammatory drugs.

Providing a semi-natural environment can reduce stress.

Ulcers are a major problem, but how much they adversely affect performance has not been determined. Researchers are still trying to find the best methods of prevention, looking at dietary, training, and medical remedies. Alfalfa hay is generally the best type of hay since it contains more calcium than grass hay, and calcium helps buffer and neutralize acid in the stomach.

Horses are also more susceptible to respiratory problems and other illnesses at times of stress, such as at weaning or after a long trailer trip. The immune system usually protects the horse from common diseases and infections, but stress can hinder the immune system and lower the horse's resistance to pathological invaders. Stress is defined as anything that poses a threat to physical or emotional well-being, temporarily or over an extended period.

During temporary stress, like acute anxiety or fear, the horse's heart rate and blood pressure rise. Circulation to the gut, skin, and other non-athletic parts of the body decreases so blood can concentrate in the muscles and lungs for the exertion needed for fleeing or fighting. After the temporary stress is over, everything returns to normal.

During more prolonged stress, the body secretes hormones called glucocorticoids. One of these, cortisol, is beneficial to the horse over the short term, because it changes the body's metabolism to help it function better under stress. Cortisol creates temporary increase in blood glucose (used as energy) and increase in fatty acids and glycerol.

Glucocorticoids break down reserves of fat, carbohydrates, and protein to release nutrients into the bloodstream. Metabolism switches from a constructive (body building) state to one of using up reserves. Growth, reproduction, and immunity are temporarily suppressed as the body prepares itself for emergency survival (fight or flight — traveling on the "reserve tank" until things get back to normal again — a coping mechanism to escape danger).

Horses under stress are also helped temporarily by increased retention of sodium and water, and increased mobilization of calcium. Probably the most beneficial reaction caused by cortisol is reduction in tissue inflammation, which provides temporary help and relief to the body during trauma and infection. Cortisol blocks the production of harmful substances and toxins, enabling the body to function more normally. All of these changes are beneficial for a day or two, but if stressful conditions prevail, the continuing production of cortisol becomes detrimental because it interferes with the immune system.

As part of the body's defense against pathogenic invaders, the immune system produces antibodies and uses white blood cells to attack germs. These processes and many other biochemical aspects of immunity are hindered when the body is creating cortisol (which is similar to other steroids in its actions). One study showed that responsiveness of white blood cells to invading bacteria was noticeably lower in fatigued horses after strenuous exercise. Overtraining can become a form of stress that leaves a horse vulnerable to illness. Several studies have indicated that the stress of long van trips reduces disease resistance; increased cortisol levels in the body can be measured after a long trip.

The lungs are especially vulnerable to lowered resistance due to stress. Harmful organisms are a natural part of the environment and always present in the air, so the immune system must be strong to protect the respiratory system. Horses tend to develop influenza, colds, rhinopneumonitis, respiratory forms of viral arteritis, as well as other respiratory problems when shipped to shows, races, or sales. Stress — and contact with other horses — gives infections a prime opportunity.

Stress may be responsible for more health problems than we realize. Traumatic experience at weaning and subjecting a foal to new things during this time of stress can make a difference in how well he does during winter. Weanlings and yearlings enduring cold, wet conditions (especially if they are also mentally stressed by unnatural conditions such as confinement in small paddocks) seem susceptible to many illnesses. Severe outbreaks of strangles and other respiratory ailments are frequent in young horses after a wet period or weaning. Salmonellosis outbreaks, ulcers, and colic are also precipitated by stress.

Various things stress various horses. Young horses experience stress in situations they are not accustomed to but learn to deal with the novelties (and become less insecure or fearful) as their training level progresses and they accept certain things as non-confrontational and part of their regular routine. Doing familiar things in a familiar environment causes less stress than being subjected to something unfamiliar.

Social Stress

Even at pasture with a group of herd mates, horses may be stressed by unnatural social structure (or constant change) imposed by humans. The horse's natural social state is living in a group of about five to twenty animals, with each one knowing where it stands in the hierarchy. Social interaction among horses is essential for mental well-being, and in a stable group the constancy of the social order gives them emotional security. To avoid stress in domestic horses, keep groups relatively stable (don't put new horses in all the time, or take some out) and group horses by status — mares with foals, mares without foals, young horses, geldings, etc.

Random mixing of horses into groups convenient for the horse owner and changing horses within a group can cause unease, fighting, or chasing within the herd. Many problems that arise when managing horses are a result of the instinctive behavior and aggression that accompany establishment of a social hierarchy. A new horse put into a group often creates a traumatic situation that can result in injury, until that horse's place is established. Constant moving of horses in and out of a group also increases risk of introducing disease.

The ironic thing about our way of managing horses is the ones we think most highly of (favorites, valuable show or racehorses) are usually the most intensely managed, living in the most unnatural conditions, which puts them more at risk for problems. The more valuable the horse, the more likely he will grow up in a stall or small paddock, being fed extra rations to make sure he reaches full potential quickly but lacking room to exercise. Often these pushed and pampered youngsters develop skeletal problems, growing up less hardy and athletic than they would if allowed to mature more naturally and slowly on low-energy, high-fiber feeds with room to run.

In paddock, pasture, or stable, the more you can approximate natural conditions, the happier and healthier your horses will be. If a horse must be in a stall, it should be roomy, well ventilated, clean, and well lit, with windows so he can see what's going on around him. Barns tend to be darker than outdoors, so good lighting is helpful. A barn should not be pitch black inside at night; horses need to be able to see movement and shapes. A horse should not be constantly stabled; if possible he should be allowed outdoors at least part of each day for exercise.

Young horses, especially, need room to exercise and need other horses for social interaction — to learn life's lessons and become well-adjusted adults.

Young horses need room to exercise and for social interaction.

Weanlings and yearlings should be kept outdoors continually (with run-in sheds for shelter) or turned out as much as possible. If they must be stalled, put them into individual stalls just for mealtimes, so they can eat without competition for feed. Turn them out with their buddies the rest of the time. They should be at pasture or turned out in small compatible groups — no more than ten or twelve youngsters who get along well. Once a group is established, don't make changes unless absolutely necessary. Living with horses he knows and feels secure with helps the young horse be more at ease and comfortable with his routine and his environment.

Whether in stall or paddock, make sure a horse has plenty of feed to keep him busy; he needs a high roughage diet that gives him something to do and keeps his digestive system working properly. Concentrated feeds fall short on both counts. The further you remove a horse from his natural eating and living patterns, the higher the risk of stress-related illnesses and metabolic or behavioral problems.

3

Practical and Safe
Horse Handling

HANDLING HORSES SAFELY, EFFICIENTLY, and in their best interest requires a working knowledge of horse psychology. Knowing how horses think and react to various stimuli can make the difference in whether your experiences with horses are good or bad — for you and the horses. Although this book is about horse care, not horse training, some of the basic aspects of "horse sense" (sensible horse handling) should be mentioned. Every time you handle a horse, even just to put a halter on him or lead him from stall to pasture, you are training him — to be easier to handle or more difficult, depending on how you go about it. This chapter looks at basic horse handling and how to prevent or minimize problem behavior and keep your day-to-day horse handling safe and productive rather than frustrating, risky, and counterproductive.

The Mind of the Horse

Horses are intelligent, sensitive animals capable of learning many things and forgetting nothing. They have better memories than humans. They don't think the way we do, and this can lead to misunderstanding, frustration, and behavioral problems, especially if you punish the horse for something he does not

Horses establish hierarchies within groups.

understand. For instance, if he spooks or jumps unexpectedly or refuses to do what you ask, he is usually reacting to something perceived as dangerous or does not understand your request; he is following his self-preservation instinct rather than purposefully trying to annoy or disobey.

To understand his reactions in certain situations and know how best to handle him, we need to realize what motivates him and consider his personality and temperament. Horses are gregarious, wanting to be with other horses, yet they also need their own space. An alpha individual, for instance, will not tolerate another horse close and will bite and kick to protect personal space. The more submissive individual, especially the "follower" who is insecure without other horses around, is less defensive of personal space and will allow other horses to come very close without retaliating.

Horses develop definite likes and dislikes for other horses; some always seem to get along well together while other individuals never do. Personality and preferences should always be considered when working with groups of horses (as when tying horses next to one another) or in stabling or pasturing arrangements. Many problems can be avoided if the handler understands the personalities and social order within the group.

The dominant-submissive relationships and instinct to imitate or follow what others in the group are doing also will affect how horses behave at pasture or on the trail. If you are riding in a group and the lead horse shies away from something, the horses behind become alert and may shy at the same place. If the horse in the lead jumps a ditch instead of stepping over it, the horses behind will try to jump it, too. If one horse is acting skittish or playful, others may become more fractious. If someone gallops past at full speed, your horse may want to run, too. These actions are survival instincts; the horse naturally does what the herd does as a way to escape possible danger.

The horse's highly developed senses constantly feed his brain information; he is mentally prepared for instant flight. This flightiness makes him seem very emotional. He expresses his feelings very obviously and his moods can change rapidly. He can be half asleep one moment and very excited the next. A person who handles horses must realize the horse's quicksilver nature and use care and consistency so the horse can trust and have confidence in the human.

The horse is a creature of habit and feels secure in the familiar. He likes to have things done the same way, at the same time, and in the same order every day. He likes consistency, especially in how he is handled. He comes to know a person and what to expect; horse and horseman can come to a mutual ease in which they trust one another and work together.

An inconsistent horse handler has less luck gaining a horse's confidence. The horse expects his human to act in a familiar and non-confrontational fashion and is surprised or annoyed if you do something contrary to his expectations. If he is accustomed to you walking out to his pasture to get him and stands quietly while you halter him, he will be startled if you come running at him. He may kick up his heels and go to the far corner as fast as he can. If he is accustomed to a soft voice and in a fit of temper you shout at him, he may be alarmed and forget what you wanted him to do. He knows you very well but reacts more to what you do and how you handle him (your outward motions and body language) than to you.

Horses become accustomed to their surroundings and like to have objects in their proper places. They become suspicious or shy of something (even a familiar thing) if it is in a different place. This is the self-preservation instinct; anything unusual could mean danger. The horse may be familiar with a wheelbarrow in his barnyard but may shy at one he sees unexpectedly along the road or out of place at home. If you are leading him in from the pasture and he must pass a wheelbarrow in an unusual spot or tipped over on its side, he may throw a fit. We

The horse should trust the rider.

think he is being silly, but in his eyes it looks so different and predatory that he wants to give it a wide berth. You must understand what sort of things might alarm a horse and be able to anticipate problems, minimize them, or be prepared for the horse's possible reaction.

Horses are usually not afraid of an object or situation if accustomed to it gradually, especially if acquainted with it while young. The youngster growing up with a variety of experiences is usually more adaptable than the overly sheltered youngster that never experiences anything new. He needs variety in his life to become a well rounded, "sane" individual that can tolerate a multitude of circumstances. Constant repetition (producing familiarity) in an atmosphere of safety, in which the horse realizes he will not be harmed by the strange object or action, can make almost anything seem ordinary or natural to him.

If he trusts you and feels secure in your leadership (as he would trust and follow the lead mare in a group of horses), he will be your willing partner under most circumstances. He will look to you for security in difficult situations. He will be more apt to stay calm and cooperative under conditions that conflict with his own instincts or desires, and be more willing to listen to you, whether you are trying to encourage him or calm him.

If he gets tangled in wire and panics, his first impulse is to escape, to run, and he may thrash and struggle to free himself, increasing risk of injury. But if he trusts you and has confidence in your leadership, your soothing voice and calmness will reassure him (like the calmness of the lead mare when she perceives that a situation is not dangerous). He'll settle down enough to allow you to free him from his predicament. This type of trust is partly due to your relationship with the horse, built on past experiences together and his previous education — your introducing him to many things while in a safe environment. Without this ability to gain trust in his human handler, the horse would always be very unreliable and hysterical in emergencies or even in everyday situations he might perceive as dangerous or frightening.

Communicating With Horses

To work with horses successfully, we must be able to communicate adequately with voice, touch, and body language. The horseman must be sensitive and sympathetic, with an intuitive feel for what is right for that particular horse at that particular moment. Successful horse handling makes use of tact and persuasion, only using force when absolutely necessary. A good horseman always thinks first of the horse and thinks ahead to possible long-term results of the handling method rather than just the convenience of the moment. The horse has an incredible memory and abusive handling will affect him a long time.

Use horse sense when introducing new things or performing routine care tasks that a horse might perceive as uncomfortable or frightening. If you are doing something new or unusual, choose a nice day and a time of day with the least distractions. Having his first foot trimming on a windy day with everything in motion and scary will make the task harder since he's already suspicious. If things go less smoothly than planned, his bad feelings about what you did to him may last awhile.

Use good judgment in rewarding proper behavior and thwarting improper behavior; make sure the horse always understands why he is being punished. He will respond by becoming easier to handle, when he knows what is expected of him. Always ask a horse to do something in a way that makes sense to him. He should be rewarded for a proper response in such a way that he'll repeat the response the next time he is asked. Often the only reward needed is praise and encouragement.

When you ask the horse to do a certain thing, such as stop or turn on cue when being led, often the reward is just a release of pressure (from the halter). When the horse starts to respond properly, release the pressure immediately. The next time he is asked, he gives the desired response because he knows it will result in release of pressure. If he realizes that stopping immediately when you say "Whoa" will result in no pressure on his nose from the halter, he will stop before you have to reinforce your request with a pull.

Horses don't use logic; you can't expect a horse to understand something he hasn't already experienced. You must build step by step on what he already knows, after first establishing a trusting relationship.

Cues and requests should be reasonable in each circumstance. If we ask the horse to do something in a manner that makes him uncomfortable or afraid, he will resist. But if the horse handler structures the request in a way that the horse thinks he is putting pressure on himself (moving into the fixed hand on the halter while being led or into the elbow situated to intercept a playful nip), it becomes the horse's own idea to give the correct response. The horse will keep a more learning, open mind instead of resenting what he perceives as something the handler is doing to him.

Regarding punishment, the important thing is not when or how much, but whether you are right in giving it; most times a horse makes a mistake or misbehaves it's your fault. If he misbehaves, figure out why. If it's your fault, do not punish him for it. Never punish a horse unless he understands why and unless you can administer the correction immediately after the misdeed; otherwise he won't know what he is being punished for.

We are always sending signals to the horse, whether we realize it or not, making things better or worse, depending on our actions and methods. Everything you do with a horse should be with some thought as to how he will respond to your action, whether you are catching him, leading him past a scary object, or asking for an advanced movement under saddle.

Working with horses is easier if you are paying attention to what the horse is doing and thinking. Control over a horse's mind involves familiarity, respect, and trust, with him being conditioned through proper handling to obey. You must be at ease in the relationship. Even if you go through the motions of being the "boss" in words and actions, your horse will sense if you are afraid; these vibes overshadow your outward actions and make him nervous, or more aggressive if he wants to test your role in the relationship. Even if he is just playful and you mistake his playful action as a sign of aggression and retreat, he will learn to take advantage of you.

Use body language and mental control to establish yourself as leader. With this relationship you can always be in control of the horse, whether leading him, holding him still for the farrier or veterinarian, putting him into a trailer, having him stand still for you to halter him, etc. To have this kind of control without coercion or nagging, you must first be in control of yourself — calm, mentally focused, and self-disciplined. If you are not aware of your own body language, you may actually be telling the horse things that you don't want him to "hear."

You can't physically dominate a horse. He is stronger than you. Instead, use body language to project your mental control, just as the alpha mare does with her herd mates. It does not require strength to handle or train horses; you con-

trol them through their minds, communicating your will to theirs. Horse handling is a mental game requiring confidence and tact, enabling you to communicate with the horse and gain his respect and trust.

The tone of your voice is very important; an approving voice can be a reward for positive behavior. A soothing voice can calm him. A disapproving voice when he misbehaves is often punishment enough, the horse realizing that his human is displeased with him.

If a physical reprimand is necessary, it should be instant and appropriate, similar to the reprimand a dominant horse would give a herd mate. You may need only a firmer leg (when mounted), a tug on the halter, or a tap with a whip, depending on the situation. Most horses understand one swat (as in a herd situation when one bite or kick is enough to keep a herd member in line), but they don't understand continual punishment. Excessive punishment will only make a horse lose his trust and respect for you. Continually pecking at a horse can confuse him. He will either quit trying to do the task right or become afraid of everything you do with him.

Physical punishment is rarely needed once you gain rapport with a horse and understand one another. You can control him more subtly, often preventing disobedience before it takes shape. This comes with perfecting communication between you and the horse, being able to predict to a certain extent what the horse will do next in any given situation. A good horse handler never lets the horse get into a position or situation in which the horse is tempted to disobey or become a danger to himself or to a person.

We may inadvertently teach a horse bad manners just by being unobservant, negligent (letting the horse get away with things), sloppy in our actions, or inconsistent in our handling methods. Many of the aggravating habits of spoiled horses are due to their handlers' inconsistency or to the horse's evasive actions (trying to escape the poor horsemanship that caused discomfort, fear, or confusion) that became habit.

An alert horse.

Understanding Equine Body Language

When handling a horse, you are better prepared for his actions and reactions if you can interpret his body language, to know whether he is at ease with what you are doing, nervous, afraid, annoyed, or resentful. Part of handling horses safely is being in tune with their feelings so you are never caught off guard. If you are aware of how a horse is feeling, you can usually be prepared to handle a difficult situation without being hurt, or defuse it and encourage the horse to become more relaxed and cooperative.

The horse's ears are one of the best indicators of mood and intent. Flicking them continually in all directions usually indicates nervousness and an attempt to learn more about what's happening in an uncertain situation. Ears flat back means the horse is uncomfortable, annoyed, or angry and prepared to defend himself. A horse with flattened ears may be ready to kick or bite. A relaxed horse has relaxed ears.

Head and neck posture indicate intent and whether the horse is about to make a move; he uses head and

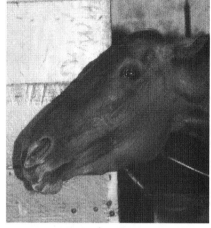
An aggressive attitude.

neck for balance and will move them as he prepares to shift his weight. Aggressive use of the head indicates anger or annoyance; as a threat the horse will make a sudden and purposeful swing (sometimes with ears back and teeth bared) toward a subordinate horse or human.

The horse reacts quickly and strongly to anything he perceives as alarming. Since his head is a very vulnerable area, he tries to get it out of the way of potential danger (such as a kick from another horse) and jerks it up. A startled, nervous, or untrusting horse may suddenly and violently jerk his head up or even rear.

. The horse's eyes give clues to what he's thinking and feeling; a sleepy eye means he's relaxed and at ease with what is going on around him. A wide

A relaxed horse.

eye (accompanied by an alert heads-up position) means he's trying to figure out what's happening and is possibly triggered for action. A horse that throws his head up and shows the whites of the eyes is very upset — either afraid or angry.

A relaxed lower lip and flaccid muscles around the mouth indicate relaxation. Nostrils also indicate mood; flared nostrils can indicate fright, excitement, or anger. A sigh indicates acceptance or relaxation. If while you are working with the horse he gives a big sigh, you know he is no longer tense but is comfortable with what you are doing.

Feet and legs are used as weapons — front feet for offense (striking) and hind feet for defense. A kick or just the threat of a kick with hind leg cocked is a warning to keep other horses from invading his space or to tell humans that he's very annoyed.

The tail is a good barometer of mood and feelings. When it is firmly clamped down, the horse is angry, defensive, or stubborn. A low, tucked tail can be a submissive gesture. A relaxed horse has a relaxed tail. Sporadic swishing signals impatience, while a violently lashing tail may mean intense discomfort or anger. A startled horse may give an involuntary movement of the tail. When working near the horse's hindquarters, a firm hold on the tail can help you feel the animal's mood and intent and can also help thwart an inclination to kick.

Safe Horse Handling

Most accidents and injuries can be prevented or minimized by anticipating what the horse might do. You're less apt to get caught in a dangerous situation. Never take any horse for granted, even one you completely trust. The most dependable horse still might move suddenly if startled. Safety-conscious defensive working habits (even when working around horses you know well and trust) can prevent stepped-on toes, bumped heads, or broken bones. Be prepared to move with your horse.

A handler can help keep the horse still during a procedure.

Sometimes you must be able to calm and restrain him and keep from being hurt by him, even though he is stronger than you are. In these instances the good horseman uses body language, leverage, and proper contact with the horse to keep him under control and to keep from being kicked or bumped.

Wound spray, an injection, or any procedure he is unfamiliar with may provoke a defensive response that could endanger the handler. Be prepared for evasive or defensive actions, handling the horse in such a way as to prevent or minimize these or be in a position where his actions cannot inflict much harm.

Safe Horse Holding

To control the horse's body, you must control his head. To control his head, you need his trust. True control comes with trust, not with physical force. If he is frightened or defensive, he will throw his head up in preparation to fight or flee. If the handler can convince the horse that it's safe and comfortable to keep his head lowered, the horse will stay more relaxed, even in a potentially tense situation. A trusting horse will lower his head readily, with very little prompting, but a horse that is afraid, suspicious, or spoiled (not wanting to submit to your wishes) will resist.

There are times you need to keep a horse still and calm for a farrier, a vet, etc. Keeping the horse totally under control may take all your attention and intuition to ensure the safety of the person working on the horse.

Use a halter that fits. If the halter is too loose, grasp it snugly under his chin, holding the loose part together, so your hand has contact with the horse's jaw.

Choose a safe area. Sometimes an open space is best, with no obstacles to run into. The horse may move in his attempts to avoid what is being done to him. If you're holding him in a barn aisle, make sure nothing is in the way or along the walls — no pitchforks, buckets, hay bales, and so on.

If the horse must remain quite still for the procedure, hold him next to a wall or solid fence. Never put him next to a wire fence or electric fence. If he lunged or backed into a wire or electric fence, he might get a foot through the wire or be shocked and jump away from it, crashing into you.

If he tends to rush backward to avoid something he doesn't like, back him up against a solid fence or wall or into a corner. With a solid barrier on one side and the handler and person working on him on the other side, the horse usually will stand still.

Stand at his shoulder, not in front of him. You will be more out of harm's way if he lunges forward or strikes out with a front foot. If you stand facing the horse's shoulder, with one hand on his halter and the other on neck or withers, you are in a better position to move when he moves. Body contact not only helps you calm and reassure him, but if you are touching him and somewhat braced against him you can move with him rather than being bumped into or stepped on if he moves.

One way to hold a halter and have more leverage is to grasp the lower part of the noseband between cheek ring and lead-shank ring. Rest your knuckles or a finger right against the horse's lower cheek (while exerting constant tension on the halter). Just by cocking your wrist you can put pressure on the side of his face with your knuckle or finger if he starts to misbehave.

By facing his shoulder while holding the halter, you can also read his intentions, and with your other hand you can rub his neck or withers to help distract him. A soothing low voice and rhythmic rubbing will help keep his mind off whatever is being done to him. Soft whistling or humming also can help distract a horse. Keeping your mind calm and focused on him can greatly help the insecure and apprehensive horse. If you are tuned in to the horse's state of mind and reactions, you can often keep him from moving during crucial moments or keep him from kicking. Raising his head or pulling it toward you can make it harder for him to kick.

If the horse indicates that he's about to blow up, warn the person working on him and try to restrain the horse. Don't try to discipline a horse for bad behavior while the farrier or vet is working on him, or you may create a worse problem. If the horse reacts adversely to your spanking or jerk on his halter, he may pull his foot away from the farrier or crash into the vet.

Safe Leading

The safest way to lead a horse and best control his movements is to walk beside his left shoulder, holding the lead shank a few inches from the halter or the halter itself. Always have a rope or shank attached to the halter; it gives you more to hold onto if he jumps, rears, or turns quickly. With a rope attached to the halter, you can let out some slack if necessary and he cannot jerk you as hard. Never wrap the end of the rope or shank around your hand; keep it in neat loops, not a coil that might get round your hand or arm.

Walk beside the horse, not in front. If he spooks or leaps forward, he won't bump into you, and you have better control over his movements. Walking beside his left shoulder enables you to move with him and control his head. If he tries to go too fast you can halt or slow him by leaning into his shoulder and pulling his head around. You can

Lead the horse on the left side.

be as strong as he is when you have body contact and leverage, making him pivot around you so he can't bolt.

Safe Tying

Halters and ropes should be strong. Web halters should be at least three-ply, with sturdy hardware. A halter is only as strong as its snap or the ring that holds the snap. If a horse pulls back and the rope, halter, or snap suddenly breaks, he could go over backward and kill himself if he hits the top of his head.

Some horsemen prefer a rope braided onto the halter ring or tied with a secure knot rather than depending on a metal snap. It's not wise to leave halters on horses and totally unnecessary if horses are trained to be caught easily. A halter can be dangerous if a horse ever catches it on something in its pen or pasture, or hooks a hind shoe or foot in it when scratching his ear. Always tie the horse with something

This tie includes a body rope...

he cannot break. Even a dependable horse may pull back if startled. If a halter breaks or a rope comes loose, he will think he can get free whenever he pulls back. This can seriously injure horse or human if the horse flies backward. A horse that becomes unpredictable, setting back at any excuse, can be dangerous

to people working around him. If he pulls back while being tied or untied, he could crash into you or take off a hand or finger that gets caught in the rope. A body rope such as the one pictured here causes a horse to pull against himself if he pulls back.

Make sure to tie the horse to something solid that won't move or break if the horse pulls back. Never tie to a wire fence or netting, as the horse could get a foot caught if he paws. If you tie to a pole fence, tie to a strong, well-set post rather than just a pole unless the pole is securely nailed to the other side of the posts and cannot be

...that pulls against the horse.

59

pulled off. It's best to loop the rope around a post as well as a pole.

Don't leave a rope so long that the horse could get a foot over it. Tie short, but with enough rope to give freedom of head and neck, or he may feel claustrophobic. About eighteen to twenty-four inches is enough. Anything longer can cause a problem if the horse puts his head down (to reach for grass or rub his head on his leg) and then puts his head back up under the rope, crossing the rope over the back of his neck. Finding his head suddenly held down can cause even a placid horse to panic and pull back.

A similar problem can occur if the rope hooks on something low when the horse puts his head down, such as the fender or taillight of a horse trailer. Make sure the rope is short, and tie it level with his head or higher; then he's less likely to get his head caught under the rope or have it catch on something. If he pulls back, he won't damage his neck muscles like he would if he were tied low, and he also won't be able to pull back as strongly.

One way to get a horse over a phobia about his head being restrained low is to let him graze while dragging a lead rope. When he first steps on the rope, he will panic and rush backward or try to fling his head up, but after a while he learns this is nothing to fear.

If tying to a tree, choose one with no sharp branches that might injure his head or eyes, and make sure the rope won't slip down the trunk. Don't tie to a horse trailer unless it is attached to the pulling vehicle or securely blocked so the wheels can't move. When tying near other horses, leave space between them so they can't kick one another. Make sure the area where you tie a horse is free of clutter or obstacles that might be hazardous if he pulls back or breaks loose.

Don't tie with bridle reins or the horse may end up with broken reins, injured mouth, or even a broken jaw. Don't tie a horse with just a rope around his neck unless you use a non-slip knot such as a bowline. If you use a knot that slips and he pulls back, he could choke himself.

When tying any horse, use a knot that will hold securely yet be easy to untie quickly. Regular knots, tied in some types of rope, can become so tight they are impossible to undo if the horse pulls. Some quick-release knots slip when pulled on, leaving the rope too long. The manger tie is a good quick-release knot (if tied tightly so it won't slip) that can be undone with a pull on the loose end. If a horse nibbles at the rope or tries to untie himself, put the loose end through the loop so he can't pull the knot loose. For a horse that plays with the rope, put the tie on the far side of the post, put the loose end through the loop of the knot and on down the post to tie to a pole below the level the horse can reach.

Another solution is to use an extra-long lead rope and dally it around the post a couple times at proper tie height, taking the end of it to another stout post for final tying. Then the rope-chewing horse can't untie the knot or tighten it by pulling back.

Safety Positions

When handling a foot, keep some body contact. You can brace against him if necessary, sense his mood (whether he is relaxed or tense), and anticipate movement. Your upper arm should be in contact with the horse's side when you are holding a front foot to clean, trim, or treat. That way, you will have more leverage if he tries to jerk the foot away. When holding a hind foot, most of the leg should be in contact with your leg. If he tries to jerk a hind foot away, firmly bend the toe upward; it will be harder for him to pull it away.

Picking a front foot correctly.

When working around the horse while his foot is on the ground, never bend over in front of the leg. Don't be right by his knee as you work on the foot. The horse can unintentionally bump you just by picking up his foot, especially a front foot. His knee can hit you in the face.

When working around the hindquarters, close contact is always safer than a short distance away (where you'd get the full force of a kick). Close contact can often prevent a kick if you are braced against the leg

Picking a hind foot correctly.

or allow you to move with the horse and not be hurt. The closer you are, the less impact you'll get from a kick; a whack at full extension of the leg may break bones.

Safety When Handling Horses in Groups

Walking among a group of loose horses can be dangerous, especially if you are in the way when a dominant horse chases a herd mate. Stay alert to what is happening. A squabble at one side of the group could create a chain reaction of movement that might affect you even if you are on the opposite side. With a group of boisterous youngsters that don't yet know their manners, you should carry a short whip or crop to help define your personal space. Use it as an extension of your arm if you need to remind some of the "gang" to keep their rough-housing a little farther away. If you are trying to catch a timid horse that might move suddenly to get away from a more domineering herd mate, you may have better luck and less chance for an accident if you catch the dominant horse first.

Always be careful when feeding horses in groups, especially feeding grain. Feeding time triggers aggressive actions with the dominant individuals trying to drive the subordinates from the food. When managing horses in groups, be aware of each horse's personality. Much conflict among horses and injuries can be avoided if compatible individuals are pastured together. They are less danger to one another and to you.

Most social problems with horses are management problems. Some of the most common causes of aggressive behavior and social distress among groups of horses are due to poor judgment about which horses are put together, over-crowding in poorly designed enclosures, and not paying attention to the equine social code.

Big problems often occur when a new horse is added to a group, disrupting the established social order as the newcomer tries to find his niche in the hier-archy. Often the aggression that is triggered to reshuffle the pecking order extends beyond the new horse as other members of the herd try to protect their status. They all have to sort out their various places again. If the dominance bat-tles and aggression do not resolve quickly, you may have to separate the individ-uals who cannot seem to get their pecking order figured out. Some horses may need more space, either in a larger pasture or with fewer herd mates, to reach a truce.

You can sometimes use the buddy system to ease a newcomer into an estab-lished herd. When a new mare is put into a broodmare band the others usually bully her and chase her away from the feed. But if you can take a compatible individual (a dominant but non-aggressive mare) from the herd and put her with the new mare for a few days in another pen or pasture, those two will often bond. They can be put into the herd together and will defend one another if the others become too inquisitive and aggressive. The new mare won't have to defend herself alone.

Horses segregated as youngsters often display problems interacting with other horses later. They don't learn the basic social skills needed to get along with other horses while growing up. Foals raised in a herd situation rather than in a stall or small paddock grow up with proper social behavior and are less apt to have trouble or cause problems in a group later. Horses accustomed to living in herds are more easily assimilated into new groups as a general rule than are hors-es that have lived most of their lives by themselves or with just one buddy.

Herd size and space are also important factors in keeping a group compatible. Bullying and aggression increase when too many horses are crowded into a small area. Putting more than ten horses in a single enclosure generally creates conflict unless the pasture is large enough for buffer zones between the two or three smaller groups that may then evolve. If you don't have that kind of space, you might resolve problems by having separate turnout time for each of the smaller groups the horses voluntarily create.

When caring for horses in groups, pay attention to feed and water arrangements to minimize risks of injury. Water sources, salt, or mineral boxes should be placed so horses have easy access to them and can get away from a dominant individual. Never situate them in a corner.

Spread feed out over a large area so the low-ranking members can get their share without being chased off. If feed is not spread out enough, skirmishes can occur, and some of the timid individuals will not get enough. Put out at least one hay pile or grain feeder per horse, plus one extra (to help reduce the "musical chairs" effect), at least twenty feet apart. If hay is fed in round bales or feed racks, have more than one in each pasture so the most dominant horse cannot guard all the feed.

Keep mares separate from geldings. Up to 30 percent of all geldings show some sexual behavior, and some may fight over mares or be kicked by indignant mares.

Safe Restraint

Sometimes a horse must stand for an unfamiliar or unpleasant procedure. A well-trained, cooperative horse might stand still just because he trusts the horseman, but a high-strung, untrained, or spoiled horse might rebel vigorously. A horse can be kept calm and immobile with a variety of restraint techniques. When using a restraint, you need to understand when and when not to use it and what works best for a particular horse.

Horses tolerate uncomfortable or threatening situations differently and may require different types of restraint. It's wise to get the horse used to restraints while he is growing up, as part of basic ground training. This is better than having to use a restraint for the first time in an emergency situation. If a restraint can be applied in an easy manner as part of the horse's handling during a training session, he will more readily tolerate it later in a crisis.

Choose a restraint acceptable to the individual horse. Some horses resent application of a twitch and fight it worse than the treatment. This is usually because a twitch has been improperly applied in the past or used only in stressful situations, and the horse associates it with pain.

For a horse that won't accept a twitch, try squeezing and twisting the loose skin at the shoulder or twisting an ear. Some horses are ear-shy, however, and that's the last thing they'll let you grab. For horses that are hard to twitch or difficult to restrain, a device called a Stableizer often works well.

Whatever restraint method you use, apply it quickly, properly, and purposefully, with enough force to hold the horse still so the desired procedure can be done and to allow the restraint to be removed as soon as possible. An improperly applied twitch or chain can do more harm than good. The horse might seem to be restrained and then explode. An inadequately applied restraint enables or encourages him to resist. If he succeeds in avoiding or resisting, he will try to avoid future attempts to restrain him. A painful or too-forceful application of a restraint will cause resentment, fear, or distrust, making the horse much harder to deal with next time.

When using a twitch, lip chain, or ear twist, be ready to perform the treatment or procedure immediately. Do not apply the restraint before getting the injection or medication ready. Most horses will tolerate such restraints for a few moments but not for an extended time.

Be careful when applying a restraint as some horses strike out with their front feet or sling their head. Stand to one side so that if the horse rears, strikes, or throws its head violently you can get out of the way. If there is someone helping you, make sure that person is out of the way of the horse's possible reactions.

Keep in mind that you have responsibility for the safety of whoever else is helping with the horse or performing the treatment. Your job is to keep the

Application of the twitch.

person from being kicked, stepped on, bitten, squashed against the wall, or run over. Pay close attention to both the horse and the person working on him. Both of you should be on the same side of the horse. Then if the horse tries to kick or becomes unruly, you can pull the horse's head in a direction that will move his body away from the person he is endangering. When restraining a horse, work with his mind. If he is timid, reassure him. If he is rebellious, remind him that you are dominant.

Using a Twitch

The twitch has been used for hundreds of years to make fidgety or fractious horses stand still. It can usually control a horse during a mildly unpleasant experience, but make sure you use good judgment in determining whether a horse will be a good candidate for twitching. A high-strung or seldom-handled horse may not respond well to twitching, nor do some foals. Trying to twitch a small foal may be unsuccessful and counterproductive; the memory of a frightening experience in application of the twitch may make him fearful of future muzzle handling. A confused or frightened horse is likewise difficult to twitch.

The traditional twitch has a wooden handle about fifteen to thirty inches long, with a loop of rope or chain attached to one end. To put a twitch on a horse, stand to one side of his head. Put your hand through the loop and grasp the horse's upper lip, then slide the chain or thong over your hand and around the lip. While putting the loop over the upper lip, tuck the twitch handle under your arm to hold it. Then twist the handle until the loop tightens around the lip. Your aim is to achieve maximum control of the horse while causing him the least amount of distress, so turn the twitch just enough to get his attention and make him stand quietly. If the horse starts to move around or react to what else is being done to him, the twitch can be tightened a bit more.

The long handle allows you enough space to stay out of the way of the horse's front feet if he misbehaves, but be sure to stand beside rather than in front of him. It is helpful to have someone hold the horse while you apply the twitch.

A chain loop has some advantages over a rope or cord. Chain tightens and loosens more quickly and easily, and pressure can be increased or decreased with little effort. A slight turn of the handle alters the pressure. A rope twitch requires many turns to get effective pressure on the lip and can be easily overdone. Since the loop is then very tight, it won't loosen as readily. Rope doesn't have the built-in limits to twisting that a chain has.

The chain or rope loop should be twisted up rather than down, since this makes it more difficult for the twitch to come off. If the horse starts objecting before the procedure is over, the twitch holder can change the angle of the handle to control the twist of the lip and put a bit more "turn" on it.

The closer the twitch handle is to vertical, the milder the effect on the nose; the closer to horizontal, the more severe. If the handle is pushed higher than the level of the horse's muzzle, the effect can be quite severe and inhumane. If the horse starts breathing heavily and rotating his head in the direction of the twist on his nose, he's probably in discomfort. By contrast, if he looks like he's standing there napping, he may have "gone dead" to the effect of the twitch, and you may not really be in control. A startling sensation may send him lunging forward. Adjustability of the long-handled twitch with chain loop enables the horse holder to "play" with the horse's lip to keep him at the right state of mind and to maintain the best control over his actions.

An important aspect of using a twitch is how you remove it. If done properly, the horse will resent it less the next time you try to twitch him. To remove it, put your hand on his upper lip, and as you untwist the chain, massage the lip firmly, rubbing the area that was twisted. Don't let the horse jerk his head away. Continue rubbing until he relaxes and accepts the massage of his nose. This gives a pleasant sensation as the numbness wears off, leaving the horse with a better attitude about the experience.

Some versions of the twitch are made of metal and clamp onto the upper lip and also to the halter, so the horse handler working alone can have both hands free to deal with the horse after adjusting the twitch. These are easy to use, but are safest if held by someone rather than affixed to the halter.

The one-man twitch that clamps the twisted upper lip in a metal frame (holding it in place with a screw-up plate) can be most dangerous. Its adjustability is limited to where you set it when you first apply it. You can't fine-tune the adjustment as you work on the horse. Nor can it be immediately removed if he suddenly decides he's had enough, making it difficult to get close to his head to loosen the screw if he throws a fit. Another type of one-man twitch clamps onto the lip like a foot-long nutcracker and can be secured by wrapping its attached rope tightly around the handles and snapping it to a halter ring.

Any type of one-man twitch can cause problems if left attached to the halter, becoming dangerous if it comes off the nose — the horse is no longer under control and is left with the tool dangling from his halter. It can become a flying missile or a deadly weapon if the horse starts throwing his head. This type of twitch should be applied properly and firmly, since a half-applied tool is more likely to come off if the horse shakes his head. The self-attaching type of twitch also can be dangerous if put on too tightly and the horse resents it and breaks away; he may run blindly in an attempt to escape the clamp on his nose.

Used properly (held by a second person rather than affixed to the halter), this type of twitch can be safer and easier to use than the traditional long-handled twitch, since there is no handle to clout you or the horse if he moves around, no chain or rope to dig into the nose. The metal clamp is also easier to apply (often less fight with a horse to get it on him, and less chance for him to learn evasive tactics). Pressure can be regulated more easily with newer versions of this metal clamp than with a traditional twitch. These "humane" twitches come in several styles, all based on the scissors-like action of the smooth metal tongs. The horse's nose is placed in the scissor jaws, which are then closed on the nose.

How a Twitch Works

Pressure on the upper lip produces a calm and relaxed (almost sedated and catatonic) state of mind. Studies done in England and the Netherlands during the 1980s found that the heart rates of twitched horses were significantly lower than those of horses not twitched, even during circumstances that ordinarily cause pain. Normally pain increases the pulse rate.

Twitching increases horses' ability to handle pain. After application of a twitch, a horse becomes quieter, appears somewhat sedated, and has drooping eyelids. Hostile or nervous attitudes subside, and the horse's interest in his surroundings decreases. It becomes difficult to make the horse move; he stands as if in a trance. If the loop is too tight or the pressure on the nose too severe, however, he will resist and might strike out with a front foot.

Proper use of a twitch, like use of acupuncture, stimulates receptor fibers in the skin that activate endorphins, which cause the heart rate to decrease and reduce sensations of pain. Endorphins also alter the animal's emotional state, making him calmer.

If a horse is in a lot of pain from injury or colic or in a highly unstable emotional state, a chemical restraint such as a sedative or tranquilizer works better than a twitch to allow safe examination or treatment of the horse. A painkiller also may be needed. Twitching is not adequate in these instances. But in many in-between situations in which the horse is too fidgety, upset, or uncomfortable to tolerate simple procedures or treatment, the twitch is often a good solution.

It quickly and easily — and only temporarily — relaxes and sedates him. As soon as you release the twitch, the horse is back to normal. You don't have to wait for effects of a sedative or tranquilizer to wear off. For best results, a twitch should not be used longer than two to five minutes.

Other Methods of Restraint

The **skin twitch** or shoulder twitch is a simple restraint that requires no tool and involves grasping a large quantity of loose skin on the neck, just in front of the shoulder. After grabbing the skin, squeeze it as hard as you can, with some twisting action. This tends to immobilize a horse due to release of endorphins that help calm him (similar to the action of a twitch). It can be used as a mild to moderate restraint technique for a variety of situations, but some horses may protest.

This type of restraint can be quite effective on young horses or foals. Grasping a handful of skin at the juncture of shoulder and neck and rolling your knuckles forward so that a fold of skin is pulled over your fingers can help keep a horse from moving forward or striking out. You can use both hands for more control.

The **hand twitch** (grasping the horse's nose with your hand and twisting or pinching the upper lip) works well on some horses and often is easier than trying to put a twitch on an evasive nose. Once you get a hold of the nose, the horse usually stands as if twitched. This type of restraint is very humane because you cannot apply enough pressure to hurt him. The disadvantage is that the horse can easily pull away. For a quick and temporary discomfort, however, such as the prick of a needle or a fast application of medicine, a hand grip on the nose often works well.

The **ear hold**, used by old-time horsemen, is also called earing down. Some people feel this is an inhumane type of restraint, but this depends on the way it is done. No mechanical type of twitch on an ear (ear tongs, etc.) should ever be used; the cartilage in the ear is very sensitive and can be permanently damaged. If done properly by hand, however, the ear hold can be very effective for short-

A hand twitch.

term restraint. When grasping the ear, line your fingers up a fraction of an inch back from the edge of the ear, resting on a ridge of cartilage at the top of the ear; your thumb under the ear will apply the pressure. You don't need to twist the ear much nor pull on it. Simply squeeze with your thumb, putting folding pressure on the ear cartilage (bending the ear's edge inward toward your palm). You can release or tighten your hold to reward or punish the horse for behaving or misbehaving. If you start with your hand position where the ear would be at normal head carriage, any evasive movements of the horse will be a form of self-punishment. Most horses find that cooperation is more comfortable.

Keep your elbow bent when grasping the ear so the horse won't hurt your shoulder if he suddenly raises his head. Some horses are effectively restrained by an ear hold, while others strongly resent it and may strike or sling the head.

An ear twitch.

A good restraint for a foal is a **tail hold**. Raising the tail upward and forward will usually quiet his struggles and immobilize him, since it triggers the reflexes that straighten his hind legs and keeps him from kicking or struggling; it also stimulates some endorphin release. On a small foal, you can put one arm around his chest and grasp the underside of his tail (at its base) with the other hand. For a larger foal, if you can't reach around him, you can grasp his mane right in front of the withers to hold his front while you lift his tail with the other hand. An aid in handling the larger foal is to pin him against the wall with your hip (pressed against his ribs) while using the tail hold and mane hold.

If you are working by yourself and need to restrain the foal and at the same time administer an injection or treatment, place a belt loosely around the foal's front (low around the base of his neck, like a breast collar). Once the belt is fastened, slide your left arm down through it, toward the rear of the foal, and then grasp the foal's tail with your right hand and place it in your left hand. Thus your left arm and hand are holding the foal at both ends, with the help of the belt "collar." With the foal between you and the stall wall and held by the belt and the tail, you have your other hand free to administer the injection or treatment.

A **bridle** can be used to restrain a horse that is accustomed to wearing one, since it gives more control than a halter if he tries to misbehave or move forward. Stand beside his head on the left, holding the reins right under his chin, where you can squeeze your hand together to put more pressure on the bit if the horse tries to move. Similarly, on a horse accustomed to a bridle, a fair degree of control can be obtained by slipping a finger into the mouth and putting pressure on the gum space between incisors and molars, as a bit would. This can often keep a horse from moving forward when a halter by itself is not enough control.

A **blindfold** is sometimes used for keeping a horse still; most horses are hesitant to move if they can't see. Even just blocking his vision on one side by cupping a hand over his eye can eliminate distractions or apprehension. If someone is giving an injection or treating a fidgety horse, he may stand calmly long enough to get the job done if he can't see. A blindfold can be applied if

A chain shank.

he must stand still for more than just a moment, but you might not want to try it on a foal or young horse as it might panic.

The traditional way to blindfold a horse is with a light jacket, pulling one arm of the jacket through the side of the halter, wrapping the back of the jacket over the horse's face to cover his eyes and tucking the other arm through the other side of the halter to hold it in place. A folded towel can also work well, and it can be easily attached to the halter with four clothespins (two on each side). It can be put on or taken off quickly and may not alarm the horse as much as stuffing a jacket under his halter. If the horse become upset, you can quickly remove the blindfold by pulling on it; the wooden clothespins will just pop off.

Holding up a leg works well to restrain some horses. Holding a front leg can keep a horse from trying to go forward. If a hind leg is being treated, you can hold up the opposite hind so the horse will keep the other foot on the ground.

Another mild restraint is to pull the horse's tail up and to the side or firmly downward. This makes it more difficult for him to kick and also helps you keep track of his movements, steadying you both as you work on the hind end.

The **chain shank** works well for mild restraint on boisterous horses. A strong lead shank with a chain on the end can be passed through the side rings on the halter and then hooked back to itself. A chain can be used several ways. One is to pass the chain through the left ring on the noseband of the halter, over the nose in direct contact with the skin, through the right ring of the noseband, then through the ring under the noseband and clipped back to itself. Or it can be passed up to the halter ring near the eye on the right side of the horse. Either way, pulling the shank puts pressure on the bridge of the nose.

It is not as effective just to pass the shank from the noseband ring on the left side to the ring on the right side; this tends to pull the halter off center into his eye every time you pull on the shank and does not put proper pressure on the horse's nose. A common mistake when using a chain is applying continuous pressure, which tends to numb the tissue and make the chain less effective; soon the horse ignores the pull. The chain shank should be used with a regular lead rope or strap, and pressure should be applied to the chain only when necessary.

If a chain over the nose is not enough restraint, the chain can be slipped down under the lip onto the upper gum surface (between gum and upper lip). The chain's pressure against the gum (**lip chain**) works well to restrain unruly horses. It puts pressure on nerves that block adrenaline release and tends to have a calming effect. If used roughly, however, a lip chain cuts into the gum or lip and may send a sensitive horse into orbit.

For best control and evenness of pressure, run the chain through the near halter ring, across the lip, and through the far ring, and then affix it to the cheek ring below the ear. You may need to lower the halter a couple of holes so the chain can be slipped under the horse's lip.

You want the chain to pass along his gums (under the upper lip) in such a way that you don't have to put any pressure on the shank to keep it in place. After lifting the lip and putting the chain against the horse's gums, you can then apply any amount of pressure needed to hold him still. If necessary, take the halter back up another hole so the chain is securely against the gums. You won't need to apply pressure if he behaves, but you can put a steady pull on the chain if needed or even a tug if he misbehaves. Some horsemen put the chain through the mouth (like a bit) for more control, but this can be inhumane.

A variation on this restraint is the **Indian war bridle**, a cord that goes over the top of the poll and through the mouth. It works well to restrain most horses, but can be hard on a horse's mouth. A similar restraint is the **Indian sliptwitch**, which goes over the poll and under the top lip, against the gum, with a loop knot in one end so it can be tightened to put more pressure on the gum and poll. This affects pressure points that activate endorphins to create a sedating effect. Used roughly, however, the cord may cut into the gum or upper lip.

The **Stableizer** is a modern adaptation of the Indian sliptwitch that is more humane and versatile. In most instances it works better than lip chains, tranquilizers, or twitches for nervous or unruly horses. It can be used in situations in which a twitch cannot — for foals, inexperienced and previously unhandled horses, prolonged restraint, and procedures where a twitch is in the way, etc.

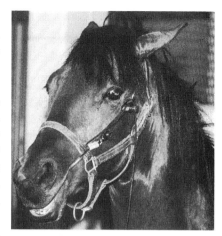

A Stableizer.

It is easy to put on (the loop can be enlarged to slip over the horse's head), won't fall off, and one person can apply it and work on the horse alone, and it's safe for horse and human. There's no handle to hit you in the head; the small plastic handle at the end of the cord is light and won't cause injury if it swings around. The Stableizer relaxes and sedates the horse, yet unlike being twitched he can still move with it on. He can be led, loaded into a trailer, or even given training lessons.

The Stableizer slips over the head and goes behind the ears and under the top lip next to the gum. It is then tightened, using its cord handle, which has small pulleys rigged like a miniature fence stretcher. The pressure points behind the ears stimulate the release of endorphins. The pressure point beneath the lip blocks the release of adrenaline and tends to relax the horse. The portion of the cord that goes under the lip is covered with plastic tubing so it won't cut into the lip or gum.

The horse experiences pleasure rather than pain while wearing it; he remembers the handling (clipping, shoeing, wound treatment) as a good experience rather than something to fear and is more cooperative the next time.

To put it on a horse, the loop is extended to its fullest size and slipped over the head, putting it behind the ears first and into the mouth (beneath the upper lip) last. Pulling the cord handle then tightens it. Once the Stableizer is in place, the horse should be turned in a short circle each direction, as you hold the handle firmly, pulling down on it at least three times and then releasing it. Then the handle can be pulled down snugly, letting the horse's head size set the pressure. The tension control button is then slid up against the top pulley. For endorphin release to have full effect, the horse must be allowed to stand for at least two minutes before you try to do anything with him.

This restraint method works just the opposite of other types of restraints, such as the twitch, ear grab, and lip chain, which work best if used as briefly as possible. With a Stableizer the horse becomes more calm and mellow the longer it is used.

Usually within sixty seconds after applying pressure, the horse relaxes. Once he is calm, he can be easily controlled for clipping, vaccination, shoeing, medical treatment, and other such procedures. If more tension is needed to manage the horse, pull down the handle and slide the control button up closer to the pulley. On most horses, the Stableizer works well the first time it is used, but on some it may require two or three sessions before they become completely manageable.

It is important to follow this gradual process — tightening the cord a few times and pulling the horse in a circle one way and then the other — because it starts the endorphin release, impresses upon the horse that you are in control, and gets him accustomed to the increased pressure you will apply in the final step of adjusting the head loop. During this time the horse's head will start to come down, the bottom lip will droop, and his eyes will soften and look sleepy. After this happens, you can go ahead with whatever procedure you need to perform.

If you must work with the horse for an extended period, ease the tension off (about one-half to three-quarters inch) on the cord by depressing the control button. If at any point you need more control again, you can take up the slack by pulling down the handle and resetting the control button up against the top pulley. You should not use maximum pressure for more than ten to fifteen minutes or there is a chance of nerve damage. Also, the constant pressure becomes ineffective for relaxing the horse after about twenty minutes and may begin to cause pain instead, which will defeat your purpose.

To remove the Stableizer, depress and slide the control button down the cord toward the plastic handle. This releases all pressure and enlarges the loop to its fullest so you can slide it off over the head. If a horse is ear shy or head shy, the loop can be taken apart at the top snap for putting it on and off.

Dealing With Problem Behavior

Problem behavior can arise or be made worse if a horse is handled improperly or can be alleviated by careful, conscientious handling. Some types of problem behavior make your job of caring for a horse more dangerous and should be diligently corrected (such as biting, kicking, rearing while being led, running over you when being caught or turned loose, and so on). Safe horse handling includes being able to nip problems in the bud or finding ways to deal with and correct a horse that already has a bad habit.

Some horses have the frustrating habit of being **hard to catch**.

You must change the horse's attitude and make him realize that being caught is something to look forward to. Horses that are handled regularly and properly from birth are usually not hard to catch. Some take longer to win over than others and a few can be challenging, but time, patience, and diligence will eventually persuade even the most resistant youngster to be caught willingly.

Every foal is different. Many are curious and friendly from the beginning and are never hard to catch. Others may need to be cornered gently for several weeks before they realize being caught is nothing to worry about. If the mare is part of the problem, work with the pair in a very small area, where you can first catch her without her running

Start handling foals early.

off and tie her in a corner so you can quietly work with the foal. Weaning time can be an opportunity to gain a foal's trust if you didn't have time to work with him before, for now the foal has to look to you for food and comfort.

Occasionally you encounter a headstrong individual who refuses to be caught. To get your hands on him you may need someone to help you gently corner him, ease him behind a gate, or run him into a barn stall. Once he's captured, leave a close-fitting halter on him for a few days in his pen. If he is elusive and won't let you get close enough to his head to grab the halter, corner him again and affix a long rope to the halter. Let him drag the rope for a few days in a small pen where there are no obstacles or protrusions that would catch a halter or entangle the dragging rope. This method is risky, since a halter or rope can some-

times get caught and should only be used as a last resort and for just a few days while you are getting the youngster accustomed to daily handling. Be sure the halter fits closely so it won't get caught on the fence, and so he can't get a foot caught if he scratches an ear with a hind foot.

With the halter and dragging rope, you can always catch him in the small pen by quietly moving around until you can pick up his trailing rope. He soon learns he cannot get away from you. If you catch and handle him several times a day, gaining his trust and

A rope can help in catching.

73

making him realize it is pointless to try to run away, he'll become easier to catch. With this method you can always catch even the most stubborn youngster and do it calmly and quietly without running.

With an older horse that is hard to catch, you must change his attitude and make him realize that being caught is pleasant. Reward him with a treat afterward. Don't take grain or treats with you to the pasture, however. Some horses try to sneak a bite and keep their freedom. The horse must learn to play by the rules and be willingly caught; he knows he'll get his treat — after you lead him out of the pasture. Don't use food as a bribe, especially in a group of horses, or the others may compete for the treat.

Confirmed catch-avoiders can be a challenge, because to persuade them that being caught is pleasant (a bite of grain afterward), you first have to catch them. You must outsmart the problem horse and catch him in a way that will help rather than hinder your purposes. If you always run him into the corral, he will never be easier to catch. He must want to be caught.

A horse must respect personal space.

Sometimes the way you go about catching a horse can make a difference in whether he will let you walk up to him. Most horses won't move away if you approach slowly and at an angle rather than too purposefully toward their heads. Stroll casually, not looking directly at the horse you need to catch. Try to keep him relaxed. Stop and loiter if he thinks about moving off; ignore him. Let him relax before you walk closer. This non-confrontational approach is less threatening and won't make him as suspicious or want to flee. Patience in the pasture often will enable you to walk up to the horse without triggering his desire to flee.

For the stubborn individual who remains elusive, keep him in a smaller pen for a few days or weeks until he resigns himself to being caught regularly. Horses that run due to habit and evasiveness rather than fear won't bother to run in a small pen. Keep the problem horse by himself and catch him several times a day to feed him, give him a treat, or take him to water. He starts to associate catching with good things. Catch him sometimes just for some petting; then turn him loose again.

Feel your way along with each problem horse and find a way to work around his hang-up and overcome it. Most spoiled horses can be rehabilitated with time and patience. Once the horse discovers you are a pleasant part of his daily routine, he'll look forward to your arrival instead of taking off whenever he sees you coming.

Reforming the **mannerless horse** also can be a challenge. Pushy horses take advantage of a timid or softhearted person who lets them do as they please. If bad manners become habit, it takes consistent firmness to convince the spoiled horse that he must respect a person.

Some horses won't stand still, stepping on your toes or bumping into you. Horses that walk on you and crowd your space lack respect for humans. Treating a horse as a pet and not being consistent in early handling and training often creates this problem. The horse doesn't have a clear picture of where he stands in the relationship; he is trying to be dominant.

A disrespectful or inattentive horse can be dangerous, whether he stomps on your toe or takes a parting shot at you with a hind foot as you turn him loose in the paddock. You must establish consistent basic rules for allowable limits of behavior. He must understand that humans are not to be touched without permission — never bumped, bitten, or kicked. If you allow him to nuzzle, rub, play, or push, he considers humans as buddies to roughhouse with.

To gain a horse's respect and keep it, you must think like a horse. Most of the horse's reactions are based on social ranking — dominance and submission — and he must figure out how humans fit into that picture. If he is successful at dominating people, he thinks he can do whatever he pleases.

The horse must learn to keep a respectful distance, and this eliminates "accidents" such as stepping on your toes, swinging his rump into you, pushing you into the gate as he crowds through, smashing your nose by swinging his head around, or swatting you in the face with his tail. The horse has precision accuracy with his tail; hitting you in the face with it is never accidental. Be alert to whenever he presses his limits or violates the rules and don't ignore things that might seem accidental. Through your own body language (holding your ground rather than moving out of the way), let the horse know you have a personal space and that you won't allow it to be violated by his disrespect.

If he invades your personal space, enforce your rule (no uninvited touching) by appropriate punishment, pushing his head or body away, giving him a quick, sharp slap, or a bump with the butt of a whip. The circumstances and severity of the horse's violation should be what dictates the reprimand you give him. Be consistent. Discourage him every time he bumps you, insisting he keep his distance. Move him back, push him away, or give him a spank (if appropriate). Most horses get the idea fairly quickly.

Some horses try to smash you up against the wall or fence when you're working with them. You must distinguish between behavior triggered by discomfort or fear and that which is deliberate and aggressive. A nervous horse needs patient, gentle work to get over his fears, but a horse that is trying to dominate you needs firm and immediate attention.

Horses that habitually bump into you must be taught to stay back. Using the butt of a whip, tap the horse on the chest to make him back up, then praise him when he responds. Whenever he moves into your space, immediately make him get back where he belongs. Having to back up makes him realize he must submit to you and that you are in control, not him.

For a really aggressive horse that tries to smash you into the wall, use a short, stout stick, holding it in such a way that the horse runs into the stick instead of you. After a few applications he learns it's not pleasant trying to move into your space.

Some horses have bad manners when you take them out of their stalls or turn them loose. To correct the habit of charging, have the horse stop and relax before you let him go. Make him stand facing you, and don't turn him loose until he stands still. Loop the rope around his neck before you unsnap him or take off

This horse resents being led.

his halter so he can't rush off the instant he thinks he's free. Make him realize you are still in control and that you are the one who will leave him. When he is calm and relaxed, quietly walk away.

Some horses misbehave when being led and become **rooters and draggers** because they resent being pulled at. They retaliate by lugging even harder into the halter. The handler may inadvertently incite this reaction by active pulling, creating a tug of war. A led horse should have some slack, accompanying you in a relaxed manner rather than being dragged or dragging you. Any pressure on the halter to slow him should be intermittent not continuous. Well-timed short tugs are more effective than a steady pull.

For a particularly overeager horse that won't heed commands to slow or halt, you may have to use a chain over the nose. You should not exert pressure with the chain unless he starts going too fast or you ask him to stop. Your right hand should be holding the end of the chain where it meets the leather shank. Have the horse on a slack lead as you walk beside or just ahead of his shoulder, an arm's length from him.

If he tries to bolt, your hand can hold the line adequately if there is a knot just back of where the chain fastens to the line. This jerks the chain on his nose with the same effect of a choke chain on a dog. If the chain is properly adjusted on the halter, it will only press into the bridge of his nose when he lugs or bolts forward. It will release and loosen when he stops. If he misbehaves, you can also engage the chain by giving one firm downward jerk. After a jerk, immediately give slack to release the pressure. This jerk and release can be effective discipline, much better than mutual pulling.

Biting is a natural defense action and a game with some horses, but no well-trained horse bites a human. Biting may be a sign of bad attitude and crankiness, wanting to be left alone, self defense in a situation he doesn't like, or his way of establishing dominance. A nervous horse may bite when frustrated or irritated. If a normally well-mannered horse tries to bite, it's a sign you are doing something wrong, causing discomfort. Most nipping can be halted by more care in handling the horse or by not giving him cause or opportunity to nip.

Often the worst biters are pets that had their way too often. Horses take advantage of an easygoing human. If a horse puts his ears back when you walk into his stall and you step back, he may decide you are the submissive one in the relationship. The next time you enter his stall, he may not only pin his ears but take a bite at you. If you fail to reprimand him at the start of his attempts to be dominant, you encourage his unacceptable behavior.

The solution to biting or any other aggressive action is to impress upon the horse that you are the dominant one. The mouthy youngster may think slapping or swatting is a game, like the mock fighting he would do with another young horse. Your discipline must be more impressive, like the reprimand he would get from an older, no-nonsense horse. A swift, growling yell coupled with a kick or a smack — something sudden and startling — should make him realize he made a big mistake. You want him to understand that this is something he should never do again.

Some young horses are so bratty in their playfulness they can become hard to handle. The best cure for this type of attitude is to put the youngster with an older horse that won't tolerate his roughhousing. The discipline the young horse gets from the older one can make the youngster realize he can't be the boss. It's easier to handle him after he has experienced what it is like to be dominated and has learned submission.

If you keep an aggressive horse by himself and you are his only influence, you must be careful and consistent in how you handle him so he will respect you and accept your role as boss. If he tries to play nipping games, be constantly alert so you can prevent or reprimand him instantly, not after the fact. Punishment for biting should be done as the act is happening or about to happen, not afterward, or it may become a game to the horse — trying to nip and then jerking his head away before you can punish him.

Always be in tune with what he is doing so you can be aware of his intentions. Prevent a nip by meeting him halfway so he bumps his nose with your elbow, hoof pick, or grooming tool. Don't jab; do it in a calm manner, so he thinks he's bumping himself. If you pay attention, and catch him when he tries to bite, his self-punishment will discourage him.

Kicking is another dangerous habit that should be halted as quickly as possible. A kick toward a human is usually due to fear or self-defense. Horses in

groups use kicking to keep subordinates in their place or to express annoyance or self-defense. A dominant horse merely threatens to kick and subordinates get out of his way. Most horses give warning signals before kicking — laying the ears back, presenting the rump, clamping the tail, lifting a hind leg threateningly, or backing toward the intruder. A startled horse may kick explosively without warning, but many times a kick can be avoided if you pay attention to the horse's mood.

Kicking can become a habit.

When approaching a horse for any reason, let him know you are there and approach his head, not his rump. Watch ears and tail for signs of mood. A horse that kicks needs to be conditioned to stand still and trust you, to learn that kicking doesn't work, that what he perceived as personal threats are not so terrible.

The key to overcoming a horse's kick reaction is to reassure him and make him realize you aren't hurting him. This is one reason it's best to work with the horse held rather than tied; he feels less trapped. Most problem behavior can be corrected, making the horse safer to handle if you take time to figure out why the horse is acting in an unacceptable way and use good horse psychology to reshape his attitude.

4

Facilities of Good
Horsekeeping

ONE OF THE MOST IMPORTANT aspects of good horsekeeping is safe and
adequate facilities. Good facilities, properly maintained, can help prevent injury
and illnesses. Poor fences, for instance, can lead to injury; a weed patch in the
pasture may contain poisonous plants; a poorly ventilated barn may lead to respiratory problems.

Fences

When it comes to keeping horses, the most crucial structures on your place
are the fences, enclosing pens, and/or pastures. Barns and shelters are nice but
not entirely necessary, whereas a fence is needed to keep a horse where he
belongs. Good fences define property lines and keep horses from wandering off.
They are crucial in the daily workings of your place; it is impossible to maintain
horses without them.

A horse fence must be safe, and secure enough to hold horses within its
boundaries. Horses are more active and skittish than other domestic animals, so
fences must be highly visible and four and a half to five-feet high. Fences should
be even taller for tall breeds and for corral fences, stallion paddocks, or foaling
and weaning pens.

A five-foot fence is the same height as fifteen hands. A general rule for small
paddocks, corrals, and stallion pens is to have the top of the fence at the horse's
eye level. Avoid acute corners in a pasture or paddock where a horse might get
trapped running along the fence line or being chased by another horse.

When constructing a new fence, your choice of materials will be influenced by
cost, the type of horses you are enclosing, and the time and maintenance they
require. You may need several types of fencing: a paddock for a stallion must be
stronger than a pasture fence for a group of mares and foals, and the latter must
be safer and more foolproof than a fence for placid old geldings. The type of fence
will also depend upon size of the area and materials suitable to the climate. No
single type of fence is best for all purposes.

If you live in a highly populated area, you might want a fence that keeps horses
in and dogs and people out. Neighborhood children climbing into your pastures or
paddocks might get hurt. Even if you have "no trespassing" signs well posted, if
someone goes in without permission and gets hurt by your horse, you may be liable.

Not all types of fence are safe for horses, and even some of the traditional types
are less safe than other types.

Barbed-wire fence.

Barbed-wire fences work well for cattle and often are used by ranchers who have both horses and cattle, but barbed wire can be dangerous for horses. A horse could seriously injure himself if he tries to paw at the fence, jump it, lean over it, or even gets pushed into it by another horse. Even horses that grow up in barbed-wire enclosures and respect fences are occasionally cut and ruined.

If your place is already enclosed by barbed wire, you may have no alternative until you can build another type of fence, but you can make the existing fence safer if you make sure the wires are tight. Sagging wires might entice a horse to reach through for grass, or he might get a foot through the fence. A tight wire fence with an electric wire along the top and one along the side to keep horses away from the barbed wire will eliminate the leaning, reaching, rubbing, and pawing that might cause injury.

Wooden fencing (poles, boards, or wooden rails) can be safe for horses under many conditions. Wood is strong and durable, more forgiving than barbed wire or metal if a horse runs into it, and cheaper than several other types of fencing.

Wooden fencing (four-plank).

In a dry climate untreated poles or boards can last twenty to thirty years and even longer if treated. Wood is most appropriate where horses have a lot of room and plenty of pasture.

Confined, bored horses will chew on wood and can demolish wooden fences in a very short time. To protect wood fencing, you may want to augment it with electrified wire or electrified tape to prevent chewing. A wood fence with electric wire along the top and another out to the side to keep horses back from it will last a long time. Wood preservatives or protective paint, reapplied when needed, is necessary in a wet climate to keep wood from rotting.

Wooden fences require a lot of maintenance. Wood can split and splinter; boards or poles can fall down, warp, swell, and contract with varying moisture conditions. Jagged edges from broken boards can be dangerous if not replaced because horses can impale themselves, and rough edges from horses chewing the boards can result in a horse getting splinters if he rubs against the board. Damaged, chewed, or rotten poles or boards must be replaced and nails driven in again if they work out. Nails may creep out an inch or more before you notice them and can be a serious hazard.

The least safe type of wooden fence for horses is the zigzag "worm fence" or "snake fence" made by interlacing logs or poles atop one another at right angles. The entire fence is a series of corners, which can be hazardous, as can the projecting log or rail ends that a horse might run into.

An alternative to boards or poles is the split rail fence, built without nails. The rails rest in holes drilled in the posts. This type of fence works fairly well if the rails or poles fit snugly and do not work themselves out. If the rails don't fit securely or are not properly

Zigzag fencing is not safe.

seasoned before installation, they may loosen and fall out. Slip-board fences work the same way; the boards are put into slots in the posts. The boards are easy to replace when repairing the fence, since no nailing is necessary.

Wood fencing for a paddock or corral will need to be protected from chewing. Even treated wood may get chewed when horses are closely confined. Electric wires in a small area are not safe since a horse may be pushed into a corner by a herd mate (and it might be necessary to crowd a horse into a corner for some reason, as when catching a young foal). A better way to protect corral fencing is to staple strips of chicken wire around the portions horses can reach to chew. A roll of chicken wire can be cut into long strips of appropriate width to cover the posts or poles and stapled on with long (two-inch) staples that will not pull out. Even the most determined wood chewers cannot bite through the chicken wire.

PVC (polyvinyl chloride) is a synthetic fencing material often used as an alternative to wood since it doesn't rot or splinter and horses won't chew it. PVC planks look like wood but without the upkeep and come in several widths, thicknesses, and colors. PVC fencing is treated to resist color changes and brittleness caused by sunlight and to reduce cracking in cold weather.

PVC fencing generally comes with a fifteen- to twenty-year warranty and may last thirty years. There are square and rounded versions. Though expensive, it requires little maintenance and usually lasts longer than wood.

PVC fencing.

Polyethylene-coated wood planks and square posts combine the advantages of wood and synthetic materials. The polymer coating makes for a good-looking fence and also protects the wood from moisture to prevent weathering and rot. It reduces the need for painting, staining, or replacing rotted wood. Like PVC planks, this fencing needs less care and maintenance than wood and is not as readily chewed. It is durable and safe and highly visible to horses; however, it is quite expensive.

Rubber and nylon strips, stretched tightly between wood posts, can be used for fencing. These strips are made from reprocessed tires and conveyer belts and are very durable with a lot of give if a horse runs into them. Strips may have to be tightened occasionally between posts, and the material may fray along the edges. If a horse chews on the strips, he might eat some of the indigestible fibers, which could lead to impaction and colic. Adding an electric wire or tape will keep horses from nibbling. A frayed or unraveled strip can be trimmed and the rough edges heat-sealed.

Vinyl-coated polyester strip fencing has strips that are six inches wide and very thin, stretched and attached to posts with special brackets. Common practice is to use three strips of this material attached to posts ten feet apart. The material is strong and flexible but lasts longer if topped by an electric wire to keep horses from nibbling or leaning over it.

Another option is a **high-tensile fence made from galvanized wire** encased in solid polymer rails or recycled-plastic strips. These strips are mounted on wood posts with brackets. Corner posts and gateposts should be very well braced or set in concrete because this fencing requires tight stretching. Its flexibility allows some bending around corners. If properly installed, this fence is quite maintenance-free but may require periodic tightening. The elastic strips give on impact (flexing six to twelve inches if a horse hits them) and then return to their original shape. Strips come in several colors and from a distance are nearly indistinguishable from board fencing.

High-tensile coated wire consists of wires covered with a solid polymer or vinyl. The strips are highly visible and somewhat elastic; if a horse hits it there is a lot of give. If he sticks his foot through, it won't cut him. Coated wire is only moderately expensive and lasts a long time. Maintenance generally consists of ratcheting it once a year to keep it tight. The exposed wire at the end of the strip should be bent and tucked around or covered with something to keep it from being a hazard to horses. This type of fencing should be installed in warm weather for maximum tightening. It may not work well in a cold climate.

Wire-mesh (net wire) fences are safer than barbed wire or smooth wire, though a pawing horse might get a foot caught if the spaces in the netting are large. The "no climb" netting with two by four-inch rectangles works well for adult horses, but a foal can get a foot through it. Netting for cattle and sheep (with larger spaces) is not safe for horses. The best type for horses is diamond mesh or V mesh since even a small hoof is less likely to go through it, and a shoe is rarely caught by it. The cross wires form hinge joints every eight inches of height, allowing the fence to fold rather than mash if a horse falls into it or a tree falls over it. The fence can be restored to original height.

Welded netting is usually less expensive than woven wire fence, but not as strong and more susceptible to rusting. If a weld breaks, a piece of wire may stick out and snag a horse. Woven wire stretches better. Galvanized wire (hot dipped in zinc oxide) won't rust as badly as untreated wire.

Diamond mesh fencing.

Wire mesh stays tight a long time if properly stretched and braced when installed. It should be topped by an electric wire, pipe, pole, or board to keep horses from leaning over it. With some netting you may need to add a pole at the bottom and a diagonal brace between posts for reinforcement. If kept properly stretched, mesh wire lasts a long time with little maintenance and is the best kind of fence for keeping horses in and dogs, coyotes, and other animals out. Install the wire on the inside of the posts for best strength and safety; the horses cannot push the wire loose (or pop the staples out) if they run into the fence or rub on it.

Vinyl mesh will not rust, rot, corrode, crack, split, or conduct electricity and can withstand extremes in temperature. This type of heavy-duty yet lightweight mesh fencing is easy to install. Some types weigh only thirty pounds per hundred feet of four-foot fencing. As with wire mesh, it works best with a solid top rail to keep horses from leaning over it.

Smooth wire, or twisted wire without barbs, can work as boundary fencing for large pastures if there isn't much pressure on the fences, but for it to be adequate it needs at least five to seven tightly stretched strands. In small enclosures, horses tend to reach through or over a smooth wire fence unless it is used with an elec-

No climb mesh wire.

tric fence or topped with a pole, pipe, or board.

High-tensile smooth wire is safe and fairly economical. It is also strong and requires little maintenance. If properly installed, horses bounce off it without injury. The 12.5-gauge wire has a breaking strength of 1,300 to 1,800 pounds. It is designed to be stretched very tightly, requiring fewer posts — up to sixty feet between posts — using wire spacers to keep the strands straight. This type of fence generally consists of ten to twelve wire strands. The wire lacks visibility, however, and you should tie brightly colored material on it until the horses learn the boundary.

New Zealand wire is a smooth, spring-loaded, tightly stretched wire that can be used where posts are far apart. It costs less than barbed wire but more than netting and may last ten to fifteen years. It is easy to put up and maintain because the spring loading helps keep the wire from breaking. It needs very solid, well-set braces at the corners. Three to seven wires are used, depending on the type of pressure the fence will receive, with reinforcement rods between posts to keep the wires properly spaced.

Chain-link fence is very expensive but long lasting and foolproof for horses or wandering children. It needs a top and bottom pipe to help brace it and keep horses from pawing it down, and it should be high enough they won't get their heads over it. Even with a top pipe, the ridges at the top of a chain link fence can cut a horse around the throat or under the jaw. Another drawback to this type of fence is that a shoe can get caught in it.

Plastic grid fencing is soft plastic mesh used around construction sites; some horsemen use it to confine foals. It is very safe and foolproof for young foals, but they do not learn to respect it, unless it has a hot wire, and will generally test fences from then on. You'll need an electric wire along the top to keep the mare from leaning or pushing on the fence.

Metal panels make good portable corrals, round pens, and fences. Panels can be used to set up a small pen or stall-size enclosure. They can be strapped to the side of a horse trailer and taken on a trail ride, camping trip, or horse show.

Pipe fence is durable and lasts forever if it doesn't rust. Some manufacturers offer a galvanized version or a baked-enamel finish to resist rust. The pipe rails are usually attached to pipe posts set in concrete. Two-inch pipe is often used for top and bottom rails, with smaller pipes, rods, or three or four strands of cable in between them. Pipe is stronger than wood and can span wider distances between posts. Pipe rails can be ten- to twenty-feet long, reducing the number of posts needed.

Since it is strong and durable, some horsemen use pipe for stallion pens or boundary fences along roads or other areas where it is crucial to have a fail-proof fence. Pipe fence can cause serious injury, however, if a horse runs into it or gets a leg or head caught. Horses have been known to put their heads through and try to chew on the next pipe down, getting mouth and jaw caught on the lower pipe. They can be strangled trying to free themselves.

Electric fences can be a quick and inexpensive way to contain horses or make existing fences safer and longer lasting, but repair and maintenance are fairly constant. Some horses become smart about electric fencing and can tell when it's not working — and may walk through it, over it, or graze under it. Electric fencing is best used with some kind of solid barrier because it is merely a psychological deterrent, not a physical barrier.

Traditional electric fencing has low visibility; a horse could run into it before he sees it. Brightly colored fence tapes or webbing strips are better in this respect. While flagging the electric wires helps, it won't stop a horse being chased by a herd mate from running into it. Most electric fencing will break if a horse hits it at full speed or decides to jump it, but plastic tape that doesn't break can cause serious injury if a horse gets a foot over it or the tape looped around a leg. Horses have been strangled by getting their heads through this type of fencing — fighting and struggling because of the electric shock. Electric fencing that breaks is safer.

A horse unaccustomed to electric fencing must learn to respect it. If you have a horse with no prior exposure to an electrified enclosure, and no solid fence to create a proper boundary in his mind, he may crash right through the hot wire. His first lesson should be in a controlled situation where he is not upset and trying to go through it. Most horses will smell the wire or tape and get a shock on the nose — and leave it alone from then on. If he does not check it out, tempt him to touch it by offering him a treat from the other side of the fence. This sounds cruel but may save him from possible injury later.

When turning any horse out in a new paddock or pasture, lead or ride him along the fence line to familiarize him with the boundary before turning him loose, especially if the fence is not highly visible. Wire or mesh fence should have flagging on it unless it has a visible top pole or some other solid portion, to help prevent your horse from running through the fence.

Match the Fencing With Its Purpose

The types of horses you are enclosing will dictate in part your choice of materials — whether you need a roomy paddock for mares and foals, a large pasture for a group of horses, a stallion pen, or a fence for rambunctious yearlings. It also

The fence should suit its purpose.

will make a difference whether other horses are nearby.

Paddocks or pasture fence for mares and foals should be very safe and durable since foals are inquisitive and can easily get into trouble putting a foot or head through the fence. The best fence for foals has some give (so a foal won't be injured if he crashes into it). It should have the bottom board, pole, or wire close to the ground to prevent a baby from rolling out of the pasture if he lies too close to the fence for a nap. An enclosure for weaning must be secure and hazard-free. A stallion paddock should be at least five-feet high or taller (preferably six to seven feet).

The fence around a paddock should be chew-proof, kick-proof, paw-proof, rub-proof, and lean-over-proof. Horses confined in small areas become bored and think up all sorts of destructive activities to entertain themselves. They may also gallop and buck around the small pen, kicking up their heels and sometimes hitting the fence.

If you have space, use double fencing between pastures, between a pasture and a roadway, or between stallion paddocks to help protect your horses and fences. Double fences with a wide alley between them reduce risk of injury, horses escaping, or spread of disease. Double fencing at a farm boundary limits contact with other horses whose health and vaccination status may be questionable.

A double fence should be wide enough to prevent nose-to-nose contact by horses and to allow access with a tractor and mower. If you don't have space for a double fence, a "T" of wood at the tops of the posts with an electric wire running along both wings of the T can keep horses from getting too close to the fence or bickering over the fence.

Building Fences

Fencing costs can be difficult to estimate. Your best source for estimates and fencing options are fence suppliers and manufacturers and your state extension specialist. Have an idea about the layout you want and measure the distances involved. Visit other horse farms to see what kinds of fencing they use, and get tips and suggestions from other horse owners. They can tell you about fencing that works best for them, the mistakes they've made, and things to avoid. Fencing is usually considered a capital expense; for tax purposes you may be able to depreciate fencing costs over a long period. Check with your tax preparer.

86

You might save money, time, and aggravation in the long run by hiring a good contractor. Some contractors will supply the materials, or you could save money by buying the materials and hiring the labor. Get suggestions from the supplier if you've never used a certain type of material before.

Before starting a fence, lay out where it will go, marking the lines with stakes and strings. Make sure you won't run into underground utility lines when digging postholes. You may want to have the property surveyed for a boundary fence even if there is an existing fence; sometimes the original fences were not on the line.

Fastening netting.

Your choice of posts depends on the type of fence you plan to build. PVC panels are designed for PVC posts; pipe fencing must be welded to pipe posts; wooden boards or rails are generally attached to wood posts. Wire or mesh fencing can be affixed to nearly any type of post. Make sure posts are set properly and well tamped or driven, or the fence will be much less durable. It will also become unsafe because the wires will sag or sections of pole or board panels can be pushed over.

Wood posts should be at least four (preferably six) inches in diameter, and eight feet long. The larger the post, the longer it will last, if well treated. Untreated posts in wet soil may last only three to five years before rotting off at ground level. The entire post should be pressure-treated to the center. Some suppliers merely dip the posts or just dip the end that goes in the ground, and these posts won't last as long. Cut off the tops at a slight angle so moisture will run off instead of sinking into the top of the post.

For a pole or board fence, posts are generally set every six to eight feet (from the center of one to the center of the next) so either twelve- or sixteen-foot boards or poles can be used. These should be spaced eight inches apart if using four, or eleven inches apart for three. You may want five or six for a stronger, safer fence. A good rule for spacing is that there should either be enough space between poles or boards so a horse can easily get his head out if he sticks it through or so little space that he can never get it through. Boards should be at least an inch thick on pasture fence and at least two inches thick for corrals or stallion pens. Standard height for a three-board fence is forty-eight inches, and sixty inches for a four- or five-board fence.

Wood posts should be set at least two and a half- to three-feet deep or below the frost line, whichever is deeper, or they will come loose, lean, or be pushed upward during freeze and thaw cycles. In wet or boggy areas, you may need to set PVC or metal posts in concrete (wood posts tend to rot in concrete, which holds the moisture next to them), or use jack fencing (buck fence) that rests on the ground. The supports (jacks) are made from two posts fastened together about two-thirds of the way up to make jacklegs, with poles or boards nailed to the side facing the pasture.

Posts for any wire or strip fence should be well braced, the wire or strips (or netting) stretched tightly. You need a very solid brace at each corner or fence end (as at a gate) and, every so often, along a lengthy straight stretch. Without good braces the pull of the wire will loosen some of the posts or pull your corner posts out of the ground. A brace usually consists of two sturdy posts set close together (six to eight feet) with a sturdy horizontal pole between them and diagonal wires (twisted tightly together) going from the top of one post to the bottom of the other. A good brace will withstand the pull of a tight fence and hold it securely in place for many years. A very large post, such as a railroad tie set in gravel, a sturdy pipe, or metal post set in concrete, can be used as a brace or gatepost.

Gates should be durable and safe.

Always attach wires, netting, boards, and rails to the inside of posts so they cannot be popped off if a horse leans or runs into the fence and to make a smooth fence line — horses won't smash their shoulders running along the fence and hitting a post. This is also important when building a riding ring or arena; you don't want to hit your knee or leg on a post if your horse goes too close to the fence. Don't put a cover board over board or pole ends in a wet climate. Though this strengthens a fence by reducing the chances of having a pole or board knocked loose, it also traps moisture to encourage rot and weakening at the nail sites. Boards or poles should be staggered so they don't all meet on the same posts.

To avoid the hazards of right-angle corners, eliminate the corner by running poles or planks across the corner (as from brace post to brace post), so a horse won't get trapped. Some horsemen construct an almost rounded corner by using a series of braces or an additional panel of fence. This makes it safer for horses and easier to mow the whole corner if you are cutting weeds or trimming the taller, ranker plants in a pasture.

Gates should be sturdy and safe. The gap between the gate and the post (on either side) should be small, so a horse or foal cannot get his head or foot caught. Never use wire or netting for a gate.

A gate should be at least as tall as the fence and fastened with a horseproof latch such as a chain with a snap. You may want a gate latch that can be opened with one hand, since you will often be leading a horse. Some gates may be handiest with two latches, such as a secure chain that a horse could never unhook and a quick and easy latch for the times you are going in and out a lot. A handy type of latch for those times is one that secures the gate

Wheelbarrow tire on gate pole.

automatically when it swings shut against the gatepost.

A gate should be wide enough for horses to go through easily without running into the gate or gatepost. Gates between pastures should be well located and wide enough that horses cannot crowd each other and cause injury. Hang a gate on the end that will best facilitate movement of horses in and out of the paddock or pasture. Plan gates so they make your daily tasks easier rather than harder. Don't leave gates open between pastures or pens, or horses may run a shoulder or stifle into a gatepost.

Some gates must be able to accommodate vehicles, tractors, or machinery, while others need only be wide enough for horse traffic. A gate for horses and people should be at least six feet, while gates for machinery may need to be twelve to sixteen feet. One gate needs to be large enough for a tractor or truck since you will have to clean out manure, mow, rake, or harrow the pasture at some point. It's always better to have the gate a little wide rather than narrow so machinery won't hit the gatepost.

The gate should be stout, yet easy to open and close (light enough or well balanced enough to open and close with one hand), and well hung on a properly braced post so it won't sag. A long and heavy gate needs a stout, well-braced post. A heavy gate will put

Gate handle for hot wire.

less stress on its post if it rests on a block of wood at the base of the post where it latches. A gate should never rest on the ground, or the bottom bar or pole may rot or rust if the gate area becomes muddy.

Aluminum gates are light and handy but not safe for horses as the sharp edges can be bent or broken if a horse rubs or leans against the gate, or tries to jump it. Wooden gates might fall apart when rubbed or pushed on; horses also chew on them. Gates made of metal tubing are generally the most safe and durable.

A heavy gate that starts to sag can be remedied by attaching a wheel to the bottom so it never drags on the ground or puts additional strain on the gate post; the wheel supports the free end of the gate and also makes it much easier to open and shut. A wheelbarrow tire or some other small wheel works well. There are also some commercially available wheels that have the necessary attachments to make it easy to put them onto a gate. Wheels on gates work best on level ground where the gate does not have the changing angle of a slope, and in climates without snow; deep snow will necessitate shoveling out the path of the wheel.

An electric fence gate needs an insulated handle so you can unhook it without getting a shock. The handle should disconnect from the side of the gate toward the charger so the gate wire is "dead" when unhooked. Then it won't shock you or a horse when in open position — or start a fire in dry grass or weeds if you put it on the ground. If you don't want the nuisance of an electric gate wire every time you go through a gate, bypass the gate by putting tall posts on both sides to run the electric wire up over the top, higher than a horse or vehicle would ever bump.

Fence Maintenance
Walk the fence lines several times a year and make a list of needed repairs and materials. Check each post to see how solid it is or if it needs retamping. Check

wood posts at ground level for signs of rot; scoop away a little dirt and stick a pocketknife into the post. Check metal posts to see if they are bent or rusted. Check wood panels to see if they are badly chewed or starting to rot from too much moisture. Check net wire for breaks (and exposed sharp wires), sagging areas that need to be stretched again, or rusted bottom wires.

Check synthetic fences for cracking. Test electric fences periodically to make sure they are working. If you have a charger with a blinking light, make a habit of glancing at it at least once a day

Check fences regularly.

when doing your chores, or check fence handles at strategic locations (that would tell you that all of the fence is working up to that point) to make sure you have a good spark. Keeping fences in good repair not only lengthens their life but also reduces risk of injuries if horses have close encounters with their boundaries.

Pasture

Pastures and paddocks have different functions. A pasture should provide high-quality forage to meet a horse's nutritional requirements. A paddock is generally a smaller area, usually an acre or less, used primarily for exercise. It may be a dry lot or it may contain grass, but providing feed is not its main purpose. It's nice to be able to keep an exercise paddock well sodded, however, since a dry lot is much dustier in dry weather and muddier in wet weather. Because a paddock gets heavy use, it should be planted with some type of hardy and persistent grass that tolerates trampling and close grazing. Paddocks are generally used year-round and must withstand a great deal of abuse by hoof action.

A pasture, by contrast, should be maintained with grass production foremost in mind. Never put more horses in (nor leave them longer) than the plants can withstand. Health of the forage plants should be the determining factor for pasture management. Many horsemen overgraze or undergraze a pasture or use it as turnout space. Over time, these practices will reduce the health and productivity of the plants, reducing forage quantity and quality.

Horses graze the same areas over and over, literally eating the grass into the ground as they seek out short and tender regrowth. This type of spot grazing reduces production of the favorite areas

Thistles overtaking pasture.

("lawns") and encourages growth of coarser plants and weeds in the ungrazed portions ("roughs"). If some of the grass gets taller than they like, these plants go to waste. Horses won't eat the grass that grows where they have defecated, often leaving tall areas by the manure piles. Horses grazing down to soil level on favorite areas may be at risk for sand colic on some types of soils. Horses should be removed from the pasture before they graze this close. The taller plants should be mowed (or grazed by cattle) to bring the plants to more uniform height.

The pasture size needed to support a horse will vary depending on climate, soil type, soil fertility, and types of grasses and/or legumes growing there. Grass grows better in a wet climate unless you irrigate. More acres of dryland grasses are needed to support a horse than well-watered green pasture. An irrigated or humid-climate pasture may support one horse on every two to four acres through the growing season, whereas a rangeland pasture in the arid West might take more than fifty acres per horse. A summer drought may reduce the productivity of a pasture, forcing you to irrigate or to supplement all or part of your horse's feed.

A thousand-pound horse needs ten to twenty pounds of dry matter per day from forage (the weight of the grass without its water content — similar to the weight of cured hay), the amount depending upon the horse's nutritional and energy needs. This means 1.8 to 3.6 tons of dry matter per year, per horse. Some productive grasses such as fescue and Bermuda grown on fertile soils with adequate moisture can produce three to five tons of dry matter per acre per year. The same grasses on less fertile, poorly managed, or drought-stricken soil will yield only one and a half to three tons of dry matter per acre per year. Other grasses in other climates have varying production per acre. Three tons of forage usually supplies the feed for one horse for three hundred days, but keep in mind that grass doesn't grow at the same rate each month. Moisture, temperature, and fertility will affect the growth rate.

Have soil tested.

Soil tests can determine soil type and fertility. Your county extension agent can help you get your soil tested. Specify that you want to grow horse pasture and need to know what fertilizers or minerals might be needed to increase your soil's fertility.

For best production, a pasture should contain several types of palatable grasses. A mix of clover or some other hardy legume with the grasses makes excellent pasture. Legumes are higher in protein and also add nitrogen to the soil, increasing fertility. While green and growing, grasses have adequate protein, even for lactating mares and growing foals. If grasses dry out, the protein level drops, and it's nice to have the legumes.

A pasture with a lot of clover may be detrimental to horses, however. Some types of clover contain dicoumarin, which is toxic. Clover can also cause photosensitization under some circumstances. There is a lot of geographic variation with clover, so check with your local extension agent. Your county agent also can advise you on the type of fertilizer you need for your soil or plants.

A grassy pasture without legumes generally needs nitrogen, while a pasture containing legumes may need phosphorus. Some soils may need potassium.

Cow manure or horse manure will provide all of these crucial plant nutrients. If you don't have a way to spread your composted manure, you may choose to purchase commercial fertilizer.

Some highly acidic soils benefit from lime to change soil pH and make it more healthy for plants (most plants grow best in soil that is only mildly acidic — with pH between six and seven (seven is neutral). Soil acidity can interfere with plants' ability to absorb minerals. With the proper pH, soil bacteria are better able to break down organic matter to add their nutrients to the soil. Lime also adds calcium and magnesium, which both aid plant growth.

How often you use lime depends on moisture levels and leaching (soil nutrients being carried away by the water). You may need to apply lime every two years or as infrequently as every ten or twenty years. If you have more than twenty-five inches of annual precipitation, nutrients and lime tend to leach out of the soil, leaving it more acidic. When adding lime to a pasture, keep the horses out of it until the lime has been dampened by dew or rain, since lime dust can cause respiratory problems.

Adding nitrogen to deficient soil can double your pasture growth (or hay yield). Late fall or early spring is usually the best time to spread composted manure on fields and pastures. The nitrogen and other soil nutrients provided by well-composted manure can give a longer-lasting benefit than commercial fertilizer when properly applied, with the beneficial effects often lasting several years unless high water content leaches away the nutrients. By contrast, commercial nitrogen fertilizer must be spread at least once a year — two or three times for best results. An established pasture may need 150 to 180 pounds of nitrogen per acre per year divided into several applications. Phosphorus, by contrast, needs to be applied only once a year, and there's a season's delay in soil response. If soil is deficient in phosphorus, you should apply it in the fall so that it will aid the spring growth of plants.

After spreading commercial fertilizer on pasture, keep horses off the pasture until the granules have dissolved and been absorbed into the soil. Rain or irrigation (preferably by sprinkler, since flood irrigation may wash nutrients away before they sink into the ground), or even several mornings of very heavy dew will dissolve the fertilizer. Be careful not to spill fertilizer in the pasture since a concentrated amount could be toxic if a horse eats it.

If you want to reseed to improve your forage plants, ask your county agent which kinds do well in your climate and soil type. The agent can also give advice on how to prepare soil before planting and how to seed it. If the land is fragile and prone to erode, a no-till method is better than plowing. If you don't have equipment to prepare the soil and plant the seeds, find a local farmer who does custom work. Grasses are usually planted in fall and legumes in the spring. If planted together, faster-growing legumes tend to shade and crowd out grass plants. Planting should be done when there is adequate moisture. Seedlings are tender and fragile. If conditions are too dry, your seedlings will die unless you irrigate. Sprinkler irrigation creates less erosion and eliminates the need for corrugations, which are undesirable in a horse pasture. Once the plants start to grow, keep horses off that pasture until plants are tall enough to bloom the next summer, then graze very lightly that first season.

Check your pasture weeds to see if any are toxic and to determine whether you need to spray them or just dig up the worst ones. Patches of thistles and other undesirable plants should be eliminated; they tend to spread and reduce pasture production. Patches of foxtail or cheat grass (downy brome) or any other grasses with sharp awns are undesirable; spears on the seed heads can become embedded in a horse's mouth. Weeds with burrs can adhere to manes, tails, fetlock hairs, or hair coat. Tiny slivers that float in the air when a burdock burr shatters can get into the horse's eye and cause severe irritation.

Spraying to control weeds.

A healthy stand of grass is the best defense to keep weeds from becoming established. Weeds are aggressive opportunists that come in when there is bare ground or disturbed soil. Wherever you disrupt the sod, as when digging a ditch or leveling a spot for a shed, weeds will come in. You'll have to control them until the grass becomes re-established.

Spraying or diligent mowing can control weeds. Check with your county agent on herbicides and how to use them, and keep horses off the pasture for two weeks after using herbicide. Spray weeds in the morning after the dew is off but before the wind comes up; you don't want wind currents taking the spray beyond the area you are treating. Learn the life cycle of the plants you are trying to eradicate and hit them when they are most vulnerable.

If you mow a weed patch before the plants mature and go to seed, you keep them from reproducing and spreading. You may have to mow several times during the growing season, but eventually this will weaken and kill the weeds. Pastures that are kept mowed down to six or eight inches can be kept nearly free of weeds while holding the grass to a height at which horses will still eat it. For best pasture health, let grass grow to at least four or five inches before you turn horses in. If it becomes much taller than that, the horses won't graze those portions as they prefer younger grass.

Giving pastures periodic rest will increase the total forage production per acre.

Uniform grazing (rather than letting some plants grow too tall) increases total forage quality. Plant growth in every pasture should be closely monitored and the horses removed after they have eaten their favorite plants down to about two-inch stubble. Walk your pastures at least twice a week to check them.

The best situation is to divide pasture into several sections. Use portable electric fence if you don't want permanent divisions. Rotate the grazing, moving horses to a new part periodically so the overgrazed spots can recover. Rotating your pastures also gives you a chance to do any maintenance such as repairing fences, fixing a water line, and clipping, harrowing, or fertilizing the pasture without the horses being in the way.

It will take several weeks for a rested parcel to regrow enough to be grazed again; the time needed depends on soil moisture and fertility. During a dry summer, plants will take longer to regrow unless you can irrigate. Plants will grow fastest during the peak of the growing season if they have water and more slowly in early spring or in the fall. With good growing conditions during summer, it takes about thirty days for the plants to regrow to grazing height.

If you cannot rotate pastures or are short on pasture in a dry year, lock the horses in a pen or paddock and limit their time on pasture to what the plants can tolerate. Let the horses graze only a few hours each day. If you are short on pasture space, you may have to use it mainly for exercise and secondarily for feed, keeping horses in adjacent dry lots where it is easy to move them back and forth when it is their turn to go out or come in.

If your largest area is merely an exercise lot rather than a pasture, your primary concern will be dust control, drainage, and erosion control rather than pasture management. You may want to establish some hardy plants that will withstand trampling and help hold the soil, even if they are not highly nutritious.

In a larger pasture, mow periodically to clip off tall mature plants, reducing them to a height of three to four inches. When those regrow, the horses will eat them. Most horse pastures are overgrazed, and horsemen neglect mowing them, thinking they should allow the grass to grow as much as possible to give the horses more to eat. But pastures that are never mowed provide less forage. Mowing keeps undesirable plants from taking over parts of the pasture and keeps less favorite grasses from getting too tall and unpalatable. Grass is healthiest and most palatable when between four and eight inches tall.

Another way to maximize use of a pasture and reduce risk of parasite infestation at the same time is to rotate horses with cattle. Cattle will eat some of the plants the horses don't and vice versa; cattle will also eat grass that grows around the horse manure. The parasites are host specific and cannot complete their life cycle in the wrong species. Thus, the horse worm larvae eaten by cattle cannot survive to lay eggs and the cycle is broken.

Good pasture management also includes manure management. In a large pasture where horses live year-round, they usually defecate wherever they happen to be, especially if they grew up on pasture. Horses that spend part of their time in a stall or paddock, however, tend to drop their manure in certain areas, creating a pile, and often do so even when at pasture. You should periodically gather manure piles to get them off the pasture (this may be most easily accomplished with a tractor and loader, putting manure into a pickup to haul off for composting, or gathering the manure more regularly with a sweeper), or break them up and drag them over the pasture with a harrow.

Harrowing to scatter manure.

In any case, you should harrow a pasture periodically to break up manure and "scratch" the sod. This stimulates more growth by allowing better penetration of water and soil nutrients from the manure or fertilizer. Several types of harrows work well, or you can improvise with old tires fastened to a railroad tie. Whatever you use to drag around the field, watch for any loose parts or wire that might come loose and be left in the field to create a hazard.

Harrowing a pasture lifts and scatters manure, old hay piles, or any other litter that might impede grass growth and spreads the manure more evenly over the pasture. Keep in mind that non-composted manure will spread parasite eggs all over the pastures unless you are keeping horses diligently dewormed. Spreading the manure will merely spread worm larvae over the areas where horses are more likely to eat them. Most worm eggs are very hardy; sunshine and drying may not kill them very quickly. Cool temperatures and moisture conditions are favorable to worm eggs and larvae. If you are rotating pastures, drag a pasture when you remove the horses, leaving them out of it while the manure dries out and the grass regrows. Irrigating the pastures to enhance regrowth, however, may keep the worms alive.

Some horsemen use a mechanical sweeper (like the type used in parks and recreation areas to remove leaves and trash) to remove manure regularly. Horses often graze a pasture more fully once the manure is gone, giving a significant increase in functional grazing area. This can offset the cost of the sweeper and the time spent pulling it around the pasture with a tractor.

Minimize Hazards

Walk a pasture now and then to check for rodent or badger holes, exposed rocks, stumps, or tree roots that might trip a horse, or low-hanging branches.

Horses that spend all their time at pasture, or even a portion of every day outside, are less apt to injure themselves than horses that are turned out briefly and irregularly. A horse that only gets out for an hour a week or every few days is most likely to blow off steam and get himself into trouble, but any horse can get hurt by coming into contact with unforgiving gates or neglected or flimsy fencing.

Some of the common things that cause injury are nails sticking out, hooks of wire, projections from broken fencing, sagging fence wires, and splinters. Make sure all bolts used in fences, gates, or stalls have smooth, round ends or are cut off flush with surrounding surfaces. Broken or unused gate hinges should be removed so a horse won't run into them. Protruding nails, wires, or bucket holders in stalls can cause eye injuries or tear an eyelid if a horse rubs on them or bumps them. A left-on halter may catch on any projection sticking out from a stall or fence. A horse rubbing on a fence or sticking its head through poles or around a post could catch the halter on a nail, staple, stub of wood, or bolt, then pull back and hang himself.

Old postholes in pastures can pull a tendon or break a leg if a horse steps in them. Wooden posts sawed off at ground level can create a hazard years later when they have rotted, leaving a hole. Wooden or metal posts broken off above ground level may puncture a foot or cause leg injuries.

Check all fences and buildings for potential hazards such as sharp edges, projecting feed mangers, narrow doorways or gateways, and tight corners where a horse might be trapped by a pasture mate. All feeders, waterers, water tanks, and mangers should have smooth edges, and there should be no spaces between feeders or waterers where a horse might get caught. All gates should be flush with the fence when closed, with no protrusions.

Don't put a pasture or pen adjacent to a metal shed with protruding corners or bottom edges — or projecting roof edges. A low roof or a guy wire from a power pole or telephone pole can be dangerous if a horse runs into it. A guy wire in a pasture can be made safer and more visible with a post and horizontal pole to shield horses from running into the wire.

Junk piles can contain poisons (lead from old batteries, for instance) or sharp objects that might injure a horse. Abandoned machinery will have sharp edges or rusty bolts that could snag a horse that rubs on it or runs into it. If your pasture borders a road, check for litter such as broken beer bottles, cans, paper, or plastic bags. Don't leave baling wire or twines where horses might get a foot entangled. Horses may chew on twine or plastic bags. Even small pieces may cause fatal colic if they block the gut. The synthetic twine does not break down as readily as the hemp twine used years ago and is not digested. Don't leave twines on bales, even big round bales, when feeding hay in feeders or leaving big bales out in the pasture for horses.

4

Water Sources, Waterers, and Feeders

Horses always should have access to fresh, clean water. The average horse drinks at least eight to twelve gallons a day and even more in hot, humid weather, during lactation, or when eating dry feeds. Some lactating mares in hot weather drink more than one hundred gallons a day. A horse may drink less than ten gallons a day when weather is cold or if eating lush pasture (high moisture content). In cold weather a horse will be more inclined to drink adequate water if it's warmed, reducing risk of impaction.

Place your waterer in an area sheltered from wind, to reduce windblown debris and dust in the water, and on a slightly elevated spot where rain or snow melt will drain away, so horses' feet won't churn the footing into a mud bog. Build up the site if necessary, and cover it with several inches of gravel. A water tank or trough should be in an open area of the pasture or paddock, or along a straight section of fence, not in a corner where low-ranking horses might get trapped. A molded plastic tank is probably the safest for outdoor horses and is also easy to move or clean. Put an automatic waterer snugly against a fence post or building wall, or a few feet away from it so a horse could never get a leg caught.

An outdoor waterer.

When selecting a pasture waterer, consider how many horses will use it. A stock tank with a float is the most inexpensive type of waterer for a number of horses. A cement tank is hardest to clean. There are round plastic waterers with a regulator valve at the bottom that opens when the water level goes down.

When installing an automatic waterer, you must dig a water line (and put in an electrical line if you want a heating unit). Locate buried phone, electrical, water, or drain lines before digging. The trench must be at least four to six inches wide, and a foot deeper than the frost line in your region — usually three to five feet — to keep the water from freezing, so you will never have the unpleasant task of having to dig it up in the winter. Water lines under driveways or areas with vehicle or horse traffic must be deeper; impact on the ground drives the frost deeper. The ground under a road will freeze deeper and stay frozen longer in spring. Install an accessible shutoff valve at some point between the waterer and main water line, so the water can be turned off if the automatic waterer malfunctions.

A hydrant should be freeze-proof and self-draining (water drains out of the upright pipe, deep into the ground, each time you turn the hydrant off) so there's no water left in it to freeze. Hydrants should be located where horses can't get to them — to prevent injury to the horses and to keep a playful horse from nibbling the handle and turning on the water.

Some stall waterers use a float; others have a moveable ball that rolls out of the way while the horse drinks (letting water in), and some use a balance beam. The latter has a drinking bowl on one end and a weight on the other end as a counterbalance. When the horse drinks, the balance is altered and the beam tips, opening a valve to refill the bowl — returning the beam to its balanced position, which closes the valve to turn off the water.

If you don't want automatic waterers in stalls, you can put a recessed faucet in each stall wall (out of the way so a horse cannot run into it or chew on it). This makes watering easier than dragging a hose through the barn.

Check for freezing.

Some waterers need electricity for a heating unit to keep them from freezing in winter; others are designed to keep the water circulating, which helps prevent freezing. The most common non-electrical waterers are insulated by a Styrofoam container and are often small, covered troughs with drinking holes protected by a floating ball. The horse pushes the ball out of the way with his nose when he drinks. Horses unaccustomed to this type of waterer may not drink. You may have to adjust the float to keep the water level low enough to allow the ball to float below the drinking hole until horses get used to drinking, then the ball can be allowed to float at normal surface level once the horses have figured it out.

In a pasture with many horses, or any large pasture, it's wise to have two or more waterers, preferably of different types. Then if one fails, the horses will still have access to water. Automatic waterers should be checked daily, preferably twice a day, to make sure they are working properly, and cleaned as often as needed. A waterer that is not checked may get dirty or have a drowned mouse or bird floating in it for days. Waterers with large bowls are often easiest to clean, as are those with removable panels on the side for easy cleaning and maintenance of internal parts. Some types have a drain at the bottom that makes them easy to clean.

In a paddock or stall you need a tub or bucket, water tank, or automatic waterer. The safest arrangement for a foaling stall is a removable tub or bucket rather than a permanent fixture that could be an obstacle to mare or foal. A manger with feed box, hay area, and water-bucket holder is often built into the front of a stall.

A plastic water bucket.

It should be thirty-eight to forty-two inches high to keep the horse from putting his feet into it and sloped inward at the bottom so he won't hit his knees when eating or drinking.

Most water and feed buckets are made of rubber or plastic — which has a lot of give if a horse falls on it or leans against it — but beware of sharp hardware (edges of hooks or grommets) embedded in them. Some rubber tubs contain nylon fibers made of a material similar to automobile tires. They are quite durable, but over time the fibers may become exposed, and a horse may chew on them. Eating the indigestible fibers can cause digestive problems and sometimes intestinal blockage. If a tub becomes ragged, replace it.

Plastic is more brittle than rubber, especially in cold weather. Recycled plastic is not as durable as virgin plastic for withstanding thumps it might get from a horse or from you beating the ice out. Many plastic buckets are made of polyethylene resin, which is more durable. Choose a tub or bucket with one-piece construction with no seams, to be most durable and crush-proof. Rubber-polymer alloy buckets rarely crack in cold temperatures. Some manufacturers put UV inhibitors in plastic to help keep it from being damaged by sunlight — sun damage makes plastic weak and brittle and more apt to crack.

In cold weather you may have to break ice out of a tub, bucket, or tank daily. Electric water warmers are sometimes used in buckets or tanks but can be dangerous if they malfunction or create a potential fire hazard in a barn.

In hot weather you may have to clean out algae or moss. It's often easier to empty and clean a tub or tank that you fill by hose than it is to clean an automatic waterer. Tanks with automatic filling devices get dirtier because they are always full and may need to be emptied and scrubbed once a week. Some horsemen use goldfish in a large tank to help keep algae under control, but fish occasionally die; their decomposing bodies pollute the water.

Feeders

There are many types of hay and grain feeders; choose the easy-to-clean ones. Many horsemen just use buckets or plastic corner feeders in a stall for feeding grain. Aluminum corner or wall-mounted feeders are also popular. Flat-backed buckets are handy for hanging against a wall. Over-the-fence feed buckets can keep the feed off the ground. Foal feeders can attach to a stall wall. Smooth bars across the opening leave room for the foal's small muzzle but keep the mare from eating the grain. There are also hay rack/grain feeder combinations, and some manufacturers of steel stall panel fronts offer a feeder built into the panel. The feeder section can swing to the outside of the stall so you can feed the horse without going into the stall.

Horses in stalls can be fed hay on the floor, in a manger or hayrack, or with a hay net. Hay nets are dangerous if a horse gets a foot caught and they must be hung high enough to prevent pawing, but not so high that leaves and dust fall into the horse's eyes. If stalls are kept clean, there is no harm in feeding hay on the floor (the most natural position for a horse to eat) unless he

A feed tub in the stall.

urinates and defecates in his hay. If a floor is sandy or gravelly, it is safer to feed in a manger or rack, since a horse may eat sand and gravel when cleaning up the last wisps of hay. A walled-off manger or bunk at floor level — kept clean — can avoid this problem. A major drawback to any type of elevated feeding system for hay is the unnatural position for eating, resulting in improper development of neck muscles (this can cause problems in performance horses).

A stall corner feeder enables the horse to eat at ground level without taking up much stall space. One sheet of plywood makes four feeders. A corner feeder saves hay, since the horse will generally stand and eat over the feeder, making hay less likely to drop on the floor. By contrast, a horse eating from a standard hay rack or off the ground may waste up to 30 percent of his hay by tromping and mixing it with manure or dirt. If you break open the flakes and shake them as you put them in the feeder, the horse won't shake and sling it around, and most of the hay will stay in the feeder.

When using hay racks, locate them in a corner out of the way, with no protrusions that might injure a horse. Put them high enough that a horse cannot get a foot caught if he paws, yet not so high that he must reach up to eat. A feeder hung too high is apt to cause respiratory problems since dust may fall into his nostrils. A hay rack should have a bin underneath it to catch the bits of hay or alfalfa leaves that fall down, so they can be eaten later and not wasted nor mixed with manure.

Some horsemen use automatic feeders that dispense a designated amount of grain or concentrate at programmed times during the day. This eliminates the

chore of measuring feed and feeding the horses and makes it possible to provide small frequent meals at regular intervals, whether you are there or not.
This equipment needs monitoring and maintenance to make sure everything
continues to work properly. The automatic feeders handle pellets and dry
grains quite well but some types of feeds, such as sweet feeds with a high concentration of molasses, leave residues in the delivery system, encouraging
mold growth. The uniformity of the feed mixture necessitated by most feeding
units is also a drawback if you have some horses in the barn that need a different ration.

An automatic feeder can never take the place of overseeing a horse's mealtime; perhaps the biggest drawback is that you might be tempted to let it do
your chores for you. There can be no substitute for personal attention at mealtime. You need to make sure the feeding system is working and that each horse
is actually getting the proper amount of feed and is healthy and eating with a
normal appetite. Feeding time is the best time to check your horse's physical
condition and to pick up on subtle signals that may indicate the early stage of
illness.

Barns and Sheds

The type of barn you need depends on climate and your situation. Your goals
(riding for pleasure, showing, breeding, running a training facility, or some other
specialized career with horses) make a lot of difference in what you need in a
barn. In many instances, barns are not built for the welfare of horses but rather
for the convenience of people. Most horses are better off outside, even in the
most severe winter weather, but they do appreciate a good windbreak, either natural or man-made.

If you have mares that might foal in bad weather or expensive show horses that
need coddling to protect their shiny hair coats year-round, you'll want a good
barn. If you live in a cold or rainy climate, outdoor horses may enjoy a run-in
shed. There are times you'll need a roof and windbreak if you have to saddle up
during a rainstorm or have a sick horse to treat. It's always nice to have adequate
shelter for a sick or injured horse.

If you build a barn, visit other horse-keeping facilities to get ideas; make sure
your barn is designed the way you want it before you start building. Take future
goals into consideration when planning a barn and any related facilities, even if
you might build it in several stages over many years. If you think you will
increase the number of stalls later or add a work area or office, put in the necessary plumbing lines during initial construction, so the water system will be adequate for the addition without digging up and changing it. If you want an indoor
or outdoor arena or more paddock space later, put the barn and access roads in
a location to leave room. Good planning at the beginning will save lots of time

and money later. A facility built for show horses will be different from one designed for broodmares, and if you switch goals later you might find you need to do some expensive remodeling. Planning ahead can minimize problems later.

Building codes, zoning ordinances, local environmental regulations, or deed covenants in your community may influence the type of barn you build. There may be restrictions on how many horses you can keep on a certain acreage, location of a barn relative to property lines or to a house site, what materials you can use, what architectural styles are acceptable, how wide the access roads must be for emergency vehicles, what type of fire safety systems must be installed, how drainage must be constructed, how manure must be handled, and so on. Before building any new facility, check the local regulations.

Select a site near all-weather roads, with higher elevation than the surrounding ground. Choosing the best place for a barn involves convenience of location and site suitability (terrain, soil, and drainage) and relationship to secondary structures such as storage sheds, hay sheds, indoor or outdoor arenas, paddocks, and space for vehicle parking or turnaround areas for delivery trucks and horse trailers. Allow at least fifty feet between buildings to reduce danger of fire spreading from one to another, or to limit the risk of contagion if you need to isolate a sick horse. Ample space between buildings and between the barn and any fences will allow for snow removal if you have to plow in winter. Otherwise you may end up shoveling snow by hand.

If you live in a cold or windy climate you need a barn that is not drafty, and one that retains heat. If you live where summers are hot and humid you'll want a barn that stays cool. Some sites on your place will probably be better than others for a barn. Consider the flow of prevailing winds. They will be important in summer for ventilation and a consideration if you are building next to close neighbors. If your barn and paddocks are upwind from a residential area, you won't be very popular.

Also consider the path of the sun — hot sun, cold shade, and strong winds will be problems instead of advantages. In North America, buildings that capture the most winter sun and summer shade have their long sides running north to south. Use the south side for most of the stalls and grooming areas and the north side for offices, hay storage, tack rooms, etc. These create a buffer between the horses and cold north winds in winter.

First priority for barn location should be a well-drained area on ground at least a foot or more above the surrounding pasture areas. If you build in a flood plain, you'll have mud around the barn, moisture seeping up through stall floors, and snow melt coming in doorways. If the ideal barn location — relative to pens, pastures, and horse traffic — is not a good spot for drainage, hire a contractor to haul in enough fill material (rocks and gravel) to build up the area. Also consider subsurface drainage around the barn foundation. You might want to put in a four-inch perforated drain tile around the outside of the building to bring the sub water to a sump where it can be pumped away.

Make sure the site is well prepared. The ground underneath a barn should be solid material with some rock in it. If it isn't, the site should be excavated at least four feet, putting in large rocks, then a layer of crushed rock, to allow for good drainage. About a foot of soil or tamped clay (or a mix of clay and sand — about three parts clay to one part sand) can be put on top of the gravel unless you want a wooden or synthetic floor. Dirt floors are often used in stalls; they are easier to keep dry if the base material has good drainage and less firm if a horse lies down a lot. You can also use rubber stall mats.

For a long-lasting barn, you'll need a good foundation, using concrete, cinder blocks, or pressure-treated wood. A simple and inexpensive barn without a foundation can be built using tall, well-treated posts set deeply into firm ground. The posts serve as supports for roof and walls. There are many designs and plans for various types of barns. Looking at different layouts can help you design the type of barn that best fits your needs and budget.

A barn can be as small or large as you want it. One popular design is a single, portable stall built on skids; it can be moved wherever you need it. A small permanent barn may consist of one or more box stalls, with a feed room and tack room. Another handy design features a single row of box stalls with an overhanging roof to provide a protected area for saddling or grooming.

Many horse owners use prefabricated barns; they are often relatively inexpensive and can be installed quickly. Some can be easily put together; others are constructed by a crew from the company that sells them. Some instant barns consist of panels in four-foot sections that snap together into a structure that can be as permanent or portable as you wish. A portable building is an advantage if you are using rented property.

A prefabricated barn can be sided to match your house, insulated as much as you want, outfitted with ventilation systems, tack and feed rooms, wash racks, plumbing, and heating. Some are constructed with steel frames set into concrete. The walls can be steel, steel covered with wood, or wood walls filled with foam. Roofs are usually steel. Most prefabricated barns have sliding doors with grates at the top. Stall interiors are usually wood-coated metal.

A barn should have windows or doors that let in sunshine but keep out harsh wind and moisture. Ventilation is important; an airtight barn holds in humidity, ammonia, and dust from hay and bedding, which can cause respiratory problems. Stall windows should be at least four feet square and covered with bars so they won't get broken. They should open from the bottom and to the inside to prevent drafts, or they should slide open sideways. They should always be protected on the inside by heavy-gauge wire to prevent breakage by horses. Window openings should face east and south if you want warmth from the sun in winter.

A good barn should stay warm in winter and cool in summer. To avoid hot summer sun, place windows only to the south. In a warm climate you may not need an enclosed barn; a row of covered stalls that open to outside paddocks may be adequate. In colder climates, most barns consist of two rows of enclosed stalls separated by a center aisle.

The aisle should be at least eight- to ten-feet wide, and twelve feet is even better if you have the space. A wide aisle is safer and more convenient if several people use the barn at once. You may need room for two horses to pass or for machinery to drive through.

Barn aisles should be kept clean and uncluttered. Don't store tack trunks, ladders, wheelbarrows, brooms, or other items along the walls. Be careful how you hang up shovels, rakes, pitchforks, and barn-cleaning forks if these must be kept in the aisle. If hung on the wall, attach them by their handles rather than by their tines (and keep tines facing toward the wall). Then if they get knocked down, the dangerous end won't crash down on you or a horse. Keep aisles clear, not only for safety and convenience when moving horses through, but also in case a horse ever gets loose in the aisle. You might want a storage closet instead.

Another convenience in a large barn is a combination grooming area, wash stall, and veterinary treatment stocks. This area should be about twelve by twenty-four feet and open at each short end. The sides can be solid walls or fence panels. A horse is led in at one end and groomed, washed, or treated, then led out the opposite end.

You may want a working area for your farrier — a place that is well lighted, level, and well away from other barn traffic and combustible material such as hay or bedding. A separate area that won't interfere with regular barn activities is best, since a horse in the aisle can be in the way and also a hazard. Allow space for the farrier's truck and tools.

Consider putting a phone in your barn or carrying a portable phone out to the barn when you are working there. A phone can make a lot of difference in an emergency — whether it's a sick or injured horse, a foaling emergency, or a situation in which someone needs to reach you. Put a list of emergency phone numbers on the wall.

Have plenty of lights in the barn, out of reach of the horses — with switches next to the main doors. Use a 150- or 200-watt bulb in each stall, or a minimum of 40-watt fluorescent light. The amount of light in a stall will be increased if the lights are positioned near the front of a stall and used with reflectors.

Barn Types

There are basically two types of barn — **shedrow** and **center aisle**. A shedrow is built with a single row of stalls or two rows of stalls back to back; the fronts open to the outside. A center-aisle barn has two rows of stalls divided by a center

A barn with center aisle.

aisle. This type of barn may be heated or unheated.

Heated barns are very expensive, needing proper insulation and a source of heat. It's usually much healthier for horses to be in an unheated barn; they have fewer colds and respiratory problems. A heat source is generally needed only in unusual conditions, such as for a seriously sick horse or new foal during cold weather, and in these situations a space heater can supply enough warmth.

When building a barn, you'll want to consider cost, durability, the amount of maintenance required for various materials, and fire resistance. Your choice of building material may depend upon climate, regional preferences, and cost.

Metal buildings can be quickly put up and are often less expensive than wood or concrete structures. They are more fireproof than wood, with less maintenance, but can be cold in winter and hot in summer, since they do not provide as much insulation as wood. They are noisy during a rain or hailstorm or in windy weather. They also can be more easily damaged if a horse rubs or kicks the walls; stalls should always have boards or poles next to the metal wall.

Wooden structures are expensive to build (materials and labor). The wood must be treated to prevent weathering, and inside structures also should be treated to help prevent chewing. Wood barns are more apt to burn quickly.

Brick, cinderblock, concrete, or **stone buildings** can be pleasantly cool in

An aluminum barn.

summer, but damp and cold in winter, needing ventilation to prevent dampness and humidity. These structures can be costly to build, but are very fireproof and quite safe in a strong wind. Concrete block barns can be painted, stuccoed, or faced with wood, natural stone, or plastic or vinyl siding. In cold climates, concrete-block walls should be insulated during construction.

Concrete or cinder blocks are not as durable as they seem; horses can kick through them because portions of the blocks are hollow. A horse kicking a concrete block wall can be injured by the sharp edges of a broken block. Blocks used in stalls should have the hollow parts filled with sand. They also should be covered with wood to reduce this risk and to keep the horse from scraping himself on the rough wall.

Another type of construction is siding over a wood frame. The siding may be made of metal, wood, brick, or plywood. **Vinyl siding** can be used on both the exterior and interior of a barn. It is easy to keep clean and needs very little maintenance. Sheds and shelters can be constructed entirely of tongue-and-groove PVC boards; they are durable and may show very little wear or aging even after fifteen or twenty years.

A wooden barn with metal roof.

Windows and skylights can make any barn lighter, saving electricity and making a more acceptable environment for horses (they don't like dark places). Ultraviolet light in sunshine kills many airborne viruses and bacteria, and some parasite eggs and larvae. Light is essential for normal body function, such as reproduction in mares, shedding winter hair in the spring, etc. If you install skylights, use plastic or UV light translucent glass, which allows more ultraviolet rays to come through.

Insulation is important for cold weather but also can help a barn in summer, lowering internal temperature by five to ten degrees by blocking the warming effect of sunshine on roof and walls. The direction and duration of sunlight on a barn's exterior determine the amount of heat that penetrates roof and walls. Insulation can deflect some of this heat at hot spots. Doors and windows under overhangs will still get winter sunshine (when you need the extra warmth) when the sun is low in the sky but not as much sun in summer. Overhangs or awnings can help cool the air moving into the building in summer. A barn roof can be constructed of metal, shingles or shakes, asphalt, or other materials. Metal is usually quickest and easiest to put on and less expensive and more

maintenance-free than most other types of roofing. You can incorporate translucent fiberglass sections in a metal roof to let in more light. The disadvantages to
a metal roof are heat during hot, sunny weather; noise during a storm; risk of
hail damage; and drips of moisture on the inside from condensation, unless you
add insulation with a moisture barrier between the metal and the insulating
material. Metal roofs may leak around the screws that hold them on. Snow may
slide off the roof all at once, making a pile next to the barn. Put doorways on the
sides that are not directly underneath the slope of the roof.

If you get a lot of rain, install rain gutters and down spouts to handle the flow
off the roof. If you get snow, put overhangs to shelter the doorways and to keep
entryways from becoming muddy from snow melt. If you have exercise runs or
paddocks attached to the barn, locate them so the rain and snow coming off the
roof won't make mud holes in the paddocks.

Wooden shakes or shingles are expensive and require a lot of labor to install.
They are a fire hazard and also cannot be used on relatively flat roofs; water will
not run off well enough for them to dry. If moisture is held there, shingles will
rot more quickly. If the moisture freezes in winter, it can damage shingles and
also allow backup of water when the ice melts, causing the roof to leak. The
advantage to wooden roofing is its insulating quality — warm in winter, cool in
summer — and no condensation inside the barn. Barrel tiles and slate are sometimes used on barn roofs (more fireproof) but are also very expensive.

Asphalt shingles and rolled roofing (installed over plywood sheeting) are
durable, some types lasting twenty years or more if properly installed. These are
less expensive than wooden shingles, fairly easy to install, and less noisy than
metal, with better insulating quality. This type of roofing can be easily damaged,
however, by extremely hot temperatures, wind, or ice buildup, and becomes brittle in cold weather.

Roof shape makes a big difference in a barn's ventilation. There should be
about six inches of roof rise for every twelve inches of roof width — a roof pitch
of six to twelve. This allows good run-off of moisture and gives more attic area
for insulation. The insulation can either be blown into the rafter area or installed
in rolls or sheets. If a barn has an exposed-beam ceiling, you won't be able to
insulate the rafter area as easily. A dropped ceiling gives you the option of filling
the entire rafter area with insulation. A dropped ceiling has other advantages,
being easier to clean (cobwebs) than open rafters and allowing better insect control and lighting. To prevent moisture from getting into the insulation and ruining it, install a vapor barrier on the inside surface.

The steeper the roof, the better the ventilation. Ridge vents along a roofpeak
can allow for air circulation without letting in rain. Older barns generally have
steeper roofs; the worst barns for ventilation are some of the newer metal ones
with relatively flat roofs. A barn in any climate needs ridge vents.

Importance of Ventilation

A horse is better off outside than in a barn, even in cold and nasty weather, because of the unnatural dampness and dustiness in a barn. Both of these conditions can lead to respiratory problems. Stalls with poor ventilation harbor contaminants suspended in the air — dust from the ground, feed, and bedding; mold spores; ammonia fumes from urine; and methane gas from decaying bedding and manure. These irritants can inflame the lung lining, setting the stage for viral invasion, which can open the way for bacterial infections. Young foals are especially vulnerable to the effects of inadequate ventilation since their lungs and immune systems are not yet fully developed.

A well-ventilated barn.

Poor air quality can cause allergic responses in many older horses. A number of performance-limiting problems are lumped under the term COPD — chronic obstructive pulmonary disease, more commonly known as heaves. A similar problem in humans is called "farmer's lung." Some types of non-allergic responses in young horses are called "small-airway disease."

Good ventilation minimizes the problems of humidity, dust, ammonia, and other irritants, providing fresh air year-round, without drafts. The livestock industry has been using principles of improved ventilation for seventy years, to better conditions for housed beef and dairy animals, hogs, and chickens. Good barn construction designs have enabled the hog industry to have a less than 1 percent incidence of respiratory problems in high-density confinement operations. These designs could benefit horses, too — but many horse owners are not aware of the principles of good ventilation or don't feel they need to worry about it. If a barn is so poorly ventilated that humans must wear face masks to clean stalls, the air quality is seriously unhealthy for horses.

Evaporation of moisture from urine and animals' exhalation creates dampness in a barn. A thousand-pound horse exhales two gallons of moisture daily. Damp air, coupled with irritation of air passages from ammonia fumes produced by urine and manure, can contribute to respiratory problems and promote growth of fungus, molds, and bacteria. In cold weather, moisture condenses on the underside of a metal or uninsulated roof, dripping down to make everything wet.

To prevent a humid barn, enough dry, fresh air must be moving through the barn to replace the damp air. Air movement within a barn sweeps away the dust and mold particles from hay and bedding, as well as airborne viruses and bacteria. By sending out warmer air (which tends to rise to ceiling level) and letting in cooler air at ground level, the dust-laden and ammonia-filled air at the lower level is constantly cleared out.

Other ways in which air moves in and out are from the pull of outside air currents (wind moving across the roof draws air out through any available opening) and wind blowing through openings in the sides or ends of the barn. The size of the barn, the height and placement of the vents and openings, and the distance between the inlets where cool air enters and the outlets where warm air escapes can all affect how well your ventilation system works.

All too often horsemen close up any gaps or openings in a barn to keep it warm, and this traps the moisture, noxious gases, and other air pollutants. Water stains and drips are signs that a barn is poorly ventilated, showing evidence of condensation. The high humidity is not only unhealthy for horses, but also damaging to the building. Large volumes of water vapor given off and condensing on walls and ceilings can deteriorate some materials and saturate insulation, ruining its effectiveness. Moisture can lead to spoilage in feed.

Check the airflow in your barn by closing all the windows and doors and walking through the barn. In a barn built for enhanced ventilation, some air movement will occur even with all the doors and windows shut. Often the most stagnant air is in the stalls. In a poorly ventilated barn, stall partitions create a barrier to air circulation. Ammonia fumes hanging low near the stall floor (being heavier than air) are a cause of lung irritation in foals, since they are not very tall and also spend a lot of time lying down. Highest concentrations will be in the lowest three feet.

Adult horses can be adversely affected, too, since they spend time with their heads lowered as they eat hay or sort through the bedding. A sick or injured horse that spends a lot of time lying down will be very vulnerable to effects of ammonia gas. Putting your own head down (sitting or lying on the stall floor) can give a rude awakening regarding the condition of the air down there.

A stall is an unhealthy environment for a foal sharing this small space with a large mother that produces heat, carbon dioxide, manure, and urine. Protein is broken down during digestion and utilization, and one of the by-products of this breakdown is urea, which is excreted in urine. Nitrogen from the urea produces ammonia when the decomposing urine contacts the air. Excess protein fed to broodmares results in greater production of ammonia.

Ammonia is irritating to eyes and lungs. If you detect the presence of ammonia gas by smell, it is twice the concentration at which it becomes harmful to any creature that must breathe it or be constantly exposed to it. Ammonia levels are often highest at the center of the stall just above the bedding surface.

Ventilation can be created in several ways. Controlled air exchange is the key to good ventilation in summer and winter. You can use natural wind currents out-doors to help cool your barn in summer, maximizing air movement by using any wind to get rid of heat. In winter your purposes are mainly to control humidity.

Windows and Other Ventilation Aids

In warm climates many barns have only grillwork or bars over windows, or nothing at all, for better air circulation. Shutters or sliding doors can be closed if necessary. In cold climates, sliding Plexiglas windows can be used on the outside of bars or grillwork. Whenever possible create a door to the outside from every stall, in addition to the one opening to the aisle. This improves ventilation and is a good safety feature in case of fire. If existing windows on the outside wall are glass, convert them to screens. Solid stall doors can be replaced with grills.

In some barns, opening windows, barn doors, and tops of stall doors can provide the best ventilation. Barns with open space at the top of each stall and walls that don't reach to the ceiling allow warm stale air to escape, and vented openings at the bottom of a stall wall can draw in fresh air. An opening at the bottom of the stall's outside wall with a matching vent at the bottom of the stall door into the aisle will greatly increase floor-level cross ventilation.

Vents can be installed, such as louvers under the eaves or roof ridge. Since hot air rises, you must give it somewhere to go. You need openings in the roof that will not weaken the structure. One of the easiest and cheapest ways is to install metal ridge vents, which are about ten feet long, over an opening about six inches wide. The vent is covered with screen or mesh. The size of the barn will determine how many ridge vents are needed; a hundred-foot long barn needs four ridge vents. A ventilating ridge cap allows warm air to move out of the attic air space but cannot move as much air out as the taller ridge vent and is often combined with louvers and cupolas. Louvers can be installed at both ends of the barn beneath the roof peak; these work best when the roof is steeply pitched.

Cupolas are typically four-sided with louvered openings or windows on each side, acting as chimneys to pull hot air up and out of the barn. Some cupolas are equipped with fans to help pull the warm air out of the barn. A spinning ventilator can pull air out of the barn, augmenting the ridge vents. In some cases you may need a fan to force the air through the barn, making sure air movement is not so much as to create a draft.

Openings at the top of the barn let air out, and fresh air must come in at a lower level. Opening barn doors at each end of the aisle is generally not enough; you need stall windows or doors to the outside or openings under the eaves along the sides of the barn. The warm air then moves up and out, replaced by fresh air.

Fans in the gable area at each end of a pitched barn roof enhance air circulation. Paddle fans above each stall (closer to the aisle than to the center of the stall) can keep air circulating throughout the barn, keeping horses cooler in hot weather. To move the most air, fans should pull it up, not blow it down. An exhaust fan or two, near the apex of the roof, help keep the air from getting stagnant even when barn doors are shut during cold weather. Fans can be on timers, running for two minutes every hour.

In winter, ventilation strategy is the reverse of summer cooling tactics. Trying to keep the barn warm by shutting doors is counterproductive, restricting air movement too much. Instead, reverse the direction of the exhaust fans to pull cold air in at ceiling level to mix with warm air in the rafters. This causes the warmer air to sink and heat the barn. The mixed air can then be expelled through adjustable ground-level louvers or through burlap-covered windows. Horses adjust to cold weather; it doesn't hurt to leave barn doors partially open except in stormy weather. Cold, fresh air is almost always better than stuffy conditions inside a barn that has been tightly sealed up to preserve heat. Part of the problem with trying to maintain proper barn temperature in winter is that people working in the barn want it warmer than what is healthy for the horses, and they tend to close up the barn or limit the fresh airflow for their own comfort.

Barn Stalls

Some stalls are too small, if you try to combine low cost with maximum occupancy. Bigger is better, especially if stalls must be used for foaling as well as for general use. A box stall twelve by twelve feet works for most horses, but a foaling stall should be at least fourteen by fourteen, preferably fourteen by sixteen or even larger.

A typical tie stall is about five feet wide and nine feet long, with a feed box or hay manger, waterer, or bucket accessible at the front. A box stall enables a horse to move around (much healthier for feet, legs, and disposition) and is much more comfortable.

A stall should be large enough that the horse has plenty of space to lie down and to eat. If the stall is too small, the horse will be stirring manure into the bedding or hay every time he moves. An extra-large stall may be needed for a foaling mare. It's handy to have a double stall divided by a moveable partition. You can use it as two stalls or as one large one. Some moveable partitions swing open. Others are constructed with removable planks. Channel iron or wood braces made of two-by-six boards are bolted to the walls to hold the partition planks in place; removing the lag bolts and braces allows the wall boards to be taken down.

Ceilings should be at least eight feet high (nine and a half feet high is better) for safe headroom. Stall partitions and fronts can be wood, concrete blocks, or prefabricated materials. Wood should be two inches thick for adequate strength. The front of a stall is usually solid up to five feet, with spaced planks or bars above that to allow ventilation. The bottom twelve to eighteen inches of a wood partition or paneling should be treated to prevent rotting. Narrowly spaced pipes, steel rods, heavy-gauge wire, or wooden slats can be used on higher parts of front or sidewalls. Partitions and stall fronts can go to the ceiling or about eight feet with air space above them.

Stall walls should be smooth. If the basic barn structure is metal, concrete, or masonry, line the stall interior with wood at least five feet high to prevent injury to feet and legs if a horse kicks the wall. You can glue exterior grade plywood (half to three-quarters of an inch thick) to the wall to give a smoother surface. If you use boards, run the wallboards vertically rather than horizontally; the shorter span will be stronger than a ten- to fourteen-foot horizontal stall board and won't give way as easily when kicked or pressed.

A complete stall lining is much safer than a few kick rails or boards, since a hoof can sometimes slip between those. Whenever you use wood for a stall interior, cap exposed edges with smooth metal or use a design that eliminates edges and corners that encourage horses to chew the wood. There should be no splinters, nails sticking out, bolt ends, or sharp edges that a horse might bump into. A bucket hook can catch a horse's blanket or

A box stall.

injure a horse. Don't use open hooks; use rounded hardware such as screw eyes if an item must project into the stall. Run your hands along the walls to feel rough spots and sharp projections that you won't notice with your eyes. If there will be a foal in the stall, kneel down and take a look (and feel) at foal level to make sure there are no projections that might snag his skin or injure his eyes.

The stall door should be at least four and a half feet wide and more than eight feet high (preferably as high as the ceiling). A door too narrow may catch a horse's hip or increase the risk of having a horse squash you when leading him in and out. Make sure stall doors (and barn doors) open easily, swing or slide fully, and are never partially blocked by hay bales or some other obstacle.

Swinging doors can be a hazard if they swing into the stall (a horse eager to come out may bang into the door before you have it completely open) and dangerous to passing horses if they swing out into the aisle. A swinging door should be hinged so it opens into the aisle and flat against the stall so it does not block the aisle when open. Swinging doors may sag if improperly installed or damaged by horses leaning on them while hanging their heads over a Dutch door. Sliding stall doors are safest. Make sure latches, handles, and locks don't protrude and that a clever horse can't open them. Latches should be functional from both sides of the door.

A traditional Dutch door enables a horse to stick his head out when the top part is open, but the door needs space to swing. Some horses will leer out into the aisle and cause trouble when others are led by. Any time a horse has access

A version of a Dutch door.

to the hardware that is keeping his door closed, he has the opportunity to figure out how to open it. A sliding door that is half wood and half grill-work is often safer. Some have grill-work that folds down so that when you are in the barn you can let a horse hang his head out into the aisle if you wish, but you can shut the opening if you don't want him leaning out while you are gone or nibbling on the latches.

The top portion of the whole front wall can be made of pipe or metal bars to enable a horse to see out of the stall. There should be very small spacing between the bars (two inches is best) so a horse can't get a foot or nose through or get his teeth or lower jaw caught when trying to chew. Full-view stall doors and fronts give good ventilation and make it easier to check on a horse.

Some horsemen feel the dividers between stalls should be solid (so horses adjacent to each other cannot start an argument if they do not get along), with a slot that can be opened if an insecure horse needs companionship of the horse next door. Many dividers are just bars or grillwork on the top portion, and this usually works fine. Two compatible horses will both be happier if they can see and smell one another, reducing the chances for developing neurotic stall vices. Considerations for having a solid or not-solid wall may depend on whether horses are living in a stall full time and need company or whether strange horses will be coming and going. Visual contact, smell, and touch are usually not a problem, as long as the stall dividers are constructed so horses cannot bite each other. The exception is when a horse has a transmittable disease. It's wise to have one stall in the barn where a horse can be isolated.

Steel stall fronts are popular in concrete or wood barns. A sliding steel door is built into the stall front. The steel will not rot or warp, and steel-frame doors need little maintenance. These doors usually have bars, steel mesh, or a combination of bars and mesh, and give improved ventilation. The sliding doors must be mounted in a track or channel. Square channels need steel rollers and must be greased regularly, but barrel tracks are cylindrical and have nylon rollers requiring no maintenance or grease.

The stall floor should be durable, resilient, and easy to keep clean, since a horse living in it may produce up to fifty pounds of manure and more than ten gallons of urine daily.

A traditional clay floor has good traction, provides some cushion and shock absorption, and is fairly warm, but moisture will not drain through as easily as through a clay and sand mixture, stone chips, or crushed rock. Sand or crushed rock may get mixed with the feed or bedding if a horse likes to paw, however. A clay floor works best if you put in stone and drain tiles underneath. Clay is easy on feet and legs, noiseless, and usually fairly dust-free. Pure clay tends to pack too tightly, without drainage, and requires a lot of work to keep level, since horses will paw holes in it. Urine can pool in holes or depressions — which softens the clay and leads to larger holes. Eventually the floor must be dug out, leveled, and tamped. It's wise to replace the top two to four inches of a clay floor annually just for sanitary reasons. A dirt floor with sand or clay mix will require regular maintenance to fill in holes and level the humps.

Tiles or stall mats can be used over wood or concrete to give more cushion and traction or over clay and dirt floors to keep horses from pawing holes or eating sand and dirt. Rubber pavers make a safe surface for wash areas, breeding sheds, and aisles. They require a curbing or edge to hold them together unless they are put over a concrete slab that is depressed for a perfect fit. Interlocking rubber pavers that look like large bricks are resilient and comfortable, providing good footing even when wet.

Wooden floors can be used for tie stalls but are too slippery for good traction in box stalls. Concrete or paved flooring is easy to clean but can be hard on feet and legs and has little traction. Sand mixed with shavings or sawdust can make a good buffer over concrete, with additional bedding on top. Concrete floors should be sloped toward a drain to remove urine and spilled water. For good drainage, a solid floor can be sloped toward a drain or sloped toward the back of the stall so fluid can drain to the outside of the barn. Usually a three-inch difference between the front and the back wall is sufficient slope.

There are several types of asphalt or blacktop flooring. Some contain large aggregate and sand, making a rough, porous floor with better footing and drainage. Straw bedding works well over asphalt. Any bedding material that packs down too tightly against the asphalt will not allow moisture to pass through.

Popcorn asphalt is relatively inexpensive, somewhat porous for drainage, easy to clean, slightly more forgiving than concrete, and less slippery. It is also less durable than concrete and needs to be replaced every few years.

Clay and dirt floors often become uneven due to pawing and barn cleaning, but if the floor is level to begin with, a mat can help keep it that way. You can generally use less bedding over a mat than over a bare floor, due to the cushion provided by the mat. Reduced bedding also means less dust and ammonia and less time spent cleaning stalls. The mats themselves are easily cleaned.

Stall mats can be made of rubber, plastic, or a combination of rubber and synthetic materials. If they have a textured surface they give good traction. The softest rubber has the most cushion but may not wear as well as harder varieties. The more dense the rubber, the harder and tougher the mat. Plastic mats are designed to let moisture through, which works well for a dirt floor but not for a solid floor. Both rubber and plastic work well over dirt. Clay or dirt should be leveled and compacted, then topped with a four- to six-inch layer of fine gravel and compacted stone dust to make a firm but well draining base.

Some rubber mats may creep or shift over time, or the edges may curl up. Since the mats are installed in sections (most rubber mats are four by six feet and weigh more than a hundred pounds), gaps between mats or around the stall edge can trap bedding or allow urine to pool beneath the mat if the flooring underneath has poor drainage. The raised edges may trip you or the horse. Much of this problem can be avoided with carefully installed, good quality mats.

The best mats are five-eighths to three-quarters of an inch thick. Thinner mats may be cheaper but won't wear as well (a horse may paw through them) and are apt to creep and curl. A smooth surface on top may be easier to clean and disinfect, but a raised surface has more traction. Plastic mats — high-strength polyethylene or PVC (polyvinyl chloride) — have holes to let moisture drain through and work well over dirt or clay floors that have good drainage. Bedding usually stays drier on a plastic mat than on a solid rubber mat.

Bedding in a barn stall or run-in shed provides a layer of insulation from cold flooring or cold ground, cushions the hard surface whether a horse is standing or lying (encouraging a horse to lie down and rest, increasing his comfort), prevents bruising of knees, elbows, hocks, and hips, and keeps the horse cleaner. If a horse is constantly exposed to urine and manure, he is more at risk for thrush, urine scald, and other skin problems. Bedding absorbs urine; if you remove soiled bedding regularly it keeps the horse's environment drier and healthier.

A cold floor without bedding can chill a horse by drawing away his body heat. Bedding creates air pockets that act as barriers between the cold ground and the horse. Piling straw bedding thicker on the sides of a stall can protect a horse from drafts in cold weather, and the padding can help him get back to his feet if he happens to roll against the wall.

Factors to consider when selecting bedding materials are cost, availability, freedom from dust and foreign material, palatability (something the horse will *not* eat). Choose material that will be compatible with your stall flooring and can be easily disposed.

Straw is fairly absorbent, and soiled straw bedding can be scattered directly on pastures and fields if necessary. Composted straw bedding mixed with manure makes good fertilizer. Wheat straw is often used, since it is less palatable than oat, rye, or barley straw and less abrasive than barley straw.

Wheat stalks in earlier times were cut at full length, which created dust-free straw, but most wheat today is harvested with combines; stalks are cut in shorter lengths, with more shattering. Choose straw that is bright and clean, with little dust and no mold. Straw makes a good bed, dries well, and stays fairly clean if manure is picked out of it often. Straw lets urine soak through it and down to the stall floor. You want the floor well covered — a deep bed to shield the horse from the liquid at floor level.

Shavings for bedding.

If you live where wood products are processed, these may be the most economical bedding, but closure of lumber mills due to public land timber lock-up has limited many good sources of wood products. If you have access to wood products, shavings are better than sawdust. The latter is usually too fine and dusty, and the horse may get particles in his nose or eyes. Shavings are usually better than wood chips; chips may be too coarse, with sharp edges, or large and uncomfortable to lie on. Wood chips also can cause choke, digestive tract obstructions, splinters, and other problems if a horse eats them.

Shavings tend to dry the horse's feet, and some can be dusty. Shavings have several advantages, however. They make a soft and well-insulated bed; some softwood shavings are more absorbent than straw; horses usually won't eat them; and they can be easy to store if bagged. Bulk shavings are difficult to store and must be kept dry. Used shavings present more disposal problems than straw, since they cannot be put directly on fields. Being more acidic than straw, wood products must first be composted for several months.

Wood products should not be used for foaling mares or mares with young foals; wood can harbor *Klebsiella* bacteria, which can cause uterine infection in the foaling mare, or navel ill in the newborn foal as well as respiratory and urinary tract infections. Straw is less likely to have microorganisms that cause problems for foals if ingested or contacted with a wet navel. *Klebsiella* bacteria from wood products can be a problem for a horse with a compromised immune system, and infection may gain entrance to the urethra of stallions or geldings bedded on shavings.

Soft woods like pine and fir make good bedding. Hardwood has less absorbency. Some hardwoods, such as black walnut, can be toxic to horses (causing laminitis), and oak has too much acid. An alkaloid found in yellow poplar wood can cause itching; horses may rub their manes and tails until the hair falls out and the flesh is raw. Shavings from other members of the poplar family are free of the alkaloid and safe to use as bedding.

It's not always easy to tell if shavings or sawdust contain black walnut, especially if several types of wood have been mixed. The color of the wood is not always a predictable clue since there are other woods that are dark, including oak and other species of walnut that are harmless. If the person delivering the shavings or sawdust doesn't know what kind they are, ask the mill to give a breakdown and description of the kind of wood and its source. If the wood cannot be identified, don't use it. Also make sure the wood has not been treated with chemicals or preservatives that might irritate skin or create allergic reactions. Shavings should be from kiln-dried wood, not green.

Shavings compress and pack down under a horse's weight, so you need extra bedding material to compensate. Most horsemen recommend bedding at least a foot deep. Composted manure and shavings create a good fertilizer, but lime may need to be added when it is put out on a field or pasture because of the acidic nature of the shavings.

Other materials that are sometimes used for bedding are shredded paper, peat moss, peanut shells, and rice hulls. Volcanic aggregate is also used as bedding, in stalls, or out in a paddock. It is lightweight and porous and can be used under other beddings to provide better drainage.

Shredded newspaper is highly absorbent and dust-free, comfortable to the horse, and fairly easy to clean out of the stall. The ink on most types of newsprint is not toxic, though it will rub off on light-colored horses and stall walls. Carbon content in the ink tends to absorb and reduce odors. Even if horses eat paper, it does not seem to be harmful. Newspapers and telephone books are printed with a nontoxic vegetable dye, but the ink on some other types of paper may not be as safe; if using shredded paper for bedding, make sure of its source.

Other bedding products include paper pulp resembling the soft cardboard used in egg cartons (highly absorbent, nontoxic, and dust-free, decomposing rapidly to make good fertilizer when composted). There is also a recycled newspaper product that is shredded and cleaned to wash out ink and chemicals.

Rice hulls are used as bedding in some areas, distributed in bags as a by-product of beer brewing. Rice hulls are lightweight and not very absorbent, working best in stalls with good drainage or with other bedding such as wood shavings. The mix acts in the same fashion as multi-layered disposable diapers; the lighter rice hulls rise to the top and the heavier shavings settle to the bottom. Moisture seeps down through the top layer of hulls into the more absorbent shavings, leaving the top surface dry and comfortable. Rice hulls also have the advantage of being less flammable than other types of bedding.

Bedding materials vary greatly in their absorbency, with rice hulls and hardwood products being least absorbent. Pinewood shavings and barley and wheat straw are moderately absorbent, while pinewood sawdust and chips are more absorbent. Long oat straw is the most absorbent type of straw; shredded newspaper is even more absorbent than any straw or wood product; and peat moss is the most absorbent type of bedding.

Straw bedding soiled with manure and urine tends to produce more ammonia gas than does sawdust or shavings. If using straw, clean the stall at least once or preferably twice a day to cut down on ammonia buildup. Sawdust reduces the amount of ammonia created but is more easily stirred around by the horse's feet than straw and tends to release clouds of ammonia gas when disturbed.

Lime has been traditionally sprinkled on the floor to neutralize ammonia odor after a stall is cleaned. There are also some commercial products that can help reduce ammonia levels. They are nontoxic and less irritating than lime.

Feed Rooms

To reduce risk of fire, hay should be stored somewhere other than the barn (in a hay shed, on high ground with a tarp over it, or in a walled-off storage room at one end of the barn). But you may want a place to put a few bales of hay in the barn, along with any grain. Traditional barns often have a hayloft, but this can be a fire hazard. The safest type of hayloft has a fire-resistant floor, such as sheets of drywall between two layers of plywood flooring. The drywall can slow down a fire, giving more time to put it out before it comes down into the main barn.

In a large barn, the handiest location for a feed room is at the middle of a long aisle with access to the outside for delivery vehicles. The feed room should be constructed of cinder blocks and shut off from the rest of the barn with steel fire doors that are always closed except when hay is being moved in. A well-constructed feed room can extend the time from minutes to hours before a fire in the hay endangers the horses in the barn. Install a horse-proof door and latch for the feed room. All grain storage containers should have lids. Don't store grain in sacks; mice or horses can get into them. The feed room should have a concrete floor for easy cleaning and for thwarting access by rodents. Rat-proof wire should be installed behind the walls and above the ceiling.

A hay shed can cut down on waste and spoilage, protecting your hay from the weather damage it would get in an uncovered haystack or under a leaky tarp. All you need is a tall roof to keep off rain and melting snow. An inexpensive shed can be constructed using tall posts for the supports, poles or lumber for the rafters and roof trusses, and a metal roof.

A hay storage shed.

Melting snow slides off the metal roof, and the hay stays dry underneath. If the base of your hay shed is on high ground and you prepare the base ahead of time by hauling in gravel or crushed rock, the bottom bales will never draw moisture or be flooded. The snow that slides off the roof may make large piles along the sides of the shed, but moisture from the melting snow in the spring will run away from the stack and not into it.

A run-in shed or outdoor shelter for horses at pasture or in paddocks may be something you'll want instead of a barn or in addition to a barn. A shed is the simplest and least expensive shelter, if horses can be fed and managed as a group instead of individually in stalls. A three-sided shed adequately protects outdoor horses in bad weather and also gives protection from flies and hot sun in summer.

When used by horses in groups, run-in sheds pose more risk of injury and less opportunity to feed each horse as an individual. Usually the social advantages of group living outweigh the benefits of individual feeding, unless it's a mixed group of horses with vastly differing nutritional needs.

A run-in shed.

The open side of a shelter should face south if your coldest winds generally come from the north. A shed with a southern exposure also gets more morning sun in winter and provides the most shade in summer since the sun is higher in the sky.

Build the shed on a high spot so horses will have dry footing, with the roof sloping away from the opening. This helps keep run-off moisture from making a bog at the front of the shed. There should be good drainage away from the shed on all sides. A four- to six-foot overhang of roof at the front will keep rain and snow from blowing inside and give more shade in summer.

The opening should be at least twelve feet high, with a minimum of nine feet at the back. This gives horses adequate headroom and allows space for a tractor with a loader or blade to clean out the manure. The shed won't need any bedding during summer and maybe not even in winter since horses may not lie down in the shed; they often prefer to nap in the open. Since horses won't spend as much time in the shed, as compared with a barn stall, manure doesn't usually build up. Some horsemen put bedding in sheds in the fall (using straw, shavings, or, sometimes, old hay — as long as it is not dusty or moldy), adding to it once or twice during winter if necessary. If horses do spend time in the shed, pick up manure piles and wet spots every ten days or so, and remove all the bedding in spring.

The shed should be large enough to accommodate all the horses in that pen or pasture without crowding. The usual estimate for shed size is to allow about 140 square feet per horse, but it's safer to provide 300 square feet. The ideal shed for four horses would be about thirty feet deep and forty feet wide.

Another option is a two-sided shed with only the north and west sides closed to the weather. There is one less confining wall to trap a horse that is being threatened by a herd mate. In a mild climate, a shed can be open on three sides with only a solid back wall. Old tires can be used to pad exposed posts where horses might run into them. A shed built with tall posts ten to twelve feet apart gives you the option of using portable panels or gates inside them to create temporary stalls if needed.

Fire Prevention in Barns and Stables

Fire is the greatest danger to a stabled horse, especially if it starts at night. With all the flammable material in a barn, a fire can escalate rapidly. A fire in straw bedding can burn more than a ten-foot circle in less than three minutes. A horse in a burning stable may have only ten minutes to live. Even if you get him out, lung tissue may be permanently damaged by smoke inhalation, and he may suffer body burns that take a long time to heal. Barns and sheds should always be built with fire safety in mind, using the most fireproof materials you can afford.

If possible, hay, straw, or other types of bedding should not be stored in the same building with horses. If separate storage is not feasible, second-story storage is better than stall level storage because heat and fire drift upward. If a fire starts in the hayloft, the flames' upward movement will allow more time to remove horses from the lower level. If hay or bedding must be stored at stall level, have it completely separate in a room with fire-resistant walls and roof. Never store hay or straw near machinery or near any type of electrical or heat source.

Any material will burn if it gets hot enough, but combustion temperature of kerosene, gasoline, paint, fertilizers, and insect repellents is low. These highly volatile and flammable substances should not be stored in a barn. Other highly flammable materials include cobwebs, dust, grain dust, horse blankets, pesticides, and herbicides. Keep papers and debris away from heat ducts and other heating elements. Other sources of heat that may cause a flammable material to ignite or smolder are cigarettes or matches, sparks from welding or machinery (trucks, tractors, mowers) or the farrier's work (especially when hot shoeing), or motors, electrical appliances, fence chargers, electrical fixtures and wires, batteries, sunlight through broken glass, or chemical reactions.

Barns built of metal, tile, stone, or concrete are safer than wood. Oak is more fireproof than pine or cedar. A new barn is not as flammable as an old one; new wood is still somewhat moist. An old wooden barn, tinder dry from years of aging, poses the most risk. All barns are less flammable in humid weather.

When building a new structure, take precautions to reduce risk of fire. County or township building codes require many of these measures. Check with the building inspector for permits and requirements in your region, and check with your insurance company before deciding about building materials. Many insurance companies will lower their premiums if fire prevention precautions are taken during construction. Some of these measures may include approved fire doors, a firewall between hay or bedding storage and the stable area, and use of materials that are flame resistant or fire resistant. Several manufacturers make fire-retardant treated wood products for interior use. Some of these products are also very resistant to termites and decay.

Use of fire-retardant paint (preferably two coats) and sealers can help. These can be applied to existing surfaces with brush, roller, or spray. A fire-retardant coating can be sprayed or fogged onto new clean surfaces. In a long row of stalls, a solid floor-to-ceiling fire-resistant partition every fourth stall can help keep flames from jumping to the next group of stalls.

Smoke detectors, sprinkler systems, and fire alarms (which can be monitored by local police or fire departments) are costly, but may give you enough time to get horses out and perhaps save the building. A water source at your barn — a good well or nearby pond — can help a fire department save the building.

Electrical problems, especially in older barns, are often the cause of fires. Anyone who uses the barn or stable should know the location of the fuse box or circuit breaker and be instructed to shut off the power if any electrical problems are noticed.

If constructing a barn, repairing an old one, or installing a new electrical system, you can take several precautions to reduce fire risk:

• Have a professional install or repair electrical wiring.

• Put the main electrical panel box in the driest and most dust-free area possible — in a tack room or utility area, never in a stall.

• The panel box should be weatherproofed even inside a building.

• Outlets and switch boxes should be metal and have dust-tight and watertight spring-loaded covers that close when released.

• Wires (even extension cords) should always be encased in conduit pipe to keep them safe from breakage and away from the teeth of curious horses, gnawing rodents, metal shoes, etc.

Often the biggest electrical mistake in barns is insufficient outlets. Overloaded extension cords can get hot and cause a fire. Electrical outlets should have spring-loaded covers to keep out dirt and moisture. They should be positioned high on the walls, rather than close to the ground. Don't have an outlet in the wash stall or wherever a lot of water will be. If any wiring is exposed, contact a qualified electrician to correct the situation. Faulty wiring is the cause of many fires.

If you are planning a new barn, locate incoming electrical wire away from a doorway, so that if a fire occurs at the panel box it will not make an exit unusable. All light fixtures, switches, and electrical wires should be out of horses' reach. All lights should have protective covers to prevent breakage, with dust and moisture-proof seals.

Motors (for air circulation fans, water pumps, hay elevators, etc.) should have moisture and dust-proof on/off switches. They should never be closer than eighteen inches from any combustible material such as hay or bedding. A fire-resistant shield should be placed between such material and the motor to protect the material from any heat given off by the motor. Electric-fence units also can be potential fire hazards. Use a charger with intermittent (not constant) current. Any appliance used in a barn such as clippers, vacuums, coffee pots, heaters, etc. should be grounded and disconnected when not in use.

Heating units and infrared lights are the biggest single cause of barn fires. Portable heaters and heat lamps should not be used in the barn area. If used in the tack room or office portion of a barn, they should not be left unattended and should always be turned off when you leave the room.

Heating appliances have no place in a barn except for a medical reason such as extra warmth for a sick foal or a newborn, and even then they should be carefully and constantly monitored and never left unattended. Heat lamps often cause barn fires when placed too close to hay or bedding or clamped to the top of a stall, where they can be knocked off and down into the bedding. Never use extension cords with heat lamps.

Heat tapes and water-tank heaters should have a thermostat. Tanks and tank heaters should be installed and manufacturers' instructions followed. Tank-heater cords and heat tapes should be adequately protected so animals cannot chew through them. Heat tapes should have a fire-retardant insulation material. Most trough heaters come with a protective cover for the electrical cord. If yours doesn't, get one at a hardware store or use fireproof foam and wrap it with electrical or duct tape. This same method can be used to protect any pipes covered with heat tape.

General fire safety involves common sense. Gasoline engines are potential spark producers, and their metal parts can get very hot, creating enough heat to ignite flammable materials. A hot tail pipe from a delivery truck can start a fire if it is touching a bale of hay. Cars, motorcycles, trucks, tractors, lawn mowers, chain saws, brush cutters, etc. are often used around barns and can cause a fire. Park vehicles at least twelve feet away from buildings. Farm equipment and trailers that are infrequently used should be parked some distance from the barn so that debris does not collect under or behind them. House vehicles and machinery in a separate building, never in the one where you have horses or hay. Smoking should not be permitted in the barn area, hay or bedding storage area, or tack room.

Weeds should be mowed or trimmed and fallen branches and other trash should be kept picked up around the barn. Keep nearby pastures or paddocks mowed to reduce risk of fire in dried weeds or brush. If your pastures border a road, mow between the fence and the road to guard against fires resulting from tossed cigarettes and sparks.

Manure piles should be at least twenty feet away from the barn to reduce risk of combustion fire. Manure that is piled too deep can generate enough heat in its fermentation to kindle flammable materials, and if it gets hot enough, manure itself will burn.

Monitor electric fences closely. A broken wire that comes into contact with dry

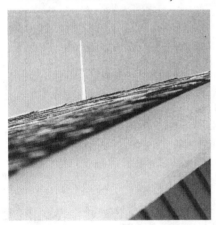

horse manure may set it afire. Dry grass or weeds too close to a fence may be ignited just from the electrical current, especially in fences designed to burn off the weeds.

Hot hay is a common cause of barn and haystack fires. When storing newly baled hay, make sure the hay does not become too hot; provide adequate ventilation for additional drying. Don't put freshly baled hay into a barn or loft or stack it next to a building. It needs more drying time so it will not generate heat. Some heating may occur even in hay baled at proper moisture

A lightning rod on a barn roof.

content.

Serious heating will occur if hay is baled too green (or with too much moisture on it from rain or heavy dew) and then put into a stack or storage area where no air can get between the bales. Such bales can eventually create spontaneous combustion. Never buy any hay that is warm. Always feel down inside a few of the bales to check. Not only can heating be a serious fire hazard but it is also an indication that hay was baled too wet and will mold, making it unhealthy as horse feed.

Heat is the result of fermentation and microbial activity. After the hay gets above 170 degrees, the microorganisms die, but the heat-producing chemical reactions can continue to drive temperatures even higher. Spontaneous combustion occurs when the hay gets hot enough and is exposed to air; the oxygen enables it to burst into flame. Hay fires can occur more than two to three weeks after the hay is put into storage. It slowly builds up temperature and then begins to smolder. It may smolder unnoticed in the center of the stack for some time before the heat reaches the surface, becoming a full-blown fire once it reaches the air.

Other fire-prevention measures include lightning protection and fire extinguishers. Barns and stables should be equipped with professionally installed (and maintained) lightning rods made of copper or aluminum, and the system should be properly grounded. Lightning rods should be checked every five years.

A fire extinguisher in a barn.

A hand-held fire extinguisher can often control a fire in its early stages. Dry-chemical fire extinguishers should be placed in all barns, stables, workshops, etc. These all-purpose extinguishers can be used to douse wood, chemical, or electrical fires. Use the kind with metal heads, not plastic. Fire extinguishers should be serviced annually and be handy at all barn entrances and exits, in the middle of long aisles, in the tack room and storage area, and near the electrical panel box, mounted in visible and accessible locations no higher than eye level, with instructions for use posted nearby. In a large barn, make sure a fire extinguisher is mounted every thirty feet and within reach just inside an exterior door. It's also a good idea to have one fire extinguisher hanging outside the barn in case a fire makes it impossible to get to the inside ones.

A fire extinguisher should be at least five pounds, preferably ten pounds, for adequate supply of fire retardant. If a unit is used, even only partially, it must then be recharged. Keep in mind that the chemicals in a fire extinguisher tend to settle and cake; each one should be shaken every six months (or according to manufacturer's directions), or it may not function properly when needed. Signs denoting the position of fire extinguishers should be very visible.

Elaborate fire-fighting systems, which automatically sprinkle water or chemicals in response to smoke alarms, may be worthwhile in large barns that house valuable horses. Other alternatives are oscillating sprinkler heads above each stall, connected to a power source that you can turn on, or a perforated garden hose running the length of the barn, attached to its own water supply. If you use the stall sprinklers, make sure the switch is near a door, for emergency access; the same applies to the hydrant you'd use for the perforated garden hose. Another alternative is to keep a hose (at least as long as the barn length) on a reel mounted next to a reliable water source. A snap-on spray nozzle can be kept by the water source if the hose is also used for other purposes.

Smoke detectors can be helpful, but residential types often do not work in a barn; dust can clog the alarm mechanism. Those designed to operate in dusty areas are more expensive. Heat detectors are more effective in a barn than smoke detectors. They are more expensive, but they don't clog.

All barns should have a minimum of two easily accessible exits. A common rule of thumb for barn size: up to twelve horses, two exits; twelve to twenty-four horses, three exits; twenty-four to thirty-six horses, four exits; thirty-six to fifty horses, five to six exits. A barn should be designed so you can lead a horse into the aisle and then directly outside in a straight line. An exit should be no more than one hundred feet from the farthest stall. Aisles should be wide enough to accommodate two handlers and horses side by side, and exit openings should be as wide as the aisle. Doors should open outward or slide completely to one side or the other and never be locked. Latches should be easy to work with just one hand. A halter and lead shank for every horse should be readily available, hung on all stall doors in case of emergencies but out of reach of horses.

Paddocks and outdoor stall runs should never have just one access (such as from the barn). Each paddock or turnout area should have its own gate to the outside in addition to the stall or barn door. If the barn is on fire and horses are in their turnout areas they can be rescued without having to take them through the barn or tear down the fence to get them out.

Have a phone in the barn and keep the fire department's number posted by it. In case of fire, notify the fire department first, and then try to rescue the horses. After that you can attempt to halt the spread of the fire or extinguish it, if you have enough help. If it's a chemical or electrical fire, use a fire extinguisher, not water. Water will conduct electricity and may deliver a fatal shock to the person handling the hose. Since many barn fires originate in wood or straw, however, your best suppression weapon is often water, so an adequate water supply is very important.

Preparedness and a cool head can help save the horses or the people involved, if a fire starts. Remove each horse as quickly and calmly as possible. If stalls have outside doors, it helps if you've given the horse a fire drill so he is familiar with going through the outside door and won't panic or balk. Horses can be completely unpredictable in a fire; dependable ones may refuse to cooperate, and nervous or unruly ones may be totally manageable. Horses may freeze up and stare at the flames. If that happens, a blindfold may help.

If you don't have a halter and lead shank, use rope, baling twine, your belt, or a scarf — anything that can be placed around his neck close to his head. Cover his eyes and nose if you have a jacket or grain sack. If a horse still refuses to cooperate, you may be able to get him moving by pulling him sideways (pivoting him around you as you press on his shoulder), using a rump rope around his hind end, tapping his hindquarters with a whip, or backing him out a door if he refuses to go forward — or two people can lock arms around his hindquarters to move him forward.

Once outside the burning barn, put him in a safe paddock, tie him, or give him to someone to hold. Never turn him loose except as a last resort. Many panicked horses will run back into the barn because it is their security. The "safe" area may be quite a ways from the barn, since the heat of a barn fire can be overwhelming even a hundred feet away. Horses must be far enough away to where they can breathe fresh air and no smoke; their lungs may already be irritated. Even if a horse comes out of a burning barn seemingly uninjured, have a veterinarian check him. Lung damage is the biggest killer in a fire; it often leads to a fatal pneumonia.

Ask someone from your local fire department to evaluate your barn's fire safety. He may notice something you overlooked. Make sure a fire truck would have adequate access to your buildings. Keep your driveway maintained and free of deep snow or mud. Much precious time could be wasted if firefighters have to stretch a hose several hundred feet.

Rodent Control

Rats, mice, and voles eat a lot of feed, contaminate more than they eat (with urine and droppings), chew baling twines in two, and damage buildings, tack, and other equipment with their gnawing and nest-building activities. They shred any handy material to make their nests and also may chew through electrical wiring and burn down the barn — or bring disease into your barn. Human illnesses associated with rodents in the United States are bubonic plague (spread by fleas from infected rats), typhus, salmonellosis, trichinosis, and listerosis. Mice can spread Lyme disease via deer ticks that use deer mice as hosts. Mice also can carry several other serious diseases, including the deadly Hantavirus.

Always be careful when cleaning barns, tack rooms, and grain storage areas, especially when sweeping or getting rid of old mouse nests, since the Hantavirus can lurk in the dust wherever the mice have been. A growing number of people in the United States have become ill or died from Hantavirus. Medical advice is to wear a dust mask when cleaning any area that has had mice nests.

Rodent droppings and urine also can cause diseases in horses. Get rid of any grain or hay that has been a feeding or nest area for mice or rats. Rodent urine is the main source of contamination with bacteria that cause leptospirosis in humans and animals; carrier rodents pass the infective organism in urine and

A mouse trap in the tack room.

other body secretions. Leptospirosis is usually not a serious disease in horses, but can have serious side effects such as abortion in pregnant mares or damage to eyes; lepto is the most common cause of moon blindness (periodic ophthalmia) in horses.

Salmonella may be present in the intestinal tract of rodents; horses may become ill and develop severe diarrhea after eating feed contaminated by infected rat droppings. Rodents also can pose a threat from botulism if dead ones end up in the feed and their decomposing bodies release deadly toxins created by the bacteria *Clostridium botulinum*.

Small animals that inhabit your barnyard may also spread EPM (equine protozoal myeloencephalitis), which is characterized by hind leg lameness, weakness, and incoordination (ataxia). This serious condition is caused by a protozoa generally spread to horses via the feces of opossums. Raccoons may harbor rabies.

Controlling Animal Pests

Good housekeeping in and around barns and outbuildings reduces the amount of food available to rodents, opossums, and raccoons. Mice and rats won't be so apt to enter in droves and multiply. Keep grain in rodent-proof containers but not airtight ones or you'll have mold growth. Metal bins tend to draw moisture from condensation and create conditions for mold.

Cracks and openings in tack rooms or feed rooms should be sealed to keep out mice. Coarse steel wool works for plugging small holes in walls and floors because you can push it into odd-shaped cracks but rodents can't chew through it easily. Wire screen or lightweight sheet metal works for larger holes. Rats and mice often enter next to water pipes, vents, or under doors. Check walls and flooring to make sure there are no cracks or separations (such as in corners) where rodents could get through.

Clear away all debris, tall grass, or weeds outside the building. These attract rodents and give them better access to the building. They don't like to travel over open space where they are vulnerable to predators. Keep your barn clean; sweep up spilled grain and dispose of it well away from the building. Store tack and horse blankets on wall racks or keep them hung properly. A pile of leather or cloth makes a good hiding place for rodents.

A good barn cat can reduce mouse numbers. The best barn cats are the ones that grew up learning to hunt with their mothers. If you bring a new cat to the barn, give it a few days to adjust to its new home, confining it to the feed room or tack room with ample food and water and a litter box, then give it access to the whole barn. Make sure the cat can get to the areas you want patrolled, even if you must put a cat-size hole in the bottom of the feed room door. Leave its feed and water in the area you want it to protect.

Some people never feed barn cats, but a hungry cat will leave the barn to hunt somewhere else (since there are probably more mice outside) instead of wasting time in the more challenging sport of chasing mice between feed sacks and around grain bins. A well-fed cat that doesn't have to worry about where its next meal is coming from will hunt and kill mice for fun. Its presence alone may deter mice from taking up residence.

A good barn cat is invaluable.

The cost of cat food is small compared with the cost of feed lost to rodents and the damage to tack. Provide a source of water for the cat, so it won't have to drink out of a horse's tub or tank and risk falling in. Keep barn cats vaccinated to protect against the common diseases that could kill them. Of primary importance is a rabies shot, since outdoor cats are at risk for coming into contact with wild animals. It's also wise to neuter your cats, especially males, since they will stay closer to home.

If you have problems with rats (a big rat may be too much challenge for a cat), you may have to use poison or traps, especially if there are areas in the barn where cats cannot patrol easily. Bait bars often work well for poisoning rats.

Inexpensive wooden-base snap traps (mouse or rat size) can be effective and safer than poison. Mice are easy to trap or poison; they are less suspicious than rats and more easily attracted to traps or bait stations. But if you are tricky and persistent, you can catch elusive rats as well. Use several traps and place them where there are droppings or signs of gnawing. Position them so the rodent must travel directly over the trigger. A trap set along a wall should extend from the wall at a right angle, with the trigger end nearly touching the wall.

Placing traps at right angles to the wall along a runway is more apt to catch the rodent than placing it parallel to the wall, since the animal uses his whiskers to follow the wall and may feel his way around a parallel trap and miss it. If using glue boards (which catch a mouse when he steps on the sticky footing) or snap traps, it helps to place them in pairs. If he jumps over the first one he may land on the second one. If taking bait from a snap trap, he may get less cautious once he's eaten the bait carefully off the first one and try for the second — and get caught. For mice that steal bait without getting caught, tie thread around the bait; then they can't get it without pulling on the thread. Use wire to secure traps to overhead rafters, beams, or pipes when dealing with roof rats or pack rats.

Reusing mouse and rat traps makes them more "user friendly." The rodent smell lulls their suspicions. You'll also have more luck if you wait a few days to set the traps, just putting bait on them at first to get the rodents accustomed to dining there. After they've taken the bait a few times, set the traps, and the rodents will be more easily caught. By contrast, a mouse or rat that has sprung a trap without being caught becomes harder to catch.

Use fresh bait. If it's been on the traps awhile it has less odor to entice rodents, and they may ignore it. Just about any food will work — peanut butter, nut meats, bacon, dried fruit, or a hunk of bread with butter on it. The traditional cheese works if you tie it to the trap so the rodent can't depart with it.

If you have a rat that won't take regular bait (suspicious of the trap), try a muskrat trap covered with a handkerchief or a piece of sheet. Rats are curious and will usually investigate and be caught. Anchor the trap securely to something heavy or solid, or he may run off with it if it only catches him by a leg.

A trap that works for mice is a flip box, which tosses mice into an escape-proof container when they pass over a triggering mechanism or go into a hole in the side of the box. These traps work well when set along mouse runways or next to their holes. Traps are safer than poison, with less risk to pets or children, but are labor intensive. You need to check traps daily and reset them or rebait them, removing any dead rodents and disposing of them.

Grain-based baits in meal or pellet form can be placed along runways or other areas of rodent activity. Rodent blocks or bait bars attract rats or mice for gnawing. Tracking powders are put in a thin layer (with a squeeze bulb) along a runway or in a bait box. The powder sticks to the fur or feet of rodents as they travel over it. They eat the poison as they groom themselves or carry it on them back to their nests where it may also kill other mice.

Be sure the poison is not where small pets or children could reach it. Collect and burn dead rodents you find. Some poisons may be harmful to your cat or dog if it eats the dead rodents. Always read labels when using poisons, and follow directions.

Seasonal Farm and Stable Management

Keeping everything working smoothly is a constant, year-round job as you deal with facility upkeep, wear and tear by horses, weather-related problems, etc. If you can keep up with or keep ahead of the seasonal demands of your horse operation, you can often avoid serious problems or costly repairs. Failing to maintain your facilities can cost more time and money later.

Fall is a good time to repair anything that might become more difficult after the ground freezes or during cold weather, such as setting or replacing (or retamping) fence posts, fixing drains, gate latches, etc. Check the thermostat on automatic waterers or water-heating units. Consider a generator if your area experiences power outages during storms.

Put heat tape around exposed pipes. Apply new paint or wood preservative on fences and wooden buildings, if you didn't get it done during summer. Winterize vehicles, equipment, farm tractors, and machinery. Check antifreeze levels. Put farm machinery under a roof or cover it with a sturdy tarp — with no low spots to collect water or melting snow that might leak through a hole in the tarp.

In the barn or stable, check electrical wiring, pipes, and flooring. Weather-strip your tack room door. Clear debris out of rain gutters. Clear your outside drain ditches before winter so there won't be blockages and water back-up later. Evaluate trees that are close to your barn or sheds; dead branches should be removed (so they won't blow onto a roof), or older trees taken out if they are close enough to the barn to cause damage if they blow over.

Make sure roadways and horse travel areas are well built up and have good drainage and all-weather surfacing so they don't become boggy. If you have a hay- or straw-storage area that is hard to get to in winter with a large truck, **Weatherizing barn trim.** improve the access so that it is feasible for winter hauling, or have your winter supplies hauled in early, well ahead of bad weather.

In winter, monitor the snow depth and roof load on barns, hay sheds, and other buildings. Metal roofs generally shed snow; on a warm afternoon the snow may all slide off. If snow does not come off a roof, however, and gets too deep, the weight may be too much for the roof, causing damage or collapse. Be prepared to shovel snow off roofs if necessary. Have a licensed contractor appraise the soundness of your buildings; reinforce the weak spots before winter snow, with supporting posts. Install a moveable roof ladder so you can get on the barn roof to shovel away a heavy snow. If hay is not under a shed, you may need to shovel snow off haystacks, to keep moisture from going down into the hay when the snow melts.

In freezing weather, maintain good footing for horse and human safety, especially on asphalt or concrete and areas where horses congregate such as around

Monitor snow on barns.

feeders or waterers. Sand or old straw in gateways can aid traction, and you can use "ice melt" or salt on bad icy patches. Don't use gravel or pebbles; sharp pieces can cause stone bruising or may work into the foot.

If mud is a problem, you may want to haul in coarse sand to build up traffic areas around farm and barnyard and to create drier areas in paddocks. You can make a mounded-up area (to give horses a dry place to lie down) by hauling in a few truckloads of gravel and covering the mound with dirt. Horses are reluctant to lie down in deep mud and may spend most of their time standing or may try to lie down in an awkward place if it's the only dry area.

When mud freezes at night, the footing becomes precarious. A horse can cut himself or strain a leg as he stumbles through deep frozen hoofprints. You might want to stockpile sand or crushed rock for winter and springtime emergencies to keep footing safer in mud or ice or smooth out travel areas with a tractor and blade in late afternoon before the mud freezes solid again at night. A combination of sawdust and sand also can aid traction in well-traveled areas or ice patches, since it doesn't freeze easily. To channel excess water away from paddocks, dig a ditch with tractor and blade. If water can be diverted away from paddocks or the barnyard, mud can be minimized or prevented.

Early spring is a good time to make a checklist of things that need to be done before another winter. Often the drier conditions of summer make us forget the cold weather or wet weather problems. If you have a problem around a barn or where there is heavy horse traffic through the barnyard, you can fix it without resorting to concrete or asphalt — which is hard on feet and legs. Dig the area down a foot or more, filling it in with about eight inches of coarse gravel or crushed rock, then put a three-inch layer of finer gravel over it. The top can be covered with unwashed sand or topsoil. It can then be seeded to hardy grass, and even if the grass gets beaten out, the surface will still stay firm and never go to mud again.

As spring arrives, it's time to clean the barn and tack room and maintain all facilities. Check roofing; spring is a good time to fix leaks. It's also time to clean out all the stalls and check for any holes in the floor or boards that need replacing, and make any repairs to doors and windows.

Check all fences, especially pasture fences, before you put horses out for grazing. Check for breaks or for trees or branches that may have fallen on the fence or into the pasture. You may need to haul these off if they create a hazard for the horses, including being toxic if eaten. Cut back limbs that might fall on the fence or short out an electric wire.

In summer have a well-planned watering system so you won't become short of water in a dry year. If you are on a city water system you may need your own well for the times when city water is restricted during drought.

A summer project is storing hay for winter. If you don't have a hay shed, select a high spot with good drainage, stack the hay well, and double tarp it. It helps if you can add a slope to the tarp, so moisture will run off. One way to put a slope on the tarp is to run a row of bales (or poles set on hay flakes) down the center of the stack, using them to create a "peaked roof" effect.

Lightning rods on your barn may be a wise precaution against lightning-caused fire. As an extra precaution always unplug all electrical devices whenever you leave the barn. Even if the building is well grounded, lightning can create a power surge that may damage electrical appliances or start a fire by destroying a plugged-in electrical device.

Lightning can be a danger to horses outdoors. They often seek shelter under trees. Lightning may strike a tall tree, killing or injuring animals under it. Horses standing along a wire fence or by a metal water trough — or anything else that conducts electricity — can also be at risk. Electricity from lightning can travel along a power line to come down poles or brace wires.

A wire fence on wood posts can carry the electricity from a lightning strike a long ways. Even if lightning hits the fence a half-mile away, a horse standing by the fence can be affected. A wood fence will not carry electricity. A wire or metal fence that has steel posts or pipe posts can be a danger if lightning hits it close to where a horse is standing next to it.

To minimize risk of lightning killing horses, house them in a well-grounded barn with lightning rods during a storm or put them in pastures without power poles, power line towers, or trees. Wooden or vinyl fencing is safer than wire.

Manure Management

A thousand-pound horse produces eight or nine tons of manure a year. One or two horses living at pasture may not create a problem, especially if the pasture is large, but if horses are in pens or stalls you'll need a plan for handling manure. Otherwise buildup will cause or contribute to odor, parasite infestations, insects, mud — and dirty conditions for horses that can make them more susceptible to skin and hoof diseases — and environmental contamination that may affect groundwater. Organic waste harbors bacteria and fungal organisms that can cause thrush and hoof abscesses, scratches, rain rot, girth itch, and ringworm.

Manure can be composted or hauled away. Some collection services make a business of converting it into fertilizer for yards and gardens. Mushroom growers will often pick it up, if you use straw bedding (a mix of straw and manure makes excellent mushroom environment) as will some organic farmers. In some instances you may be able to sell manure or compost, or give it away.

Fresh horse manure makes the best fertilizer for roses, evergreens, azaleas, and other plants that prefer an acidic environment. For most plants, however, horse manure is good fertilizer only after it has been composted and is less acidic. Composted manure is better for pastures; fresh manure contains more weed seeds and worm eggs — and can kill out the grass if spread too thickly (due to acids, ammonia, and salts).

If properly handled, manure is better for plants and for the environment than commercial fertilizers. Though they contain the same nutrients, the concentrations of phosphorus, potassium, and nitrogen are lower in manure. Nitrogen is essential to plant health and growth, but in high concentrations it can burn the roots, kill the earthworms necessary for aeration, and leach into water supplies and kill fish. The nitrogen in manure has a more natural slow-release effect and is less apt to wash away.

If you grow pasture, hay, or grain, you can use manure for fertilizer after composting. One horse produces about $150 worth of good fertilizer per year. About one-fifth of the plant nutrients a horse eats passes through in manure and urine, and much of these valuable nutrients can be recycled and used by pasture plants or crops. A ton of horse manure supplies plant nutrients equivalent to those in a hundred-pound sack of fertilizer, as well as adding valuable organic matter and trace minerals to the soil, giving a much longer-lasting beneficial effect.

A compost pile is a good source for fertilizer.

Composting reduces the bulk and concentrates the nutrients of stall cleanings while reducing the nitrogen — the component that can contaminate water sources. Your manure piles should be more than a hundred feet away from wells or water sources and not in a low area where moisture would collect. In a populated area, keep your pile some distance from neighbors, though a properly composted pile will not have a foul odor, just an earthy smell. It also will not attract flies; once the pile heats up it will kill most fly larvae and is not attractive to insects.

Composting is a fermentation process that creates heat, which kills some parasites and weed seeds (and many pathogenic bacteria), reduces odor, and eliminates some of the water in the manure. The manure pile shrinks in size and weight and turns into a dark, loam-like fertilizer with an earthy smell.

A manure pile breaks down quickly if it has the correct ratio of manure, bulking agent (straw or wood chips from bedding), water, and oxygen. A compost pile should be least one cubic yard in volume to obtain high enough temperature for efficient breakdown and have 55 percent moisture content, a minimum of 5.5 percent oxygen, plus necessary microorganisms and a carbon-nitrogen ratio of thirty to one. This ratio is found in most stall cleanings; manure contains the necessary nitrogen, and bedding material supplies the carbon. If the stall cleanings contain a lot of shavings and very little manure, however, the ratio of carbon to nitrogen may be too high for good fertilizer. Decomposing shavings rob nitrogen from the soil and turn the pasture plants yellow.

A compost pile that is properly constructed and maintained (turning the material periodically and monitoring the moisture content, heat production, etc.) can become fertilizer within ninety days, although the average time is about 120 days. A pile that does not have the correct mix of manure and bedding or is not cared for will take longer, taking six to twelve months or more to become good fertilizer. Even poor compost eventually breaks down, but it may take several years. You'll be able to tell when compost is ready to use as fertilizer; the pile will be about half its original size and the material will be crumbly like soil.

In a pile of manure, fermentation raises the temperature. If a pile gets too hot it tends to combust rather than become compost. A heap that is more than ten feet high and fifteen feet in diameter gets so hot inside that it slowly burns. If it becomes too moist (from rain) the combustion process speeds up and the pile may actually flame up — just like wet hay that burns from spontaneous combustion. Even if the pile does not actually catch fire, the high heat will damage the nutrients in it.

If a pile gets too hot, it should be made smaller; if it gets too cool, it should be made larger. A five- to six-foot depth of material works about the best. Most horsemen don't bother with turning the pile, just making a new one periodically and allowing the old one a year or more to mature. If you have a lot of manure to dispose of, it's usually best to have three piles — one that is old and ready to spread, one in the process of composting, and one you are adding to daily. Locate them in a place convenient for dumping and for hauling away, preferably on a sloped concrete surface or on a sloping rock base with rock walls. You can cover them with plastic or with dirt to keep them from drying out too much or having the nutrients leached out by rain or snow melt.

Pens and paddocks need periodic cleaning if manure is not picked up. If you don't have machinery, borrow or rent a tractor and blade or loader, or hire someone to scrape and pile manure and haul it out. Depending on the size of the paddock and number of horses in it, this may need to be done annually or every few years. Otherwise the muck becomes knee deep in wet seasons. Periodic pen cleaning will be appreciated by your horses and also gives you another good source of fertilizer. The pen cleanings generally do not need composting; the old manure is already broken down and ready to spread on fields or pastures.

Feed and Water:
General Nutrition

YOUR FEEDING PROGRAM is probably the most important factor in maintaining your horse's physical and mental welfare. The quality and quantity of feed determine how well the young horse grows, how well the athletic horse performs, and how well any horse maintains proper body condition and health. Horses should not be fat; obesity impairs endurance, fertility, athletic ability, health, and longevity. Too much body weight adds stress to the body and can lead to lameness or make a mild lameness worse. Inadequate feed or deficiencies in diet can interfere with proper growth and health, making the horse more vulnerable to many problems and illnesses, or can contribute to a poor disposition.

The goal of any feeding program should be to provide each horse with: 1) Enough energy for his job. 2) Enough protein for growth if he is young and for repairing body wear and tear if mature. 3) Enough vitamins and minerals to keep all body parts healthy and to assist in the body's chemical processes. 4) Enough fiber to supply energy and other nutrients (and keep him busy as long as possible when he is not working and to aid in proper digestion). 5) Enough water to maintain the delicate balances within his body and to keep everything in the digestive tract moving along.

Nutritional needs differ depending on age and use.

The goal in feeding horses is to provide each one with a diet that satisfies nutritional needs but does not hinder nor overburden any part of his digestive system. The further away from a natural grass diet we get, the more likely a horse might suffer digestive problems and colic, imbalances that result in serious problems like laminitis, skeletal problems in young growing horses, or behavioral problems. The safest feeding program relies as heavily as possible on grass or good hay, adding grains, fats, extra protein, vitamins, minerals, or other supplements only as needed.

Every horse has individual needs, so feeding horses is a very inexact science. You must know each horse well and tailor feeding to meet his needs according to his age, level of activity, lifestyle, and metabolism. You must keep a fine-tuned "feel" for his body condition, his appetite, and health.

The National Research Council has established approximate nutrient requirements (energy, protein, vitamins, minerals) based on weight, type of horse, and work level. These guidelines represent an average and are used by nutritionists and feed formulators. Using these figures, horse owners can devise a feed program to meet those requirements, using forage as a basis, and fine-tuning the ration to fit the individual horse.

In many cases the horse's needs can be met with a simple forage diet of pasture or good hay, free choice salt, and in some cases a mineral or vitamin/mineral supplement. In other cases, such as when a horse is young and growing, lactating, or doing strenuous work, he might need concentrates or supplements in addition to forages.

Equine Digestion

The equine digestive system is designed to process forage and works best if the horse eats more or less continually rather than loading up once or twice a day on high-energy feeds. He is happiest and healthiest on a steady diet of grass. He can digest large quantities of forage per day by eating only a little at a time. The horse, like the cow, is a roughage-eater, but unlike the ruminant he has a simple stomach similar to that of a pig or human and only chews his food once. The equine stomach holds only two to five gallons; his digestive system is designed for eating small amounts often.

The ruminant processes roughages in the largest stomach, the rumen, where microorganisms break down cellulose and other fibrous material into usable nutrients. Horses have a similar fermentation vat (the cecum) farther along the tract. Ruminants and horses can therefore utilize roughage while humans cannot— as our simple stomach has no way to break it down.

About 70 percent of the protein and 75 percent of the soluble carbohydrates in the horse's feed can be digested and absorbed by the time ingested material goes through the small intestine, but the remainder isn't broken down until it reaches the hindgut — the cecum and large colon, which process and digest liquids, left-over fats, cellulose, and other fibrous parts of feed.

The cell walls of plants are composed primarily of cellulose, which is unaffected by enzymes of the stomach and small intestine. All grass-eating animals rely on special microbes to digest cellulose through fermentation, changing it into energy-producing fatty acids. Chemical changes during this digestion process produce heat energy, which can help keep a horse warm in cold weather. In winter, a horse is better served by an increase in his hay ration than from extra grain because the digestion and breakdown of roughage create more body heat. This is the reason horses crave roughage during cold weather and will chew on trees, fences, and stalls if you don't feed them enough hay.

During the breakdown of roughages in the hindgut, the microorganisms also manufacture amino acids, from which the horse gets usable proteins and vitamin B. These B vitamins are essential to health and proper function of the body. The microorganisms also yield additional protein, vitamins, and energy.

The cecum and colon also serve as a water conservation unit, absorbing and recycling the fluid needed for digestion. As much as 20 percent of the horse's total body fluid (the average horse has about eighty-five gallons) crosses through the gut wall every day. Most of it comes in through the six to ten gallons of saliva that are added to the feed during chewing. Much of the water a horse drinks is used in creating saliva to aid chewing and digestion.

If a horse is fed infrequent large (grain) meals that he eats rapidly, extra fluids must be pulled from the body — mostly through the salivary glands — to aid the digestive effort. In some instances, this rapid shift in fluid balance can trigger a reaction in the body's major blood flow control mechanisms, which are normally only triggered during extreme blood loss, shock, and laminitis. This hormonal reaction pulls the fluid from the digestive tract back into wider circulation, often before the feed has gotten very far into the large intestine, a situation that can occasionally lead to imbalances and impaction. Large carbohydrate meals cause more severe fluid shifts than do roughages.

Hormonal action created by infrequent large feedings can put a horse at risk for colic. Spasmodic colic can occur after the evening feeding on a hot summer day, for instance, as a result of heat stress combined with the sudden fluid shift that concentrates too much body fluid in the gut. Horses can adjust to twice-daily feedings, however, becoming less affected by the fluid dislocation than when first started on this routine.

Yet if other stresses are added, such as exercise right after eating or physical or emotional stress just before eating, the blood flow to the gut is reduced and rerouted to the muscles, impairing the motility of the digestive tract. Reduced gut circulation plus a large fluctuation in body fluid balance make it difficult for the horse to digest his large meal; colic or laminitis may result. Dividing a horse's ration into three or four meals instead of two and never having any meals as much as twelve hours apart put less stress on his digestive system.

Unnatural feeds (high-protein alfalfa or grain) also can cause trouble. Abrupt changes in feed can upset the population of microbes and lead to laminitis or colic due to a change in the rate of feed breakdown, excessive gas, or creation of toxins.

Ordinarily the microbes in the fermentation vat multiply as needed, and the population of "gut bugs" stays in balance with the digestive jobs at hand. Sudden changes of feed, however, such as from hay to lush pasture or to a larger portion of grain, can upset the delicate balance in the gut. A sudden grain increase also can cause fermentation in the stomach and small intestine — a very abnormal situation.

A common problem is overfeeding soluble carbohydrates and starch (in concentrate feeds like grain). The horse has a small stomach, and grain will start passing into the small intestine before digestion properly begins. A big feeding can overwhelm the small intestine's ability to digest and absorb; some grain goes through undigested. If starches are not totally digested in the small intestine and travel to the cecum, they are quickly fermented by bacteria into lactic acid, disturbing normal gut function.

The increase in lactic acid rapidly lowers the pH of the cecum and colon, increasing the rate of food passage and decreasing the nutrient absorption — and creating an inhospitable environment for the microflora necessary for proper fermentation and digestion. The death of bacteria in large numbers can lead to production of endotoxins (endotoxemia) and colic, damage to the gut wall, and subsequent leakage of toxins into the bloodstream, which can put the horse into shock. Even if the grain overload does not cause colic or laminitis, it can interfere with proper mineral absorption, due to low pH in the cecum. In young growing horses this can lead to improper bone development and skeletal problems.

To avoid overtaxing the horse's small stomach, a guideline for feeding concentrates is not to exceed five pounds of grain per feeding. If a horse needs more energy, supplements, such as fat in the form of vegetable oil, can be more beneficial than overdoing the grain ration. Horses use fats well, but fats must be added gradually to the diet and are best fed in multiple feedings. Horses have no gall bladder to store the bile necessary to digest fats, so it takes time for them to adjust.

All changes in diet should be made over several days or longer to allow the tract to adjust. An increase in feed should be gradual, taking at least a week to accomplish. The more drastic the change, the longer and more gradual a transition period should be. When changing the grain or concentrate portion of the diet, compare the labels on the feed mix. If the total levels of digestible energy (DE) and protein are similar, the change won't affect your horse's digestion much; two or three days (feeding increasingly more of the new feed and less of the old) will be an adequate adjustment. If the protein or the energy content is more than 5 percent higher in the new feed, take a full week to switch. If making a major change, such as switching from a low-fat to a high-fat feed or greatly increasing both the energy and the protein, take two weeks to make the transition.

A change in roughage from poor or "average" quality pasture or hay to nutrient-rich feed like alfalfa hay should also take two weeks. A switch from hay to lush pasture should take at least a week. Put the horse out for only a short time the first day, and gradually increase his turnout time. Take a full three weeks to introduce a thin animal (on a low plane of nutrition) to a high-calorie, nutrient-rich diet. A debilitated horse does not do well on grain; he must be well started on good roughage before you introduce concentrates into his diet.

When making any feed change, monitor the horse closely to make sure he is handling the new feed without digestive problems. Any hint of colic or diarrhea should be a warning sign to back off on the change until his gut is working normally again.

How the Horse Eats and Processes Food

The horse uses his incisors (front teeth) to bite off grass. His back teeth chew and grind food, mixing it with saliva to make it easier to chew and swallow. If teeth wear unevenly, he can't chew properly; this can lead to indigestion, colic, impaction, or even starvation.

The horse has three sets of paired salivary glands, secreting up to ten gallons of saliva daily. Some authorities state that horses on a diet of continual grazing or roughages produce twenty-five to thirty gallons of saliva per day. Not only does saliva moisten feed so it can be swallowed and passed through the gut, but it also acts as a buffering solution to help maintain proper pH — to counteract bile in the small intestine and keep the ingesta at a pH between 6.8 and 6.5 (for optimal fermentation in the cecum and large colon).

The esophagus is a muscular tube going from the pharynx down the left side of the neck (alongside the centrally located windpipe) into the stomach. The esophagus is basically a one-way street, with peristalsis (contracting movements that go along the tube in rhythmic waves) traveling only toward the stomach. This one-way movement, along with the acute angle at which the esophagus joins the stomach and the one-way valve at the stomach, makes the horse practically unable to vomit. If a horse eats spoiled feed or has a blockage between stomach and intestine and tries to vomit, the food may come out through his nose and get into his windpipe.

After food moves into the stomach, digestive enzymes secreted by the stomach walls begin breaking down the feed and start the digestion of proteins. The stomach is small, holding only about 8 percent of the total capacity of the digestive tract, and most feeds pass through it rapidly, often entering the small intestine within fifteen minutes of being eaten.

The stomach is healthiest when food is passing through it more or less continually. The outer lining of the stomach has little protection against the hydrochloric acid produced for digestion by the inner glandular lining. If horses are fed often (or grazing at pasture), the stomach always has food in it to absorb the acid, greatly reducing the risk of ulcers. The type of feed given to a horse also can be a factor in whether he develops ulcers. Diets containing a lot of grain can put a horse at risk for ulcers. A horse that eats forage produces more saliva, which acts as a buffer in the stomach. Alfalfa hay is a good forage for ulcer prevention since it contains high levels of calcium—which helps neutralize the stomach acid.

After food leaves the stomach, digestion of protein continues in the small intestine. Breakdown of starches and sugars, and to some extent fats, begins. Even though feed passes through the small intestine rapidly, most of the digestion and absorption take place there; the majority of proteins and starches are absorbed through intestinal walls. The end products of digestion of soluble carbohydrates are glucose and other sugars. It is important that they be digested efficiently in the small intestine. Large amounts of carbohydrates passing to the large intestine raise the risk for colic. This can happen when a horse is fed too much grain or is worked hard too soon after eating grain; exercise can hinder the digestion process. Inadequately digested carbohydrates passing into the large intestine can disrupt the fermentation process and alter the population of microbes.

Because the horse has no gall bladder, bile is secreted continually in the small intestine. It was earlier thought that horses could not use fat due to the absence of a gall bladder, but research has shown they can handle diets containing as much as 18 percent fat. Weanlings gain weight faster with less total feed when fat is added to their rations, and performance horses can use fat for energy, reducing the amount of grain needed (thus reducing risks of founder and colic). Fat as an energy source can help a hard-working horse exert longer without fatigue. Since fat slows the emptying of the stomach, it should not be fed just before strenuous exertion or during an athletic event. A horse doing sustained activity needs a good roughage fill instead and can be started on fats again after the event.

Some nutrients pass through the digestive tract without being absorbed, because they're in a form not readily used by the horse or he doesn't need them. The healthy horse's fine-tuned system supervises absorption of certain nutrients on an as-needed basis; the intestine acts as a regulatory gateway to help maintain a constant blood level of important nutrients. Overfeeding can cause some problems with the regulatory system, resulting in high levels of trace elements that can be toxic.

Enzymes aid in digestion in the first part of the digestive tract. In the latter part of the tract, microbes break down and digest fiber through fermentation.

The cecum and large colon have a unique structure; their walls are pursed out with many small ridges and sacs that slow food passage so microbes have more time to work. The remaining water from the food material is absorbed from the residue passing through the small colon, forming balls of feces that then pass out through the rectum and anus. The horse normally passes thirty to fifty pounds of manure daily. The quantity of manure and its moisture content depend on the types of feed being eaten and whether the horse is drinking sufficient water.

The color, smell, and texture of a horse's manure can give a clue as to the digestive system's health and function. Check the horse's teeth if long stems of roughage or pieces of grain are coming through. Manure that is too fluid could indicate infection or irritation that needs medical attention. Laxative feeds such as lush green grass, rich alfalfa hay, or bran produce softer manure than a grass hay diet. If feces are small and hard, the horse may be suffering from impaction and constipation or might not be drinking enough water.

The horse does not start life with a digestive system that can handle roughage. At birth his cecum is not yet functional (having no microorganisms to facilitate fermentation), and he depends on his simple stomach and small intestine for digesting milk. As he comes into contact with bacteria, he develops the ability to digest starches and cellulose. Foals instinctively eat some of their mother's fresh manure to gain the proper microflora that set up housekeeping in the cecum and large intestine. A foal utilizes roughages quite well by two months of age, though the amount of hay or pasture he can consume is still somewhat limited. As the hindgut increases in size and function as he grows, he has more need for forage and less dependency on milk.

Basic Nutritional Needs

The horse in nature has all his requirements met by natural forages, salt, and water. Native grasses provide all the vitamins and minerals needed except for salt; no forages contain sufficient sodium or chloride. The wild horse meets this need by using natural salt licks (salt deposits in soil) and by developing body systems that retain and conserve salt. Horses are also well suited to handling fluctuations in vitamin and mineral content of feed since various regions and seasons affect availability of some of these micronutrients. Dry grass in winter does not have carotene (from which the horse manufactures vitamin A), but this vitamin can be stored in the liver for long periods; the horse's body has enough to last until green grass appears the next spring.

Horses are very good at storing, conserving, and manufacturing vitamins and minerals; pasture, hay, and grain provide most horses with more than enough of the essentials. The exception might be a sick horse that could benefit from C and B-complex vitamins (since illness may have impaired his ability to create them) or a horse with more athletic demands on his body than any wild horse.

The energy content of grasses provides adequate fuel for the wild horse's activities. Foals grow up healthy and fit on grass and milk, nursing their dams until just before birth of the next foal. They might have been thin during winter but grow up sound with none or few of the structural problems of overfed and underexercised domesticated youngsters, though it takes the wild horse longer to reach full maturity. With domestication, we demand more of horses, wanting youngsters to grow fast and be ready for sale or athletic careers at a young age, pushing them far beyond the normal activities of their wild counterparts.

We confine horses and provide very little natural exercise. In many instances a horse is not allowed to graze but is expected to eat concentrated feeds at widely spaced intervals, leaving him nothing else to do. Others are worked much harder than any wild horse and would not have time to consume enough grass to provide the needed energy.

The amount of exercise a horse gets affects how much feed he needs and how well he digests it. Mild exercise can aid the digestive process (it's healthier for the horse to travel slowly grazing than to stand all day in a stall), while strenuous exercise can hinder it.

Roughage benefits a horse that works hard all day by providing nutrients to the hindgut. These horses get more than half their energy from volatile fatty acids (created by fiber breakdown in the hindgut), and the forage also provides electrolyte reserves and fluid storage. The main problem with green grass for hard work is a high moisture content that limits the total amount the horse can eat. Horses can get more total nutrients in hay.

Horses that compete in strenuous sports often cannot give peak performances on fuel that green grass provides (due to inability to eat enough), and their bodies may not be able to handle stresses involved in these activities without additional minerals and other nutrients to balance losses. How much supplementation with concentrated energy feeds, vitamins, and minerals a horse needs depends upon how hard he is working and upon the efficiency of his metabolism. Some horses require more dietary additions than others for peak performance. Sprinters generally need a more concentrated and readily metabolized energy source than do distance horses; many endurance horses and ranch horses that travel many miles a day do well on a basic roughage diet, especially if they have an efficient body metabolism. Horses bred for endurance can perform well on good hay alone or with a small amount of concentrate added to the ration. The amount of high-energy feed required by any horse depends on the individual as well as on how he is being used.

Protein

Protein helps build bones, blood, skin, hair, hooves, and muscle. Lack of quality protein will impair a young horse's growth and interfere with hoof development. A horse lacking protein will have a poor hair coat and reduced appetite and shed slowly in spring. Protein requirements of adult horses, however, are so low that true deficiencies are rare, occurring only when a horse is on poor pasture or hay for a long time. If protein is added to the diet, signs of protein deficiency in an adult horse can be resolved in about a week. Young growing horses may suffer more serious damage, however, if they receive insufficient protein. The National Research Council recommends that weanlings' diets consist of 14.5 percent protein; yearlings, 12.6 percent; and two-year-olds, 10.4 percent. A mare needs extra protein during the last trimester of pregnancy (10.6 percent) when the fetus is growing fastest. She needs the most protein, however, when she is producing milk (11 percent). Excess protein in the diet is metabolized as energy and produces heat when digested; high protein feeds are a good choice in cold weather but detrimental when a horse is working hard in hot weather.

Mature horses have very low protein needs, even when working hard (8 to 10 percent). Protein is a poor energy source compared with carbohydrates, fats, and volatile fatty acids from roughages — all metabolized far more efficiently. Once a horse matures, his protein needs can usually be met by low-protein feeds such as pasture or grass hay.

Amino Acids

Protein is created from building blocks called amino acids. Chemically, protein resembles a knotted and tangled bead necklace, each bead being an amino acid. The order in which amino acids are combined determines the protein and its structure and functions. In the horse, there are twenty-two amino acid beads in this necklace, ten of which must be supplied by diet. The body can synthesize the others from any source of nitrogen. The body can change some amino acids into different combinations, but others can only be created by green plants, which a horse must eat.

The ten that can't be synthesized by the body are essential amino acids. If one essential amino acid for a certain protein is missing from the diet, the synthesis of that particular protein cannot continue. Its absence may prevent normal growth even if the diet contains an adequate supply of all the other ingredients. The growing horse is similar to a house being built. Even if all the other materials are there, the structure cannot progress if the carpenter runs out of nails. But the other materials cannot be stored until the necessary amino acid shows up. Unable to create the growth protein needed, the body converts the rest of the amino acids into energy instead — an inefficient form of fuel.

Lysine is considered the most important essential amino acid for growth; without it the body has trouble using any of the other amino acids. Feeds that are rich in lysine include alfalfa, soybean meal, and milk casein (such as dried skim milk); grains and grass hay are much lower in this important nutrient.

Young horses on feeds that are low in lysine grow more slowly than those on a high lysine diet, even if the crude protein levels of their rations are similar. The amino acid content of a feed is more important to a growing horse than to a mature animal; the adult is much less sensitive to differences in protein quality. Lysine and methionine are often deficient in hay and are routinely added synthetically to commercial feed mixes.

Meat-eating animals get all the essential amino acids needed by the body — because meat contains them all, but herbivores (like human vegetarians) are more at risk for protein deficiencies, especially while young and growing. Most grains are low in lysine, so a well-balanced ration adds other sources of high-quality protein. If a growing horse is on grass hay, a supplement of leafy alfalfa hay or soybean meal can provide lysine.

How Much Protein Is Enough?

How do pregnant mares and young horses manage in the wild on a diet of grasses? Mares foal in late spring or early summer when grass is green and growing, at its peak for protein quality and quantity. New spring grass may be as much as 22 percent digestible protein. The mare that foals in late spring or early summer has adequate protein for late pregnancy and her first months of lactation. Problems in equine nutrition come with the artificial conditions we impose with domestication by having mares foal early, before green grass; keeping them in stalls or paddocks without access to good quality pasture (necessitating a hay and grain diet); and having to balance the diet appropriately for protein quantity and quality.

Protein requirements diminish as a horse grows up. Primary development of bone and muscle occurs early in life (during the last trimester of gestation and in the first months after birth when he is growing fastest). By the time the foal is weaned, his protein needs are much less.

Domestic horses are more often overfed than underfed. Many people assume that if a little protein is good, more is better. It's true that a deficiency in protein can make a young horse slow growing, but most well-fed horses receive more protein than they need. The overfed mature horse on a generous ration of alfalfa hay and high-protein sweet feed must break down the excess to be used as energy or stored as fat, an inefficient process that produces six times more heat than the breakdown of carbohydrates or fats, while yielding less energy. Protein not used immediately by the body is broken down to release nitrogen atoms, which then combine with other atoms to become ammonia and urea molecules, which are excreted in urine.

A horse on a high protein diet drinks more water than normal to help flush the by-products of protein breakdown, and thus produces more urine. This can lead to wet bedding in stalls, plus irritation of respiratory passages from increased ammonia. Some researchers think the high levels of ammonia in stalls where racehorses are confined — on high-protein diets — contribute to exercise-induced lung bleeding, due to the respiratory irritation.

Feeding the Pregnant and Lactating Mare

By the end of the seventh month of gestation, the growing fetus has used only 10 percent of the total protein necessary for full-term development. During the final four months, the fetus uses the remaining 90 percent, and the mare herself needs extra protein for growth of the placenta and amniotic tissues surrounding the fast-growing fetus. Most mares have adequate protein if some good alfalfa hay is added to their diet. If alfalfa is not available, a few pounds of 13 to 16 percent protein feed mix can supply what's needed.

A pregnant mare needs more protein.

Some broodmares become too fat if given grain in addition to pasture or hay; instead, use a small amount of concentrated protein supplement to keep the energy content of the ration lower. Two pounds of protein concentrate gives the same amount of protein as 4 pounds of a 15 percent protein grain mix, with about half the calories. The protein in the concentrated supplement is usually derived from high-lysine sources such as soybean meal, which is a good choice for the developing fetus or the lactating mare.

Lactating mares need nearly twice as much protein as mares in early gestation, because during peak milk production a mare produces more than a pound of protein each day in the four to six gallons of milk she produces. Milk protein is high in lysine, just what the foal needs for fast growth. A mare's milk production diminishes greatly if her protein intake is limited.

Lactating mares need even more.

She'll still produce milk if her diet is short on energy, as she can rob her body reserves, but she has no protein reserves. Protein must be provided continually in the feed. Overfeeding a mare protein can be detrimental, however. On many farms where fast-growing foals are nursing overfed mares, the youngsters develop skeletal and joint problems.

Under natural conditions, young horses don't reach mature size as quickly as domesticated horses, but they stay more sound. Often a horseman thinks foals must be pushed to maximum ability to grow; this is the challenge for anyone raising horses for competitive careers in which youngsters are asked for peak performance. Nursing mares and young foals are often overfed. Foals raised to compete in early life are at risk for problems when pushed quickly to their full growth potential, often becoming unsound before they ever start their careers.

Feeding the Weanling

After weaning, a foal is usually fed a high concentrate ration. Young horses on a high forage diet don't grow as fast because of limited gut capacity (they can't eat enough roughage to supply the body's needs for protein and energy, when weaned young), so many horsemen feed a lot of grain and 16 percent sweet feed or comparable protein concentrate. This type of feeding program, however, may hinder a foal from ever fully developing his capacity to utilize roughage properly. Balancing the diet to provide adequate protein and energy without overdoing one or the other for the fast-growing weanling is a real challenge.

Supplementing a diet of grass or hay to meet the weanling's protein needs can produce a ration in which the concentrate portion outweighs the roughage portion, which is very unnatural and can be risky for the digestive tract. Feeding the youngster for maximum growth is also very questionable for his future soundness. Lean youngsters are generally more fit and healthy. Horsemen who want their animals to stay sound through a long, useful life are wise to let them grow a little more slowly, as nature intended.

Carbohydrates

Carbohydrates are major energy sources and include sugars, starches, and cellulose. Oats, barley, corn, and other concentrated feeds may be as much as 60 percent sugar and starch. The carbohydrates from cellulose (the fibrous part of grass and hay) are derived as it is broken down in the cecum by microbes' fermentation action.

Simple carbohydrates, found in concentrate feeds like grain that contain sugars and starches are easily digested by enzymes in the small intestine, but the complex structural carbohydrates that make up plant cell walls are not broken down until they reach the cecum and colon. The hindgut absorbs the energy-rich fermentation by-products (volatile fatty acids). Cellulose, found in all forages, is less easily digested than grain and must be eaten in larger amounts to produce the same amount of energy, but the energy yield from forage is steadier — and more natural for the horse.

Carbohydrates provide glucose and glycogen to fuel the body processes (maintaining temperature and heartbeat, respiration, digestion) and the energy for exercise. Carbohydrates also can be building blocks for other nutrients; when eaten in excess of what the horse needs for immediate use they can be stored as fat for future energy.

A most important dietary need is energy. Even growing horses and lactating mares that need more protein and minerals than the average horse, need energy-rich feed. If a horse uses more energy daily than what he eats, he draws on body stores and loses weight; if he expends less energy than what he eats, he stores the extra and becomes fat.

In young horses, the amount of energy-producing foods consumed determines growth rate. Protein, vitamins, minerals, and other nutrients are crucial, but utilization hinges upon the feeds' energy content. New tissue growth requires a lot of energy; a weanling needs almost as much energy daily as an idle horse weighing three times as much. Too much energy, however, especially in the form of concentrated carbohydrates, can make a youngster gain too much weight too fast. If a young horse carries too much body weight for his skeleton, he could fall prey to a number of developmental problems including OCD (osteochondritis dessicans) or physitis. Fast-growing youngsters fed too much energy often become unsound before adulthood.

At the other extreme is the youngster on a low-energy diet — poor quality forages and no concentrates. He will take much longer to reach mature size and may develop problems due to insufficient nutrients. Somewhere in between is the balance — feeding a growing horse enough energy to reach optimum growth while keeping him healthy and sound.

The energy needs of every horse are different. The horseman must take into consideration not only the age, status, and activity of each horse but also differences in body metabolism (some need less feed than others, while doing the same work), climate, and temperature. Cold weather will increase a horse's energy needs.

A basic ration should start with forages, as the carbohydrate content of cellulose is adequate for most horses. A horse that can't keep optimum weight on pasture or hay may need grain. If several small feedings of oats or barley are still not adequate, a more energy-dense grain such as corn may be needed. If the horse still needs more energy (as do some high-performance athletes or lactating mares), it is better to add some fat to the diet than to risk the danger of carbohydrate overload in the gut.

Fats

Natural feeds such as grass and hay contain little fat and most grains fed to horses only contain about 2 percent to 3.5 percent fat. Barley is about 1.9 percent fat; oats can be as high as 4.5 percent fat and corn, 6.6 percent. Good-quality grass or legume hay may contain about 2 percent fat, dropping to 1.5 percent or less when overly dry. Alfalfa meal can be about 2.8 percent fat and wheat bran about 4.1 percent.

Though the horse's natural diet is low in fat, these small amounts are important for helping him absorb fat-soluble vitamins (especially A, D, and E), and furnish fatty acids necessary for cell membrane health. The only fatty acid he cannot manufacture for himself is linoleic acid, and it is found in the vegetable fats in forages and grain. Fats provide energy and are crucial for healthy skin and hair. A little bit of fat is also important in production of joint fluid, muscle tissue, and hormones.

The horses most likely to be deficient in dietary fat are those on dried out pastures or fed poor-quality hay with no grain. The usual signs of insufficient dietary fat are a dull coat, poor hoof quality, and dry, flaky skin. Changing to better hay or adding a little grain or two ounces of corn oil to the diet can correct these problems.

Some hard-working horses in racing or endurance careers are given fats (vegetable oil) as an energy supplement. Fats contain more than twice the energy of an equal weight of carbohydrate like grain. Feeding fat can reduce the amount of grain needed to give a hard-working horse adequate energy. A fat supplement should be fed carefully, however, starting with a small amount and increasing it gradually. Feeding more than a cup of oil can be too laxative and also can have an adverse affect on absorption and utilization of certain vitamins and minerals, especially vitamins A and E. The horse needs time to gear up his digestive capacity to handle fats.

Vitamins

Vitamins are organic compounds required by the body in small amounts to help regulate the chemical reactions for normal function, keeping the body operating smoothly. There are two kinds of vitamins: fat soluble A, D, E, and K, which can be stored in the body and used during times the diet may be inadequate, and water soluble B vitamins and C. The fat soluble ones can occasionally build up to toxic levels if overfed, while the water soluble ones can be excreted if any excess is not used quickly by the body.

All green forages are rich in most of the vitamins the horse needs. A horse on good pasture doesn't need additional vitamins. Under normal conditions, the horse produces his own C, D, and some B vitamins. His "gut bugs" produce all the other B vitamins and vitamin K during fermenting of feed.

Vitamin supplementation has become common practice and may be needed when horses don't get enough natural vitamins at pasture or in hay. But if good quality natural feeds are available, your horse may not need the supplements. Vitamin requirements generally don't increase when a horse's workload increases; an idle horse and horses in strenuous athletic careers have basically the same needs, with the possible exception of vitamin E.

Vitamin A is manufactured by the horse from the beta-carotene in plants. Green pasture is an excellent source of carotene, as is green, leafy alfalfa hay. Grass hay is a little lower, especially if harvested when mature. The carotene in stored feeds is subject to oxidation. Weathering, improper curing, exposure to sunlight or long storage may reduce Vitamin A in hay, but green alfalfa may contain up to 70 times the amount a horse needs.

Horses need vitamin A for maintaining reproductive health, normal bone metabolism, proper skin and hoof growth, and health of the eyes and the lining of the respiratory tract. Vitamin A deficiency can make horses prone to digestive upsets and colic, respiratory ailments, and brittle bones, and it can lead to blindness, loss of appetite, impaired disease resistance. A horse that lacks enough vitamin A may have dry, dull, brittle hair; skin lesions; cracked hooves; and dry skin.

Vitamin A is fat soluble, which means it can be stored in the body. Some beta-carotene is absorbed intact rather than converted to vitamin A, and is stored and used in skin, fat, and the ovaries, where it helps control progesterone secretion. It also plays a major role in ovulation, embryo implantation in the uterus, and maintaining pregnancy. A beta-carotene deficiency interferes with these reproductive functions and can result in abortion or weak and poorly developed foals. A deficiency can't be corrected by vitamin A supplements, only by feeding more beta-carotene in natural feeds.

Most of the vitamin A in the body is stored in the liver, which can stockpile a three- to six-month supply and release it back into the bloodstream as needed. Horses at pasture during summer usually store enough of this vitamin to last through winter. However, if a horse is never on pasture, is fed overly mature grass hay, or is pregnant during winter, vitamin A should be included when making up a ration or supplementing the diet.

Vitamin A toxicity occasionally occurs. Extreme overdose can cause bones to break down. Extra vitamin A is often given to young animals in an effort to make bones and bodies stronger, but it can have the opposite effect; large overdoses retard growth and cause joint problems and thin bones. Green alfalfa can contain many times the amount of vitamin A needed, but this is generally not a problem unless the horse is also receiving vitamin A supplements.

Vitamin D is produced in the skin if a horse is exposed to sunlight. Sun-dried hay is a good source; vitamin D accumulates in dead leaves. Under normal conditions, a horse should never be short on vitamin D, unless he is kept in a barn all the time and fed something other than hay. Hay contains plenty of vitamin D when freshly baled, though it tends to degrade over time. Hay more than a year old might not meet a horse's needs for vitamin D, but as long as he gets a few hours of sun each day this is no problem.

Vitamin D plays an important role in calcium and phosphorus absorption and utilization, especially conversion of calcium and phosphorus into bones. Lack of vitamin D can cause rickets (bones become soft and bendable) and skeletal deformities in growing horses and osteomalacia (soft bones) in mature horses. Vitamin D also is involved in proper absorption of zinc, iron, cobalt, and magnesium and may influence the depositing of these minerals in bone.

Due to its important role in calcium metabolism, some horsemen overfeed vitamin D, but this is risky. Massive dietary doses of vitamin D can be toxic, damaging the parathyroid gland and kidneys and upsetting calcium-phosphorus metabolism. This can result in calcification of bruises and soft tissue, especially the skeletal muscles and the heart. Calcium deposits collect in the heart valves and walls, along the walls of major blood vessels, and in the kidney, diaphragm, salivary glands, and stomach lining.

You shouldn't need to supplement vitamin D, but if you do, the amount should never exceed 10 percent of the vitamin A being given. Vitamin D toxicity is probably the most common of all vitamin overdoses, due to oral or injectable supplementation.

Vitamin E is needed for proper muscle development and function and for healthy reproductive and immune systems. It helps maintain cell membrane stability and red blood cell integrity. This vitamin is a powerful antioxidant, helping to prevent or delay deterioration of tissues in its role as a free-radical scavenger. Free radicals are a type of oxygen molecule with an unpaired electron in their composition, which makes them very unstable and quick to react with other molecules, stealing electrons from their outer orbits. This damages the other molecules, contributing to tissue damage at the cellular level in a process called oxidation.

Free radicals are produced in small amounts during normal body processes such as energy production, but increase during stress, trauma, or disease. They weaken cell wall membranes, and the cell ruptures and dies. Vitamin E helps stabilize the free radicals and stop destructive processes. This fat-soluble vitamin becomes embedded in each cell's protective fatty layer and disables free radicals before they can damage the cell wall. Nerves and muscle cells are most commonly damaged; vitamin E is helpful in warding off diseases that affect the nerves (such as degenerative diseases like wobbles and equine protozoal myeloencephalitis), and myopathies (muscle diseases).

Vitamin E and selenium, a trace mineral found in plants, work together in this task and help prevent tying up and other muscle problems in hard-working horses. Vitamin E helps prevent stiffness and soreness after exercise, and some researchers feel that high levels of vitamin E may enhance performance. Symptoms of vitamin E deficiency are grouped with those of selenium deficiency since the two work together. A mild deficiency may produce a decrease in a horse's immune response to illness, or show up as slower growth rate in foals.

Vitamin E overdose is not dangerous, since it is non-toxic, but even small overdoses of its partner selenium can cause serious trouble.

High levels of vitamin E can interfere with absorption of other fat-soluble vitamins, however, so most equine nutritionists recommend a maximum of 1,000 International Units per kilogram of body weight in the diet. This vitamin is usually adequate in natural feeds. Green forages, properly cured hay, unprocessed cereal grains, and wheat germ oil are good sources of vitamin E. Processing (heating, grinding, pelleting) and long storage of feeds can decrease vitamin E content. Hay subjected to rain, sun, or storage at high temperatures can lose vitamin E. A deficiency usually occurs in horses whose natural diet of fresh forage has been replaced by highly processed feeds.

In periods of stress, supplemental vitamin E can be helpful. Even if a horse is getting plenty of this vitamin, it may be poorly utilized in some situations; as a fat-soluble vitamin, it must mix with fat molecules in the small intestine to be absorbed. If you supplement vitamin E, always give it with a meal. Any illness that interferes with intestinal function can limit the amount of vitamin E absorbed through the gut lining.

Vitamin K is essential for forming prothrombin, a blood-clotting ingredient manufactured in the liver; it also helps activate certain proteins in the body. Vitamin K is made by bacteria in the horse's cecum and is absorbed slowly; some of it passes out with the manure. The cecum or large intestine constantly produces vitamin K, so manure is a good source of this vitamin. Eating manure enables a horse to absorb more vitamin K, which is well absorbed in the small intestine. Most horses eat some manure, so they should not be deficient in vitamin K.

Occasionally a horse may need vitamin K supplements. Foals needing surgery or injured soon after birth may be at risk of hemorrhage and death because their digestive tracts don't yet have the bacteria to synthesize vitamin K or digest fiber. Most foals eat some of their dams' manure, which gives them a start of necessary microbes and also supplies them with vitamin K. Foals begin making their own vitamin K within one to four weeks after birth.

There are instances in which certain feeds or molds interfere with vitamin K absorption or increase the need for this vitamin. Moldy sweet clover hay or haylage may contain an anti-coagulant called dicoumarol (related to warfarin, used in rat poison) and can interfere with blood clotting. If a horse eats moldy hay over a period of several weeks, synthesis of vitamin K-dependent clotting factors is impaired, putting him at risk for bleeding.

B vitamins (thiamine, riboflavin, niacin, pyridoxine, pantothenic acid, biotin, choline, folic acid, and B12) are created in the cecum and large colon by bacterial action. B vitamins are involved in energy metabolism. The horse generally does not need B vitamins added to his diet unless he is ill, anemic, or unable to produce them. The need for B vitamins may increase with stress. Some researchers think that young, rapidly growing horses or athletes subjected to high levels of work may not produce enough B vitamins to satisfy their requirements and may benefit from supplementation.

Thiamine (vitamin B1) plays an important role in nerve transmission and stimulation and carbohydrate metabolism. Horses obtain a high level of thiamine from intestinal bacteria but also may need some in their diet. Green forage is an excellent source as is brewer's yeast. Deficiency can occur if a horse eats bracken fern, which contains a chemical that inhibits absorption.

Fresh forage or yeast supplements also adequately supply the other B vitamins that are also synthesized in the horse's gut. Horses have no known naturally occurring B vitamin deficiencies or toxicities, though some horsemen supplement biotin to improve hoof health. Biotin seems to help some horses with thin, shelly hooves, though results vary from horse to horse and it may take six to nine months to see improvement. No optimal level of biotin for horses has been established, and the amounts included in most of the popular hoof supplements are well above what is considered the horse's basic needs.

Vitamin B12 and folic acid are needed for synthesis of red blood cells; a deficiency of either can result in anemia. Folic acid is found in green forage but B12 is not found in any plants. Produced in the horse's gut, it can be synthesized by microbes. Some horsemen supplement with B12 thinking it will enhance performance, stimulate appetite, or prevent anemia, but the normal healthy horse has plenty. Supplemental B12 can temporarily help a severely anemic horse but should be used in conjunction with correcting the original cause of the problem.

Vitamin C is an antioxidant that protects fats, proteins, and cell membranes from damage by free radicals. It plays a role in forming bones and teeth, helps utilize several B vitamins, and improves intestinal absorption of iron. It is also a component of several amino acids and the connective tissue collagen.

Horses synthesize vitamin C from glucose in the liver. Horses have no known dietary requirement or known deficiency of this vitamin. A horse usually does not need supplementation but stress or illness can disrupt his production of vitamin C. Supplementation can help when a horse is being treated for a viral infection. Some viruses seem to inhibit the production of vitamin C.

Older horses may lose their ability to produce vitamin C, and some nutritionists recommend supplementing vitamin C in horses past eighteen years of age. Horses that have been ill or stressed sometimes have low plasma concentrations of ascorbic acid, which may make them more susceptible to disease, nosebleeds, and wound infections. Some horsemen believe that infertility in mares and stallions can sometimes be helped with vitamin C supplements. Vitamin C seems to help horses that are prone to runny nose and chronic cough in the winter. Vitamin C helps repair joint cartilage. Supplements are often used in various stress and disease situations.

Minerals

Minerals are inorganic elements (not produced by living things) required in small amounts for body function. Minerals help metabolize carbohydrates, proteins, and fats; they are crucial to nerve conductivity and muscle contraction, and give strength and substance to bones. Certain minerals help the blood transport oxygen; maintain the body's acid/base, electrolyte, and fluid balances; and are important components of enzymes the horse creates for body metabolism. Minerals are also necessary for the production of certain vitamins, hormones, and amino acids.

More has been written in the last twenty-five years about the roles of various minerals in helping prevent problems and diseases than was written in the last two hundred years. But much of what we read today about various minerals' importance is still speculative and often overstated (from companies selling mineral supplements and feed additives). This has led some horsemen to overuse minerals, which is wasteful, expensive, and potentially dangerous.

Under natural conditions the horse gets minerals by eating plants that store them from the soil. The major minerals needed are calcium, phosphorus, magnesium, sodium, chlorine, and potassium. Others needed in minute (trace) amounts are iodine, cobalt, copper, iron, zinc, manganese, and selenium. Supplements are only necessary in regions where certain minerals are lacking in soil. Overdose can be toxic, and some have little margin for error. Feeding the minimum amount of a mineral is just as effective as feeding the maximum amount. Check with your veterinarian or an equine nutritionist before giving mineral supplements.

Some minerals work together or influence one another. The amount of one can affect absorption and utilization of the other. Calcium and phosphorus, for instance, are both essential to growth and repair of bones but must be present in the proper proportions to be most effective. Copper, zinc, and iron are also linked in their performance, and abnormal amounts may play a role in developmental bone disease in young, growing horses. Excessive zinc, iron, and/or manganese can hinder the absorption of calcium and phosphorus. Excessive calcium can interfere with proper absorption of some of the trace minerals, such as zinc.

Certain minerals also can combine in the gut to form different compounds with differing "digestibility"; some don't break down as well and are therefore less utilized by the body. The amount of a certain mineral listed in a feed product's ingredients may only be partially available for actual use by the horse. The type of calcium in a commercial feed, for instance, may not be efficiently utilized, and actual absorption can vary as much as 10 to 40 percent (phosphorus is usually more consistently utilized, at about 70 percent). Iron utilization ranges from about 2 to 20 percent, depending on the compound being added to the feed, and zinc can range from 5 percent to 90 percent utilization.

Feed companies have tried to improve the absorption rates of certain minerals because the inorganic forms they use for bolstering a feed's component are often not as readily absorbed as the organic forms in natural feeds (forages and grains). Some minerals can be made more readily utilized by a process known as chelation, which bonds the mineral to two or more amino acids, forming stable biological compounds that are metabolized as much as 300 to 500 percent more effectively than their inorganic counterparts.

Calcium and Phosphorus

These two minerals make up the major ingredients of bones and teeth. A lack of either can hinder growth or lead to unsoundness. During a foal's development, cartilage forms and is replaced by bone. Milk is the best source of calcium and phosphorus for foals.

Calcium is important for nerve conductivity and energy metabolism, contractions of muscles (especially the heart muscle), health of cell membranes, body temperature regulation, secretions from various glands, and blood clotting. A horse's ability to absorb calcium often declines with age; a young horse may absorb 70 percent of the calcium in his diet while an older horse may absorb 50 percent or less. Phosphorus is essential for growth and repair of bones and teeth, along with many functions of the body cells and energy metabolism. During late pregnancy and throughout lactation, a mare's needs for phosphorus increases.

Forages are usually high in calcium, and grain is high in phosphorus. The ratio of calcium to phosphorus in the horse's diet is very important; he needs at least as much calcium as phosphorus. Most researchers feel that the balance should be somewhere between 1:1 and 2:1 (1.2 parts calcium to one part phosphorus is ideal) and should not exceed four parts calcium to one part phosphorus. The usual ratio in pasture grass is about 1.2:1, which is perfect for horses. Young horses are often fed grain to speed their growth, but if grain (with its higher phosphorus content) is added to the diet then more calcium should be added (alfalfa hay is a good source) to balance it.

Too much phosphorus in a ration binds with calcium and prevents its absorption (but excess calcium has little effect on the absorption of phosphorus). Feeding too much grain can be detrimental because the grain not only provides more phosphorus than needed but also ties up the calcium in a compound that is not absorbed. Feeding more calcium does not solve the problem because it is not properly absorbed. Thus overfeeding a young horse with grain can result in soft bones, crooked legs, and unsoundness.

Signs of calcium deficiency include abnormal bone development in foals and yearlings, decreased bone density in adult horses (and sometimes stiffness and lameness), weight loss, fragile bones, and loose teeth. "Big head" in adult horses (enlargement of the jaws, from bone being replaced by fibrous connective tissue) is caused by overfeeding phosphorus and is often due to reliance on bran in the diet, which is very high in phosphorus and low in calcium.

Deficiencies of either calcium or phosphorus can result in the body drawing upon bone supply to maintain other functions dependent upon that mineral. In adult horses, this results in weakening of bones (or osteoporosis, in which bones become fragile and brittle). A calcium deficiency can cause rickets in young horses. Under most circumstances, however, a horse eating forage never develops a calcium shortage because hay is high in calcium.

Inappropriate calcium metabolism (too high or too low) can affect athletic performance because calcium plays a role in muscle contraction. The ability to mobilize calcium is regulated by the hormone calcitonin, the production of which is affected by dietary calcium. If dietary calcium is high, the body is lulled into a false sense of plenty and calcitonin production is low; the horse may suddenly face a shortage during athletic activity. This is a big factor in some cases of muscle tying up or metabolic collapse. It also can be a factor in post-exertion colics when decreased gut motility occurs due to insufficient calcium.

Excess calcium in a diet may interfere with absorption of trace minerals (especially iron, zinc, and copper) and in the young horse can lead to skeletal problems such as OCD lesions. Too much calcium in the bloodstream can occur from kidney disease. If the kidneys are not working properly to excrete calcium in the urine, calcium quickly builds up.

Salt: Sodium Chloride

Salt is a combination of two very important minerals: sodium and chloride. Forages do not contain adequate salt, so always provide it for horses. Some commercial feeds contain salt, but it may not be enough if a horse is sweating or lactating. Horses should have free access to salt in a stall or pasture, even if receiving a feed containing salt. The horse can regulate his salt intake so it's best to feed salt free choice rather than use a feed that is high in salt content.

Even if the horse licks his salt block for something to do and eats more than he needs, the excess is flushed out with urine and does no harm as long as he has enough water to drink. Horses are not at risk for high blood pressure when consuming extra salt, as some humans are. Salt is the only mineral that can be safely fed free choice since overdoses are not harmful. This is why it's best to offer plain salt rather than mineralized salt, especially in hot weather or when a horse is working. A horse that sweats a lot replenishes his salt losses by consuming more salt. If it contains trace minerals, he may eat more of them than is healthy.

Working horses need salt.

5

Salt performs many important functions in the body. It stimulates secretion of saliva, and saliva contains enzymes that are important in digestion. A sodium deficiency reduces the horse's utilization of digested protein and energy, and a lack of salt can decrease growth rate in young horses.

The sodium and chlorine (chloride in compound form) in salt are the main ingredients of the fluid circulating within the body and between the body cells. These minerals help maintain fluid pressure of the cells and aid fluid movement through the cell membranes (to move nutrients and wastes). Sodium and chlorine help keep the proper water balance in the body and aid in the release of water through the skin pores as sweat. Sodium is necessary for production of bile, which helps digest fats. Chlorine is necessary for hydrochloric acid, the gastric juice for digesting protein. The components of salt are the most important of the minerals called electrolytes.

Horses need more salt when they sweat profusely to prevent fatigue, dehydration, and collapse. Horses doing moderate work lose fifty to sixty grams of salt in sweat each day, and about thirty-five grams of salt in urine (a total of about a fifth of a pound of salt daily). The more a horse exerts, the more salt is lost through sweat and the more he requires to replace it. Unless salt is replaced, a horse will show signs of fatigue and electrolyte imbalance.

Horses have a wide variation in individual salt needs and consumption, depending on level of activity, weather temperature, humidity, and individual factors. The best and safest way to provide salt is to give horses free access to salt at all times, along with plenty of water. Thus, the horse can balance his own salt and water intake and never be deficient. When salt intake is low, the body adjusts to conserve its supply; urine output of sodium and chlorine nearly stops. A high salt intake triggers greater secretion of sodium and chlorine, filtered out of the blood by the kidneys; the horse drinks more water to flush out the salt.

Shortage of salt over long periods can cause loss of appetite, weight loss, stunted growth, rough hair coat, depression, and depraved appetite; the horse tries to eat anything that might contain salt or have salty flavor. These abnormal cravings may be dangerous if the horse tries to eat rocks or wood or consumes a lot of sand. Beach sand or river sand may contain salty substances and a salt-hungry horse will eat the sand. He may continually lick toxic substances such as painted fences or fence posts treated with wood preservatives, which may poison him.

Under normal conditions, horses doing minimal work eat about half a pound of salt per week, depending on the salt content of any prepared feeds given and how much the horse sweats. Loose salt can be provided in a salt box. Blocks work well if they're not too hard. If your region lacks natural iodine, use salt containing iodine unless your horses are getting a mineral supplement. Iodized salt should be used only if feeds are short on natural iodine; if fed in excess, iodine is toxic.

Potassium

Potassium helps body cells keep proper fluid balance and pressure, and maintains proper pH balance in the body. It is one of the electrolytes and is included with sodium chloride when replacing the important salts that a horse loses through sweating or diarrhea. Without adequate potassium, the horse is more easily fatigued, suffering muscle weakness and loss of appetite. Under normal conditions, potassium deficiency is very rare because most forages contain from 1 percent to 4 percent potassium, which is more than adequate for supplying the horse's daily requirement of about 0.4 percent (or a hard-working horse's need for about 0.6 percent). Cereal grains also contain potassium (between 0.3 percent and 0.5 percent).

Excess potassium is readily excreted in the horse's urine and thus is not harmful. One exception is the horse that suffers from HYPP (hyperkalemic periodic paralysis), a genetic problem inherited by certain Quarter Horses, Paints, and Appaloosas descended from the Quarter Horse Impressive. In these animals, potassium is not properly excreted and tends to build up within the body. This condition is dealt with nutritionally by keeping the horse's dietary intake of potassium very low (under 1 percent), usually by feeding a high grain, low forage diet and avoiding green forage and molasses.

For horses that need more potassium (hard-working horses that lose this element through excessive sweating), electrolyte products can be given, or fifty to one hundred grams of "lite" salt (half sodium chloride, half potassium chloride) can be added to the feed.

Magnesium

A horse's bones contain more than half its body reserves of magnesium. This element is important to the function of many enzymes. Most horse feeds contain more than adequate amounts. Horses fed normal diets never suffer deficiencies or overdoses, but occasionally a lactating mare may develop muscle spasms (tetany) because of a high potassium, low magnesium diet; high levels of magnesium are lost to the body through milk production.

Sulfur

Sulfur is an important ingredient for production of several amino acids and for the B vitamins biotin and thiamine. Sulfur is also crucial for production of insulin, taurine (an organic acid occurring in bile salts), and chondroitin sulfate (a component of bone, cartilage, tendons, and blood vessels). Keratin, one of the proteins that make up hoof and hair tissue, is 4 percent sulfur. Sulfur requirements for horses have not yet been determined, but most feeds contain organic sulfur, which seems to meet daily requirements.

Trace minerals — ones needed by the horse in very tiny amounts — are iodine, selenium, iron, copper, zinc, manganese, and cobalt.

Iodine

Iodine is necessary for production of thyroxin (T4) and tri-iodothyronine (T3), hormones that help control metabolism. The proper amount is important; overdose and deficiency both cause goiter (enlargement of the thyroid gland).

The estimated daily requirement of iodine is about 0.1 part per million. As little as 5 parts per million can be toxic. Most horse feeds contain between 0.05 and 0.2 parts per million, but some have as much as 2 parts per million, depending upon soil where the feed was grown. Certain areas in the United States are short on iodine, including the Great Lakes region, Pacific Coast, Rocky Mountains, northern Great Plains, and upper Mississippi Valley. A number of other regions have high concentrations of iodine. If your forages are already high in iodine, avoid iodine supplements, trace mineral mixes, or salt containing iodine.

Iodine deficiency and iodine overdose can produce similar symptoms, including hair loss, dull hair coat, slow growth, and decreased bone calcification in young horses. An imbalance also can cause drowsiness and lethargy, inability to handle cold weather, and occasionally hypothermia (low body temperature). Sometimes an iodine deficiency causes thickened skin.

Pregnancy creates greater demand for iodine. A pregnant mare with an iodine deficiency may give birth to a weak or stillborn foal. Foals that survive may have bone and joint abnormalities or have enlarged thyroid glands. Goiters can be large enough to make birth difficult.

The tiny amount of iodine required by a horse (about one milligram daily) can be supplied by iodized salt or mineral salt if your region is deficient. A horse may get an overdose, however, if he is getting trace mineral salt, a grain mix that contains iodine, and a vitamin-mineral supplement or "shiny hair coat" supplement. Kelp products contain a lot of iodine.

It is worse to overfeed iodine than to have a deficiency. High levels of iodine fed to a pregnant or lactating mare can cause goiter in her foal. In recent years there have been more problems with iodine toxicity than with deficiencies, possibly because of over-supplementation by well-meaning horse owners. Check feed labels. Don't use supplements containing iodine (except for iodized salt in a deficient area) except when advised by your veterinarian.

Selenium

Selenium can be deadly if it isn't in the diet, and deadly if there's too much. Without adequate selenium, horses may develop muscle disease and weakness, reproductive problems, and immune deficiencies. Mild deficiencies may go unnoticed by the horse owner; the only symptoms might be decreased fertility or increased susceptibility to disease. Less common are severe deficiencies, which can result in muscle weakness, difficulty in swallowing, impaired heart function, and respiratory distress.

Foals are at risk if their dams received inadequate selenium during pregnancy. Foals may be stillborn, die within a few days of birth, or develop symptoms of deficiency (muscle pain, inability to nurse, hindquarter lameness) during the first four weeks of life. Contracted tendons and angular limb deformities are common in selenium-deficient foals, and retained placentas are common in mares.

If the mare's milk is selenium-deficient, a foal can develop "white muscle disease" soon after birth. In milder cases the foal may have a stiff gait because the lack of selenium affects muscle mobility. Areas in the neck and hindquarters become swollen and painful. Nursing becomes difficult and the foal spends a lot of time lying down. In acute cases the foal may become depressed, with high temperature, fast respiration, and pale mucous membranes. Death can occur within thirty-six hours of birth. Post-mortem examination shows muscle degeneration; large areas are white or streaked with white instead of the normal red, thus the disease's name. Damaged muscles have less myoglobin, the red iron-containing protein pigment of normal muscles. Scar tissue may build up in the heart, reducing its elasticity; the foal may die of heart failure. Scarred tissue can't regenerate, so the damage from selenium deficiency in foals is usually irreversible. In selenium deficient regions, mares should receive selenium supplementation throughout pregnancy and foals can be given vitamin E and selenium injections after birth.

Like vitamin E, selenium is an antioxidant and is essential for proper immune function. Vitamin E and selenium have similar actions in the body; they each do some good separately but together have an enhanced effect by working together to maintain muscle health, growth, and performance, and to protect body tissues from damage and degeneration that occurs during oxidation (loss of electrons during chemical processes in the body). The partnership of selenium and vitamin E for protecting cells works best when both are present in proper amounts. A combination of the two is often prescribed for horses prone to muscle problems and tying up.

Selenium deficiency is a problem in most of the United States (portions of forty-two states), including the eastern third of the country, much of the Pacific Northwest and northern California, along with parts of Ohio, Indiana, Minnesota, Michigan, Wisconsin, and central Iowa. Much of Canada is also selenium deficient. Sandy and acidic soils tend to be more selenium deficient, and bottomlands that are irrigated are often short on this trace mineral because it tends to leach out. Horsemen who purchase hay from some of these areas may have a serious problem with deficiencies in their horses.

Sulfur and zinc in feeds can prevent proper utilization of selenium. The horse's body cannot utilize these elements when they are bound together. Growing plants usually accumulate selenium in adequate amounts for maintaining the health of grazing animals, but in some soils there isn't enough selenium. Clover and alfalfa do not pick it up as readily as do grasses. Sulfur in soil also can retard a plant's ability to absorb selenium. High crop yields and intensive irrigation and fertilization have increased the incidence of selenium deficiency; the higher the crop yield, the smaller the concentration of selenium. Slower growing plants (less yield per acre or cuttings per season) have time to accumulate a little more.

Many commercial grain mixes include supplemental selenium, usually appearing on the feed tag as sodium selenite. Routinely adding selenium to the feed is a controversial issue, however, since some areas of the country have an excess of selenium, and even a small overdose can be toxic. The United States and Canada now have regulations requiring feed companies to print a warning on the label if there has been selenium added to the feed.

Selenium has a narrow safety margin for horses — only a few parts per million above recommended levels. Feed companies often add 0.1 to 0.4 parts per million to feed mixes (0.1 part per million is very adequate for most horses, but during training, after injury or illness, or in a mare's last trimester of pregnancy, that need may double). Selenium can be toxic, however, when total daily intake is 3 to 5 parts per million or more. The selenium level currently recommended for horses is between 0.1 part per million and 0.3 parts per million (dry matter), though some equine nutritionists believe this is somewhat conservative.

Selenium toxicity causes patchy sweating, colic, diarrhea, increased heart and respiration rates, blind staggers (in an acute situation, as when a horse is given a selenium injection), loss of hair (especially mane and tail), joint stiffness, cracks around the hoof just under the coronary band, and sometimes loss of a hoof. The excess selenium replaces the sulfur in proteins, causing hair loss and brittle hooves. The horse becomes anemic and has a poor appetite and rough hair coat. If a pregnant mare has too much selenium in her diet, the foal may be deformed at birth or be born with symptoms of selenium poisoning.

Selenium content of feeds can vary greatly. In some regions, areas with adequate levels of selenium and inadequate spots occur very close together, and elsewhere small pockets with toxic concentrations occur in regions that otherwise have proper selenium levels. Toxic levels exist in numerous locations in California, Nevada, Oregon, Idaho, Utah, Montana, Wyoming, North and South Dakota, Nebraska, Colorado, Arizona, and New Mexico — most of the Midwest and Rocky Mountain regions from the Dakotas to Texas. The main danger is when horses eat certain plants that are selenium accumulators, storing excess selenium from the soil. Selenium poisoning is most often seen when pastures are overgrazed or when good feed is short (and horses start eating plants they might not otherwise consume) or when toxic plants end up in harvested hay.

Copper and Zinc
The roles played by these two minerals in equine nutrition are not yet completely understood. Copper is a component of several enzymes that help synthesize and maintain connective tissue. Copper also is important in synthesis of the

skin pigment melanin and in stabilizing bone collagen (the fibrous protein portion). Zinc is contained in some of the enzymes that help metabolize proteins and carbohydrates. Some researchers think zinc is important in maintaining healthy cell membranes and a healthy immune system. Feed companies generally include copper in concentrate feeds at a level of 30 to 50 parts per million and zinc level at 80 to 120 parts per million. Zinc and copper are usually supplied in feeds at a 4:1 ratio (four parts zinc to one part copper), although this practice is not supported by research.

It is difficult to estimate how much copper horses utilize, since absorption in the digestive tract can be influenced by zinc, iron, or molybdenum. Horses rarely have deficiencies, though earlier research suggested that lack of copper can play a role in developmental bone disease in young horses (a theory now thought to have been overrated). Deficiency also has been implicated in rupture of uterine arteries in older mares during foaling or rupture of the aorta during exercise.

Horses have a fairly high tolerance for excess copper in their diet; they have the ability to decrease absorption of this mineral when the intake increases. Zinc is also well tolerated in excess, but absorption can vary greatly since the level of many other minerals, including copper and iron, affects it. Zinc poisoning does not occur under normal circumstances (usually only when horses graze pastures contaminated by nearby smelters, mines, foundries, or other industrial plants). Symptoms of zinc poisoning include limb deformities in foals. The average level of zinc in most natural feeds is quite low (feed companies often add this mineral), but no symptoms of deficiency have been noted in horses.

Iron

Iron is crucial to formation of red blood cells and the hemoglobin that transports oxygen. About 60 percent of the body's iron supply is used for this purpose and the rest is involved in production of various enzymes and muscle myoglobin. Horsemen sometimes give iron supplements, thinking the mineral will increase the horse's endurance or athletic performance, but this practice is dangerous. Foals given supplemental iron at birth have died, and deaths also have occurred in mature horses given large doses.

The horse's need for iron is very low, estimated at about 50 parts per million per day for pregnancy, lactation, and growth, and 40 parts per million for mature horses. Most forages contain between 50 and 250 parts per million (sometimes as much as 400 parts per million). The horse is very efficient at processing and reusing his iron supply. As red blood cells become old and die, the iron in their hemoglobin is salvaged and stored, then used again to make new red blood cells. Thus iron deficiencies in horses are truly rare, generally occurring only with severe or chronic blood loss (such as from internal or external parasites).

Iron deficiency results in impaired performance and anemia (low red blood cell count). If a horse is short of iron, the cause should be determined and corrected. Supplemental iron should not be given until a blood test has shown the horse to be anemic.

Iron toxicity is more common in horses than iron deficiency, due to over-supplementation. It also can be a problem in regions with high iron content in the water. High levels of iron can make a horse more susceptible to bacterial infections. Foals are very susceptible to iron toxicity; excess iron is stored in tissues, primarily in the liver. Foals can develop diarrhea, dehydration, and liver failure. The body has no way to excrete excess iron except through blood loss; its only defense is decreased absorption. This works to some extent with oral supplements but not with injections. The body stores iron, whether it needs it or not, and this can cause problems in the bone marrow as well as the liver.

Manganese

Manganese plays a role in metabolism of fatty acids and carbohydrates and is essential for synthesis of chondroitin sulfate (necessary for cartilage production). It also is important for reproduction and growth. The amount of manganese needed by horses has not been determined.

Cobalt

Cobalt is a component of vitamin B12 — its only known function as a nutrient. Cobalt deficiency can result in B12 deficiency. Researchers have not yet determined the optimum level for cobalt in feed, but based on recommendations for cattle, a minimum of 0.1 part per million and a maximum of 10 parts per million have been suggested for horses. Cobalt deficiency does not seem to cause problems in horses. But cobalt supplements (given with intent of preventing vitamin B12 deficiency) have sometimes caused severe liver and kidney damage when used in high doses.

Water Requirements of Horses

Water is necessary for nearly every bodily function. This plentiful and inexpensive "nutrient" makes up 65 to 85 percent of a foal's body weight, and 68 to 72 percent of an adult horse's body weight. A thousand-pound horse's body contains about eighty gallons of water. Even small changes in total body water can have a large negative impact on a horse's health and well-being.

A thousand-pound horse usually drinks ten to twelve gallons of water per day, the actual amount depending on his work and the weather. During ninety to one hundred degree weather, the idle horse drinks at least 16 gallons just to replace fluid lost through sweat. Horses that work or lactate in hot weather can consume more than one hundred gallons a day. In freezing weather, most horses drink only four to five gallons daily. Dehydration can be caused by a horse not drinking enough or by excessive water loss. Fever, diarrhea, excessive sweating, and many other factors can reduce the body's water supply.

When a horse is short on fluid, the first sign of imbalance may be colic; water is pulled from the gut for more important functions. If dehydration is gradual, the first symptoms are often a decrease in appetite and impaction; there is little moisture in the digestive tract and manure becomes firm and scant.

Much of the water requirement is obtained through drinking, but some is sup-plied by moisture in feeds (such as green pasture grass) or generated within the body or recycled as saliva. A horse's water requirements are influenced by what he's eating. Lush grass may be fifty to ninety percent water, while hay may be only 5 to 8 percent water. Water intake is related to dry-matter intake and salt consumption.

Water loss occurs through sweat, evaporation, urine, manure, and moisture lost from the lungs while breathing. Lactation will increase water requirement 50 to 70 percent above average intake (many mares secrete

Water requirements vary.

five to six gallons of water daily in milk). Horses doing hard work may sweat eight to ten gallons of fluid. Endurance horses in hot weather can lose 5 to 10 percent of their body weight in fluid loss. Any time a horse loses 10 percent of his body water, he is at risk for digestive disturbances, and a loss of 20 percent of body fluid will result in death.

To avoid dangerous water loss in summer, don't work a horse hard when tem-perature and/or humidity are high. Always allow the horse water when riding, even when he is hot from exertion. It is safe to water a hot horse as long as the water is not cold and he continues working after drinking. Cold water may cause intestinal cramping and muscle problems, especially if the horse is standing idle after drinking, with blood rushing from his muscles to warm the cold water in his gut. Lukewarm water is safer. Water that sits in the sun may get too warm, however, and horses won't drink.

Most horses prefer water between sixty and seventy-five degrees in summer and above forty degrees in winter. Horse owners usually realize that their animals need more water in hot weather or during exertion but sometimes fail to make sure hors-es are drinking enough water in cold weather. A sudden cold spell may make hors-es refuse to drink, and the abrupt drop in available body fluid often results in colic.

The quality of water is also important. Horses may refuse to drink dirty water or water with manure in it. Water supplies can be toxic if they contain certain minerals in high concentrations or too much salt or contaminants. You may need to have the water tested.

Natural Feeds: The Importance of Fiber

Forage is defined as a feed with a minimum fiber content of 18 percent and relatively low energy content. Roughage (stem fibers, plant stalks, and leaves) should always be the mainstay of a horse's diet. Even performance horses, growing horses, and lactating broodmares can often have their requirements (or a very large proportion) supplied by good pasture and/or hay. Forages contribute more to a horse's general good health and well being than any other feed, greatly reducing the incidence of colic, laminitis, and behavioral problems arising from confinement and boredom.

Cellulose, lignin, and hemicellulose give plants strength and rigidity. Lignin acts as a binder for the cellulose fibers and is the portion of the plant that is totally indigestible. Cellulose and hemicellulose are part of the non-seed and non-fruit portions of a plant (leaves, stems, and hulls), also called insoluble fiber. The soluble fiber is a much smaller proportion of the plant — the liquid in resin, sap, or other plant juices. Fiber content of pasture plants and hay will vary, depending on time of year, stage of maturity, and available moisture, whereas the fiber content of most grains will not vary much and is considerably lower.

Cellulose and hemicellulose are about 50 percent digestible by the bacteria in the hindgut and they provide an important source of energy. Lignin passes through completely undigested, making up the major component of manure. Some fiber is necessary to the horse's digestion; the bulk is needed to help keep things moving, and to provide for a balanced population of microbes in the hindgut. It also prevents too-quick digestion of carbohydrates, which can sometimes cause digestive problems if they are not buffered and cushioned by the presence of fiber in the large intestine.

Without adequate fiber, the gut loses its ability to conserve water and electrolytes; the bulky fiber helps hold fluid, like a large sponge. Without fiber in the gut to keep things moving, high carbohydrate feeds such as grains may block the tract, putting the horse at risk for colic and dehydration.

Pasture

Forages are divided into two categories — grasses and legumes. Both can be excellent sources of nutrition for horses, but legumes are often higher in protein and other nutrients. Horses generally don't need the abundance of nutrients supplied by legumes alone, and a pasture growing only legumes is not as hardy — these plants generally don't withstand trampling and grazing as well as grasses. A good mix of grasses or a mix of grass and a legume makes the best pasture.

When living at pasture, adult horses usually spend 60 to 80 percent of their time grazing. Feed intake varies, depending on season, types of plants, and quality of pasture. Horses living full time on good pasture may graze leisurely, eating a pound or more of forage per hour of grazing, whereas horses with limited turnout may eat three times that much per hour. Most horses can take in enough forage during four to five hours of grazing (on good pasture) to meet their daily nutrient requirements. On sparse dry ranges, however, or poor pasture (weedy, dry and mature, or overgrazed) a horse may spend most of his time grazing in order to get enough food.

Nutritional value of forages is highest when plants are young and growing; the more immature the plant, the more palatable and nutritious it is. As plants mature, they develop more structural strength (more indigestible lignin). Mature horses can become fat on lush pasture and must be limited in grazing time unless they are worked hard. If pasture is too lush, however, horses may have a hard time eating enough of it to provide their needs for fiber because of the high water content.

Many horses tend to overeat on early spring pasture, and this overindulgence can lead to colic or founder. Horsemen generally think that the reason a horse overeats on lush pasture is because it tastes good and he's greedy, but lush green grass is high in water content and does not fill a horse up as more mature grasses would. A horse needs to eat about 2 percent of his body weight per day in fiber just to keep his digestive tract functioning properly. On green pasture he may not be getting enough fiber and just keeps eating, gorging himself in an attempt to feel full and satisfied.

As grasses mature, nutrient value drops and percentage of fiber increases. Irrigated pastures or those that are well watered by rain can keep their nutrient content high all summer if they are grazed or mowed periodically to keep them continually regrowing and in a "young" vegetative stage.

A horse may get too much fiber in comparison to nutrient values if he has to eat dry, overly mature plants or large amounts of poor quality forage. The horse's gut may be distended with feed because of his attempt to eat enough forage but he may actually be underweight. The large volume of indigestible fiber may not supply the calories he needs to maintain body weight. In these instances the horse needs better-quality forage (and in some cases, grain) to provide the necessary energy with less bulk.

Legumes most commonly used in horse pastures are alfalfa, clovers, lespedeza, and birdsfoot trefoil. These plants are higher in protein, calcium, and phosphorus than grasses, and contain more lysine, the amino acid needed for growth in young animals. Of the protein found in grasses, only about 2.5 percent to 3 percent of it is lysine, whereas the protein in legumes is 4.5 percent to 5 percent lysine.

Feeding Hay

The mainstay of many horses' diets is hay, whether fed for part of the year when pastures are dry or snow-covered, or year-round for horses that don't have access to pasture. Hay supplies the necessary fiber, and next to pasture, good quality hay is the ideal feed. In many instances, a good hay diet is superior to pasture because you have more control over how much a horse consumes. You can limit the idle, fat horse or easy keeper to the nutrition he needs, or enable a hard-working horse to eat more total nutrients per pound of feed. The hard-working horse that does not have all day to graze can get his requirements more quickly by eating hay morning and evening (with the larger feeding at night when he has more time to work on it). With hay, you can get more pounds of dry matter into him — hence more energy.

Hay is categorized as grass, legume, or mixed (grasses and a legume). Some of the popular grass hays are timothy, orchard grass, bluegrass, and brome. Grass hay often has a slightly lower level of digestible energy and crude protein than green pasture grass, since some values are lost as the hay matures and is dried at harvest. But it is still adequate for most horses except growing youngsters and lactating mares. Timothy is widely grown, tolerating cold weather and growing early in spring. It doesn't do as well in extreme heat and humidity. Growers in the central and southern United States often use Coastal Bermuda grass, brome, or orchard grass. Other grasses used for hay are bluegrass, fescue, reed canary grass, rye grass, and Sudan grass. Many horsemen prefer grass because it tends to be less dusty than legume hay, with no risk of blister beetles and a lower protein content (which makes it ideal for mature horses and for hard-working horses that don't need the heat created).

Several types of legumes are used as horse hay, with alfalfa being the most popular. Other legume hays include clover (red, crimson, alsike ,and ladino), lespedeza, birdsfoot trefoil, vetch, and cowpeas. Good legume hay generally has a slightly higher level of digestible energy, vitamin A, many minerals, and more than twice the protein (and three times the level of calcium) than grass hay. Early bloom alfalfa hay is about 18 percent crude protein, compared with 9.8 percent for early bloom timothy, and 11.4 percent for early bloom orchard grass. Alfalfa cut in full bloom drops to 15.5 percent crude protein, compared to 6.9 percent for late-bloom timothy and 7.6 percent for late-bloom orchard grass. Thus, legume hay comes closer to meeting protein and mineral needs of young growing horses and lactating mares than does grass hay.

About two-thirds of the energy and three-fourths of the protein (as well as most other nutrients) are in the leaves of a forage plant. Coarse, thick-stemmed hay has more fiber and less nutrition than leafy hay with finer stems. One way to assess the maturity of alfalfa hay, for instance, is the snap test. If a handful of hay bends easily in your hand, its fiber is more digestible (with less woody lignin) than if the stems snap like twigs. For horses, alfalfa should have a moderate stem to give some fiber content. Really fine, palatable alfalfa (rabbit hay or dairy hay) is too rich for horses and does not have enough lignin content for proper digestion. At the other extreme, overly mature alfalfa, already bloomed, may be too coarse.

In many regions that get only two or three cuttings of hay, first cutting alfalfa is usually the preferred feed for horses, not only because it often has a little grass mixed with it but also because it tends to have coarser stems due to the fact that it grows the fastest. Later cuttings tend to grow more slowly and stems are finer, sometimes too fine (too many nutrients per pound, with very little fiber) for most horses. In other

Hay supplies most requirements.

regions, first cutting hay is less desirable because it tends to have more weeds. If there is a long growing season, the second and third cuttings will be the coarsest because they grow the fastest, during the hottest weather, and the later cuttings will have the finest stems, growing more slowly during cooler days of fall. The nutrient value and coarseness also depend upon when the hay was cut (before, during, or after blooming).

Alfalfa hay is valued by horsemen for its high-quality nutrition and high protein content. Horses usually do well on alfalfa or grass hay. Alfalfa hay cut before it blooms is higher in protein, calcium, and carotene (vitamin A) than grass hay. The mature, idle horse does not need this much protein, however; he just converts it into fat. He also will urinate more frequently to get rid of nitrogen created by breakdown of extra protein (one reason horsemen used to think alfalfa damaged a horse's kidneys). This is not harmful as long as he has enough water to replace lost fluid; horses eating alfalfa hay drink more water than horses on grass hay (which can make for more stall clean-up if they are confined). Protein is composed of amino acids that contain nitrogen and hydrogen. As the kidneys process excess amino acids, they turn some into ammonia. A barn where a lot of alfalfa hay is fed has more ammonia problem in stalls than a barn where grass hay is fed.

A hard-working horse needs more nutrients than an idle horse, and some horse owners like to feed a mix of grass and alfalfa when trying to keep a hard-working horse in good condition. Too much protein can be detrimental for the performance horse, however; horses in strenuous careers may do poorly if fed alfalfa hay alone. High protein levels are not needed for muscular activity and can be counterproductive because of the problem of getting rid of the wastes and heat created. Alfalfa's high protein and calcium content make some horses more likely to develop thumps, tie up, overheat, and become dehydrated when being worked. Thumps, also called diaphramgamtic flutter, is a condition in which the diaphragm contracts in time with the heartbeat, creating a rapid, jerking movement of the flanks, often accompanied by a thumping sound.

Alfalfa, because it is leafy, tends to be dustier than grass hay unless harvested in almost perfect conditions. If the leaves are too dry, they shatter and create a dust of fine particles that can irritate the respiratory tract and cause coughing, or allergic sensitivities and heaves — similar to an asthma attack in humans. Avoid feeding dusty hay (whether grass or alfalfa). If it's a little dusty you may be able to shake it up thoroughly to remove the dust. If there's still some dust you can sprinkle it with water to settle the rest. Sprinkled hay must be eaten right away, however; otherwise it can begin to mold.

If baled even slightly too green or wet, alfalfa tends to mold more readily than grass because it is richer in nutrients, making an ideal environment for mold to flourish. Good grass hay is often safer to feed under variable conditions; it can tolerate a wider range of situations during harvest.

A problem that sometimes occurs with alfalfa hay harvested after it blooms is blister beetle poisoning. The small flying beetles are attracted to the blossoms to feed on pollen and are sometimes injured or killed by haying machinery and end up in the bales. It only takes a few beetles to kill a horse. A horse can die within a few hours if he eats very many beetles, or a fatal dose may accumulate over several days if he is continually fed the contaminated hay and ingests a beetle or two with each meal. The chemical cantharidin is just as toxic in dead beetles as in live ones; remains of beetles in year-old hay are as deadly as a freshly killed beetle.

Blister beetle.

Though mature alfalfa is preferable to early cut alfalfa for feeding adult horses, the risk of blister beetle poisoning always exists when you use hay that was cut after blooming. To avoid poisoning, first cutting alfalfa, harvested before it blooms (few blister beetle species hatch that early in the season), is usually the safest hay.

Not all hay (whether grass or alfalfa) is the same in weight or nutrition. It may take twice as much poor hay as good hay to keep a horse in good condition; the horse may have a hay belly and still lose weight. Poor hay is never a bargain; it can lead to nutritional deficiencies, digestive or respiratory problems, or even fatal colic if it contains toxic molds or poisonous weeds.

When you feed hay, know exactly how much you are feeding (you should always feed hay by weight, not by volume). There can be a big difference in size and weight of bales. Weigh a few bales from each load of hay you get. If you can't weigh the bales, weigh some flakes (the portion you would feed a horse), using a bathroom scale. Weigh yourself and then weigh while holding a flake of hay and subtract the difference. Some bales are loosely packed, or the hay is quite dry and will not weigh much even though they look big. Other bales may be heavy because they are moist and moldy.

A thousand-pound idle horse needs about twenty-five pounds of good grass hay daily (but only about ten pounds of good alfalfa), split into two or three feedings. If his work increases, the amount of hay should be increased. Some horses get by on less; others need more.

Alfalfa hay is usually heavier (same volume) than grass hay. Because it has more nutrients, horses need less total weight per feeding than grass hay, which means feeding much less volume of alfalfa. The exact amount depends on how much of the alfalfa is leaves versus stems. The leaves, being more energy rich, are where much of the weight is. Alfalfa hay that is mostly stems will not weigh as much and can be fed more liberally without risk of digestive problems. Stemmy, overmature alfalfa hay may contain enough lignin to satisfy the horse's need for fiber.

Leafy, rich alfalfa hay is so palatable that mature horses become too fat if allowed to eat as much as they want, and some get indigestion or colic unless the amount is rationed. But if you restrict them to the amount they need, they will eat it quickly and want something more to nibble on. Unless you give the horse another source of fiber along with it, such as grass hay, he will start chewing wood. Grass hay takes longer to eat and provides more normal fill. Rich alfalfa hay is best used like a supplement — to complement a basic diet of grass hay. Don't feed more than one pound of alfalfa hay per one hundred pounds of body weight; fill in with another type of roughage.

Selecting Hay

Hay quality varies greatly depending on growing conditions, stage of maturity at harvest, weather, and moisture conditions at harvest. Poor hay will not provide adequate nutrition and also causes health problems if it is dusty, moldy, or contains toxic plants. Certain types of molds can kill a horse or cause colic or abortions in pregnant mares. Some molds create allergies in young horses and cause coughing in older horses.

The best way to check hay is to open a few bales and look closely at the hay inside — its texture, maturity, color, leafiness — and check for weeds, mold, dust, discoloration from weathering, heat, and foreign material in the bales (bal-

Check the interior of a bale.

ing twines, wire, sticks). Rained-on hay that had to be redried may be dull in color, more yellow or brown than bright green. All hay tends to weather after it has been stacked awhile; the sun bleaches the outside edge. The inside should still be green, however.

The hay should smell good, not musty, sour, or moldy. The flakes should not stick together; moldy hay is usually heavy, stuck together, and dusty. Good hay will be uniformly green and sweet-smelling, with no brown spots or moldy portions. Try to buy hay that has been protected from weather by a tarp or hay shed unless you are buying it directly out of the field after baling. Heavy rain on a stack of hay may ruin the top layers of bales, soaking down into them and causing mold. The bottom layer also may be moldy if the stack sat on moist ground. When buying hay that has been stored for any time outdoors, specify that you do not want any top or bottom bales. They not only

Weight of hay can vary.

weigh more because of the extra moisture (adding to the cost of the load) but will likely have mold spoilage.

Stage of maturity is crucial for all hay, especially alfalfa; it loses food value much more rapidly than grass hay when mature. Mature plants have longer, coarser, and more fibrous stems; fewer leaves; and may have already bloomed (or gone to seed, in the case of grass hay).

Many factors can influence the nutrition level of hay. A certain crop may be higher or lower than average, depending on the way it was harvested (maturity and degree of moisture).

Soils vary from farm to farm or even from field to field, being acid or alkaline, wet bottomland or well-drained high ground. Slow-growing hay has more nutrition per pound than fast-growing hay. Hay grows faster during a hot season and may be lower in total nutrients and protein than slow-growing hay in a cool season. Often the fast-growing hay becomes coarse and stemmy while the slower-growing plants are more fine and palatable.

Hay with too much moisture in it when baled will heat (due to fermentation and chemical reactions) and mold. With too little moisture it will be dry and lose its leaves, and most of its nutritional value. It is difficult to estimate the protein level (or percentage of other nutrients) in a load of hay. The only way to know the actual protein or mineral content is to test the nutritional value (protein content, crude fiber, and moisture content) of your hay. To take a hay sample for testing, borrow a tool from your extension agent to drill into several bales for core samples, or break open at least five bales to take handfuls from the center and near the ends to mix in a bag. The National Forage Testing Association (phone number: 402-466-7677) can give you the name of a certified laboratory near you. Testing cost may vary, depending on the tests you want. Determining moisture level and crude protein level are fairly inexpensive tests; it will cost more to check the levels of specific vitamins and minerals.

Alfalfa hay, for example, is generally acceptable if it tests at least 17 percent crude protein (roughly 11 percent digestible protein) with maximum of 37 percent crude fiber, and no more than 12 percent moisture.

Round bales and large square bales are sometimes used for horses. These large bales can be convenient in a pasture situation or large paddock where horses have access to them in bale feeders or out on the ground. They can be handy for horses that need free choice access to hay, eliminating the several-times-a-day feeding chore for broodmares or young horses that need to eat often.

Large bales should be situated in a safe area where horses can have easy access. In a large pasture with many horses, bales should be put out in sev-

Round bales.

eral locations so that the more timid individuals can always get to the hay without being run off by the bossier ones.

Ease of feeding and having forage constantly available for horses that need it are the biggest advantages to using the large bales. The drawbacks include wasted hay, less quality control (you can't tell what the inside of the bale is like, as you can when feeding small bales flake by flake), and more risk of certain contaminants. When baled under questionable conditions, large bales are more likely to heat and spoil since there is more volume of airless hay that has no chance to finish drying. There's also more risk for botulism if a small animal such as a mouse is inadvertently baled; this deadly bacteria can proliferate more readily in the airtight conditions.

Horses with respiratory issues such as sensitivity to dust and molds or that are prone to "heaves" may not do well when eating big bales. They inhale more particles while their faces are deep in the hay.

Alternative Fiber Sources

Even though hay and pasture are the most commonly used roughages for horses, other feeds can be used when hay or pasture is scarce. Straw should not be fed because it is too coarse, but chopped straw or low-quality hay can be added to a high concentrate diet. Called chaff, the chopped material is used as a fiber supplement to mix with grain. Chaff helps slow down a horse that bolts his grain, gives more chew time to idle or fat horses, and adds fiber for a horse that tends to colic on high concentrate feeds. Chopped straw adds bulk rather than nutrients. It tends to be dusty and increases risk of choke.

If cut while green and growing, before the grain heads mature, some types of straw make good hay. Oat hay is quite palatable and can be used as part of a ration, but grains other than oats or beardless barley have rough beards and seed awns. If cut for hay, they aren't suitable for horses because rough pieces can irritate the mouth and throat. Be careful when using oat hay; it can cause nitrate poisoning under certain conditions (harvested after a growth spurt, such as after a rain following a dry spell). Horses are not as susceptible to nitrate poisoning as cattle are, but hay with extremely high nitrate levels could cause problems. If you use oat hay, first have it checked for nitrates.

Grain hulls can be used to add roughage to the diet, as they have more fiber than grass hay and are low in energy. The hulls of most grains can be fed to horses to replace some or all of the forage in a ration. Oat hulls and coarsely ground corn cobs are often used to add fiber. This type of feed tends to be dusty, however, and is best mixed with a little water or molasses.

Silage can be fed to horses but can be dangerous; molds are common in this type of feed. Corn silage, if moldy (particularly if it contains some corn along with the stalks), can be more dangerous than grass silage; the latter is usually safer for horses. Silage that is spoiled, moldy, or frozen should never be fed to horses. It can cause digestive upsets and colic, or even poisoning. Horses are more susceptible to poisoning from spoiled silage than are cattle.

Botulism is a possible risk with silage or haylage (and baled hay, for that matter), if a small animal or bird becomes trapped in it. The bacteria that cause botulism *Clostridium botulinum* live in the intestine of the animal. If the animal dies in the hay or silage (killed by the harvesting equipment), its decomposition releases anaerobic bacteria that thrive in the moist airless environment, especially if the silage or bale has a pH greater than 4.5.

Beet pulp is sometimes fed to horses. This is the fibrous by-product of sugar beet processing (after the sugar is extracted). In North America it is most commonly available in dehydrated form. It's best to soak it in water before feeding, since dry beet pulp expands in the stomach and can cause problems (or draw too much fluid from the gut to rehydrate it). Properly prepared, it is succulent and palatable with a somewhat laxative effect because of its high water content. It is a very digestible source of fiber.

In dry form, beet pulp has almost as many calories as barley (its energy content is very similar to oats) and much more than hay, but when prepared with water its nutritional level per pound drops, because the water makes up much of the weight. Prepared beet pulp has about one-third the calories of oats. It should be soaked in enough water to increase its weight threefold (two pounds of water added to each pound of beet pulp). If you add the right amount of hot water to the beet pulp and soak it for several hours until the water is completely absorbed, the pulp will be quite palatable to most horses. Some horsemen like to add molasses to improve the taste.

Beet pulp can be substituted for part of a hay ration, though nutritionists recommend that it not exceed one-third of the roughage portion of the diet to avoid digestive problems. Beet pulp can benefit older horses with bad teeth because it is easier to chew than hay, and in winter, its high water content helps reduce risk of impaction in geriatric equines. It can stimulate the appetite of an older horse or finicky eater, and is often used to help put

Beet pulp.

weight on horses that have difficulty maintaining weight. It's easier to disguise oral medications in beet pulp than in grain; the horse is less aware of the additive and less able to sort it out and leave it.

Bran is another way to add fiber to the horse's diet but is not as nutritious. Wheat bran is the by-product of milling wheat and consists of the coarse outer covering of wheat kernels. It can be mixed with concentrates for additional bulk or be given as a laxative. Some horsemen feed a hot bran mash on a cold winter evening or as a tonic for a tired or sick horse, or for a mare after foaling to keep her from becoming constipated. It is often fed to older horses to help prevent impaction.

A bran mash is made by adding hot water to about two pounds of bran, stirring until crumbly but not soupy. When used as a way to get more moisture into the gut (in the case of a sick or dehydrated horse) it should be soupy. Bran should never be fed dry.

Wheat bran is high in fiber, protein (about 17 percent protein), and phosphorus, but very low in calcium. Bran adds bulk to the diet — it's twice as bulky as oats — but it's poorly digested and low in energy. Because it is poorly digested, it increases the intestinal fill and the amount of manure passed.

The main drawback to feeding bran regularly is its calcium-phosphorus ratio. Bran is about one part calcium to ten parts phosphorus, causing a serious imbalance in diet if fed frequently, interfering with proper absorption of calcium. This can damage a young horse's growing bones and can cause deformed bones in adults. Wheat bran is the most common type fed to horses, but rice bran (in small quantities) is sometimes used as a fat supplement.

Lawn clippings are usually not a safe feed for horses and often cause serious problems. A horse can bolt down lawn clippings much faster than he can bite and chew green grass. In some instances this hurried eating can lead to impaction, choke, bloating and indigestion, or even founder in a susceptible animal.

Spoilage is a common risk because moist green grass will begin to ferment if it is piled for a time. The top part of the pile will dry, but the grass underneath starts to ferment and generate heat, which can happen very quickly on a hot, humid day. The same kind of process can occur inside a canvas lawn-mower bag. There is no "safe" rule of thumb for how long you can allow grass to lie on the ground or sit in a pile before feeding it; this depends on ground moisture, the maturity of the grass, and weather and wind conditions. If you can't gather the grass within ten to fifteen minutes of cutting, or if you feed more than the horse can eat within a few minutes, it's probably not safe to feed.

Concentrates

Concentrates include grains and grain by-products. They are low in fiber and high in digestible nutrients. Grains are classified in two groups — cereal grains and protein grains. Cereal grains include oats, wheat, corn, milo, barley, and rice. They are monocotyledons like other grasses, and the protein they contain is only 2.5 to 3 percent lysine. Protein grains include soybean, linseed or flax, canola, and cottonseed. These are dicotyledons like alfalfa and other legumes; their protein is about 4 to 6.5 percent lysine. Different grains vary in the amounts of protein, calories, fat, and fiber they contain. Grain is the plant's seedhead. Some have a fibrous hull (oats, barley, rice, and husked milo) while others do not (corn, wheat, rye, and millet).

The grains most often used for horses in the United States are oats, barley, corn, and milo. Not all concentrates are the same in nutrient density; some are bulkier than others, with more volume and less weight (less nutrition in an equal volume). A quart of oats, for instance, weighs about one pound, a quart of barley weighs 1.5 pounds, while a quart of corn weighs about 1.75 pounds. Therefore, oats are bulkier than corn; the corn weighs more for its volume. The more weight, the more energy available in the feed; hence the name concentrates —

grains contain more nutrients for their volume than do forages. Always take weight into consideration when changing grains. Changing a ration without adjusting for the weight of the new feed may lead to digestive problems or colic.

Some grains are easier to digest than others due to chemical structure. In harder-to-digest grains, a greater amount of starch travels to the hindgut intact, where it is fermented, creating lactic acid. This lowers the pH in the cecum, which can lead to acidosis (too much acid in the gut, which leads to accumulation of acid in the blood and body tissues). Fermentation digestion is greatly reduced when pH drops below 6.0. With the decreased digestion the gut draws fluid from the rest of the body. This increases the rate of movement through the tract, making manure looser and decreasing absorption of nutrients, along with creating a strong acidic odor in the manure. Corn and red milo are the most difficult grains for the horse's enzymes to break down. They also have the least fiber, and when fed in excess are most likely to cause digestive upsets, colic, or laminitis.

Processing grains by rolling, crimping, cracking, steaming, dry heating, or extruding them can help the horse break down the feed easier. This increases absorption of nutrients in the small intestine, enabling more of the grain to be digested and absorbed before it gets to the hindgut and causes problems.

Processing grain can greatly improve digestibility and feed efficiency, but it also has disadvantages. Whenever the hard outer seed coating is broken, it is more vulnerable to invasion from insects, molds, and other microorganisms. There is also more rapid breakdown of the nutrients stored within the seed. Breaking open the kernel exposes the grain to oxidation and deterioration, making it become stale faster and less palatable. Some feed companies add antioxidants and mold inhibitors to their processed grains to help combat these problems. Grains that have been processed cannot be stored as long as whole grains without losing their nutrient values and must be watched more closely for signs of mold and spoilage. Don't store processed grain for more than two weeks.

Oats weigh thirty-two to forty pounds to the bushel and are about 70 percent total digestible nutrients, with 9.4 percent digestible protein and about 11 percent crude fiber. Oats are a little less vulnerable to molds and mycotoxins than other grains. Standard varieties are also the safest grain to feed; they are about 30 percent hull, which provides bulk and fiber. Some of the other concentrates — shelled corn, wheat, or oilseed meals — are heavy feeds without much bulk. They tend to form a doughy mass in the stomach (which can cause colic), whereas oats form a loose mass that is more easily digested and move through the tract at a normal rate.

Crimping or rolling oats increases their food value because they can be even more easily chewed and digested, though most adult horses have no difficulty chewing and digesting them since oats have a relatively soft kernel. It is wise to use grain that has been steam rolled. Veterinarians recommend that all grains be heat processed in some manner to kill the organism that causes EPM.

Naked oats are a genetically altered variety with loose hulls that fall off the kernels as the grain is harvested. They are popular with horsemen who are trying to increase their horses' calories and nutrition without changing to a more energy-dense feed like corn. The use of naked oats can often make a diet of oats and grass adequate for even the hardest working horse.

A pound of naked oats has 20 to 30 percent more calories and 20 percent more total digestible nutrients per pound than conventional oats. This means that seven to eight pounds of naked oats can give a horse the energy equivalent of ten pounds of regular oats. The new variety has 50 percent more protein, with higher levels of important amino acids such as lysine and methionine, which are crucial for young, growing horses. Part of their extra energy comes from high oil content; normal oats have only about 5 percent fat while naked oats may con-

Oats.

tain 9 to 12 percent fat, providing much more digestible energy.

Naked oats complement a diet of grass hay or grass/alfalfa for the mature horse. When feeding young horses, naked oats help keep the calcium/phosphorus ratio in balance when fed with straight alfalfa. Naked oats have 30 percent more phosphorus than conventional oats to complement the extra calcium in the alfalfa. Naked oats can be used as the only concentrate source, rather than mixing grains.

Barley is heavier than oats; a bushel of barley weighs about forty-eight pounds. This grain is 78 percent digestible nutrients, with 10 percent digestible protein and about 5.9 percent crude fiber. Barley hulls provide less bulk than oat hulls. A portion of conventional oats or wheat bran is sometimes added to barley feeds to increase the bulk. Barley kernels are very hard and are best for horses if rolled or steam rolled. Ground barley should never be used for horse feed because it is too dusty and fine, becoming a doughy mass in the stomach.

Corn weighs about fifty-six pounds per bushel and is 80 percent digestible nutrients, but only 6.7 percent digestible protein and 2 percent fiber. It has no hulls and is low in bulk (unless processed with part of the cob included). Corn is rich in energy and should be fed sparingly. Large quantities may make a horse too fat or cause founder. Corn is low in protein; if fed to growing horses or pregnant mares it should be supplemented with a high protein feed. To be efficiently digested, corn usually needs to be processed by cracking (breaking the kernels) or flaking (flattening kernels with a roller). This makes it easier to digest, but also exposes the kernels to more risk of mold and mycotoxins, which can cause fatal disease if eaten. Of all the grains fed to horses, corn is most likely to develop molds if exposed to moisture.

Wheat is sometimes fed to horses when the price is low enough. Wheat should be rolled or crushed to make it easier to chew and digest. It should be fed in small amounts (usually less than 20 percent of the concentrate portion of the ration) and mixed with a bulky grain or with bran, to avoid colic. Wheat is a high-energy feed that is also high in protein. It weighs about sixty pounds to the bushel and contains 80 percent digestible nutrients. Wheat is about 11 percent protein and only 2.6 percent fiber.

Milo (sorghum grain) is fed to horses in areas where it is grown. This hard, round grain should be rolled, crushed, or steam flaked, and because it is lacking in bulk it should be mixed with bran, oats, or barley — or some other bulky feed — to avoid constipation. Milo weighs about fifty-six pounds to the bushel and is about 80 percent digestible nutrients and only 2.3 percent crude fiber. It contains about 8.5 percent digestible protein.

Molasses (a by-product of sugar refining) is often added to grain to reduce dustiness and to increase the energy content. Molasses is about 54 percent digestible nutrients. The proportion of molasses in the grain should never be more than 10 percent or it may be too laxative. Refined sugars may create muscle problems in horses that are prone to tying up.

Oilseed meals — linseed meal, soybean meal, and cottonseed meal — are by-products of extraction of oil from

Grain mixes have advantages.

seeds. They are high in protein and often added to a grain ration to increase protein content. These are very concentrated feeds and a horse should never be fed more than a pound per day.

Grain mixes are usually more expensive than buying grain in bulk to mix yourself, but many horsemen like the convenience of commercial feed mixes. Fortified grain mixes are designed to provide energy, protein, minerals, and vitamins that might be lacking in low-quality forage or to supplement the horse that needs extra nutrients for performance, growth, or reproduction. Many good products are available, but read labels carefully to find out what's in the feed, in what quantities, or you may overfeed certain nutrients, especially if you are also giving supplements or mineralized salt, which may have the same ingredients. Make sure the feed mix you use is appropriate for the horse (growing horse, idle mature horse, lactating broodmare, lightly used pleasure horse, or hard-working performance horse), and for the forage part of the diet.

Protein and mineral levels in a grain mix are usually meant to complement a certain type of forage, so together the forage and the grain mix meet all the nutrient requirements of certain horses. A 10 percent protein concentrate with a calcium-phosphorus ratio of 1:1 is a good choice for a horse on legume hay (since that hay is higher in both protein and calcium than grass hay). For a horse on grass hay, a grain mix with higher protein might be better, especially for a lactating mare or a young, growing horse. In these instances, a mix with 16 percent protein and a calcium-phosphorus ratio of 1.5:1 is more appropriate. Most commercial horse feeds are well balanced nutritionally when fed according to label directions.

Pelleted feeds are handy and easy to feed. Pelleting cereal grain can improve digestibility and increase feed efficiency, but mixed grain pellets may not hold together. Each type of grain requires a different temperature to change its starch structure, and if gelatinization does not occur, the pellets crumble apart.

Hay pellets are an economical option if hay is expensive and can be beneficial for a horse that has respiratory problems. Most pellets are not as dusty as hay. There are three types of pelleted feeds: pelleted grains, pelleted hay, and "complete" pellets that contain hay, grain, vitamins, and minerals. Hay cubes are simply hay chopped up and pressed (with an adhesive material added to help hold them together). They have the advantage of a guaranteed nutrient content; you know what the horse is getting. Hay pellets come in a variety of sizes and textures, from

Pellets are easy to feed.

soft and crumbly to very hard. There are alfalfa cubes, grass cubes, mixed-hay cubes, or hay mixed with other products such as ground corn cobs.

Grain pellets are made by grinding grain into small particles, held together with a binding material such as molasses. Grain pellets should not have a high fiber content. If the fiber is more than 8 percent, the product has too much filler. If the fiber is less than 8 percent, the level of digestible nutrients is higher and the pellet has a greater food and energy content.

Complete pellets are designed to supply all the horse's requirements. These have crude fiber levels above 12 percent (usually about 20 to 30 percent) and may use various sources of fiber — such as beet pulp, chopped hay, oat hulls, or soy hulls. It's actually best if fiber makes up at least 50 percent of the pellet to give the horse enough roughage to maintain his gut function if he is eating no other forage. Some horsemen like to feed a complete pellet in addition to hay, using the pellet as a low-energy alternative to grain.

Pellets have advantages and disadvantages. Some of the plus points are easy measuring, uniform contents, and ease of transport and storage. Pelleted feeds take up less space than hay; a ton of baled hay takes 200 to 330 cubic feet of storage space whereas a ton of hay pellets needs only sixty to seventy cubic feet. Once bagged and properly stored (in dry conditions, away from extreme heat), they keep for up to one or two years with very little loss of nutrients. Unless they get wet, pelleted feeds generally won't mold. Pellets work well with automated feeding systems because they are dry — not sticky like sweet feed mixes.

When pellets are fed, there is little waste — ingredients are nearly all utilized. Horses with bad teeth, older horses, and horses with breathing problems often do better on pellets than on hay. Most horses generally prefer hard, crunchy pellets as they help satisfy the chewing urge. Softer ones are better for toothless older horses. The harder pellets can be soaked in water if necessary for easier consumption by old horses or sick ones.

When selecting pellets for a horse that cannot tolerate dust, choose hard pellets (less crumbling) and fairly long ones. Short pellets increase the chance for dust and crumbs. Because the contents of a pellet are uniform, horses can't sort out and leave certain ingredients as they might in a grain mix, nor waste the fine leaf particles of hay. Pellets can be an advantage when trying to put weight on a horse or feed a hard-working horse more calories, since the product is already compacted and dense; you can feed a horse 20 to 30 percent more "food" in pelleted form than in hay. Since they are already ground, they are easier to digest than whole grains or hay, and they are easier to handle in cold weather than sweet feeds, which are coated with molasses and can freeze solid.

A big disadvantage to a complete pellet feed is the lack of bulk (fiber). Pellet-fed horses usually chew wood because they crave more fiber. Complete pellets do contain hay, but it is all finely ground. The horse eats less total bulk and does not feel full; lack of adequate fiber also robs him of important digestive function. Dividing the daily ration of pellets into at least four small portions rather than feeding only twice a day may help, since horses eat this type of feed very quickly (and the rate of passage through the gut is quite swift because of the ease of digestion). Most horses chew wood badly when first changed from forage to pellets. If a horse on a pellet diet suddenly finds access to pasture or hay, he may be in danger of colic or impaction because his gut capacity has decreased and cannot handle the extra bulk.

Though a complete pellet is designed to be a total replacement for hay or pasture, it's a good idea to allow a horse a little time each day at pasture, or feed him at least a half pound of forage per hundred pounds of body weight per day in addition to the pelleted ration. This reduces wood chewing and digestive problems. The only time you might want to use pellets exclusively is when forage is not available or when feeding a horse with respiratory problems that cannot tolerate hay.

Some greedy eaters are at risk of choke when eating pellets, especially if they bolt their feed. This often can be resolved by adding some chopped hay or soaked beet pulp to the feed, putting a few large, smooth rocks in the feed tub to make the horse eat more slowly, or using smaller pellets (more difficult for the horse to pick up with his lips) spread thinly over a large feed tub to make the horse work harder at eating.

Sweet Feed

Also called textured feed, sweet feed is usually a mix of grains, vitamins, and minerals. Molasses is added to bind the smaller particles to the larger ones (so they don't sift to the bottom of the feed tub) and to create a uniform taste from batch

to batch. The grains are usually rolled or cracked (or ground, in the case of milo, since it has such a hard seed coat), then mixed together in proper proportions to create the specific nutritional requirements of the product.

The mix may vary greatly from one product to another. Some "dry" sweet feeds contain only about fifty pounds of molasses per ton, while "wet" feeds may have as much as 240 pounds of molasses per ton. Protein may range from 10 percent to 18 percent, depending on the grains used. The products high in protein have less corn and oats,

Sweet feed.

and more soybeans. The high-protein mixes for young, growing horses often contain high levels of vitamins and minerals. Drier forms do not stick together as readily as the wetter ones, and some horses may sort out their favorite ingredients and leave the rest.

Supplements

A feed supplement is anything that is fed to horses besides the basics of pasture, hay, salt, and water. Technically grain is a supplement, but the term as used by most horsemen has come to refer to any additional ingredient such as preparations of vitamins, minerals, proteins, fats, energy, etc. As a general rule, a supplement should be added only when the hay/grain (or pasture) diet does not supply adequate levels of protein, certain vitamins, or other basic nutrients.

In these situations, a commercial ration-balancer product may be the only supplement needed. Some horses need more protein than they can obtain from hay or pasture, but have adequate energy. These horses don't need grain, but ration-balancer products can play a beneficial role in their diet. Most ration balancers contain protein as well as the necessary vitamins and minerals, but the protein content may vary in different products. When choosing a balancer, read labels to know how they are intended to be fed. Some are created to be fed with a grass hay while others are intended to be fed with a legume or alfalfa hay. Others contain just the basic vitamins and minerals—for horses that have adequate protein in their diet.

Protein supplements can be used if a horse needs more protein than forages provide or if good pasture or alfalfa hay is not available. Soybean, linseed, or cottonseed meal are good supplemental sources, but extra protein can come from plant or animal sources. Animal protein is usually more expensive per unit than vegetable protein. But animal protein supplements such as dried skim milk, bone meal, fish meal, or meat meal can be good sources since they provide a higher amount of lysine as well as significant amounts of calcium and phosphorus. Most vegetable sources of protein have a relatively low lysine content and more phos-

phorus than calcium (and can disrupt proper calcium-phosphorus ratio in the diet). Soybean meal is usually an economical protein source with more lysine than other oil-seed meals.

Feeding fat as a supplement has become a common practice for horses that need more total energy, especially those in stressful athletic careers, older horses, or broodmares. Adding fat to the diet can safely increase the total energy content, providing 2.25 times as much energy as an equal weight of carbohydrates such as grain, and can thus reduce the amount of grain needed, reducing the risks for founder and digestive problems.

Supplements are popular.

The horse's body must adjust to this energy source and adapt to using it, and this may take several weeks. For best results, add fat gradually during a horse's fitness training.

Supplemental fat can create a shinier hair coat and put weight on thin horses. Older horses can be kept in better body condition, especially if they have bad teeth or reduced digestive efficiency. Fat supplements can help a broodmare that has trouble keeping her weight during the stress of lactation.

Fat can be fed as vegetable oil (corn and soy oil are often used), poured over the grain ration, or as a feed additive such as rice bran (which is relatively high in fat, available as a powder or in pellet form). The rice bran may keep better in a hot climate; oils and animal fats become rancid if they become too warm or have exposure to sunlight. For young horses, extruded soybeans can be a good product, since they are high in both fat and protein.

Some commercial feed mixes have fats added, and often contain anti-oxidants to minimize spoilage. If your horse does not like oil or rice bran on his grain, a commercial fat-supplemented feed (in which the fat is better disguised and hence more palatable to the fussy eater) might be easier. Choose a feed that has the proper protein level for the type of horse you are feeding.

Vitamin supplements are often given to breeding stock, young horses, and performance horses, but a person should carefully analyze the basic feeding program (pasture, hay, pellets, commercial grain mixes) first to see if the horse really needs supplemental vitamins in addition to the basic ration. Consult your veterinarian or an equine nutritionist.

Mineral supplements can be the most dangerous when overdone. Some horsemen worry that modern farming practices (chemical fertilizers and high production per acre) have put heavy demands on soil and that many feeds are mineral deficient. However, analysis of hay and grain grown on most soils has not shown enough change that would cause deficiency in the horse's diet. Supplements are usually necessary only in regions where the soil has no natural iodine or selenium. Overdose of either of these trace minerals is toxic, so check with your veterinarian or agricultural agent before you add mineral supplements.

Iron is another trace mineral that is often over-supplemented. Toxicity from misuse of iron supplements is much more harmful than iron deficiency, and deficiency is very rare. Injectable iron carries the risk of anaphylactic shock. Don't supplement iron unless a veterinarian diagnoses a true deficiency in a horse, along with laboratory analysis of the feed and water. Horsemen who feed or inject vitamin or mineral supplements without knowing if these are actually needed can cause serious harm or even kill the horse. Injectable supplements are especially dangerous and should never be used unless a horse has been clinically determined to need them.

Older horses, especially older broodmares that have the added stress of pregnancy and lactation, may need supplements to keep from becoming thin or deficient because their digestive systems may not be as efficient as that of a younger horse. Older broodmares may have placental insufficiency, needing more supplementation just to get adequate nutrients to the fetus. Hard-working horses sometimes benefit from supplements, but supplementation must be done on an individual basis.

Be careful when adding supplements to a commercial feed mix (as some horsemen do to try to increase growth or performance). Adding a protein supplement (for a lactating mare or growing horse) may unbalance the dietary amounts of minerals if the supplement also supplies certain vitamins and minerals, as many do. Adding oats also can unbalance the calcium-phosphorus ratio. Some horsemen add oats to try to reduce the overall energy level of a grain mix and add more fiber, but it's usually better to just feed less of the grain mix and add more hay. Another alternative would be to add a different high-fiber feed such as alfalfa meal if you want to increase the fiber content of the diet for a horse on restricted forage. Alfalfa meal reduces the energy density of a grain mix while maintaining the proper mineral balance, moreso than the addition of oats, since the alfalfa has more calcium than oats.

Check contents of all commercial feeds and supplements you use. If a product exceeds recommended daily amounts of vitamins or minerals (as most supplements do), law requires that the specific ingredients be itemized by amount. If you check the labels, you will be able to tell if you are doubling up too many nutrients and possibly creating problems for your horse.

New types of supplements have come on the market in recent years. Several feed companies cater to performance horses with a highly palatable product containing oils, fatty acids, vitamins, and minerals in a mix that is easily digested and converted to energy. Some supplements also contain yeast culture, which provides lysine when digested. These supplements are aimed at horses that are stressed.

Yeast is used by some horsemen to increase digestibility of feeds and stabilize fermentation in the hindgut, particularly in horses prone to colic or laminitis. Yeast improves the utiliza-

Older mares might need supplements.

tion of feed, enhances palatability (encouraging the fussy eater to eat more), aids in absorption of vitamins and minerals, improves condition of hooves and hair coat, and boosts growth rate.

Some yeast preparations are a strain of live yeast culture, but the regular "brewer's yeast" sold in grocery stores for making bread will also work and is an inexpensive and readily available supplement that provides a natural source of B complex vitamins. Either type of yeast added to the horse's diet daily seems to increase the efficiency of fiber digestion and the absorption of phosphorus, possibly through stimulation of certain bacteria in the cecum and colon. The yeast passes through the stomach and becomes active in the hindgut, where fermentation takes place.

Another group of feed additives is the probiotics, which contain live bacteria that help break down certain feeds. The bacteria used in equine probiotics are generally the lactic acid fermenters *Lactobacilli* that work on starch and soluble sugars rather than those needed for fermentation of plant cell walls (and therefore the probiotics do not improve fiber digestibility). Probiotics are most often used in foals with diarrhea to lower the pH of the gut to a point where the harmful, infection-causing bacteria cannot survive. Other probiotics are sometimes used in adult horses that have had their normal microbe colony disrupted due to illness and extensive antibiotic treatment.

Flaxseed and flaxseed oil are rich sources of essential fatty acids, which are thought to help prevent laminitis due to excessive grain consumption. The unsaturated fatty acids found in flaxseed oil (especially omega-3) are essential nutrients; they cannot be manufactured by the horse and can only be obtained by eating certain types of feed. A natural diet of fresh grass contains very adequate amounts of essential fatty acids, but a horse being fed cured hay (especially older hay) and processed feeds may not get enough. A horse needs a higher proportion of omega-3 (Alpha-linolenic acid) than omega-6 (linoleic acid), or he may develop muscle problems, arthritis, or laminitis.

A horse on a high corn diet (high in omega-6) becomes more susceptible to laminitis. Supplemental sources of essential fatty acids, such as flaxseed oil, making a diet rich in omega-3, can drastically reduce a horse's production of some of the potent inflammatory and blood vessel constricting mediators that are thought to be involved in laminitis.

However, omega-3 is extremely fragile and oxidizes if exposed to light or heat. Oxidation changes the chemical structure of the essential fatty acid into toxic derivatives called lipid peroxides. If you use flaxseed oil as a supplement, make sure it is fresh and that it has not been altered with a heating process that damages the oil. A flaxseed oil supplement should be kept frozen or covered with an antioxidant and kept out of the light and heat. Tasting the oil can tell you if it's fresh; if it has been damaged, it will be bitter and rancid. The more bitter it is, the more lipid peroxide it contains.

Flax can be fed as meal rather than as oil. Feeding a pound of flaxseed daily is the equivalent of a half pound of oil. A pound of flaxseed meal can cut two pounds of corn from a horse's diet. The energy value of flaxseed is twice that of corn.

A number of feed supplements called nutraceuticals are popular with horsemen. These fall into a category of their own, being not quite nutrients and not quite drugs but something in between. Sprinkled on feed or given orally as pills or paste, nutraceuticals are being used to treat a wide assortment of disorders.

Glycosaminoglycan (GAG) is a natural joint lubricant used in granular form as a feed additive or as an intramuscular injection to help the body repair normal cartilage wear and tear in joints and prevent inflammation in connective tissue disease. Chondroitin sulfate (a component of cartilage, skin, vertebral discs, and other body tissues) belongs to the GAG family and is thought to keep cartilage spongy and healthy by attracting fluid. Injectable forms of synthetic GAGs have been used for years to treat joint disease, and more recently oral products have come into use as feed additives. Studies have shown that they help relieve inflammation associated with arthritis and slow the degenerative process.

Glucosamine is one of the building blocks for chondroitin sulfate and is part of the chemical that gives synovial fluid (joint lubricant) its resilience and provides nourishment for the joint surfaces Hailed as a wonder drug, glucosamine is being used by an increasing number of horsemen as a natural alternative to steroids and nonsteroidal anti-inflammatory drugs (NSAIDs) in treating degenerative joint disease. It is commercially formulated as a salt — a white powder that resembles non-dairy coffee creamer.

Dimethyl glycine (DMG) is a compound found in seeds and nuts, and seems to help some equine athletes increase work output while recovering faster; it also improves appetite and seems to reduce lactic acid levels.

Methylsulfonyl methane (MSM) is an organic compound derived from DMSO (dimethyl sulfoxide, a topical anti-inflammatory agent). Some horsemen use it as a supplement to prevent muscle soreness, as an aid in better hoof growth, and for many other conditions. It is a dietary source of sulfur (necessary for formation of connective tissue) and also seems to have some antioxidant properties. Some horsemen feel it is helpful for horses with heaves. It also seems to help mares with unhealthy uterine lining.

New Discoveries

Research in the early 1990s identified a possible essential nutrient for performance horses — a little known trace mineral called chromium. Though it has been recognized for a number of years as an essential nutrient for humans (in tiny amounts), its function for horses is still being studied. At present chromium's only known role is as a component of glucose tolerance factor, which makes possible (and increases) the action of insulin. Insulin helps direct the flow of nutrients to various tissues in the horse's body, aiding the uptake of glucose and amino acids.

Equine nutritionists and researchers continue to study whether certain dietary elements or factors (changes in feed, various feed programs, or supplements) improve performance. Many research trials are being done to evaluate the effect that different feeds and supplements have on performance horses, growing horses, and reproduction. Now and then an ingredient like supplemental fat or yeast culture is found to produce a consistently beneficial response.

Feeding the Problem Horse

Some horses present special challenges, such as being too thin, too fat, or sick. Some horses are finicky and are hard to keep weight on, especially when working. The first option is to increase the feed's energy density by adding grain or fat to the diet. Weight loss in spite of plentiful feed may be a sign the horse is being overconditioned.

Increasing good roughage or adding nutrient-rich legume hay can usually help the thin, idle horse or one doing moderate work. A hard-working horse, however, will not tolerate the extra protein some feeds (such as alfalfa) provide, with heat produced during digestion. A better choice might be rehydrated beet pulp, with its highly digestible fiber, low protein, low vitamin-mineral content (unlikely to upset the diet's mineral balance), and palatability. Unlike grain, it is safe to feed in relatively large quantities and can be added to a grain ration to give greater digestibility. For horses that just pick at hay, beet pulp often can be a good substitute for part of it.

The hard-working horse cannot eat enough roughage to supply his needs, particularly if he is finicky, tired, or dehydrated. If a horse won't eat enough hay, he can usually be tempted with something more lush and palatable, such as fresh green grass, or rehydrated beet pulp. A tired, dehydrated horse often will eat green grass when he won't touch anything else. You can also soak a flake of hay in water.

The fat horse needs fewer calories and/or more work. When cutting down his nutrients, however, don't cut down the total amount of feed or he will look for something else to chew on. Cut down the quality of his ration rather than the quantity. A mature thousand-pound horse still needs about twenty pounds of feed to meet his dry matter requirements, and if you cut him back to fifteen pounds he will start eating the fences or bedding. Feed him clean grass hay (no grain), cut mature enough to be low in nutrients.

Keeping on weight can be hard.

The sick or injured horse needs special care in feeding because nutrition plays an important role in recovery. If he was fit and active before his injury or illness, he may need his total ration reduced as he can't use as many calories in his inactivity. Keep in mind, however, that illness may make other demands on his body. Pain, fever, and infection all increase his metabolic rate and his need for energy and protein. A horse that is fighting infection needs extra protein. The immune system needs amino acids to create antibodies and other infection-fighting cells.

A shivering horse needs more calories to help generate body heat. The best way to help him is to increase protein — with its increased heat of digestion. In a sick horse, the body's metabolic rate (the speed at which energy and nutrients are burned) may increase up to three times the normal rate. If he is not eating enough (which is often the case if he doesn't feel well),

Fat horses need more work.

he will lose weight. A well-fleshed idle horse usually has enough body reserves to get him through a mild illness, but a fit, athletic horse may have very little fat to spare when illness or injury decreases his appetite.

The sick or injured horse should always have access to salt and water. He may not drink enough, so be sure his water is always clean and fresh and at acceptable temperature (cool, but not cold, in summer; warm, but not hot, in winter). Water him in a bucket or tub so you can monitor how much he actually drinks.

Make sure feed is palatable and of high nutrient quality if he has poor appetite. His illness may dictate what is best to feed. A horse with a respiratory problem irritated by dusty feed should have his hay soaked in water or be fed pellets or special feed for horses with heaves. A horse with a small intestine disorder (reduced ability to digest grain) should be fed a nutritious fiber diet with little or no grain. A horse with a large intestine disorder (less ability to digest and absorb protein and

A hard-working horse needs fuel.

roughage, and phosphorus) will do better on alfalfa or pellets and additional grain. A horse with gastric ulcers should be fed fine grass hay and no grain; the latter tends to irritate the stomach lining and causes wider swings in gastric activity, which can accentuate an ulcer. A horse with diarrhea should generally be fed grass hay and no grain.

A horse whose digestive capacity has been diminished (by parasites, antibiotic therapy, or some other situation that has reduced the population of beneficial microbes) may benefit from yeast supplementation and vitamin B complex or other micronutrients to help restore proper gut function. Horses that don't eat enough for an extended time may have difficulty extracting the necessary nutrients from feed and could benefit from supplements that supply an increase in nutrients or feeds that have been processed to enhance digestibility. If a sick horse refuses to eat, tempt him with lush green grass or something he really likes in small frequent meals. If he refuses feed because you have put medication in it, take that feed away and give him some without medicine.

Spoiled Feed and Food Poisoning

Evaluating feed quality is an important responsibility. Spoiled or moldy feeds can be deadly to horses. Fungi, molds, or bacteria can contaminate hay or grain while it is growing, or during harvest or storage. The problem's severity may be influenced by weather conditions during the growing season or by exposure to moisture during or after harvest. The same kind of hay or grain may be fed for years — grown, processed, and stored the same way each year — and then suddenly a horse will be poisoned as a result of some unusual weather factor that allows harmful organisms to flourish.

Some types of mold are harmless when eaten, but others are highly toxic. Many strains of *Aspergillus* produce aflatoxins, which cause cancer of the liver in the animals or humans that eat them. Other strains of *Aspergillus* produce toxins that are rapidly fatal ("moldy corn disease") with symptoms that may be mistaken for encephalomyelitis (sleeping sickness) since the brain is affected.

Corn is usually a good feed for horses, but only high-quality, disease-free corn should be fed, with moisture content below 15 percent. Corn should be stored where it cannot draw moisture. Condensation inside a metal grain bin can be a problem unless the old grain is always cleaned out before a new batch is put in. With shelled corn, bad kernels sometimes get mixed with good corn. Usually only a small percentage of kernels in a moldy batch contain high levels of toxin. This is the reason some horses may develop fatal poisoning even though others fed the same feed are unaffected. It takes only a few kernels of bad corn to produce problems if a horse eats them. Corn that has not been adequately dried in the field or in a drier after harvest may spoil and mold when stored. Some of the visible molds are not as deadly as the aflatoxins that can develop on corn during a wet growing season.

Another problem that sometimes occurs on grains and grasses while growing is a fungus called ergot. Plants susceptible include wheat, rye, barley, bluegrass, red top, brome, and reed canarygrass. Eating small amounts of ergot daily can lead to circulation problems, especially in extremities; blood vessels constrict and shut off blood supply to feet, ears, and tail, causing tissue death. The horse may lose ear tips or develop gangrene in the feet and legs, causing death. If horses are removed from the offending pasture or feeds in the early stages of poisoning, they usually recover, if the tissue damage has not been too great.

Other fungi such as rusts and smut may contaminate grain or pastures. Rusts infect leaves and stalks of grasses in reddish-brown patches. Smuts look like black, powdery clumps replacing the grass heads or grains. Eating smutty grain may cause convulsions, paralysis, and death. Rusts and smut also can cause colic.

Clovers and other legumes sometimes develop an irritating and toxic fungus, *Rhizoctonia leguminicola* ("black patch disease"), which spots the stems and leaves and causes chemical changes in the plant. Red clover, alsike, white clover, soybeans, and alfalfa are legumes most commonly affected. The fungus can survive winter conditions (living at least two years on infected seeds) and persist in a field or pasture once established. The fungus produces toxic alkaloids that irritate the horse's salivary glands, causing slobbering. The alkaloids can cause malformation of a fetus or abortion, diarrhea, frequent urination, weight loss, or even death, depending on how much is eaten.

Fungal toxins, called mycotoxins, can be very deadly, damaging liver and kidneys, destroying red blood cells, or producing other serious effects. Abnormal weather conditions may promote fungal growth on pastures or hay crops. A storm in late summer or early fall, followed by cool weather, may produce an ideal environment for fungi to flourish. Mowed hay that gets rained on before it is baled may create the right conditions for molds or fungi.

Another hazard that can lurk in feed is botulism, a potent and lethal toxin produced by *Clostridium botulinum*, a bacteria that thrives in the absence of oxygen and produces spores that are very hardy. Toxins produced by these bacteria are responsible for many mysterious deaths every year. Like other clostridia (tetanus, malignant edema, etc.) botulism lurks nearly everywhere, especially where there is rotting organic matter such as old bedding, spoiled hay, or dead animals.

The most common source of botulism is spoiled feed, and this can be difficult to detect. The bacteria may not change the smell, taste, or appearance of feed. Carcasses of dead mice, birds, cats, snakes, etc. in feed or bedding may be the source of contamination. It is common for small animals to be killed by the mowing machine or baler, ending up in the hay. The toxins that build up in the carcasses may then spread to surrounding hay, sometimes reaching such a high concentration that it may take less than a quarter pound of hay to kill a horse. If you find a dead animal in feed, discard all feed surrounding it. If hay or grain smells sour or rotten, organisms are present that grow in the absence of oxygen.

The best way to avoid food poisoning is to select feeds carefully and always be sure what your horse is eating. Make sure feeds are properly harvested and stored. Always check for unusual odor, appearance, or texture, and discard suspicious feed in a place where horses won't have access to it. Keep feed tubs and water tubs clean. Keep grain and watering areas widely separated. Grain or hay in water can ferment and produce harmful microbe growth. Never leave uneaten feed in a bucket or tub more than a day. Even the moisture from the horse's mouth may be enough to promote growth of mold or other fungi.

Monensin poisoning is another problem that can quickly kill a horse, if he is fed a livestock or poultry feed containing this drug. Monensin (trade name Rumensin®) is often added to livestock rations to improve feed efficiency, or to poultry feed to help prevent coccidiosis, a disease caused by certain protozoa. It is fatal when eaten by horses, however, causing muscle damage and heart failure. Signs of monensin poisoning in the horse include rapid heartbeat, weak and irregular pulse, blue mucous membranes, and abnormal lung sounds.

Horses eating pellets or feed supplements put out for cattle, or eating commercial feeds contaminated with even a small amount of this drug, have died. It only takes a few crumbs of contaminated feed to kill a horse. Horses that survive may suffer permanent heart damage. Public awareness has reduced the frequency with which monensin poisoning occurs, but a few tragedies still happen. To be safe, buy feeds made specifically for horses, and purchase from a feed mill that does not also process cattle or poultry feeds. If a feed label ever states "For Ruminant Animals Only," never feed the bag's contents to horses.

Be observant when feeding. In a typical poisoning situation, problems generally start when the horses are fed a new batch of feed. Watch to see if they eat it willingly. A fussy horse may detect something different about the feed. Horses may at first refuse the new feed, eat it reluctantly, or only after they become hungry. The best thing to do if horses are hesitant is to take away the new feed at first hint of refusal. It's always a good idea to introduce a new batch of feed before you run out of the old, so you have an alternate feed if your horses ever "turn up their noses" at the new feed. If there is any question about a new batch of feed, return the unused portion to the supplier. It's not worth taking a chance.

6

Foot Care and
Hoof Health

ONE OF THE MOST IMPORTANT aspects of caring for a horse is regular hoof care. In the wild, a horse wears down his feet at nearly the same rate they grow. His feet never become too long or worn down to the quick unless he has to travel excessively to find feed or water. The domestic horse, however, is often shod (eliminating hoof wear) or kept in a small pen or pasture with soft footing, where feet do not wear normally. In these situations the horse owner must make sure the feet are properly trimmed (or shod) and not subjected to cracking or breaking.

Foot Facts

The domesticated horse was brought from grasslands to hard roads; from light exercise to hard work; from healthy, clean rangeland to confined housing or small, sometimes muddy pens. Feet may grow long from lack of exercise or they may need shoeing to prevent excessive wear while being worked. Long feet can make a horse lame or put limbs out of balance due to uneven wear on split or broken hoof walls (causing strained joints, crooked legs, or a crippled horse). If feet wear too much from excessive use, the horse loses the protective outer covering of the hoof and becomes lame from walking on the sensitive tissues of the foot.

A regularly ridden horse often needs protection for his feet as he may travel more than a wild horse. Humans discovered this almost as soon as they started using the horse for their own purposes. Thousands of years ago, humans devised ways to protect their horses' feet, using everything from socks to sandals. Nailing iron shoes to the hoof was not tried until the second century B.C. and did not become common practice until the end of the fifth century A.D. Shoeing as we know it came into regular use by the Middle Ages. It hasn't changed much until recently. New materials and modern science have given us more knowledge about hoof health and new techniques for dealing with hoof problems. This learning process is ongoing.

Horses are individuals. The feet of each horse have their own shape, hardness, and rate of hoof growth. Breed and climate account for some differences. Draft horses have relatively flat feet; their ancestors evolved in moist, marshy conditions of northern Europe. A large, flat hoof enabled the big horse to travel over boggy ground without sinking. Concussion was not a big factor on soft ground, so it didn't matter if the hoof was flat. The Arabian, by contrast, lived in dry desert country, where a hoof needed to be smaller, blockier, and tougher, with a concave sole, to prevent bruising and for more flex to allow for greater concussion. A concave sole has more give as it can flatten as it hits the ground and then spring back into place when picked up. Arabians (of traditional breeding) rarely have flat feet or shallow heels.

Non-pigmented hooves tend to be less resilient than pigmented ones; some horses with white feet have more problems. Hooves are softer when wet, more brittle when dry, and thus more prone to chipping and cracking. White feet usually wear faster than pigmented ones. The unpigmented hoof horn, like unpigmented skin, may not be as tough or resistant to the effects of sunshine and drying.

As a general rule, when a horse has both pigmented feet and white feet, the white ones tend to be less resilient. When the horse is barefoot, the white feet may chip, crack, break, or spread more readily than the dark ones.

Anatomy of the Foot

The hoof is a specialized horny shell that covers sensitive inner tissues. This hoof wall grows continually (from the corium of the coronary band at the hairline) to make up for normal wear and broken edges. The hoof wall itself is made up of tiny, hollow tubules (like drinking straws) bundled tightly together, running from the coronary band to the ground surface of the foot. These tubules have no nerve endings or blood supply. On the inside of the hoof, these tubules interface with the sensitive laminae that carry blood and nerve endings.

The foot's tough, outer covering consists of hoof wall, sole, frog, and bars. The outer part of the wall is keratinized to form a hard shell. When you look at the bottom of the foot, the bars are seen as an inward continuation of the hoof wall, serving as a brace to keep the heels from contracting. The V-shaped frog serves as a cushion in the middle of the hoof; it helps absorb concussion and also acts as a regulator for hoof moisture.

The junction where sole and hoof wall meet is called the white line and is very obvious on a freshly trimmed foot. This line is yellowish at the sole edge, whiter toward the hoof wall edge, and is usually of uniform width. A thick white line indicates a hoof with density and strength, whereas a thin one (especially if it has points of separation or tendency to flake apart) may indicate a structural weakness.

The horny tissue outside the white line is insensitive hoof wall and everything inside it is "alive." Between ground surface and coronary band, this white line area is where the insensitive laminae (tubular "fingers") from the bloodless, nerveless hoof wall meet and interlock with sensitive laminae from the living tissues inside the hoof. The area at the bottom where they meet (white line) has some elasticity, to create a link between the solid hoof wall and the softer sole, facilitating expansion and contraction of the rear parts of the foot.

The hoof wall carries most of the weight when the foot is on the ground (especially when the horse is shod), and the bars serve as a brace to prevent over-expansion and contraction of the foot. The sole is somewhat concave to give grip and allow for expansion when weight is placed on the foot. Front feet are usually rounder, larger, and stronger than hind feet because the front legs support nearly two-thirds of the horse's weight and experience more concussion and wear.

Conformation

Hoof conformation is a big factor in whether the foot will hold up under long, heavy use. Feet should be well-shaped and proportionate to the size of the horse. He needs enough hoof to support his weight, but not so much he'll be clumsy. If his feet are too small for his body structure, he will not hold up under strenuous use; the increased shock of concussion in the small hoof area can lead to navicular syndrome, which results from too much trauma and stress on the navicular bone and/or bursa, laminitis, or joint problems in the leg caused by excessive concussion. A large, heavy horse needs feet of adequate size and strength to carry the extra weight during strenuous activity while a smaller horse needs smaller feet or he loses agility.

Hooves should be wide at the heels to "give" and spring farther apart when the foot hits the ground; this helps absorb concussion. Otherwise, the jarring would be transmitted directly to the bones of the foot, leg, and joints. A foot should be fairly deep at the heel, not shallow and close to the ground. A strong, deep heel is less apt to bruise and also tends to have stronger bars. Bars of the foot help take additional weight upon the heels and act as wedges to keep the foot strong and resilient.

The sole should be almost round, with a healthy frog, good strong bars, and definite grooves (sulci) on each side of the frog. Soles should be slightly concave in the front feet and more concave in hinds. Flat feet are a detriment since the soles bruise more easily. The frog should be centered in the sole with the point of the frog pointing to the toe of the foot.

The wall grows a quarter to three-eighths of an inch per month; the entire hoof wall can be replaced by new horn every eight to ten months, though some individuals have slower or faster rates of hoof growth. If a horse is shod, his shoes need to be reset or replaced every three to ten weeks (six weeks is an average), depending on the rate of hoof growth.

If a horse has good conformation, his feet usually wear evenly because the foot breaks over squarely at the center of the toe; he won't wear one side of the foot or toe more than the other. A horse with crooked legs usually has feet that are unbalanced and wear crookedly; one side of the foot will be a different shape than the other and the frog will usually be pointed off center.

Hoof Growth

The hoof wall grows downward from the coronary band; any injury to the coronary band affects hoof growth in that area. The normal hoof wall is smooth, with no rings or ridges. Rings and ripples indicate patterns of uneven growth and may mean the horse experienced illness, nutritional stress, or some other stress while that part of the hoof wall was forming. A single ring on all four feet at the same location may be the aftereffect of an illness. Ripples may indicate a mild case of laminitis. Some rings can be caused by seasonal variations of hoof growth (warm weather and green grass tend to make a hoof grow faster), dietary changes, or a fever that temporarily altered hoof growth.

The horny sole continually grows downward from the sensitive inner sole; little cracks develop in the old sole and help it flake away — the outer layer is dead tissue. This self-trimming process is called exfoliation. A horse's sole generally needs no trimming. Trimming it may expose sensitive tissues. Occasionally, however, the dead material on the sole builds up (especially if the horse is kept in wet conditions where the sole never dries out). The dead sole must be carefully peeled away with a hoof knife to the proper level. Otherwise the foot wall cannot be trimmed adequately and the layer of dead sole may continue to build up and provide a place for bacteria to grow.

The Frog

The open heels and wedge-shaped frog allow the hoof to expand and contract as weight is placed on it and then released, and also provide more traction for the ground surface of the foot. The frog is the softest part of the hoof, made up of the same fibrous material as the rest of the external hoof except that the frog contains oil glands, making it more rubbery, and it usually contains more water. The frog is 50 percent water, by weight. It generally becomes smaller and more shriveled during dry summers.

Horses that live in soft, wet pastures tend to have bigger, softer frogs than horses traveling dry, rocky desert terrain. Wet footing tends to make a hoof expand and flatten out, and the frog is always in contact with the ground since the foot sinks into the soft ground. A horse living in dry country develops harder and more upright hoof walls, pulling the frog off the ground, out of the way of sharp rocks. A soft, flat foot would wear away too quickly and also stone bruise in dry, rocky terrain.

The "pancake" feet of draft horses kept these large animals from sinking into soft ground, spreading the weight over a larger area; these horses have large frogs that have complete contact with the ground. The opposite extreme is the desert animal (donkey or burro) with a narrow, upright, contracted foot and a frog so high it never hits the ground. Some zebras have no frog at all. Most riding horses are between these two extremes, with feet and frogs that can adapt to different conditions.

The Natural Foot

The art and science of shoeing have progressed in fits and starts since the first innovative horseman nailed shoes to the equine foot. As farriers learned more about hoof anatomy and ways to attach a shoe without crippling or hindering the horse, shoeing became the norm. Farriery has come a long way from its infancy in the Middle Ages and has contributed much in the challenge of keeping hard-working horses sound. There is still a lot to learn, however, and during the 1980s and '90s, some farriers began to take a more scrutinizing look at the natural foot of the wild horse to help fine-tune their ideas and techniques for creating a healthier shod foot.

One of the most interesting findings was that the hoof wall of the wild horse makes only four points of contact with a flat surface — at each heel and at each side of the toe — for a square support pattern. The toe itself is dubbed off, and the wall at the quarters is generally gone (this is the weakest part of the hoof wall on any hoof — wild or domestic). Since the hoof wall is usually worn away except at the heels and at each side of the toe, the sole and frog may bear part of the weight if the hoof is packed with dirt. By contrast, the shod horse carries more weight on the hoof wall and laminae, even though the frog and sole are better suited for weight bearing.

With the toe dubbed off, a wild horse's hoof has a relatively consistent breakover point about one to one and a half inches in front of the tip of the frog — the actual length depending on the size of the horse and his hooves. The shod domestic horse generally has a much longer toe, with the breakover point being two inches or more from the tip of the frog. This creates a different hoof angle and also forces the foot to land flat or toe first instead of heel first. The heel is where the fatty and more resilient tissues are, such as the digital cushion, the foot cartilage, and frog. Many domestic horses land flat-footed rather than on the heel, creating more shock and trauma for the navicular bone, tendons, and coffin joints. These tissues are not very well designed for shock absorption and can be damaged by excessive concussion.

A wild horse tends to wear off his toe and has a much shorter toe than most domestic horses. The hoof at the toe on a wild horse is rarely more than three inches in length (distance from coronary band to ground surface), whereas the domestic horse of same body weight and hoof size often has a toe length of three and a half inches or more, creating a different foot angle and forcing the point of hoof breakover farther forward. This creates a different type of foot flight, landing flat-footed or sometimes even on the toe — a very unnatural and potentially damaging situation.

Four-Point Trim

Some farriers now use the "four-point trim" to simulate the natural hoof wear of the wild horse's foot. This trimming involves shortening the toe so the hoof is more naturally shaped — a bit more square and blocky, without such a long toe, which gives many horses more support to the leg and not so much strain on the tendons.

When a problem foot is first trimmed this way, it looks vastly different from the symmetrical, circular foot that farriery has considered ideal, but over time it attains a structural integrity that enables it to maintain itself at or near ideal shape without having to continue the four-point trim. Often the quickest and most

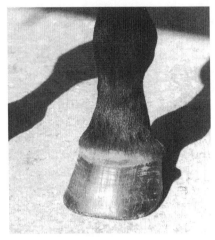

A four-point trim.

effective way to correct some problem feet is to let a horse go barefoot on dry ground in the four-point trim for a few months. Putting the hoof at a more natural angle allows the foot to remodel itself if it has become unbalanced from improper trimming or shoeing, and it can often become healthier in the process, with its structures working more as nature intended.

Foot Care

If horses are confined, the most important aspect of hoof care is regular cleaning and inspection. The feet should be cleaned daily if possible and always before riding. You can remove mud or manure that may otherwise stay packed in the foot and lead to thrush or any rocks that might be stuck in the feet.

If you handle the feet often, you will know when they need to be trimmed or shod again. You will notice any chips or cracks in an unshod foot or pink spots in the sole from bruising. You will be able to see the beginnings of any wall separations. As you handle legs and feet, you also will likely notice any heat in the leg or hoof or swelling in the lower leg, which could indicate injury or infection.

Cleaning the Feet

A hoof pick is the best instrument for cleaning the hoof, though you also can use the blunt edge of a hoof knife to get all the dirt out. Never use a sharp or pointed instrument for cleaning the foot; you might injure yourself or the horse if he jerks his foot. Use a blunt instrument when cleaning dirt or muck out of the cleft between frog and sole because anything sharp can injure sensitive tissues beneath the cleft, especially back toward the heel where soft tissues are closer to the surface. If you clean the clefts from heel to toe, you're less likely to poke too hard into the heel area than if cleaning them from toe to heel.

Any dead tissue along the sole can be removed with a hoof knife. If the horse's foot is healthy, the frog probably needs no other trimming than just smoothing it up and getting rid of loose tatters. An overgrown frog that is shedding might need more trimming. Most horses shed the frog a couple of times during the year.

Sometimes the old part is still hanging there or sticking out the back of the foot while attached at the heel area. If this happens it should be carefully trimmed away with the hoof knife or cut away with hoof cutters. Otherwise the shedding portion may become dried out and stiff, sometimes curling up and poking the skin above the back of the heel. As the frog is shed, new healthy tissue grows underneath it to replace it, but this takes a little time. For a while the hoof may look like it has no frog until the new one grows in.

If a horse is barefoot and there's a chip in the hoof wall, it can be smoothed with a rasp (or hoof nippers and rasp if necessary) so it won't break more or create a crack. If the horse travels on rocky ground, the frog should be trimmed a bit if it's quite large to prevent excessive contact with sharp rocks. A thrushy frog (which can occur in wet, muddy conditions) may have to be trimmed to get rid of the pockets of infection and get down to healthy frog tissue. If the frog is undermined and rotten with thrush, all abnormal portions should be trimmed away so the area can be treated, to eliminate the thrush infection. Thrush is a type of hoof rot, characterized by black necrotic (dead) tissue in affected areas.

Trimming and Shoeing

Even if you never do your own shoeing or trimming, it's good to learn as much as you can about your horse's feet so you will know whether a farrier is doing a good job. You should be familiar with how your horse travels. Do his feet move forward in relatively straight lines, wing inward, or paddle outward? Notice the point at which a foot breaks over and leaves the ground and whether the breakover point is at the center of the toe or off to one side.

Look at the bottom of the horse's feet or his old shoes. Uneven wear shows that the horse is not traveling straight but is breaking over and landing crookedly. A horse that travels straight on sound feet and legs will wear his feet (or shoes) evenly, with slightly more wear at the center of the toe. You will be able to tell if the old shoe fit properly or not; if it wasn't wide enough to allow for hoof expansion, the hoof wall at heel and quarters will start to grow down around the shoe. This can sometimes happen even in a well-fitted shoe if the shoes were left on too long.

When you look at the shoe after removal, the properly fit shoe will have developed grooves at the heel (on the

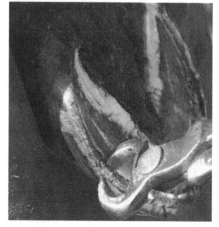

Nippers remove excess growth.

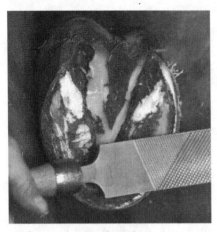

A rasp smooths the edges.

side that was next to the foot) where constant expansion and contraction of the hoof have worn a little of the shoe away. If the hoof side of a used shoe is as smooth as new at the heel areas, then the heel was probably "nail-bound" to the shoe, could not expand and contract, and was pinched every time the horse put weight on that foot.

The old shoe can give you clues about how the horse should be shod or better ways to shoe him. Thin or worn spots in the old shoe are evidence of some type of imbalance that caused the horse to put more weight on that area of the foot, such as landing on the inside or outside branch or breaking over one side of the toe instead of the center. An off-center wear spot means the horse's foot is not facing forward but toeing in (if the wear spot is to the outside of the toe) or toeing out (if the wear is on the inside).

Compare right and left shoes (front and hind feet) and also front and back shoes on the same side. Differences in shoe wear between right and left indicate unequal use, either from an uneven gait (possibly an indication of a subtle lameness that can make a horse use the lame and sound leg differently) or a one-sided rider. Always posting on the same diagonal at the trot, for instance, may cause a horse to use his legs unevenly. A sound, properly shod horse travels symmetrically and wears the feet or shoes evenly unless improper riding hinders his gait.

A rasp takes back the toe.

When he's standing squarely, the slope of the foot and pastern should be the same. The most commonly measured aspect of foot balance is toe angle, the angle between the ground surface and the slope of the foot and pastern. Long ago, someone decided forty-five degrees was the proper angle for front feet and fifty-five degrees for the hind feet. This "ideal" angle has been touted in books on conformation and shoeing for more than two centuries but is not correct for most horses.

Such a foot is too sloping for many horses, creating too long a toe, excessive weight on the heels, and stress on the deep flexor tendon (and hence the navicular bone). Rather than try for a mythical ideal angle, each horse's feet should be balanced to fit his own conformation. There is no ideal foot or foot angle; the angle must be correct for that specific individual.

Some horses have more upright feet and pasterns than other horses, but the feet should be trimmed so that the pastern and hoof form an unbroken line, whatever the angle is for that horse. If toes are left too long, the angle will be broken, putting strain on the tendons and other parts of the leg. If the heel is too long, the line will be broken the other direction. Study the foot when the horse is standing squarely to judge how much hoof must be trimmed to make the foot level at its proper angle. The hind foot will be a little steeper than the front.

Worn areas on old shoes.

When viewed from the side, the heels should have the same slope as the front of the foot; the hoof wall at the toe has the same angle with the ground as the hoof wall at the heel. If the heels are more upright than the toe, the horse has a clubfoot. If the heels are more sloped than the toe, they are underrun. Either condition needs special attention when trimming and shoeing. The horse's base of support (the ground surface of the foot) should extend back to a line continued down from the center of the cannon bone to the ground, when the horse is standing squarely. The back of the heel should be at that point.

The foot also should be balanced from side to side as well as front to back. Lack of balance in the hoof causes uneven stress distribution, which can lead to strain on the leg, problems with hoof wear and gait, and interference when one limb hits another. Assess foot balance by watching a horse move to see whether one side of the foot lands before the other and by "looking down the leg" when you pick up a foot — holding the cannon bone just below the knee or hock to let the

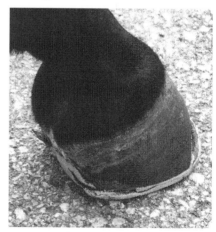

Example of a clubfoot.

foot hang loosely. This gives you a view of the ground surface of the foot and whether it is hanging in balance, perpendicular to a line continued down from the center of the cannon bone, with the inside and outside heels level.

Some right-handed farriers have trouble leveling a horse's right front foot and left-handed farriers have trouble leveling the left front, since the movement of that hand and arm is hindered by the horse's body. Right-handed farriers tend to leave the outside portion of the toe and inside of the heel on the right front foot a little long. The foot becomes unbalanced, concentrating the weight load in these areas. This condition is so common it has been nicknamed "right front foot disease." It can be corrected by more careful trimming, gradually adjusting the trimming to bring the hoof back into proper balance and restore uniform weight bearing and proper hoof wear.

The basic goal of shoeing is to make sure the horse can land evenly on the foot, with weight distributed across the whole bottom surface. An unbalanced foot often has a flare on one side — a distortion of hoof wall caused by an uneven weight load. Any hoof that is non-symmetrical is functionally out of balance, with uneven weight distribution. A flare makes a foot unbalanced from side to side, puts stress on the leg, and alters the gait. If uncorrected, flares will only get worse, adding more stress to the leg. This may lead to hoof cracking, since the hoof wall is so distorted.

Shoe Fit

The shoe should fit evenly on the foot and rest flat against the bottom of the hoof wall. The shoe should fit the foot so the outer edge of the shoe closely follows the outline of the trimmed hoof at the toe and sides. Take into consideration that the toe should be trimmed back a bit, like a natural barefoot hoof, which also helps a horse break over center if the shoe has a square toe. The shoe should be slightly wider than the hoof at quarters and heels to allow for expansion when weight is placed on the foot and should extend just beyond the heels of the horse to provide support and protection.

If the shoe is too short or does not fit properly at the quarters and heel, the shoe may cut into the foot as the hoof wall grows (the hoof may grow down around the outside of the shoe) or cause corns or other problems that could make the horse lame. To allow for hoof expansion, branches of the shoe should extend about one-sixteenth of an inch wider than the hoof wall at the heel and quarter, and the heel of the shoe should extend about that much behind the horse's heel. If the shoe sticks out too much at the heel, the horse might step on it with another foot and pull off the shoe. The horse is also more likely to interfere if the shoe is too long or wide at the heels. Some horses, when lying down, will also bump their elbows on the heel of a shoe.

Since the foot should be allowed to expand when weight is placed on it, especially at the heel, nails should never be driven into the hoof too far to the rear. The last nail hole of the shoe should not be farther back than the bend of the quarter.

The shoe should be properly centered on the foot. For horses with good leg conformation and normal feet (straight and well-balanced), the shoe can be centered by using the point of the frog as a guide. The frog divides the bottom of the foot into equal halves and points toward the center of the toe. In horses that are pigeon-toed or splay-footed, however, the frog usually points off center and cannot be used as a guide.

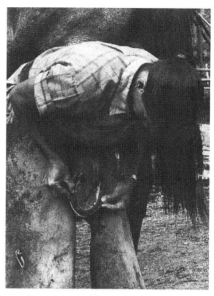

Fitting the shoe to the foot.

Types of Shoes

There are many kinds of horseshoes. Select shoes that will suit your horse's work while hindering him the least. A horse with a problem may need a special shoe created by your farrier, but most horses get along fine with factory made shoes.

Shoes should be as light as possible, taking into consideration the wear demanded of them, so they will interfere as little as possible with the normal flight of the horse's foot. Weight, no matter how it's added to the foot, always reduces speed and agility and can make a minor deviation in foot flight more noticeable. Any deviation takes the form of an arc, either to the outside or the inside of normal foot flight. Adding weight to the foot increases the arc because of the additional swing it makes. Ordinary shoeing thus accentuates foot flight and any gait defect. This is the reason many horses overreach or interfere only when shod. A horse that tends to interfere (strike one front limb against the other, or one hind against the other hind) or forge (strike his front heel or sole with his hind toe) does so even more when shod. He must be carefully shod, with proper foot balance.

A horse that toes in (pigeon-footed) tends to break over to the outside and swing his foot outward (paddling) while a horse that toes out (splay-footed) tends to break over to the inside and swing the foot inward (winging). The toed-out horse tends to interfere more than a toed-in horse. A short-backed horse with long legs is more apt to forge than a horse with legs proportionate to his body length. These are generalizations; some individuals don't fit the pattern due to different aspects of conformation. If you have a horse with a problem in how he travels (not corrected enough by squaring of the toe to help him break over straight instead of crooked), he needs special shoeing to keep him traveling straight or to keep him from hitting himself when shod.

For ordinary shoeing, steel shoes are commonly used because steel is easy to work with and durable. Unless a horse is being used hard, a steel shoe generally lasts until the next shoeing. The disadvantages of steel are its heaviness and its poor ability to dissipate shock and concussion. Aluminum shoes are lighter but are expensive and wear out more quickly. Cast aluminum is about a third the weight of steel, but it is not as durable and harder to weld and work with than steel. Titanium shoes are light and more durable than aluminum but more expensive. Plastic, rubber, and glue-on shoes have come into use in recent years, but generally are used for foals or hoof injuries — situations in which nails should not be put into the hoof wall. Plastic and glue-on shoes usually do not hold up well enough for horses doing athletic work.

Ground surface of a shoe, for most horses, should be plain. A plain plate shoe will interfere least with the horse's way of going, partly because it's lighter than a shoe with a toe grab or heel caulks. In some instances, however, a horse used for athletic activity needs better traction. Even a ranch horse or pleasure horse used in the mountains may need some buildup at toe and heel for traction on rocks and slippery hillsides.

Traction

Horses that work at speed on various types of surfaces need appropriate traction to perform with adequate speed and agility without risk of falling down. In these cases, use the proper type of traction for the activity — enough to help the horse travel safely and work at peak performance, but not so much that it makes the hoof grab too abruptly. Too much traction hinders the hoof's ability to slide. The abrupt grab increases shock and concussion and can cause injuries (torn ligaments or broken legs) due to the jerk and strain on joints and tendons. You need enough traction so the horse will not slip (or suffer strained, hyperextended joints or pulled muscles from scrambling), yet not so much that it puts unnatural stress on tendons and ligaments. Concussion also increases when less surface area hits the ground.

Traction devices include various types of toe or heel caulks, studs, spots of borium (tungsten carbide) welded to the shoe, and removable studs of various shapes and sizes for various types of footing. These devices are best used for specific situations, such as slow work on ice, jumpers on wet grass, or some other type of very slippery footing. In these instances, removable caulks are handy as they can be taken off when not needed.

Shoe design can also add or decrease traction. A flat, wide-webbed shoe with a beveled edge that does not cut into the ground gives the least traction, while a shoe with a sharp edge or a "rim shoe" will cut into the ground more and give better traction. Polo plates are rim shoes with a high inside rim to give traction while still enabling the foot to have a flexible and rapid breakover.

Borium

If a horse wears out his shoes faster than his feet grow (as happens with some endurance horses and other hard-used horses), you may need a few spots of hard-surfacing added to the wearing surface to make it last longer. Borium (tungsten carbide, used on drill bits for drilling through rocks) is often used for this purpose and can be spot-welded to the shoe. The rough surface that results is harder than steel and will not wear away, and also gives good traction on rocks, concrete, ice, and other slippery surfaces.

Borium should be added to the wear points or the basic four points of natural hoof contact — a spot on each heel and one on each side of the toe. Putting the borium on each side of the toe (rather than at the front of the toe) is best, since you don't want to interfere with the horse's breakover point. Having the borium on each side of the toe makes the foot break over center and can correct a horse with a mild crookedness, making the foot start its flight straight. This is often the simplest solution for a horse that interferes.

Corrective Shoeing and Therapeutic Shoeing

The term corrective shoeing has been overused and often misunderstood. It implies that a farrier can correct conformational faults of a horse's feet and legs. Your farrier cannot change the conformation of a mature horse and to try would only put more stress on certain parts of the limb, but the farrier can make small corrections with each trimming or shoeing to keep the feet as well-balanced as possible to prevent limb interference. True corrections are only effective on foals and are generally done by trimming, not shoeing.

The optimum time to attempt actual changes (to influence bone structure and make a young limb grow more normally) is during the first four months of a foal's life. After seven months the leg bones are not as malleable. After the bones stop growing, there's nothing you can do to make a permanent correction (each "correc-

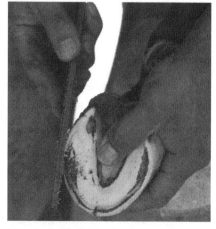

Trimming a foal's foot.

tion" is only temporary from this point on), and any drastic changes to the balance of the foot may cause lameness.

Without proper foot trimming to help balance it, a leg that is slightly out of line may get worse as a foal grows. A leg that is crooked or a foot that toes in or out will produce uneven wear on the hoof. As the hoof wears unevenly, the problem compounds and becomes a vicious cycle — the more the foot wears unevenly, the more crooked the foot or leg becomes, and the more uneven it wears. Many small problems can be corrected or kept from becoming larger problems just with regular, careful trimming when the horse is a foal. Corrective trimming is usually a matter of balancing the foot. Once a horse is grown, the farrier strives to shoe him with proper support to enhance rather than interfere with leg movement and balance. Shoes should promote ease of movement for the entire leg, rather than try to change that movement at the foot.

An egg bar shoe for extra support.

Overcorrection can be harmful. If a foot is lowered too much on one side, it may create pinching of the growth plate directly above it in the pastern or fetlock joint. Overcorrection can cause problems farther up the leg, since changing the foot puts the rest of the leg off balance and violates that horse's conformational integrity. Also, keep in mind that many young foals toe out due to lack of muscle development. These youngsters generally straighten up on their own as they fill out. If you try to "correct" them, they will become crooked later.

If a horse toes in or out because of rotation at the fetlock joint or of the entire leg, foot trimming can't correct it. The farrier must look at the whole leg. Knowing which deviations trimming can and cannot help is very important because corrections may sometimes hinder or injure the horse.

Forging or interference can be helped with corrective shoeing; in these cases the farrier is not so much trying to change the foot or leg, but trying to enable the horse to travel in a more normal fashion, minimizing the adverse effects caused by the extra weight on the foot from wearing shoes. If a horse forges, for instance, you can change the weight of the shoe or change the breakover by using a rolled or rocker toe or squaring the toe so the front foot is picked up faster — to get out of the way of the hind foot.

Therapeutic shoeing refers to shoeing designed to help a hoof with a medical problem or some kind of functional impairment, such as glue-on shoes for horses whose feet can't hold nails because of thin walls or special shoes for horses with bruised soles or founder. If a horse has a lameness problem or an injury, your farrier may use or create a special shoe to help resolve the problem or allow the foot to function more normally while it heals.

Hoof pads can be used to protect a sole from bruising, to reduce concussion with better shock absorption, or to compensate for hoof imbalance. Rim pads can reduce shock on the weight-bearing walls while leaving the center open. Wedge pads are thicker at one end than at the other and can be used to elevate the toe or the heel (to reduce stress on certain tendons or the suspensory ligament). Heel and frog supports can be used in conjunction with bar shoes or egg bar shoes for treating coffin bone fractures, corns, and bruises. Pads with frog supports can be used to relieve pressure on quarter cracks.

Glue-on shoes of various designs can be used to protect an injured foot or alter foot angle for medical purposes, such as for giving extra frog or sole support. In a foundered horse, the hoof wall is already compromised, and driving nails into it just adds more trauma and further weakens the hoof. An innovative farrier, working with a veterinarian, can create a special shoe to fit any purpose, designing it to help a specific hoof problem, even to the point of reconstructing much of the hoof wall with synthetic materials to support the foot while a new hoof grows.

Pulling a Shoe

The worst thing about horseshoeing in general is when shoes are left on too long. A horse whose feet have grown too long because shoes are left on may suffer leg wounds from striking himself, strained legs, contracted feet, corns, and other injuries due to long feet and shoe pressure. Since the hoof wall grows out perpendicularly from the coronary band, the horse's base of support actually grows out from under him if shoes are left on too long. This puts great strain on flexor tendons and on the navicular bone inside the hoof, as well as all foot and leg joints. Shoes worn too long may become thin and loose, sometimes bending and shifting, causing corns (from pressure on bars or sole) or nail punctures.

Even if you have a farrier do your shoeing you should still learn how to pull a shoe properly. There are situations where you should not wait for a farrier. A shoe may loosen when caught in a bog, hooked on a fence or some other obstacle, or stepped on by a hind foot. In these cases you should pull the shoe immediately so it won't injure the horse. If it's hanging loose on one side or is at risk of catching on something or causing a corn or bruise because it has slipped, it needs to come off. If it catches on something or the horse steps on it with another foot, it may break the hoof wall or take a chunk out, making it harder to shoe the foot properly again.

A shoe is easy to remove without breaking the hoof wall if you have a few shoeing and trimming tools. A shoeing hammer, clinch cutter, nippers, and rasp work

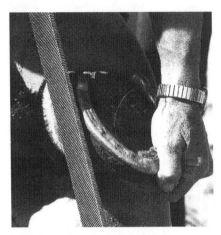

Rasping off the clinches.

best, but you also can use a flat-edged screwdriver instead of a clinch cutter and a carpenter's hammer. Hoof nippers or pulling nippers work well for pulling a shoe, but if the shoe is fairly loose you can use a pair of vice grips or pliers to hold onto the shoe and give you some leverage.

The shoe is less likely to break the hoof wall as you pull it and is easier to remove if you first unclinch the nails that are still in place. Cut the clinched nails on the hoof wall with a clinch cutter or unbend them with hoof nippers. You can use a hammer to drive a clinch cutter or a flat screwdriver under each nail end so you can pry up the clinch, then cut off the straightened nail end with nippers.

Another option is to rasp off the clinched nail ends with a rasp or file. Rest the horse's foot on your knee and rasp each clinch until it is gone or rasped off enough so it can no longer hold. Then

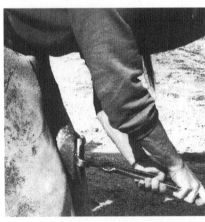

Start at the heels to remove shoe.

you can pull the shoe easily, even if you don't have nippers or pullers. Slip the claws of a carpenter's hammer under the heel of the shoe, push the head of the hammer toward the frog to pry up the shoe at the heel, then slowly work the hammer claws around the shoe until it comes off.

If you have shoeing tools, use pulling pincers or old hoof cutters to pull the shoe. It is better to pull the shoe than to just cut the nails between the shoe and hoof as some people try to do to remove the shoe. Cutting the nails leaves pieces in the hoof wall that will have to be removed after the shoe is off. Pulling out nail pieces with nippers, pincers, or pliers is not as easy as when the pieces are still attached to the shoe, and they are much more likely to break or crack the horse's hoof wall than when pulling the shoe properly.

To pull a shoe, hold the foot in shoeing position and place pulling pincers, nippers, or vice grips between the shoe and hoof at the heel, starting on the loosest side to make it easier. Close the handle and push it away from you to loosen the heel branch of the shoe, pushing slightly toward the middle line of the foot. Always push the tool's handle inward toward the center of the sole rather than outward; prying outward may tear off a chunk of hoof wall. Use a downward force to pry and loosen the shoe, working alternately along each branch and toward the toe as it comes loose.

Remove each nail as you loosen it. As you pull the shoe loose, hold the foot securely and never twist the pincers or pull crookedly or you might strain or injure the fetlock joint (the horse will protest if you pull his joint). Continue working down both branches alternately until the entire shoe is loosened.

If you have not been able to undo the clinches or rasp them off, you can still remove the shoe as described, but it will take more strength and leverage because you must pull the clinches loose and on through the hoof wall. If some of the clinches are still quite tight, however, the hoof wall may break unless you take each nail out as you loosen it.

To get hold of a nail head, you may first have to pound the shoe gently back against the hoof so the loosened nail head will protrude enough to grasp it with nippers, pliers, or your hammer claws. Take it out, and then pull on the shoe again to loosen it enough to take out the next nail, alternating down each side of the shoe. If a nail breaks off in the hoof wall, pull the nail out with nippers or pliers.

Tightening a Clinch

If a shoe has loose clinches but is not in real danger of coming off, you can tighten the clinches and keep the shoe from coming loose for a few more days until your farrier has time to reshoe the horse. It's not wise to leave it clanking or it may come off. Also, the movement on the loose clinches will enlarge the nail holes and weaken the surrounding hoof horn. If the shoe gets looser, it may shift position on the foot and put pressure on the bars or sole to create a corn. The loose clinches may stick out from the hoof wall, increasing the likelihood of the horse hitting himself with them.

If you don't want to take the shoe off (you have to ride the horse again before you can schedule a reshoeing, or you don't want him barefoot for fear of hoof wall breakage or cracking), you can reclinch it. It's not wise to tap the protruding clinches down with a hammer, because this may just roll them under and damage the hoof wall, and the balled-up clinch still sticks out.

To do a good job of reclinching, straighten out the old clinch first. Once you've straightened the clinch, you can cut the long end off with clinch cutters or hoof nippers if it is quite long, then rasp a small notch under the protruding nail tip. Reclinch the nail by placing any square-edged piece of metal (even the side of your rasp) against the tip that is protruding from the hoof wall while you tap the nail head down firmly into the shoe crease. Your metal edge turns the nail as you pound it down. After you flatten the nail, use a clinching tool to squeeze the tip over tightly, pushing it down into the small groove you made with the rasp right beneath it. If you don't have a clinching tool, hold a piece of metal against the nail head while you pound the clinch over into the groove with your hammer, or pound it down while the horse is standing with his foot on the ground. The retightened clinch should hold until the shoe is ready to be replaced.

Lost Shoes

Shoes sometimes come off because they are left on too long and the nail heads wear off. Wet conditions can soften the hoof wall, causing the hoof to spread and the clinches to loosen. The constant change of weather conditions from wet to dry to wet again causes repeated hoof wall expansion and contraction that makes the foot more brittle and easily cracked. Exposure to alternating moisture and dryness can make hooves dry out just as human hands do when constantly in and out of water. A hoof may deteriorate so much that it's hard to find a solid place to hold a nail.

Wet footing also can result in many lost shoes. Horsemen generally blame mud for pulling off shoes, but the actual culprit is often excessive moisture that softens up hooves so they don't hold the nails as well. A horse also can pull a shoe while struggling through a mud hole and stepping on himself. Deep footing can hinder a horse's balance and stride; when the mud slows and holds one foot, another leg may be quickly needed for balance, or the foot may suddenly become unstuck and land out of sequence and out of place, pulling off the shoe on another foot. Horses that run and play hard on wet, slippery footing also may grab a shoe.

If your farrier has shod the horse in front to give more support to underrun heels, or to allow plenty of room for hoof expansion, the horse may pull a front shoe with a hind foot. A base narrow horse that toes out may occasionally step on a front foot with his other front (if the shoe projects past the hoof in the heel and quarters), because he stands with his feet so close together. A horse with long hind legs (withers lower than croup) or a horse with a short back and long legs may forge or overreach, pulling off a front shoe. If a horse repeatedly pulls off his front shoes, your farrier may have to shoe him differently to prevent this problem.

If a shoe comes off while riding, you must protect the foot until you can get home. If the shoe is still dangling, remove it if you can, trying not to tear off any of the hoof wall with it. Even if the hoof wall is not damaged when the shoe comes off, the wall will chip and crack because of the sharp edges (unlike the rounded edges of a horse that has been going barefoot), and the horse may also stone bruise. His feet are not very tough; the shoe was protecting the vulnerable areas.

A hoof boot is the ideal solution, but most riders don't carry these. You'll have to improvise some type of hoof protection. A sweater or sweatshirt can be folded to use as padding, tying the sleeves around the foot and pastern to hold it in place. You can then lead the horse home without damaging the foot.

If the horse won't be reshod for a few days, put a more effective "hoof cover" on him at home. Clean the foot and use a protective boot, or apply duct tape over the bottom of the foot and around the lower portion of the hoof wall. If the horse is tender-footed, add more sole protection — a hoof pad or folded towel — taped to the bottom of the foot. If the horse is in a stall or dry paddock and is not being ridden, this temporary protection should suffice. If a chunk of hoof wall is missing, a farrier can repair it with one of several good hoof filler repair products before the new shoe is put on.

Common Hoof Problems

Many of the hoof problems that affect horses are caused by the conditions in which they live. These include the environment, nutrition, genetics (some horses have thin soles or hoof walls, or feet and leg conformation that makes them more susceptible to foot problems), or the way feet are trimmed or shod. Not every horse is blessed with ideal feet, but in most instances the horse owner can prevent serious problems with good care and diligent efforts to correct small problems before they become large ones.

Thrush

Organisms found in the barnyard, stable, or pasture that thrive in wet or decaying material such as mud or manure cause thrush, which affects the cleft and grooves of the frog and sometimes the sole. If the hoof is packed with dirt, mud, or manure, lack of air next to the frog and constant moisture make a perfect situation for infection. A hoof that is always clean and dry will not develop thrush.

Improper trimming and shoeing and poor hoof health make a frog more susceptible to thrush. Horses with contracted feet have deep grooves along the frog; dirt and manure are apt to accumulate in those clefts. Frequent cleaning of feet helps prevent thrush. Torn or ragged pieces of frog should be trimmed off. They are no longer useful to the foot and just provide nooks and crevices where thrush can start. Keeping the frog properly trimmed helps make its grooves more self-cleaning; they won't collect mud and debris so easily, and flexing of the foot (expanding and contracting) when the horse exercises enables the lodged material to fall out.

Thrush is easily recognized by the dark color along the frog (and sometimes dark soft patches up into the sole, especially along the white line) and by the strong, offensive smell. There is black, slimy moisture in the clefts of the frog, which tends to stick to the hoof pick when you clean the foot. When the clefts are cleaned out they are deeper than normal and may extend into sensitive tissues of the foot, making the horse flinch as they are cleaned. The frog may be undermined; any large loose areas should be removed. If thrush is neglected it can make the horse lame; the infection erodes more and more of the foot. It may penetrate the horny outer structures and invade the sensitive inner tissues.

Thrush in its early stages is recognized by the dark coloration and grime around the frog or in spots along the white line — and the bad odor. At this point it can be quickly cleared up by keeping the feet clean and applying iodine (strong tincture), chlorine bleach (a mix of equal parts bleach and water), or any commercial thrush medication daily for a few days to the affected areas after cleaning the foot. Don't spill any on the horse's skin.

If the horse is kept in a muddy, dirty environment, however, and his feet are not cleaned (and never have a chance to dry out), the condition may progress to unsoundness; he will show pain when his feet are cleaned or trimmed. In severe cases there will be discharge from the frog. The horse will be quite lame, with the infection causing swelling in the leg above the hoof. A neglected case of thrush can eventually infect the coffin joint.

Regular hoof care and a clean environment can prevent or halt thrush, as can daily riding or exercise on dry surfaces. This enables the horse's feet to dry out, and air can get to all parts of the foot. Keeping the feet clean and dry is the best solution; medication won't cure or keep thrush from recurring if the horse's feet are continually packed with mud or manure between treatments.

A problem that can occur in wet climates is "canker," an infectious hoof disease that involves the frog and surrounding sole. Canker results in an abnormal growth of horn, sometimes creating a white to yellowish mound of soft material with a foul smell. Treatment consists of removing the abnormal tissue and applying metronidazole or chloramphenicol (strong antibiotics) to the foot. The affected area may need to be trimmed off more than once during the healing process (to make sure the daily medication can get to the infection), since the abnormal tissue may regrow for a while. It may take several weeks to halt the infection completely.

Another condition similar to thrush consists of inflammation of skin between the bulbs of the heel. This condition should not be treated with iodine or harsh chemicals, however, because they will cause more damage to the skin. If a horse has contracted heels, the bulbs of the heels grow closer together and a deep crevice may form between the heel bulbs. Moisture and dirt in this crevice can lead to a painful infection. It smells and looks like thrush, so some horsemen treat it like thrush, causing a chemical burn that makes the condition worse.

To treat a thrush-like infection between the heel bulbs, clean and dry the affected area, then saturate some gauze strips with nitrofurazone ointment and work the medicated strips, one at a time, down into the groove between the heel bulbs. The protruding ends of the strips can then be cut off. Remove the old strips daily and insert newly medicated clean strips. After a few days the space between the heel bulbs will widen a bit and the infection will clear up. If heels are contracted due to improper shoeing, correct the shoeing.

Contracted Feet

Contracted heels or feet have been traditionally classed as an unsoundness in a horse. Even if your horse is not lame, this condition makes him likely to become lame. The contracted foot is unable to absorb and dissipate concussion properly, making him more susceptible to problems such as navicular syndrome or concussion-related breakdowns in other structures of the foot and leg.

A contracted foot is more narrow than normal, especially at the heels and quarters, and the frog becomes small and atrophied. Contraction is more common in front feet than in hinds, especially if the condition is due to improper shoeing. Sometimes only one foot becomes contracted due to injury and lameness (and subsequent disuse of that foot). Front feet are normally quite round, and hind feet more narrow and concave at the sole, but it is easy to tell the difference between a normal foot and a contracted one; the normal foot has a healthy frog and wide heels. The heels of a contracted foot are too close together.

Some breeds have feet more oval than round, but the feet are not contracted. The construction and health of the heels, bars, sole, and frog can help a horseman tell the difference between a normal, healthy narrow foot and a contracted one. In some horses, one front foot is narrower than the other as an inherited condition; it may or may not cause problems.

The true contracted foot is an abnormal, pathological condition in which many of the important structures of the foot have suffered degenerative changes. Contracted heels can be due to injury, disuse of the foot and lack of frog pressure, or the result of improper shoeing that does not allow heel and quarters to expand when weight is placed on the foot. Leaving shoes on too long (the hoof wall grows too long and inhibits hoof expansion at heel and quarters) or keeping a horse shod year-round and never letting the foot function more naturally can contribute to foot contraction, especially if shoeing does not allow for proper heel expansion.

Foot expansion is essential to hoof health. Contraction results from the breakdown in the foot's shock absorption mechanisms; the hoof has lost its ability to expand and becomes smaller. It's a vicious cycle; once contraction gets started, the foot function, especially in the heel area, is badly impaired and the condition just becomes worse.

If the foot bears weight properly, the heels won't contract. With proper trimming and shoeing, allowing for heel expansion and weight bearing, most contracted feet will expand back to their natural shape within a few shoeings. If the feet have contracted due to disuse from pain, special shoeing may help. A special shoe can help decrease pain enough so the horse can bear weight more normally on the foot again and the contracted heels can began to re-expand.

The best way to treat contracted heels is to identify the original cause and deal with it while at the same time enabling the foot to expand at the heel when weight is placed on it. In most horses, balancing the foot and correcting any deviation from normal foot angle will suffice, especially if the shoe can be fitted so it's slightly wider than the foot at heel and quarters and the last nail is placed ahead of the bend of the quarters, so as not to inhibit expansion.

Flat Feet and Use of Hoof Pads

A horse with flat feet tends to bruise more readily than a horse with normal concave soles. A flat-footed horse that is well shod and never used in rocky terrain may never become tender, but if he's ridden on gravel roads or rocks he may go lame.

Horses with flat feet or thin soles, laminitis, or dropped soles may need added protection. The flat-footed horse's sole is right down on the ground and all the sensitive tissues above it are subjected to jarring or bruising if the horse hits a rock. If the inner tissues bruise badly enough, a foot abscess can develop, causing great pain (from pressure inside the hoof) and lameness. A hoof abscess can lay up a horse for several weeks or months, especially if the sole must be opened for drainage and then has to grow new horn to fill the hole. A deep bruise, even if it doesn't abscess, may take weeks to heal. A horse with a bruise that doesn't abscess will heal without treatment but will need a long rest from work.

Using hoof pads to protect a thin or flat sole can prevent stone bruising. If you only ride occasionally on rocky ground you may want to use Easyboots, which can be removed when you're not riding, rather than hoof pads. Easyboots can be used on a barefoot or shod horse if sized properly for the foot. The boots can be put on over the shoes when traveling in rocky areas and removed when footing is softer.

If you use hoof pads, the pad goes between the hoof and the shoe when the shoe is nailed on. Choose pad material carefully. If a horse is ridden a lot, you

A pad goes between sole and shoe.

need something more durable than some of the commercial hoof pads, especially the softer cushion pads used as shock absorbers to reduce concussion. Many of these pads will wear clear through before it's time to reshoe the horse.

Shock-absorbing pads are ideal for a horse recovering from founder or a horse with arthritic joints, navicular disease, or other problems associated with or aggravated by concussion. These pads may help an otherwise lame horse travel sound for light work. They are not adequate, however, for the horse that needs durable protection from the rocks.

The synthetic material used by shoe repair shops for resoling human shoes works well. Neoprene is about a quarter-inch thick and very tough and durable. It will last as long as a steel horseshoe. Most flat-footed horses only need hoof pads in front; very few have problems with hind feet, which are usually more concave and do not carry as much weight. You rarely find a flat hind foot.

A horse with pads doesn't get much air next to the sole, and if he's in a wet pasture or muddy pen, moisture may

A protective boot.

get trapped under the pad, keeping his sole wet and creating an ideal situation for thrush. Iodine can prevent or halt a case of thrush under a pad. The easiest way to apply iodine or any other liquid thrush medication is to squirt it under the pad with a small syringe. It's less messy than trying to pour it between pad and sole, and you are less apt to spill it. Hold the foot up so that the iodine from the syringe will flow down under the pad, covering the sole as you squirt it in.

Thrush usually isn't a problem if the pad is cut out for the frog (a technique that works well on a flat foot; the pad doesn't have to bend up over the frog). The frog can stay clean and dry, exposed to the air. If you keep a horse padded all season, however, you may want to put iodine under the pads occasionally. Don't do it too often, or you may corrode the shoe nails.

The key to caring for the flat-footed horse that bruises easily is to shoe him protectively with pads *before* he bruises or gets too tender-footed. The area most susceptible to bruising is the front part of the sole, right behind the toe. Pads can prevent trouble before it starts. Proper shoeing, with protection for the sole area, can enable the horse to perform at his best, without becoming lame or worrying about his feet. Many flat-footed or thin-soled horses get into the habit of shortening their stride in rocks or gravel, but with adequate hoof protection they can travel with confidence.

Use of Iodine To Toughen Tender Feet

Some horses are borderline on whether they need hoof pads and can often be kept from getting tender-footed just by regular use of iodine or a commercial hoof product for toughening the sole. Strong tincture of iodine acts as an astringent and helps toughen soles and drive the quick (sensitive tissue next to the horny sole) back deeper.

Iodine also works well for any freshly trimmed or newly shod horse that might be tender for a few days after trimming. If you use iodine to toughen soles, use 7 percent tincture of iodine and apply it only to the sole area; you don't need it on the frog. Be careful not to spill any on the heels or let it run down onto the hoof wall or onto the coronary band or skin. Iodine is a very strong chemical and can irritate the skin or dry out a hoof wall.

Suck a little iodine into a small syringe, then slowly squirt the medication onto the sole, applying it only in the areas needed. If you accidentally get too much out, you can immediately suck the extra back up into the syringe. Take care to apply only enough to cover the sole so the iodine won't run under the shoe and onto the hoof wall.

When riding a flat-footed, thin-soled, or freshly shod tender-footed horse on rocky ground, apply iodine a time or two before you start riding him and then daily each time you take him out. On a freshly shod horse that usually has tough feet, you may only need to use the iodine a few days until he gets over being tender.

Corns and Stone Bruises

Trauma to the inner tissues of the foot beneath the horny sole can rupture small blood vessels, creating a bruise. When the horse steps on a sharp rock, for instance, the crushing of blood vessels between the sole and the bone inside the foot causes bleeding beneath the sole and pressure buildup that can create pain, sometimes so much the horse is reluctant to bear weight. A mild bruise may just produce tenderness. The horse may travel fine on soft ground but "gimp" on gravel or rocks when those hard surfaces put more pressure on the sore spot.

A heel bruise causes the horse to put more weight on the toe. When standing, he may try to bear weight on the toe, resting the foot with the knee forward, to decrease heel pressure. A horse with a bruise in the toe area lands on the heel. The horse with a mild sole bruise may just seem tender and short-strided or stumble in his efforts to walk gingerly on the sore foot.

Hoof testers can help locate the bruise. The horse will flinch when the bruised area is pressed. A serious bruise may abscess and require veterinary treatment in opening and draining the abscess, soaking the foot, and applying iodine. The abscess usually heals quickly once drained and treated, but the hole in the sole will take several months to fill in with new hoof horn. During that time, the horse is susceptible to reinjury and should not be ridden unless the hole can be covered with a protective shoe until it fills in. If the hole is just behind the toe (a place that is commonly bruised), your farrier can add some extra metal to a steel shoe to cover the hole. This would allow the horse to be ridden again much sooner.

Any sole bruise is subject to infection and abscess if there's a crack in the sole to the outside, which allows bacteria to enter. The resulting abscess needs to be opened and drained or it will cause lameness and may eventually break out in the heel bulb area. Signs of an abscess include heat and swelling in the pastern and fetlock joint region. If the abscess is neglected and "travels" in the foot, the inner structures of the foot could be damaged.

There are several types of sole bruises. A bruise where the hoof wall and bars come together is called a corn. Corns are often caused by improper shoeing (especially shoes too narrow) or shoes left on too long. Sometimes a farrier bends the inside branch of the shoe (at the heel) toward the frog to keep the horse from stepping on the back of the front shoe with the hind foot. If the shoe is not fitted properly when this is done, there may be direct pressure on the sole at the angle of the bars instead of on the hoof wall, and the repeated concussion in this vulnerable area can cause bruising. Use of a shoe that is slightly too small for the foot also can increase the pressure on the sole in this area, and heel caulks can aggravate this effect. The extra pressure bruises the sole and creates a corn.

A "push corn" occurs when an upright or pinched heel puts too much of the horse's weight directly onto the sensitive heel tissues. A shoe left on too long can cause a bruise in that area, especially if the hoof wall starts to grow down around the outside of the shoe at the heel. This puts too much pressure inside the hoof wall at the bars — where the shoe is pressing — and crushes the tissues near the back corner of the coffin bone inside the hoof.

A "pull corn" can be caused by the horse's toe being too long, putting extra leverage and stress on some parts of the hoof wall with each step. The juncture where the horny sole meets the sensitive laminae inside the foot can become injured.

A sharp rock can create a bruise anywhere on the sole. A minor bruise causes blood to leak from broken blood vessels into the horny tissue. The hemorrhage within the inner surface of the hoof horn usually causes red stains. A serious bruise may cause more internal blood seepage, creating a blood-filled space within the inner sole. Severe injury results in collection of serum beneath the injured horn. The region may have a bluish coloration, which you can see after scraping the flaky part of the sole surface away, especially if a sole abscess is developing.

In some thin-soled horses used on rough or rocky ground, sole bruising can become chronic, eventually causing inflammation of the coffin bone and permanent lameness. The coffin bone is only about three-eighths of an inch away from the sole in a normal foot, so a thin sole doesn't give it much protection. Soles also can be compromised with too much moisture (making them softer) and by bathing. Detergent shampoos can weaken the horn (just as washing dishes can soften fingernails to the point of bending). A soft or brittle sole from too much wetting and drying can bruise more easily.

If your horse is lame, your veterinarian can pare the sore area down with a hoof knife to see if the surface is cracked, giving bacteria access to the bruise and the sensitive inner foot tissues. If a crack exists, that area should be pared down so the blood and serum can drain out, and the foot should be soaked to draw out any remaining infection.

Soak the foot daily, twenty minutes at a time, in hot water and Epsom salts. Antibiotic injections are usually not much help in bruised sole abscesses since the area is not well reached by blood circulation. The bruised area is best treated

Use cotton to cover the wound.

locally. Opening the area for drainage and daily soaking (for three or four days) usually clear up the infection so the bruised area can heal. The foot should be bandaged between soakings to keep the area from becoming contaminated with dirt and mud. Squirt a little iodine into the drainage area, cover the area with cotton, then bandage the foot and put it into a boot or waterproof wrap to keep it clean and dry between soakings.

Even if the infection clears up quickly, keep the foot bandaged or in a protective boot to keep out dirt until the area begins to grow new horn. Once the horse walks sound again and the area is healing, a shoe and hoof pad can keep out dirt and protect the hole in the sole until adequate new horn has regrown, or you can use a special shoe that covers the hole.

Standing a horse in crushed ice sometimes can reduce pressure and inflammation caused by a mild, fresh bruise. If bruising does not create an abscess, this ice treatment may be all that is needed to relieve soreness.

Bruising can also occur in the hoof wall as well as the sole if the hoof strikes a rock or a fence rail when jumping, or hits a solid object. A bruise in the wall can be easily seen in a non-pigmented hoof but not in a dark one. A red stain in the white line (usually discovered when trimming the foot) is indication of a past injury that is growing out.

Puncture Wounds in the Foot

A puncture wound (at any location in the body) is always serious, since it can lead to tetanus. The penetrating object (a stick, wire, nail, broken glass) may take bacteria with it into the wound, and the airless environment and damaged tissue create ideal conditions for tetanus bacteria to multiply. Spores of this bacteria are commonly found in the soil. A wound that bleeds and heals from the inside out is rarely at risk for tetanus, but punctures tend to close over before the inner part has healed, leaving dirt and infection inside.

A puncture in the foot can damage the inner tissues. It may be hard to locate if the foreign object is no longer embedded. A puncture wound in the frog can be especially difficult to find if the spongy material of the frog closes up again after the object makes its hole. The horse's gait may give a clue about which area of the foot was punctured; he may try to land on a portion of the foot that puts least pressure on the punctured area. If the foot is infected, he may be reluctant to put weight on it at all. A hoof tester can often help pinpoint the spot.

If you suspect a puncture or if the object is still embedded, consult your veterinarian. Don't remove the penetrating object; a veterinarian will have a much better idea of which structures might be involved (and may be able to take X-rays to check the exact location). Treatment may depend upon where the puncture is located and how deeply the object penetrated. If the navicular bursa is involved and surgery needed, the horse has a better chance of recovery if this is recognized early.

You may not know the horse stepped on something sharp until an abscess develops and he goes lame. It's best, however, to start treatment immediately after a puncture occurs. The horse should have a tetanus shot if he hasn't had a booster yet for the year.

If the puncture is not treated and infection has no drainage, the infection will spread until it can burst out at the coronary band. If this happens, don't assume the infection is from an injury to the coronary band; check the bottom of the foot for a possible puncture wound, especially if the horse is lame. A serious puncture wound infection can cause the lower leg to swell and the horse may have a fever due to septicemia from infection entering the body. Antibiotics are needed.

"Gravel" Infection

"Gravel" is an old term for a foot infection that breaks out at the heel or coronary band after traveling up through the hoof. It is usually accompanied by varying degrees of lameness. Modern veterinary texts and most veterinarians will tell you that the old theory about pieces of gravel migrating up through the bottom of the foot is not valid. Traditional thought was that the horse picked up a piece of gravel at the bottom of his foot at the white line and the gravel then worked its way up into the foot. The gravel supposedly migrated, along with the infection it caused, eventually coming out at the heel or right above the coronary band.

Gravel pieces do sometimes lodge at the white line in a barefoot horse, especially if there's some separation or cracking there, but these foreign bodies usually do not go up into the foot. What actually happens is that a crack or damaged area, such as a hoof puncture or separation at the white line, allows infection to invade the foot. If the infection goes up into sensitive tissues and no drainage is established to get rid of it, the pus moves to the nearest outer surface to erupt.

Inside the hoof, the nearest outer surface is the sole or hoof wall, which is a solid barrier, so the infection must follow the line of least resistance in the soft tissues, making a vertical track up the white line between the sensitive and insensitive laminae, and eventually breaking out at the coronary band or heel area. The coronet at that spot becomes hot and swollen, and before the infection erupts, the area can be quite painful, causing lameness. As soon as drainage begins, the lameness subsides.

Foreign bodies that do occasionally penetrate a hoof at the white line to work upward are small stones, glass shards, broken slivers of sharp flint, sharp pieces of porous volcanic rock, or even sharp plant parts such as Canadian "spear grass." This problem rarely occurs in light horses (whose hoof walls do not expand much) but can happen in heavy athletes when racing or doing fast work barefoot, such as unshod rodeo horses competing in high-speed performance events such as roping, racing, or bulldogging. Concussion occurring in the unshod hoof of the heavyweight horse doing speed work or jumping makes the hoof more susceptible to wall and sole separation at the white line, creating a vulnerable opening. If the ground surface is hazardous with sharp gravel or other sharp fragments, these may enter deeply between the wall and sole when the hoof is expanded at the white line during the weight-bearing phase of the stride.

The object may then migrate upward from the point of entry, traveling between the coffin bone and hoof wall in soft tissues to come out the coronary band, or move sideways beneath the coffin bone's bottom side (between coffin bone and sole) to come out the heel. Painful lameness results from this migration. Infection and pus follow the path created by the migrating object, but the foreign body breaks out and exits the foot before the pus tract comes through the path made by it.

More commonly, however, the pus that erupts is from infection due to puncture or cracks that open the way for bacteria. This is a frequent cause of sudden lameness in barefoot horses at pasture, especially if hooves are not regularly cared for. If feet are allowed to become long (chipping or cracking) or brittle, it is not unusual for infection to enter. Cases of lameness occur most readily when conditions are extremely dry (leading to brittle feet that crack readily), extremely wet (the hoof becomes soft and more vulnerable to punctures that can penetrate the white line), or when horses have foundered and have some separation at the white line. Wet footing containing sand or gravel may soften the hoof and allow particles to be forced up into the white line. If infection results, it travels upward to break out at the coronary band and may also cause a crack. Infection can also occur shortly after a horse is shod, entering the white line area through a hole made by a driven nail, if the nail pricks sensitive tissues.

A careful examination of the white line and sole should reveal one or more black spots that result from an infection originating from a crack in the sole.

These spots should be probed carefully to check for deeper infection. If the horse is checked with a hoof tester to pinpoint location soon after he goes lame, the offending crack can be found and dug out with a hoof knife, establishing drainage and getting rid of the pus. Recovery can thus begin before the infection has to travel up through the hoof to find a way out.

If the problem is not caught early and infection has begun to move up through the foot, opening the sole does little good; the pus pocket has traveled too far upward. Soaking the foot can hasten the travel, however, and help bring the infection to the surface faster to break out and drain. The exit site may need to be enlarged and flushed out.

Except in severe cases, recovery rate is usually very good, especially if the condition is discovered and treated soon, before infection travels through the foot. Even when the pus pocket migrates to the heel or coronary band and breaks open to drain, the horse is usually none the worse for it. Exceptions are horses with chronic laminitis; the deformed feet and dropped sole make the problem more likely to recur. Some horses that suffer gravel infections for long periods without treatment may not recover full soundness as permanent damage can occur within the foot.

Prevention of "gravel" can be difficult, especially in horses at pasture, such as broodmares or retired horses that are not being used (whose feet may not get regular care) and in horses that have previously foundered. Keeping the feet smoothed and trimmed to prevent chipping and cracking and not allowing them to become dry and brittle can help reduce the chances of gravel infection.

Opening, Draining, and Soaking an Infection
A hoof infection or abscess, whether caused by a puncture wound, infected stone bruise, deep hoof crack, neglected thrush that penetrates sensitive inner tissues, "gravel," or a quicked horseshoe nail should usually be opened to drain, soaked, cleaned with a disinfectant, and kept bandaged until healing is well begun. The entire bottom of the foot should be thoroughly cleaned and washed before soaking.

A veterinarian can open the area, making at least a quarter-inch hole into the infected tissue, with the walls of the drainage hole widening toward the ground surface so it won't become obstructed. When a puncture wound is in the frog, that portion of the frog should be trimmed away at the site of the puncture until adequate drainage for the infection is established.

After draining, the opened area should be flushed out with an antiseptic solution, such as 1 percent povidone iodine solution. If the wound does not need to be soaked, the opening can be packed with cotton soaked in povidone iodine, and the foot bandaged to keep it clean and dry. If the infection is serious or has created drainage from the coronary band, it will heal much faster if the foot can

Soaking a foot.

be soaked for several days in Epsom salts (magnesium sulfate solution). Soaking the foot in the warm salt-water solution helps pull out any remaining infection and also makes the sore foot feel better.

If the horse has never had a foot soaked, make it a good experience for him so he will cooperate rather than resist. The tub used should be pliable, such as a plastic dish pan or rubber feed tub, and not too tall. A tall bucket is not as easy to get his foot into and he may be more suspicious about it. Don't use a metal bucket or stiff plastic. These make too much noise, which could frighten the horse, and the horse could rap his shin if he tries to take his foot out or move around. A bucket may tip up and hit his leg. Use a very pliable tub so that if the horse does move around and step on it, the sides will harmlessly collapse and give, without banging the horse. The tub only needs to hold about four to six inches of water. A couple inches will

Applying an antiseptic.

be adequate if you are soaking the bottom of the foot, whereas you will need more water if soaking the coronary band.

To get your horse used to the tub, put his foot into an empty one. Once he realizes it's not dangerous and stands there quietly, wash his foot thoroughly and put it into a clean, well-rinsed tub. Carefully add water, slightly warmer than body temperature. After he accepts that, add several tablespoons of Epsom salts (magnesium sulfate) to the water. Slowly pouring water into the tub while the horse is standing in it may be less alarming to him than having to put his foot into a tub with water already in it.

Once he's standing in the warm salt-water solution, add hotter water until the water in the tub is comfortably warm (but not hot). Keep the water as warm as the horse can comfortably tolerate it. If you have a helper, one person can monitor the horse to keep him from spilling the tub if he picks up the foot (the person can hold the foot and guide it back into the tub so he won't put it on the ground and get the hoof dirty) and one can take care of the hot water refills.

If a horse is nervous about having his foot soaked, hand feed the horse to occupy his mind during the soaking and keep him happy and relaxed. Most horses stand very nicely once they get used to the warm water; it makes the foot feel better.

A soaking boot can be used if a horse won't stand with his foot in a tub. A soaking boot can also be handy for applying a poultice to the foot. The boot fits loosely on the foot, with room for the poultice material or soaking fluid to surround the foot. A boot works well in instances in which a foot requires a longer period of contact with a poultice or medicated material.

After soaking a foot to pull out infection, bandage the area to keep it clean and dry until the next treatment. Dry the foot and apply a thin coating of petroleum jelly around the heel bulbs and coronary band if soaking chaps the skin, then pack the drainage hole in the sole with cotton soaked in povidone iodine, pad the foot with cotton, a section of towel, or even a disposable baby diaper, then wrap the foot with stretchy self-adhering tape or gauze bandaging.

When using stretchy tape, don't wrap any higher than the middle of the hoof wall. You can then use duct tape to cover it and tape it directly to the hoof to hold it. Finish covering the whole bandage with duct tape; it holds very well and can be an adequate protective covering if the ground is dry. If the ground is wet or muddy, make a smooth initial wrap (not too bulky) so the bandaged foot will then fit into an Easyboot or some other waterproof boot to keep the bandage clean and dry.

Injury to the Coronary Band

Coronary band injuries can occur if a horse steps on himself with a shod foot, runs into something solid or sharp (a nail, sharp rock, piece of metal, or gets the foot caught in a fence and suffers a wire cut), or has his foot stepped on by another horse. Sometimes a horse will hit the coronary band when loading or unloading from a trailer. A horse can also strike himself during fast work. A horse wearing studs or caulks on his shoes may injure the coronary band and should wear bell boots to protect his feet when doing fast work.

A deep wound at the coronet should receive immediate veterinary attention. Unless properly repaired, it can result in scar tissue that may disrupt the hoof's growing cells and compromise the area. A serious gap may disrupt hoof growth completely. A wound in the coronary band can also develop proud flesh(excess granulation tissue that grows out from a wound) if not treated properly.

Sometimes a deep scrape or injury to the coronary band causes a horny growth that protrudes and keeps growing. This process is called metaplasia, which means transformation of a cell into abnormal tissue. In the case of an injured coronary band (involving the transitional tissue between skin and hoof), the skin cells on the resulting scar may change into horny tissue. Some of the cell layers in the skin of the scar tissue may protrude and produce a large mass of hoof horn.

The excess horny growth may need to be clipped regularly with hoof nippers to keep it flush with the coronary band. Frequent applications of hoof dressing can keep the abnormal area soft and pliable so it won't crack and bleed. If the excess callus at the coronary band causes pain and lameness or is struck by another hoof and bleeds, a veterinarian may have to remove the growth surgically.

Hoof Cracks

Cracks in the hoof wall are sometimes hard to get rid of once they become established. The hoof tends to keep splitting as it grows out, due to pressure on the crack when it bears weight. Cracks are usually the result of long bare feet that chip and split, excessive concussion and forces on a brittle foot, or injury. Chips and cracks in a bare foot are usually not serious unless neglected; long, untrimmed feet can develop serious cracks that become deep, traveling into sensitive tissues and making the horse lame. If the hoof is kept short, minor cracks and chips grow out and don't become problems.

Brittle feet, caused by dry conditions, genetics, or nutrition (or combination of these factors) make a horse more susceptible to hoof cracks. If a horse has brittle feet, a good hoof dressing can sometimes help by reducing moisture loss in the hoof wall, as can certain feed supplements if the problem is nutritional.

Quarter cracks are common in horses that have a lot of stress on the foot (such as racehorses) since quarters are the thinnest and most delicate part of the hoof wall. A quarter crack can be caused by thin walls (a genetic weakness), improperly trimmed feet, concussion on hard ground, stones, exercise on uneven ground, or a misplaced shoe nail. With some horses, quarter cracks are a lifelong problem; the hoof needs constant care and treatment to keep cracks from recurring or getting worse.

Toe cracks, quarter cracks, and heel cracks are vertical splits between the hoof horn tubules. Those that start at ground surface are often called grass cracks. Sometimes a crack will start in the heel and quarter area and travel horizontally around the foot, due to a weakness in the hoof wall at that area from an injury, as when a horse strikes the hoof forcefully against a rock.

A hoof with cracks.

Sometimes a crack starts at the coronary band because of an injury or defect in the coronet or from an infection in the foot that breaks out at the coronet. This type of crack is called a sand crack. It travels downward because of hoof wall weakness at that spot. A horizontal crack in the hoof wall is called a blow-out, and is usually caused by injury to the coronary band or by a blow to the hoof wall. A blow-out rarely spreads, and seldom requires any treatment, but because the hoof wall is weakened at that spot it may set the stage for a vertical crack if other factors put additional stress on the hoof wall.

Horizontal hoof cracks can be caused by selenium toxicity. These cracks often appear near the top of the hoof, just beneath the coronary band. Selenium excess in the body alters the normal chemical bonding of the keratin that forms hoof horn. If a horse continues to eat feed that contains high levels of selenium, the poor hoof quality can progress to complete separation of the hoof wall from the foot, with the horny capsule sloughing off. Usually the horse will be showing other signs of selenium toxicity before this happens, such as hair loss (especially mane and tail) and the horizontal hoof cracks. Consult a veterinarian.

Thin hoof walls and soles make a barefoot horse susceptible to cracks because the hoof is more easily chipped when traveling on uneven ground. A horse with this type of hoof should be trimmed often and the edges of the foot smoothed to help prevent chipping. A ragged edge is more likely to crack than a smooth one, so frequent smoothing with a rasp can help prevent cracks.

The biggest cause of cracks is letting bare feet grow too long between trimming. Growing out a bad crack on a barefoot horse can be difficult because it may be impossible to take all the pressure off the crack and keep it from spreading unless your farrier applies a special glue to hold it together while the hoof grows out. The farrier may decide to put a shoe on the foot to help hold the crack together until it grows out.

A shoe can help keep stress off the hoof wall at the area of the crack, and keep it from continuing to split. If the crack is at or near the toe, it helps to put a clip on each side of the crack to keep the hoof wall from expanding there when weight is placed on the foot. For a quarter crack, a half bar shoe is sometimes helpful, for it enables the frog to bear some of the weight that would ordinarily be borne by the hoof wall.

When trimming the foot, the farrier should cut away the hoof at the crack

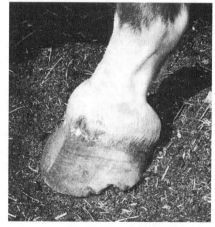

Excessive length leads to cracks.

so it doesn't bear weight and expand. For a toe crack, the toe should be trimmed and shortened. For a quarter or heel crack, the hoof wall at the heel should be trimmed from the point of the crack to the back of the hoof so the heel and quarter areas will not take weight. Then the crack cannot spread apart and split more. If the horse is to be shod, this leaves a gap between the shoe and the hoof wall at the location of the crack. Thus the weight is distributed along the rest of the shoe, with none at the crack. This allows the hoof to grow out without widening the crack and sending it on up the hoof. For a toe crack, a square-toed shoe and clips can often help keep the crack from progressing by minimizing the stress effect during breakover.

If a serious crack persists in spite of careful and frequent trimming, consult your veterinarian or farrier. The crack should be corrected, not only to halt its progress but also to protect the underlying tissues from contamination and infection.

Remedies for Dry, Brittle Feet

Hooves are healthiest when the hoof horn has proper moisture levels. Moisture is conducted up and down the hoof by tiny tubules in the horn. Dry feet often develop cracks and chips; the dry foot doesn't have the elasticity and resilience of one with proper moisture content. The dried-out hoof becomes more brittle and readily chipped. Hoof nippers may break or shatter the wall. It's harder to nail a shoe securely to a dry, brittle, shelly hoof.

A hoof is healthiest when footing is dry, not wet, and when the horse is getting regular exercise. Hoof moisture comes from within via a healthy blood supply, so a horse that gets little or no exercise may not have sufficient moisture delivered to the hoof and his feet may also contract. If a hoof becomes too soft from wet weather, mud, or frequent bathing, the wall may spread and its layers may separate. A dry environment is actually more natural and healthy for the hoof than a wet one; feet that are constantly wet are more subject to breakdown and disease. Horsemen in wet climates often protect their horses' feet from the effects of excessive moisture by using waterproofing hoof dressings and hoof hardeners.

You can't add moisture to a hoof with a hoof dressing, but you can reduce moisture loss by holding in the moisture that is already there. The hoof's natural protective coating is sometimes damaged or compromised by environmental conditions, and you can use a hoof dressing to serve as a temporary coating. A hoof dressing's protective layer only lasts a short time, but if applied frequently it may help minimize moisture loss from the hoof.

The hoof dries out when moisture evaporates through the hoof wall faster than it can be replaced. A hoof sealer can help feet that are covered with tiny surface cracks caused by moisture changes (similar to cracked and chapped hands). Unlike a thick, greasy hoof dressing, a hoof sealer soaks into the hoof wall and helps keep external moisture from damaging the hoof and internal moisture from evaporating. This can help counter effects of environmental changes such as dewy pastures at night that dry out during the day, or wet feet (from bathing) put into stall bedding that dries out hooves. While drying out, the hoof develops cracks.

Mud that dries on a hoof may pull out the hoof wall's natural oils. Horsemen used to think that mud made a good treatment for dry or cracked hooves, but a hoof constantly in mud has soft walls that tend to spread and get flares. Horses with soft hooves standing in mud can get bacterial infections in the hoof walls or abscesses in the feet. The healthiest feet are actually found on desert horses, and the poorest quality feet are those that are wet all the time. External moisture is not really good for hooves. All the moisture a hoof needs can be supplied by the blood circulation; external moisture merely softens and weakens the hoof wall. This is the rea-

son the hoof has a natural "varnish" to keep out external moisture. The worst type of moisture is urine, since ammonia breaks down the hoof horn.

Some horses' hooves are very dry, and dressings may help. You may have to try several products before finding one that works for your horse. Not all feet need help retaining moisture; if a hoof is not cracked and is holding a shoe properly, it's best not to interfere with its moisture balance. If a horse is standing in mud or in a wet environment that prevents normal hoof mois-

Application of hoof dressing.

ture evaporation, the last thing you want to do is further hinder the hoof's ability to get rid of excess moisture.

Various ways to prevent excessive moisture loss from hoof horn include using sealant on clean, dry hooves before riding or turning a stabled horse out, making sure hooves are dry after bathing a horse (before you put him back into a stall), and using good straw or shredded paper for bedding instead of wood products. Some types of sawdust and shavings can dry out the feet, pulling the moisture from the hooves. Pine is one of the worst. If shavings smell of pine resin, use a sealant on your horse's feet.

One of the best ways to create a healthier, more resilient hoof is to take horses out of stalls or hard, dry paddocks and put them on grass pasture. Grass provides the ideal environment for the foot, moisture-wise (neither too wet nor too dry), and also provides nutrients a horse needs for growing a healthy hoof wall.

Diet and Hoof Health

Much research has been done in the past two decades on the correlation between diet and hoof health — the link between nutrition and horn strength and growth. Healthy hoof horn cannot be created without proper nutrition. Yet what might be adequate for one horse's hooves might be inadequate for another.

Feet reflect a horse's individuality — influenced by genetics, basic health, environment, foot care, and level of activity. Two horses can be in the same barn, on the same diet, shod by the same farrier, competing in the same sport, yet one might have tough, healthy feet while the other has weak walls, unable to hold a shoe. The difference may be due to genetics and nutrition. Even though their diets are the same, these otherwise similar horses may have genetic differences, not only in construction of their feet, but also in the way they utilize and absorb nutrients. Inability to absorb nutrients properly may be as simple as poor teeth. Other factors might be a less efficient digestive system (as in an older horse or one with parasite damage), or a hormone problem, such as thyroid, that can cause poor hoof health and dull hair.

The hoof needs certain basic ingredients to grow. The hoof wall's dry matter is about 93 percent protein, mainly the insoluble protein called keratin, which constitutes the tough outer layer of hoof and skin. Protein is made up of amino acids; hoof horn gets its strength from the cross-linking of sulfur-bearing amino acids like methionine, cystine, and cysteine.

Many commercial hoof supplement products contain methionine and claim it is essential to hoof health, but in reality all of the dietary essential amino acids are needed for healthy hoof horn. If a horse's total protein requirements are not met, hoof growth will be adversely affected. Good hooves require proper nutrition, which includes adequate amounts of protein, vitamins, and minerals. A natural diet of grasses supplies all the horse's needs, in proper balance and mineral ratios. This is the reason a horse on high-protein green grass experiences excellent hoof growth. A horse fed poor-quality hay, however, may need supplements.

Biotin (a water-soluble B vitamin) assists chemical reactions in the body, including synthesis of protein for keratin formation. It has been shown to improve weak, thin-walled feet when fed over a long period (at least nine to twelve months, since it takes that long to grow a new hoof), but most horses don't need biotin unless they are stressed — working hard, stabled for long periods, fed low-quality feeds, etc. The horse creates biotin in his gut and has a very adequate amount under normal conditions. Horses that respond to biotin supplementation (about 5 percent of the horses that have poor quality hoof horn) are usually stressed horses or young horses in poor body condition.

Many horse owners think that just feeding a biotin supplement will create stronger and better hoof growth, but biotin by itself is not enough to correct poor horn quality; it is just one of many nutrients needed by the adult horse for healthy hoof horn. Even among stressed horses, a true biotin deficiency is relatively rare and usually accompanied by other deficiencies. To see if your horse is truly biotin deficient, your veterinarian can give your horse a relatively inexpensive blood test.

Many horses with brittle, poor quality hoof horn don't respond to biotin supplements but do show improvement in horn quality when diets are better balanced for calcium. Grain is high in phosphorus and phytates (the latter blocks absorption of calcium in the gut) and can alter the calcium-phosphorus ratio that is so crucial for proper bone and hoof growth. Alfalfa can supply the necessary calcium, but the horse won't utilize much of it if his diet contains too much grain. Good-quality pasture grasses grown on fertile soils contain ideal calcium-phosphorus balance for horses.

Another feed that can interfere with proper hoof health is bran, which is very high in phosphorus. High phosphorus level and phytates not only block proper absorption of calcium but interfere with protein utilization as well. Whether as wheat bran (commonly used for bran mashes), rice bran, oats (their hulls), or other grains, bran can be detrimental to horses with problem feet.

Some horses on high-fat diets (adding vegetable oil to feed) have shown improvement in hoof quality, though no research has yet determined why. Some farriers and veterinarians feel anything that promotes hair growth and condition will also promote hoof growth and health, and this would include vitamin A, extra fat in the diet, etc. Nutritional supplements aimed at skin and hair tissues can also help unhealthy hooves.

For some horses, selenium may be needed for good hoof health. Selenium works with vitamin E to help protect the fatty phospholipids that form the "mortar" that holds the hoof wall together. The amount and quality of these fats help determine the hardness and resilience of the hoof wall. Too much selenium, however, causes poor-quality hoof growth, pain in the feet, and cracks around the hoof (or even loss of a hoof). Excessive vitamin A can cause brittle feet, and excessive sulfur can block collagen production and halt hoof growth. Too much of these essential ingredients can be as harmful as too little. Never use more than one supplement, and only use a supplement if you are very sure your horse needs it.

When considering nutrition as a cause of poor hoof quality, also remember that it can be months before a change in diet produces visible results. If you notice in late summer that your horse's hoof walls seem weak and crumbling, even though the horse is on good pasture, you need to realize that the trouble probably started six to eight months earlier when that part of the hoof was growing. Poor-quality hay during winter might be the reason his feet are unhealthy now. When poor diet is corrected, hoof problems caused by inadequate nutrition should begin to show improvement (the new horn emerging from the coronary band) in about eight to ten weeks, but total replacement of the old, weak hoof wall will take nine to twelve months.

A horse with healthy hooves does not need supplements. Some farriers and veterinarians feel that most bad feet are the result of genetics and bad management (which includes poor trimming and shoeing) rather than nutrition, but some problems can be resolved with proper nutrition. If you feel a hoof problem is nutrition-related, carefully analyze your horse's feeds and try to correct any imbalances. In today's world of fancy feeds and dozens of supplements, overfeeding horses causes more problems than underfeeding them. Focus on the diet as a whole to keep it adequate and balanced. Don't try a shotgun treatment to correct poor hooves or you may create problems with oversupplementation.

White Line Disease

White line disease is a progressive separation of the hoof wall from the foot. It starts at the bottom of the foot and travels upward, involving the thickest layer of the hoof wall — the portion attached to the insensitive laminae (the tiny "leaves" from the bloodless outer wall that interlock with the sensitive laminae at the edge of the foot's inner structures). It is called white line disease only because it begins at the white line.

The hoof horn just outside the white line is the structure affected, though in advanced cases the white line may be involved. This disease creates soft or chalky horn tissue. In years past, the term "seedy toe" was sometimes used to describe the condition. The material in the ever-widening space is soft and crumbly.

The wall separation begins at the bottom of the foot, anywhere along its circumference. The disease may create a bulge in the hoof wall, a gray or black area of debris at the edge of the hoof wall, or a shelly, crumbly consistency (hoof material that is very easily pulled off or picked away). There may be a powdery or greasy spot at the toe, a lesion on the front of the hoof (usually in a triangular shape or inverted "U"), rotten odor (not as overwhelming as that of thrush), or black pus oozing from the affected area.

The separation may start mechanically if the hoof wall is too long; weight placed on the foot at each step tends to pry the hoof wall away from the sole. The separation collects dirt and manure that are forced up into the opening, making a moist, dark place for microbes that like to grow in hoof horn. Barefoot horses with long feet may suffer wall separation due to mud or fine gravel packing into the bottom of the foot and white line area, forced up between the hoof wall and the sole. As the horse travels and puts weight on the foot, the mud is forced higher, creating a separation where the horn-digesting fungi get started.

In a long-standing case, the outer wall becomes completely detached and the coffin bone may sink, rotating downward toward the sole of the foot at the toe. This factor (and subsequent lameness) often leads to misdiagnosis as laminitis. White line disease does not result in lameness, however, unless it progresses to a dropping of the coffin bone, whereas laminitis is always very painful.

Anaerobic pathogens (yeast, fungi, or certain bacteria) seem to be the cause of white line disease. All of the implicated microbes are found in the soil in most geographic regions. Environmental factors, mechanical stresses, and opportunistic microbes may combine to cause the hoof horn's disintegration. Many farriers and veterinarians feel that the most common cause of this problem is fungal infection of the hoof wall that develops due to mechanical stresses created by poor management or other disease processes.

White line disease can be treated by removing all the diseased hoof horn with clippers, grinding away all the remaining residue of affected horn, and treating the underlying tissue with a good fungicide. This can leave a large hole, so reconstructive shoeing is usually necessary to support that part of the foot and prevent further separation of hoof from coffin bone. A patch of fiberglass or some other hoof repair material can be used to help stabilize the shoe while the foot grows out again.

Recovery time depends on how much hoof wall was lost. An advanced case where much of the wall had to be removed might take six months to a year for new horn to grow. During this time the foot must be protected against reinfection. With treatment and protection, however, even feet with massive destruction will recover; some horses have lost more than 80 percent of the hoof wall and still grew back a normal healthy hoof.

A small separation at the heel and quarter area can often be treated with less drastic measures. These heel holes can be dug out, removing as much of the decomposed hoof horn as possible, and filling the hole with a medicated packing. A shoe can be put on the foot to keep the packing in and prevent further contamination of the hole. If the horse is kept in a dry place and the shoes are reset regularly to replace the medicated packing until the hoof wall grows out, the hoof deterioration will be halted.

Best prevention is to keep footing clean and dry, minimize foot washing, check feet regularly, use clean tools (a rasp can harbor fungal spores), have your farrier disinfect his tools between horses, and feed a balanced diet. Nutritional supplements containing biotin, amino acids, and trace minerals help promote hoof growth and healthy horn, but remember that oversupplementation can be damaging and may actually make a horse more vulnerable to hoof problems.

Laminitis

Laminitis is an inflammation of the interlocking fingers or laminae that attach the horny outer covering to the living tissues inside. The laminae are vital to the survival and health of the hoof wall. Tiny capillaries provide a steady flow of oxygen and nutrients to the sensitive laminae, the inner portion of the attachment that connects the hoof capsule to the coffin bone.

One of the hoof's unique adaptations to protect itself from frostbite also makes it more vulnerable to laminitis. The hoof's circulatory system has shunts that can channel blood directly from the arteries into the veins, by-passing the tiny capillaries. When the hoof gets cold, these shunts open up and allow the blood to hurry through the foot without slowing down in the tiny capillary network. This large blood flow in the central area of the foot keeps it warm, while the reduced blood in the outer portion makes it less vulnerable to freezing.

Toxins in the blood from grain overload (and the resulting endotoxemia from a malfunctioning microbe population in the gut) or from systemic illness or uterine infection due to a retained placenta (foaling founder) create chemical imbalances in the body. The shunts in the feet are adversely affected and the tiny capillaries in the laminae are deprived of blood. This is a more complete shutdown than when the horse's foot is protecting itself from cold. Reduced blood flow to the laminae leads to blood clots and cell death, destroying vital structures of the foot. Death of enough of the laminae tissue destroys the attachment between the coffin bone and the hoof wall and the bone begins to sink within the foot.

This can create permanent damage; the foot becomes deformed, with the sole dropping down and hoof wall spreading and developing rings and ridges. The slope of the front part of the foot becomes concave as the toe turns upward. The sinking of the coffin bone is called founder (like a sinking ship).

Laminitis may result in founder, depending upon how serious it is and how much damage is done to the laminae. Since the laminae at the toes of the front

feet are under the greatest stress, most cases of founder involve separation of the laminae in that area. The coffin bone begins to separate from the hoof at the front tip and rotates toward the bottom of the sole, causing bruising in the sole and a flat or convex sole. The hoof wall at the toe is loose from its attachment and begins to peel away from the coffin bone, turning upward. These separations in the hoof structure, loss of circulation, and tissue death can all make the hoof susceptible to infection and abscesses.

The painful stance of laminitis.

Sometimes all the laminae around the wall are so compromised that the coffin bone becomes completely detached (not just at the toe) and slides down inside the hoof, tearing and destroying the areas that are crucial for normal hoof growth. The hoof may then grow in deformed fashion (with rings, ridges, and a curling-up toe) or die completely and slough off, like a person losing a damaged fingernail. The horse has to support his weight and try to walk on these damaged areas, which is quite painful. The inflammation within the foot causes swelling, and because the foot is encased in solid walls that can't expand to accommodate the swelling, the pain can be excruciating.

In severe cases the horse will not put any weight on his feet, spending most of his time lying down or rolling around in agony. Lameness is usually most severe in the front feet because they carry more weight. The horse may stand with his front feet propped out ahead and hind feet well under the body in an attempt to carry more of the weight behind. If he walks, he hobbles painfully, trying to put as little weight on the front feet as possible. He may shiver or sweat and have a fast pulse rate and rapid, shallow respiration. If all four feet are affected, he may stand with all his feet bunched together under his body, with his back arched upward. He doesn't want to move, and when he does, he stumbles and shuffles.

If you ever suspect laminitis, a veterinarian should treat the horse immediately to deal with the cause of the toxic condition (endotoxemia from grain overload, retained placenta, systemic illness, "grass founder," though about 20 percent of all laminitis cases have no detectable cause) and try to reverse the damaging process in the feet. This usually means treatment with drugs for pain relief and to promote better capillary circulation and enhance blood flow. If laminae attachments are not destroyed, the horse can recover. Laminitis can be a one-time illness followed by recovery or may become chronic if permanent changes occur in the foot, necessitating continual corrective trimming.

Many farriers will create a special shoe for the foundered foot. Several types are used, including the rockered-toe egg-bar shoe, backward shoe, heart-bar shoe, to give extra support to the rear of the foot, minimize stress of breakover, and reduce stress on the deep digital flexor tendon, as this tendon normally pulls on the underside of the coffin bone and can thus contribute to its rotation. The pull on the underside of the bone tends to pull the backside of it up, and the front tip of it downward.

The toe of the sole is already stressed by the sinking tip of the coffin bone, so you don't want a shoe that puts pressure on the toe at all, but you do need to protect the dropped sole from ground pressure. Shoe pressure has to be applied correctly and in the right places, or it can do more harm than good. You need a good farrier who is experienced in handling foundered horses to assess the situation and figure out which approach will work best for this particular horse. He may combine or change methods as the horse's condition improves.

Laminitis usually can be prevented by conscientious care. Feed-related laminitis is rare in horses on a well-balanced ration with most of their diet consisting of forages (a minimum of grain), with adjustments made slowly when feed changes are made. Other ways to reduce risk of laminitis include limiting grazing time on early spring grass, conditioning a horse gradually, not working him to the point of exhaustion, cooling him out properly after workouts, protecting him from heat exhaustion and heat stroke, avoiding excessive concussion on hard surfaces, keeping him in proper condition (fat horses are more prone to laminitis than fit horses), and making sure he has adequate exercise.

Navicular Syndrome

Navicular syndrome has been called the "man-made crippler," and is the most common cause of front leg lameness in domestic horses; it is rarely seen in wild ones. Several factors in our use and confinement of horses can lead to navicular syndrome. It was first described in the eighteenth century, and horsemen thought it was hereditary. What is actually inherited is conformation — small feet, upright shoulders, and upright pasterns that increase concussion.

The small, boat-shaped navicular bone lies behind the coffin bone and short pastern bone. It provides a leverage point for the deep digital flexor tendon, serving as a bearing surface and shock absorber. It stabilizes the attachment of the flexor tendon to the coffin bone, and keeps the coffin bone and short pastern bone in proper alignment, helping decrease wear and tear on the coffin joint and the flexor tendon.

The impact and concussion when the foot hits the ground are transmitted through the coffin bone and navicular bone to the short pastern bone and on up the leg. The smaller the hoof in relation to the horse's weight, the greater the shock to the navicular bone and its associated tendons and ligaments. Upright pasterns or extra stress when landing from a jump squeeze the bone between the vertical pull of the deep digital flexor tendon and the vertical pressure from the short pastern bone. The ligaments holding the navicular bone in place are also stretched, straining their attachments and sometimes causing bone spurs.

The deep digital flexor tendon runs down the back of the leg to the coffin bone, and the navicular bone acts as a pulley to keep the angle of this tendon's attachment to the bone constant — to keep the tendon from being torn away from the bone when the leg is under extreme stress (such as landing after a jump). Damage to this tendon in the navicular area can cause pain, as when adhesions form between the tendon and the navicular bone. The ligaments that connect the navicular bone to the other bones in the foot (coffin bone and short pastern bone) can also be a pain source.

The coffin joint (between coffin bone and short pastern bone) where the navicular bone is located is very vulnerable to wear and concussion and may degenerate and become arthritic. As a result, treatment of navicular lameness with medications for arthritis and joint disease often will help. To treat a case of navicular syndrome, the veterinarian needs to know which area is hurting and why.

Certain kinds of horses are more prone to navicular syndrome due to conformation and use. The highest incidence of navicular syndrome occurs in performance horses, usually seven to fourteen years old. Quarter Horses and

Thoroughbreds seem to be affected more commonly than other breeds. Quarter Horses often have large heavy bodies and small feet. Thoroughbreds seldom have navicular problems when young and racing, but in second careers as jumpers, eventers, etc., they are more at risk due to wear and tear on joints and soft tissues.

Factors that can lead to navicular problems are small feet, contracted heels, underrun heels, sheared heels, improper hoof angles, long toes, and incorrect breakover point. Other factors are confinement and lack of exercise. Continually standing in a stall puts constant pressure on feet and impairs circulation. In most instances, navicular syndrome occurs only in front feet, due to the extra stress and concussion on them.

In the early stages of navicular trouble (which may encompass several years), the horse may be intermittently lame, improving with rest, but the lameness reappears when he's used again. He may not show severe lameness, just a mild lameness when he circles (putting more stress on the inside foot), or his gimp may shift back and forth from one leg to the other when traveling in a straight line. Lameness may be present in both front feet, or seem worse in one. The horse owner may not notice that both feet are sore until a veterinarian does a nerve block on the worst foot.

Lameness may be observed when the horse is turning or walking on gravel or rocks. He takes shorter, lighter steps, trying to keep weight off his front feet. He may point one foot forward when standing, or stand with both front feet too far forward. The horseman might think he's foundered, but there's no heat in the hooves.

When the horse gallops, he has a short, choppy stride. He stumbles a lot because he tries to put his toe down first and not take weight on the heel, often stabbing his toes into the ground. He has decreased suppleness, may be reluctant to pick up a certain lead, or starts balking at jumps. The horseman might think the horse is sore in the shoulders, has chronic laminitis, or is going sour in his work because of reluctance to perform. The horse may be short strided and stiff when going downhill.

Over time, the foot changes shape. The horse's effort to avoid frog pressure and weight on the heels causes the heels to rise and contract. The sole becomes more concave and the foot narrows across the quarters. If just one front foot is affected, it will be more contracted than the other.

Treatment for navicular syndrome varies with each individual case. For best results, the veterinarian must try to determine the source of the horse's pain (tendons, ligaments, joints, cartilage, or the bone itself), and figure out what led the horse to injure that area and how best to resolve it. Treatment can include proper shoeing to correct the problems that caused the condition and anti-inflammatory drugs such as phenylbutazone to ease the discomfort and enable the horse to use the foot normally again.

The sooner navicular problems can be treated and the pain alleviated, the greater the horse's chances of recovery, even if you and your veterinarian are not exactly sure what caused the pain. If a horse shows signs of mild discomfort, don't postpone diagnostic attempts, waiting until symptoms are more obvious; by then he may have suffered more damage. Helping the horse use the foot normally again can prevent more damage from occurring.

Pain relievers will not cure the problem, but can aid healing by allowing the horse to use the foot properly. Corticosteroids (such as dexamethasone and prednisone) and nonsteroidal anti-inflammatory drugs can provide pain relief and reduce swelling. Drugs like bute and aspirin also reduce blood clotting. Arthritis medications like polysulfated glycosaminoglycans (PSGAGs) can help halt joint degeneration if the problem involves arthritis. PSGAGs inhibit the enzymes that contribute to joint inflammation and help protect the joint cartilage from further damage.

Mild navicular pain often can be relieved with a change in management. If the problem is due to poor circulation or mild joint stiffness, exercise can help; the horse should be turned out instead of in a stall, or given light work. On the other hand, if the problem is due to excessive stress and concussion, the horse needs time off from hard work. Pasture turnout can be beneficial.

Surgery to cut the palmar digital nerve (neurectomy) may be necessary if proper shoeing and pain relievers fail to relieve the condition. This may be only a temporary solution, however, since the condition itself is not cured and may eventually deteriorate to the point at which lameness returns. Palmar digital neurectomy involves cutting the nerves running along either side of the back of the pastern and into the heels. The horse can no longer feel anything in his heels. This usually enables him to travel sound again, though in some cases the pain relief does not last more than a year because the nerves regenerate. A neurectomy has other drawbacks; with no feeling in the foot, the horse cannot feel any other problems either.

In recent years, as an alternative to surgery, chemicals have been used to provide long-term nerve blocking. The chemical block, using ammonium chloride or an alcohol extract, lasts about six weeks, which is long enough for the horse to start healing. If the horse doesn't feel any pain for a while, he can use the foot normally again and get the proper mechanics of motion back. When a horse feels pain in the heel area, he often compensates by trying to land on his toes, putting too much load on his fetlock joint and the navicular bone via the pulley-support system. This may explain why damage to the navicular bone can be a result, rather than a cause, of heel pain in some other structure (such as the tendon, coffin joint, or cartilage).

Ringbone and Sidebone

Ringbone is a lameness-causing enlargement at the pastern or coffin joint; new bone growth is caused by injury to one of these joints. High ringbone refers to the condition when it affects the pastern joint — between the long pastern bone and short pastern bone, above the hoof. Low ringbone is a bony enlargement at the coffin joint — between the coffin bone and short pastern bone, inside the hoof. Ringbone is further classified as articular (involving the joint itself, which always causes lameness) and periarticular (bone spurs near the joint but not involving the joint surface). Periarticular ringbone may not cause lameness. Articular ringbone is more common and more serious.

Periarticular ringbone is most common in high ringbone. Low ringbone usually affects the joint and is very serious because it occurs beneath the coronary band, inside the hoof, where it causes severe pain and lameness. Chronic low ringbone has been called pyramidal disease or buttress foot because of the bulging of the coronary band at the front of the foot.

The most common cause of arthritic ringbone is injury to the joint from strain and stress (including concussion) during athletic activity or constant strain caused by poor conformation. A crooked leg, especially from the fetlock joint down (toes turned in or out), puts greater stress on the pastern or coffin joint, and work increases this stress. Ringbone is more common in horses that compete in stock horse and western performance events, dressage, and polo (activities that call for sudden maneuvers or unusual stresses to these joints) than in racing.

The first sign of trouble is intermittent lameness, heat, and tender swelling around the joint. As the condition becomes chronic, the soft tissue around the joint becomes firm and cool. Pigeon-toed horses are more apt to develop ringbone on the outside of the joints, while splay-footed horses develop it on the inside, due to the extra stress placed on these areas.

A horse diagnosed with ringbone should be rested and treated with anti-inflammatory drugs. High ringbone sometimes heals if the pastern joint grows together. When fusion is complete, lameness disappears. Sometimes surgical fusion of the joint is recommended. Low ringbone usually results in permanent unsoundness.

Sidebones are ossification of the cartilage on the sides of a horse's foot. In a normal horse these cartilage areas on each side of the foot (back toward the heel and above the coronary band) are firm but movable structures. They become sidebones if they calcify and turn to bone. Concussion is a major cause of sidebones, especially in horses with upright pasterns for this causes more trauma to the cartilages. Splay-footed horses tend to get medial sidebones (inside of the foot) while pigeon-toed horses tend to get lateral (outside) sidebones, though it's not uncommon for sidebones to develop in both cartilages eventually.

Sidebones are primarily a problem in front feet because they receive more concussion than hind feet. Wire cuts that damage the cartilage can cause sidebones. Poor shoeing also can be a factor. Long heel caulks can increase concussion, and shoeing a horse unevenly can put more strain on one side of the foot, increasing concussion to one of the cartilages. Foundered horses or horses with contracted heels are also prone to sidebones since their feet are less able to handle concussion. Sidebones may cause lameness in the early stages when inflammation occurs, but many horses with healed, calcified sidebones are not lame.

Pinpointing Lameness

Approximately 80 percent of all lameness problems are in the foot rather than higher up the leg (though some foot lamenesses are caused by back problems that increase concussion; chiropractic care can sometimes relieve strain on the legs and feet). When a horse's foot is sore, it may be very obvious, but sometimes a careful examination is needed to figure out which foot is sore, and where. If you are familiar with how a sound horse moves (the perfect regularity of gait and stride) at walk and trot, you can more readily detect when a horse is "off." Lameness is merely an alteration of gait as he tries to reduce pain of weight bearing.

Your ability to identify which foot is lame will be greater if you know what the normal rhythm should be, watching the movement and listening to the sound of the hoof beats on firm ground. The walk may not reveal much unless the horse is quite sore, whereas the trot is an ideal gait for pinpointing lameness. The horse will make more obvious deviation, since the trot is the most regular and symmetrical gait, with diagonal legs striking the ground together. It's harder to pick the lame leg at a canter or gallop; these are not symmetrical gaits, so a horse can more easily minimize lameness, especially if he uses the lead that reduces strain on his sore leg.

The horse compensates for pain by getting off the sore leg as quickly as possible, moving his other legs and his body in such a way to take more of the weight. These compensatory movements signal lameness. Head carriage is the most obvious clue, since he uses his head and neck for balance. His head and neck make up about 20 percent of his weight, and he uses them the way a human swings the arms for balance while walking or running. At the walk and canter, the horse's head bobs at each stride.

At the trot, however, the horse's head remains steady because he always has a leg at each side and at each end of his body striking the ground at the same time. He doesn't need to use his head for balance. If there is any hint of head-bobbing at the trot, the horse is lame and trying to shift his weight off a sore leg or foot by making extra balancing movements with head and neck.

Have someone lead the horse directly away from you at a trot in a straight line and back again. The handler should have enough slack in the rope so the horse's head is free and you'll be able to see any hint of head bobbing. Also watch the horse from the side as he is led by you at a trot, using a straight background like a fence to give you a reference point. The horse should also be longed or led in a circle in both directions, since some lameness is easier to see when the horse is making a turn.

In almost every type of front-leg lameness, and even in a serious hind-leg lameness, the horse's head will bob at the trot as he tries to take weight off the sore leg and put it more quickly onto the good leg. His head will go up just before nodding it down, taking as much weight as possible off the bad leg as it strikes the ground and then throwing it onto the good leg. Thus he will lift his head when the sore leg is hitting the ground and drop his head when the good foot lands. If it is difficult for you to watch his head and his feet at the same time, you can make it easier by saying "right, left, right, left" as each front foot comes to the ground, then shift your vision to his head while you keep up the rhythm. If his head rises every time you are saying "right," the soreness is in his right front.

If the horse has equal pain in both front legs (as from founder or navicular syndrome), he will not bob his head but may hold his head higher than normal as he tries to keep weight off his front legs while pushing his hind legs farther under himself to take more of the weight.

Compensatory movements for hind-leg lameness are more difficult to detect; the horse will only bob his head for severe hind-leg pain, and this might be mis-

Jogging a horse to check for lameness.

interpreted as lameness in a front leg. A more reliable way to pinpoint hind-leg lameness is to stand behind the horse as he is led directly away from you, so you can compare the up-and-down movement of his hip bones. If the pain occurs as the lame foot takes weight, the rest of the stride will be quite shortened and the hip will pop up as the horse gets off that leg quickly. To evaluate the hip movement better, it helps to imagine a big "T" on the back end of the horse, with the tail dividing the hindquarters in half and the horizontal top of the "T" connecting the points of the hips. As the horse moves, the rise and fall of the hips will be quite obvious as you envision this horizontal line.

Other ways to tell which foot is lame is to lead the horse in circles and on hard ground. A hard surface accentuates some types of lameness, due to more concussion. A turn or circle will put more stress on certain parts of his feet or legs and cause him to make more obvious compensatory movements. Another clue is how the horse stands while at rest — whether he puts weight squarely on all four feet or tries to take weight off a foot by standing with it more forward of the usual position (front), or resting it (hind).

After determining which leg is sore, the next step is to locate the problem. The first place to look, if a horse is reluctant to put full weight on a leg, is the foot. The problem may be as simple as a rock caught in the hoof or wedged in the shoe. There may be some indication of trauma or infection, such as a puncture or an advanced case of thrush. If there is nothing obvious, you may need a hoof tester to check for a sore area, which might indicate a bruise or abscess under the sole's exterior. If the bottom of the foot seems fine, check for heat in the hoof wall and compare it with the warmth or coolness of the other feet. Check for pain around the coronary band by squeezing the coronet and the heels. If you are still at a loss, check the leg from top to bottom, and check the sound leg also, to compare the joints for thickness and swelling, heat or sensitivity. Your hands can often give you clues that are hard to see, and the horse's reaction to your touch or pressing can also tell you if an area is sore.

Once you locate the sore area, you then need to determine what caused the soreness — an injury or infection — and what to do about it. Contact your veterinarian for a proper diagnosis and advice on what might be the most effective treatment. Sometimes the soreness is actually a secondary problem; your veterinarian can help you track down the root of the matter.

7

Aspects of Care in Various Seasons

SOME ASPECTS OF HORSE CARE vary with the changing seasons, particularly if you live in a cold northern climate, a southern area with mild winters and hot summers, or an area with a lot of moisture.

Spring Care

During the spring, many horsemen get back to work with their horses if they've taken time off from riding during the winter. Before resuming training or picking up where you left off last fall, check your horses' body condition and look for any health and soundness problems that might have escaped notice during their vacation.

Spring is a good time to check teeth and feet. Have your veterinarian or equine dentist examine your horses' teeth and take care of any dental problems that have developed. Young horses often have mouth problems due to shedding of baby teeth and eruption of permanent teeth, and mature horses may develop hooks and other problems due to uneven wear.

Hooves need care if they weren't regularly trimmed through winter, and might require shoes if you want to start riding. If hooves were continually packed with mud and manure during the winter, frogs may be soft and mushy; thrush may have gained a toehold. You might have to apply iodine a few times along the clefts to clear up thrush before you start riding.

There are several kinds of internal parasites that are damaging to horses. Since the advent of modern deworming drugs (the various benzimidazoles in the 1960s and ivermectin in the 1980s), most horse owners have routinely dewormed their horses to keep these parasites under control. The problem now is that some of our best deworming drugs are no longer as effective as they were in the past. Some parasites have become resistant to their effects, and we need to develop different strategies. Rotating dewormers can help (and knowing how and when to change drugs) but isn't a complete answer to this challenge.

Knowing the parasites' life cycles helps us create a more effective plan for dealing with them, utilizing a combination of chemical dewormers and pasture management. Routine deworming, based on a calendar schedule, is an inefficient way to get rid of parasites and can also be detrimental, leading to more resistant worms. There have been resistance problems with the benzimidazole dewormers for many years. Now there is increasing ascarid resistance to the avermectins (ivermectin and moxidectin).

The pharmaceutical companies have not come up with any new drugs, so we need to try to break the parasite cycle by determining which horses are shedding parasite eggs onto the pasture. Fecal samples and egg counts can help us monitor worm loads. A relatively small percentage of horses in any group are shedding the highest number of eggs. If we treat those individuals, and minimize recontamination of the pasture, the rest of the herd will stay relatively free of worms. If we reduce the use of dewormers, targeting just the shedders, we prolong the effectiveness of deworming drugs.

One deworming in early spring, however, should be aimed at bots, before mature grubs detach from the stomach lining and pass out with manure to pupate in the ground and become bot flies. A spring deworming for bots kills any that might have been missed in the fall and helps to ensure there are fewer bot flies during summer to pester and reinfect your horses.

A soundness check is a good idea before you start a horse back into fitness training. Have someone lead the horse straight toward and straight away from you (the trot is the easiest gait in which to pinpoint lameness or soreness), and in a thirty-foot circle both directions. Trotting on hard ground often reveals concussion-related problems (affecting bones and joints). Trotting on soft footing may reveal muscular problems. If the horse checks out sound and healthy, start his spring conditioning program but take it slowly to get his muscles, tendons, and ligaments back to strength without injuring them.

Daily grooming is often neglected in winter when horses have long winter coats, especially if they are at pasture. You may have a major grooming job to help the horse get rid of winter hair. If he has been in a stall, there may be skin inflammation on hocks, elbows, shoulders, or other parts of his body that contact the floor when he's lying down, especially if acid and ammonia from manure and urine accumulate in his hair coat. By spring this can result in a matted coat with sores underneath. You may have to clean the affected areas thoroughly and apply a soothing ointment to clear up the infection or inflammation in the raw areas.

Shedding

Unless you live in a warm climate, your horses grow long, thick winter coats during winter and shed this extra insulation in the spring. A number of hormonal, nutritional, and environmental factors influence shedding and hair growth. Longer days stimulate a horse to shed his winter coat. In fall, the shorter days stimulate growth of winter hair, though you won't begin to notice the summer hairs falling out until you've had some cold nights. The summer hair starts growing in among the long winter hairs in very early spring, long before he starts to shed.

Hormones affect shedding; a stallion often has a sleeker, shinier hair coat than a gelding, shedding faster in the spring and keeping a sleeker hair coat longer in

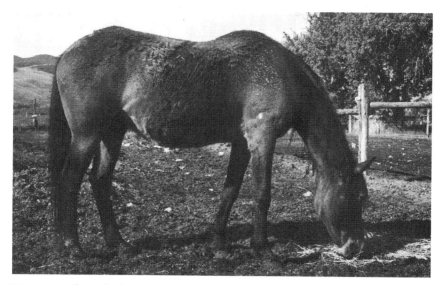

Horses tend to shed in patterns.

the fall. Thyroid imbalance or Cushing's syndrome may cause a horse to shed slowly or not shed at all; these horses must be clipped. Cushing's syndrome mainly affects older horses in their twenties or thirties.

Mineral deficiencies can cause slow shedding. A normal well-fed horse that is on a balanced diet will shed faster than a horse with a dietary deficiency. Hair is created from protein; a horse must have adequate protein to grow a healthy hair coat. A heavy infestation of internal parasites can result in dull hair coat or slow shedding; worms rob the horse of nutrients. Deficiencies of copper, selenium, and certain vitamins can make the coat dull and lifeless and slow to make proper changes from season to season. Stress, illness, and other factors that create abnormal conditions in the body can cause slow shedding.

Some horsemen like to feed a couple of ounces of vegetable oil daily in the grain ration to promote a shinier coat and hasten shedding. The oil may stimulate more secretion from the hair's oil glands or add the needed calories for a little more body condition, which makes the horse more prompt to shed when days get warm. Oil can make a noticeable difference if a horse was slightly underfed during winter. The best remedy for helping a horse shed faster, however, is a balanced diet and daily grooming and body massage. Blanketing, brushing, exercise, light, and heat all help a horse shed faster. If he sweats, his body thinks it's time to get rid of extra hair.

Horses often rub on fences and trees or roll when shedding to help loosen old hair. If a horse exercises and sweats, he becomes itchy. If he seems exceptionally itchy — rubbing vigorously and damaging his skin — or has excessive dandruff or greasy skin, this could indicate skin disease or parasites such as lice or pin-worms. If you live in an area where spring weather is humid or rainy, the horse's winter hair may harbor fungi or bacteria. Dirt, moisture, and dead hair make an ideal place for rain rot and other skin problems.

You can speed the shedding process and minimize the chances for skin diseases by daily grooming, using a rubber curry comb or shedding blade to remove dead hair, followed by brisk brushing and massage. This increases circulation to the skin and stimulates the oil glands, contributing to a healthy hair coat. If a horse has a skin problem, bathing with an antiseptic shampoo may help.

Dealing With Scratches

Spring mud can cause problems, including fungal skin lesions on horses' lower legs. This condition can occur when the lower legs are often wet or in contact with mud and manure (and may occur at other times of the year as well, depending on climate and pasture or paddock conditions).

Scratches is the common term for a skin problem that is often caused by fungi and bacteria. The affected area becomes crusted, scabby, and thickened. The skin may ooze or the whole lower leg may swell, and in severe cases the horse becomes lame. This condition generally affects unpigmented skin (the white leg markings) more readily than dark skin; the latter is thicker and tougher and more resistant to small injuries that open the way for the fungal infection.

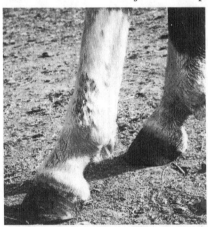

Scratches on unpigmented skin.

Traditional treatments for scratches were astringents like methylene blue, iodine mixed with glycerin, or ointments made with zinc oxide, nitrofurazone, and steroids. A very effective treatment is a mix of equal parts nitrofurazone, DMSO (dimethyl sulfoxide), and thiabendazole (a dewormer that's also a good fungicide). This dewormer paste is hard to find now, but you can substitute one of the other benzimidazole dewormers such as fenbendazole, cambendazole, oxybendazole, oxfendizole, or mebendazole. Any deworming paste that contains one of these drugs as its main ingredient will work.

The affected area should be scrubbed thoroughly to remove all dirt or mud and dried with a clean towel. Then the medication mixture can be applied to the affected part of the leg. The DMSO reduces swelling and inflammation and helps the other medication penetrate the area thoroughly. The nitrofurazone combats bacterial infection that may accompany the fungus and also buffers the DMSO so it won't burn or irritate the tissues. The paste dewormer is the safest fungicide to use in conjunction with DMSO, since it is an oral medication (safe to use internally). Harsh or poisonous fungicides like iodine should never be used with DMSO, a powerful solvent that is immediately absorbed by the body. It carries anything else with it.

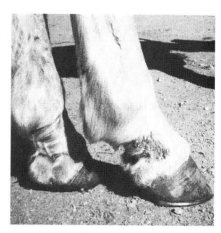

Cracked and chapped pasterns.

The best prevention for scratches is to keep white-legged horses out of muddy or wet pastures because the pink skin chaps and cracks more readily than dark skin. Fungus, once introduced into the soil, remains there, and horses may pick it up if they have cracks or breaks in the skin, especially around the heels or pasterns. Scratches also can be a problem in winter pastures or dry summer pastures if the fungus exists in the dust and dirt and is introduced through breaks in the skin. If caught early, however, a few treatments will clear this condition up quickly.

Spring Grass

New grass is high in protein and easily digested carbohydrates. Though it is high in water content and low on filler, horses crave it after a winter on dry grass or hay and tend to overeat. Cases of colic, diarrhea, and grass founder increase in the spring and sometimes botulism (in certain regions) due to the horse eating toxic materials along with the new grass.

Spring grass can pose dangers.

Most of these problems can be avoided if horses are removed from pastures during spring thaw, kept off during early grass growth, and not put back until grass is well grown. Pastures also benefit from not having horses trampling the muddy grass or nipping off new green grass before it can grow.

Horses in large pastures can generally make the transition from winter-dry grass to new spring grass without problems, but some years new grass comes so suddenly that horses don't have time to adjust. If pastures go from bleak to lush all at once, horses can be at risk for founder because of the vastly higher level of easily digestible carbohydrates in young grass. Some horses are easy keepers and prone to founder. They should be locked up and adjusted gradually to the new grass. Some individuals should be kept off grass completely or put out for short periods after the grass is no longer so lush. Animals with a history of grass founder should never be turned out on pasture in early spring.

Spring Vaccinations

Spring is the usual time for vaccinations, partly because many diseases are summer problems. Some are spread by summer insects such as mosquitoes (equine encephalomyelitis and West Nile virus), occur seasonally (Potomac horse fever), or are likely to be spread from horse to horse during summer shows and competitions (influenza, strangles, and other respiratory diseases). Some may occur any time of year (tetanus or botulism), but an annual vaccination for each of these will generally protect horses. How often you vaccinate (some diseases need multiple booster shots for best protection) and which diseases you vaccinate against will depend on your geographic location and the amount of exposure your horses have to other horses.

Not every horse should be vaccinated against every preventable disease. Some vaccinations are unnecessary in certain regions or circumstances. All horses should be vaccinated against the highly fatal disease tetanus; the spore-forming bacteria that cause it lurk nearly everywhere in the soil, especially in regions that

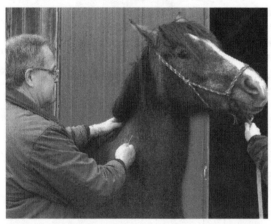

have been intensely cultivated for many years. There are a few small areas, however, including parts of the Rocky Mountains, where tetanus is not a problem.

Potomac horse fever (caused by a bacteria found in fluke larvae that parasitize fresh-water snails) is a threat in many regions (especially where there are rivers and streams). Rabies is also a threat in many areas. This deadly viral dis-

Spring is the season for many vaccinations.

ease occurs in cycles in wildlife populations and is such a health risk to pets, livestock, and humans that all pets and horses should be vaccinated if there's evidence of rabies in your area.

Venezuelan equine encephalomyelitis (VEE) occasionally threatens horses (and humans) in the Southwest when this viral disease comes north from Central America, but it is not a concern for horses in other parts of the United States. Eastern (EEE) and western (WEE) encephalomyelitis, however, are a threat to most horses in North America. These two diseases should be included in an annual vaccination program and can be given in a combination injection that protects against tetanus and influenza as well. In northern regions an annual booster is sufficient to give protection (after the initial series the first year the horse is vaccinated), but in southern areas with a long mosquito season horses may need two shots: one in early spring and another in late summer.

West Nile virus is another mosquito-borne disease that affects horses and humans. After coming into this country in the late 1990s, it has now spread to nearly all parts of the United States. Horses need an annual booster (before each mosquito season) after the initial series of shots. As with EEE and WEE, horses in warm climates with a very long mosquito season may need two boosters.

Viral diseases that cause respiratory problems in horses such as influenza, rhinopneumonitis, and equine viral arteritis (EVA) need to be included in a vaccination program if your horse comes in contact with other horses. EVA may not be a problem in your area, so ask your veterinarian. Some of these respiratory infections also can cause abortion in pregnant mares. Vaccinate mares that leave your farm to be bred or are stabled where strange horses come and go. Transmission occurs through direct exposure to infected horses or to the equipment or facilities contaminated by a sick horse. If a horse leaves your place only during summer (and no strange horses come to your place), time the vaccinations to give peak protection during the period your horse is exposed to other horses. Horses at high risk (on farms with lots of horse traffic, breeding stallions, mares sent to other farms to be bred, horses stabled at racetracks or fairgrounds) can be vaccinated as often as every two months.

Strangles vaccine should be given to horses with risk of exposure or living where strangles has occurred in the past. An intranasal vaccine for strangles now exists that is safer and more effective than the injectable vaccines. Horses that are not likely to be exposed to strangles do not need to be vaccinated. The same is true for botulism. Unless a horse lives on a farm or visits one where there are cases, vaccination for botulism is unnecessary unless you live in an area where these bacteria lurk in the soil.

There are also vaccines against enterotoxemia, Salmonella, and equine protozoal myeloencephalitis (EPM). Weigh these options against the risks for your horses and discuss with your veterinarian. Many horses need only one or two vaccines each year, while other horses may need the protection of several. You don't want to leave your horses unprotected from a serious disease, but you also don't need to vaccinate against the ones that are very low risk for your particular animals.

Vaccines are not 100 percent effective in preventing disease and can sometimes cause harmful reactions, but they are still the best tool for protecting horses against certain deadly and disabling illnesses. The vaccine stimulates the body to create antibodies that recognize and react with that virus or bacterium if it enters the body again. Production of antibodies and other immune substances from vaccination takes about seven to ten days in a healthy horse.

Varying degrees of vaccination failure occur in vaccinated horses. Most horses develop a fairly good immune response but some have only a partial or poor response to a vaccination and may not be protected against that disease. Stress, heavy parasite infestation, malnutrition, and other adverse situations may hinder an animal's ability to mount a good response to vaccination. Some vaccination failures are due to the horse's incubating the disease at the time of vaccination. If foals are vaccinated too young, immunity may not develop because of interference from maternal antibodies gained via colostrum; the body already has a passive immunity and does not bother to create a defense. When vaccinating foals, discuss a vaccination schedule with your veterinarian; different diseases have different optimum times (age of foal) and number of boosters for best results.

Giving a Vaccination

If you vaccinate your own horses, develop a good technique for giving injections using proper locations on the horse's body. Also be aware of possible vaccination reactions and how to deal with them. If you haven't given injections, have your veterinarian show you how. Watching the smooth technique of an experienced person can help you learn to do it properly and with little discomfort to the horse. Make sure the injection site is clean and dry, free of dirt or mud. Wet hair and skin are more likely to cause contamination when the needle is inserted.

Giving a shot in the rump muscle.

Intramuscular injections should always be given into thick muscle, such as the buttocks. This is the best site for large shots, such as antibiotics. A smaller injection (one or two cc) can be put into neck or breast muscles; most vaccines are small enough injections to use these sites. Never put more than two cc into the neck or breast. These muscles are not large enough to absorb a large shot and the tissue could swell. If you have a larger shot but don't want to use the buttocks, the dosage can be split into two or more portions and put into several locations, such as each side of the neck or into each breast muscle.

Veterinarians differ in which sites they recommend. Some veterinarians advise horsemen to use only the neck or buttocks (back of the hind leg) for vaccinations, saying the breast muscle is a bad place since a reaction might work directly into the chest. Others say the side of the neck, in a triangular location above the shoulder and below the mane, is a bad place, especially for vaccines that might cause reactions (some vets no longer give *any* shots in the neck) because horses may have difficulty eating or drinking with sore necks. An abscess, which can occur following a vaccination, in the neck is dangerous as the infection can follow the spaces between the muscle layers down into the chest. The neck is not as muscular as the rump or buttocks (it has more ligamentous tissue) and is not as good for absorbing the injection.

Horsemen traditionally used the large rump muscle for many injections. But many veterinarians do not recommend this site because of its horizontal position, which makes it difficult for proper drainage should an abscess develop. A properly administered injection has little risk of contamination but there is always the possibility. The buttock, neck, and breast muscles are more vertical locations; an infection at these sites would have better drainage. The buttock muscle is a good site unless a horse is inclined to kick. If using this location, stand close to the horse to avoid the full force of a kick.

If a horse is fidgety or resents injections, the easiest site is the muscle on either side of the breastbone, partly because this location is less mobile than his neck and he is also less sensitive here and less apt to feel the needle. If someone is holding and feeding him a treat to distract him, you can slip the needle in without his knowing it.

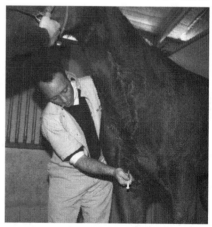

Make sure the injection site is clean, detach the needle from the syringe, and gently thump or press the area with the side of your hand holding the needle. Thump quickly two or three times and immediately insert the needle. Thumping tends to desensitize the area and mask the prick of the needle

Giving a shot in the chest.

so it will not startle the horse. If a horse is suspicious about the thumping because he's had it done many times before, just press the area firmly before inserting the needle. You also can desensitize the neck by pinching the skin just before inserting the needle.

If blood starts to ooze or drip from the inserted needle, remove the needle and start over; you don't want to inject vaccine into a vein. Double check by pulling the plunger back after you attach your syringe to the inserted needle. If blood appears in the syringe, remove the needle and try again. If no blood appears, give the injection, pushing the plunger in steadily but not too quickly. If using a screw-on needle and syringe, make sure it is well screwed together before pushing the plunger or it will come apart and lose the vaccine. With a slip-on needle make sure it's fully on, and hold the syringe and needle firmly together as you depress the plunger to make sure they don't come apart as you give the injection.

When finished, withdraw the needle and syringe and then rub or press the injection site to keep the fluid from leaking out until the hole in the skin constricts (and to desensitize the skin a bit longer). If fluid starts oozing out afterward, press that spot until it stops.

Vaccination Reactions

Sometimes a muscle will swell at the injection site, staying swollen for a few days. Vaccines are more apt to cause swellings than are injections of antibiotics, since the vaccine stimulates more tissue response. The amount of swelling from a vaccination depends upon the type of vaccine given and upon the individual horse's reaction to it. Some horses are more sensitive to certain products than others. In most cases the swelling is temporary; it might make the horse a little stiff for a few days. Mild exercise after a vaccination can often help prevent or resorb the swelling. Discuss a large swelling with your veterinarian because it may mean the horse is more sensitive to that vaccine.

There is some risk of serious reaction whenever you inject a foreign material into the body. Every horseman should be aware of these possibilities and be prepared to act swiftly if this happens. Horses can react to certain vaccines or to the carrier substance with which the vaccine ingredient is mixed. If a horse has a history of problems with vaccination, you may have to change vaccines or even delete one from his annual vaccination program. Discuss this with your veterinarian.

Vaccine reactions can include immediate response to the antigen being injected and range from anaphylactic shock (an acute allergic reaction affecting the whole body with life-threatening respiratory and circulatory failure) to a breathing problem (like asthma) caused by histamine release. Other types of reaction include damage from antibodies (such as destruction of kidney cells); damage from the antigen/antibody complex, such as serum sickness; and development of swelling and tissue death after the injection.

A mild reaction from an injection may create excessive local tissue swelling or hives all over the body. A severe allergic reaction may cause shortness of breath, like an asthma attack in a human. Giving the horse antihistamines can usually halt these reactions, but if a reaction is too severe the horse may go into shock and die unless treated with steroids and adrenaline to reverse the shock.

Though rare, anaphylactic shock is a potential risk with any injection. A horse going into shock may react in various ways. Skin, lungs, feet, or circulatory system may be affected. The horse may have trouble breathing and may suffocate. He may develop acute laminitis. He may collapse and die even before a veterinarian who just gave the injection causing it can give treatment. Usually the more serious the reaction, the sooner it will occur after the injection.

Another type of injection-related complication is infection; fatal clostridial infection can occur occasionally, even with scrupulous cleanliness. A non-antibiotic injection (vaccine, vitamins, and various drugs) may trigger a fatal infection if there are clostridial spores in the muscle tissue. Spores of clostridial organisms absorbed from the gut may lie dormant in the muscle until muscle trauma creates an environment for the bacteria to proliferate. If the horse's muscle harbors such bacteria, any injection other than an antibiotic would cause enough tissue damage to set the stage for infection.

Ticks

Many warm-weather pests that bother horses don't come out in force until summer, but a few are a nuisance in spring. Some species of ticks are springtime parasites looking for a host to latch onto for a blood meal. Checking a horse (and yourself) for ticks should be part of daily grooming after every spring ride. Horses at pasture in spring may pick up numerous ticks daily. The ticks wait on grass or bushes for a victim, then latch onto any part of the horse (or you) that brushes the plant.

Various types of ticks have similar life cycles — they live for two years or more, depending on species. Adult female ticks feed on warm-blooded hosts in order to produce eggs, which they lay in late spring to mid-summer. The resulting larvae do not feed on warm-blooded hosts until the following spring when they feed, molt, develop into nymphs, feed again, and then become adults ready to mate and lay eggs. On the host, they crawl to a preferred location (such as the underside of a horse's belly, on the sheath or udder, root of the tail or mane, or in the ears — depending on the preference of the species), pierce the skin, and start feeding on blood. Once attached with mouthparts and head buried in the skin, they can be difficult to dislodge.

There are many types of ticks. Some are hard-bodied, like the wood tick or dog tick, while others are soft. Many are round and reddish brown or light brown with gray-white speckles on the back and near the head. They are small and flat when they first attach to the host, then become plump and round when filled with blood. Some get twenty times larger, drinking up to two milliliters of blood. A heavy tick infestation can irritate the horse enough to interfere with grazing and may lead to weight loss or anemia.

Ticks are vectors (carriers and spreaders) of many protozoan diseases, including piroplasmosis. The protozoa in most cases survive from one generation of ticks to the next by infecting the ticks' eggs. Some ticks also spread diseases caused by bacteria, viruses, and rickettsia. The latter type of organism includes the one that causes Rocky Mountain spotted fever, a serious disease of humans. A viral disease sometimes spread by ticks is western equine encephalomyelitis. Tiny deer ticks can spread the bacteria that cause Lyme disease in humans and animals.

When removing a tick from your horse, be careful to extract the head along with the body. It's better to use a tool than your fingers. Using pliers, forceps, or tweezers, grasp the tick as close to its head as possible and work it loose gently so as not to leave the head or mouthparts embedded in the flesh. Don't squash the tick and get its fluids on your hands since you may be vulnerable to disease. If you can grasp the tick close to the skin and pull it straight out, you'll usually get the head and it won't matter if some of the mouthparts are left in the skin. Apply antiseptic to the site. You may want to preserve an unusual-looking tick in a jar to show to your veterinarian for species identification or to be tested for possible disease.

If horses have a heavy infestation they can be sprayed with an insecticide solution. Check with your veterinarian or agricultural extension agent for advice on insecticides and use one the ticks in your area have not yet developed resistance to. Be sure that the product is safe for horses. One chemical that is effective against ticks, mites, and lice on cattle and pigs is amitraz, but it is not safe for horses and can cause colic, impaction, and sometimes death. Before applying any product for ticks, read the label.

Another way to reduce the tick problem on horses is to deworm with ivermectin every six weeks during spring and summer. This drug paralyzes any blood-sucking parasite, and they soon die, including any tick that is attached to the horse at that time.

Summer Care

Summer brings its own problems, which can include heat and humidity, flies or harmful insects, summer storms, and in some areas excessive exposure to sunlight.

Heat and Humidity

Some regions have consistently hot weather in summer while others may have only a few days that get hot enough to be a problem for horses. Increased athletic activity and high summer temperatures can present special hazards. Temperatures above eighty degrees Fahrenheit, especially if relative humidity gets above 50 percent and there is no breeze, can greatly increase the chance for heat stroke. The horse has difficulty cooling himself because sweat does not evaporate when air is humid.

During extremely hot weather, try to transport horses at night when temperatures are cooler. To prevent problems, be sure trailer vents are open, don't blanket the horse, and remove back curtains or top doors for more ventilation. Horses should not be left inside a stationary trailer. Traveling will create an airflow to prevent heat buildup and encourage the evaporation of sweat to help cool the horses. Most trailers today have fans or can be equipped with fans to keep air moving over the horses even when the trailer is stopped.

Insufficient water can cause impaction.

In paddock or pasture, horses will benefit from shade during the hottest part of summer. If there is no natural shade, a shed or sunroof can be built. If weather is extremely hot, you may need to stable horses during the day (in a well-ventilated barn with individual stall fans) and put them out to graze only at night.

Shortage of water during hot weather can be a cause of heat stroke. If an automatic waterer quits working, you may not know soon enough that horses have no water. Unless you can check the waterers several times a day, it may be better to water a horse in a large tub so you know he has water and how much he's drinking.

The type of feed a horse eats also can make a difference in whether extreme heat will adversely affect him. Horses generate more body heat when digesting large amounts of protein. Some horses tend to colic in hot weather; in the process of cooling the body much of the blood flow is directed to the skin for cooling and sweat production, leaving less blood available for digestion. Digestive problems are compounded if a horse is exercised soon after being fed (a big problem with grains and concentrates, but not with forages), when blood is needed in the gut and the body temperature is already somewhat elevated by digestion. Large grain feedings should be given in the evening

Access to salt is important.

after the horse is done working and has more time for digestion in the cooler hours of night.

If a horse is short on water, a diet of coarse hay may lead to impaction in summer. A horse's water requirements increase if he has to sweat. If additional water is not provided, the digestive tract is shortchanged, making the horse more prone to constipation and impaction. He'll need adequate fresh water at all times, not just morning and evening. If weather is quite hot, a horse may have a poor appetite.

Access to salt is very important when horses are sweating. A horse may lose as much as one-third of a pound or more of salt per day. It's easier for a horse to consume loose salt than block salt when he needs to replace a lot at once. Use plain salt, especially in hot weather. Salt and trace minerals should not be fed in combined form, as the horse's needs for these are quite different; his salt need (aside from body metabolism) is based almost entirely on how much he sweats, whereas his need for most trace minerals remains steady and independent of exercise and hot weather. If a horse only has access to trace mineralized salt, he is being force- fed extra minerals via his salt needs. This can become dangerous, since some of the extra minerals are not easily excreted and can reach toxic levels.

Use good judgment when riding in hot weather or participating in strenuous athletic events. Don't make demands on your horse beyond his fitness level. Overexertion in hot weather is a common problem and can seriously endanger the life of your horse. Heat stroke or heat exhaustion occurs most often in horses being overworked in hot and humid weather, especially if they are not properly conditioned. The physical exertion and hot weather create competing demands on the horse's cooling system. His body cannot regulate its own temperature as tissues become dehydrated from excessive sweating, with resulting loss of fluid and vital electrolytes. A rider alert to early warning signs can halt the exercise before this dangerous situation becomes life-threatening or give electrolytes and provide water to replace the losses.

The Cooling Effects of Sweat

During hot weather, ability to keep cool is vitally important. The horse's normal temperature range is 99 to 100.5 degrees Fahrenheit, so a temperature that stays above 103 is serious. Above 105 is dangerous, and a temperature above 107 can be deadly. To dissipate body heat, the blood transports heat from the inner parts of the body to the skin, where the heat radiates into the air. Air exchange in the lungs also helps cool the blood. In milder temperatures, a hard-working horse may temporarily develop a rectal temperature as high as 105 degrees, but if he's healthy and fit, his temperature should rapidly drop back down to normal when exercise stops and he is cooled out.

However, the hotter the air temperature, the less efficient the horse's cooling efforts will be through air exchange or radiation from the skin, and he will have to rely upon sweat evaporation to dissipate heat.

Sweat glands open and allow fluid from blood vessels to escape to the body surface for evaporation, producing a cooling effect. It cools the skin surface and the blood passing through the vessels just under the skin. This cooled blood then circulates through and helps cool the rest of the body. Sweat is the primary source of water loss during hot weather or exertion. When exercising and sweating, a horse may lose up to four gallons per hour.

Sweating helps cool the body.

The effectiveness of sweating depends on the rate of heat production (how much the horse is exerting), the air temperature, relative humidity, and wind velocity. A breeze will speed the evaporation process greatly, cooling the horse much more rapidly than when the air is still.

In a dry climate, the horse may not seem to be sweating — the sweat evaporates almost as soon as it is produced, reducing body temperature. If air is humid, however, evaporation is hindered. Sweat may cover the body and run off in streams or turn to lather. Without evaporation, the body cannot cool efficiently, and signals for more sweating. Sweat production increases but does little good; the horse stays wet but does not become cooler. If he continues to work in hot, humid weather, he quickly dehydrates and overheats.

Fluid loss and electrolyte loss in horses working hard in hot weather may lead to fatigue, muscle spasms and cramps, dehydration, thumps (spasm of the diaphragm muscle triggered by a decrease in calcium and potassium), or heat stroke. Anything that inhibits a horse's ability to cool himself (long hair coat, too much fat, a blanket) may lead to heat stroke.

Heat Stroke

Early symptoms of heat stroke include unexpected fatigue, stumbling, and increased respiratory rate. The horse may become restless and anxious, progressing to erratic or irrational behavior, depression or excitability, disorientation, and rapid pulse and respiration. A horse with mild heat stress may have a respiration rate of forty and pulse of sixty; a horse with severe heat stress may have a respiration rate above fifty and pulse above eighty, at rest. Muscle tremors also can occur. A horse suffering from heat stress has dark gums (dark pink or maroon

Hosing with cool water helps.

instead of normal bubble-gum pink), and with severe heat stress they will be dark red or purple. His pulse may be very weak. Rectal temperature may reach 106 to 110 degrees. At first the horse will be drenched with sweat, but in severe cases sweating stops once the horse has run out of water. Hot, dry skin is another clue to impending heat stroke. He may be oblivious to his surroundings, won't eat, and has difficulty moving. If he's being hauled, he may go down in the trailer, or if he is being ridden, he may suddenly refuse to go on. Heat stroke also can occur in an idle horse if he is confined in a hot or poorly ventilated area, but more often the victim is being ridden and exerting in the heat.

Heat stroke is always an emergency; seek medical help at once. If untreated, the horse could collapse and go into convulsions or a coma and die within a few hours. Move him into shade if possible. Keep air moving with fans or manual fanning. Try to lower his temperature while you wait for the veterinarian. Do not blanket him. Hosing with cool water will help, especially if you can apply cool water to the inside of his legs and thighs and to the head and lower part of the neck. It's usually not wise to put cold water over the large muscles of the hindquarters or shoulders because of risk for muscle cramps, but in a horse with heat stroke, applying cold water over the entire body is the fastest way to cool him. The life-threatening danger of heat stroke is more important than worrying about muscle cramps.

If air is humid, scrape off excess water to take body heat with it. In humid conditions, removal of water (which is warm after touching the horse) is important; put cold water on, scrape it off, and keep adding more cold water and scraping it off. After thirty seconds of cold water cooling, walk the horse for twenty to thirty seconds, then apply cold water again. Alternately walking and cooling promote blood flow to the skin, and air movement aids evaporation. Keep checking his temperature. It should drop about two degrees Fahrenheit within ten minutes. Stop cooling when his temperature comes below 101, when his skin feels cool over the hindquarters after walking, or when his respiration rate drops below thirty or you may chill him. Definitely stop if he begins to shiver.

Don't use ice packs since this may constrict the blood vessels and hinder blood flow to the area under the pack, which will actually slow the cooling process. If using wet towels on the neck or head, continually pour cold water on them. A cold, wet towel left in place without constantly adding cold water will warm up and act as insulation, retaining heat and hindering heat loss unless you keep it cold. Sponge or spray cold water (or alcohol) over the areas where large blood vessels bring overheated blood to the surface (legs, head, and neck). Eating grass or drinking water will help the horse lower his internal temperature.

In a case of heat stroke, a veterinarian will give the horse large volumes of intravenous fluids to restore what has been lost and to help increase proper circulation. Cold water enemas may be necessary to reduce internal temperature. Once he seems back to normal, you can let the horse have all the green grass, grass hay, water, and salt he wants, but do not give him grain. His body is still stressed; concentrates may cause digestive problems. It may take a week or more for the horse to recover, and he may not be able to go back to work again for several months. A horse recovering from any heat-related illness should be on a diet of green grass or some other feed with high water content.

Preventing heat stroke is always better than having to treat it. In most instances you can prevent trouble through careful conditioning and training and by paying close attention to the horse's vital signs and sweating and avoiding situations that might lead to heat stroke. Fat horses and heavily muscled horses that don't dissipate heat well should be watched closely in hot, humid weather. Limit exercise when temperatures and humidity are dangerously high. A rule of thumb about danger zones: when temperature and humidity figures are added together and the total exceeds 130 (such as 80 degrees Fahrenheit with 50 percent humidity), the danger of overheating increases. This is also true whenever the air temperature approaches 100 degrees, even if humidity is low. These guidelines are only estimates, however, since they do not take wind speed into consideration. Use common sense and monitor your horse.

Know what is normal for your horse. Check pulse, respiration, and temperature after a workout to see how overheated he is and how quickly he recovers. When cooling him, walk in the shade if possible and in a big circle if there's a breeze to cool him on all sides. Check him fifteen minutes after you've cooled him and put him away, and again thirty minutes after that. If he is not completely cooled out (still retaining internal heat), he'll break out in a sweat again. This may happen if a breeze dries the horse; he seems dry and cool, but his internal temperature is still high.

If he does break out in another sweat, walk him and cool him out again. After a strenuous workout in hot weather, you should also check on him again several hours later, since he may be at risk for colic or founder. Try to avoid strenuous work during the hottest part of the day. During periods of extreme heat, ride very early in the morning or late in the evening.

Anhidrosis

Sometimes horses develop a sweating disorder called anhidrosis, which liter-ally means without sweat. Usually the sweating reflex goes into action during hot weather or exertion, but in hot, humid weather there may not be much differ-ence between the air temperature and the horse's body temperature. Sweat does not evaporate properly and the horse's cooling system doesn't work. After sweat-ing profusely for a time, the horse may quit sweating.

This is a problem for horses in tropical countries and some areas of the United States (especially the Gulf Coast states). Anhidrosis is not restricted to humid southern regions, however. Cases have been reported as far north as Minnesota and Michigan and in arid climates like Arizona and California. It has been esti-mated that 20 to 30 percent of Thoroughbreds in training in hot, humid regions suffer from some degree of anhidrosis. Even horses that grow up in hot areas can lose their ability to sweat, though the problem is most common in horses brought from other regions.

Foals and young horses are rarely affected, since their smaller bodies are more efficient in getting rid of body heat and they are usually not exerting themselves hard in hot weather. The ability to dissipate heat is related to body size and mass. Body mass and surface area are big factors in heat retention. A larger animal has a larger volume-to-surface area ratio and holds the heat in more readily; a big, heavy horse will overheat faster than a small one.

Anhidrosis usually develops during summer, may come on quickly or gradu-ally over several weeks, and continue until cooler weather. An affected horse starts panting and his performance drops off. Horses that do most of their hard work early in the morning (such as racehorses training before sunup) don't have as much problem as those that work during hotter parts of the day.

If a horse has to sweat continually to cool himself, as when working hard or liv-ing in a hot, stuffy stall, the sweat glands have to work overtime and eventually shut down because of over-stimulation. The horse becomes dry-skinned, pants with his mouth open, and has a temperature of 103 degrees or higher. He may have a few patches of sweat behind his ears, under his mane, and at the elbows and flanks, but no moisture over his body. Other signs of anhidrosis are dry, flaky skin and hair loss, especially around the eyes. Oils from the sebaceous glands are no longer taken out onto the skin by sweat. The dry skin may become itchy.

Prolonged inability to sweat puts a horse at risk for heat stroke and other prob-lems, but if discovered early, resting his cooling system can reverse anhidrosis. He should be bathed with cool water or sprayed with mist to bring temperature down to normal. Then his temperature should be monitored and kept low so he doesn't need to sweat. He must stay out of the sun but not in a hot, humid stall. A portable fan may be adequate to stabilize body temperature until his sweating reflex recovers. If anhidrosis is treated as soon as it occurs and the horse has not suffered this problem before, sweating ability may recover in a few days. If the problem is longstanding, however, the horse may need help for several weeks to maintain proper body temperature while he recovers. Misting fans can lower stall temperature as much as fifteen degrees. The horse should not exert himself in hot weather until he recovers. Some horses do not regain their ability to handle humidity and must be moved to a cooler climate.

The severely anhidrotic horse should be kept in an air-conditioned stall during the heat of day and turned

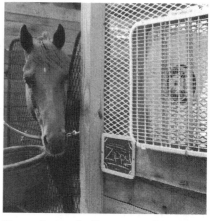

Try to keep the horse comfortable.

out only at night. A low-protein diet also can help, which means no alfalfa hay. A high-fat, low-protein diet produces less body heat during digestion. The horse should have access to salt.

Sunshine Problems

Long days of summer and the intensity of the sun's rays can sometimes cause problems for horses with white markings or light-colored skin. Dark skin has better protection against ultraviolet rays. Skin is pink under white markings and a few horses have light-colored or pink skin all over their bodies, heightening their risk for sunburn and skin cancer.

Horses with white faces or white markings around the eyes also can suffer from sun glare; their eyes may water from the constant irritation. Dark skin around the eyes helps absorb the sun's rays and protect the eyes from bright light, whereas light skin or white markings tend to reflect it into the eyes. The thin-haired eyelid area may also become sun-damaged and susceptible to cancer.

If a horse with white around his eyes squints in bright summer sunlight, you can protect his eyes by applying dark

Protecting skin with purple dye.

mascara or a purple-colored pinkeye spray for cattle around the affected eye. The purple dye in the pinkeye medication will not hurt the eye and stay dark on the skin for many days, reducing glare and reflected light. Theatrical grease paint (used by stage actors and athletes) also can be used. The screen mesh of a fly mask also can help cut down on the bright light and glare.

Sunburn can be a problem for horses with white markings (especially on the face) or for light-skinned horses, and is more prevalent in regions with intense summer sun. Irritated, red skin that sometimes blisters usually occurs where hair is thin (giving little protection against the sun's rays) and has no protective dark pigment. If a horse sunburns, use human sunscreen lotion (choose one with no PABA, which is harmful to animals). You can use ointment containing zinc oxide or an organic dye such as methylene blue or gentian violet. There are also some non-toxic protective lotions specially designed for horses.

In some instances the sunburn on white markings is caused by photosensitization. This condition occurs when a horse eats plants containing substances that cause a toxic reaction in unpigmented skin. The photodynamic agent in the plant is absorbed from the digestive tract into the bloodstream and travels to the skin tissues, where it is activated by sunlight in the unprotected white areas, killing the skin cells. The affected skin turns dark before it sloughs off.

A horse with this problem can be put in a barn during the day and turned out at pasture at night. Soothing ointment can be applied to the affected areas until they heal. To keep the problem from recurring, the horse should be removed from the feed or pasture that caused the reaction.

Squamous Cell Carcinoma

This type of skin cancer often occurs on the eyelids or around the vulva or sheath if skin is unpigmented. Cancer of the eyelid is fairly common in horses with pink eyelids (Paints, Appaloosas, Pintos) or any horses with white faces, light skin, or large white markings on the face with pink skin around one or both eyes. Tumors surrounding the eyeball are common in sunny areas like California and the Southwest. Intense sunlight can encourage the growth of cancer.

Cancer of the eyelid can spread to surrounding tissues, and unless caught early will necessitate removal of the eye. Most squamous cell carcinomas occur on the third eyelid or lower eyelid on the inner surface and may appear as a raised bump or a raw surface, looking like a runny sore. A bump or reddened area is not always cancer, but if the abnormality becomes larger, redder, or more irritated, the chances of its being cancer are great; the horse should have immediate veterinary attention to have the growth removed. If left untreated, the cancer will continue to grow and spread to nearby tissues, eventually killing the horse. To prevent cancer, horses with unpigmented eyelids should be protected from bright sunlight by keeping them stabled, providing shade during bright days, or painting a non-toxic substance carefully around the eye during bright sunny weather.

Squamous cell carcinoma can also appear on the male genitals (sheath and penis) and occurs most often on older horses. The pre-cancerous lesions are small, white, slightly raised plaques, less than five millimeters in diameter. Once lesions become cancerous, they can enlarge into growths with a cauliflower appearance or look like shallow, crusted ulcerations that fail to heal. Any persistent sore on a horse's penis or sheath should be checked by your veterinarian. These cancers tend to remain localized until spreading into the lymphatic system, so there is usually a chance to treat them successfully if discovered early.

Summer Storms

Summer lightning storms occur frequently in many regions. A shod horse, with four feet and metal shoes, is so well grounded he is at great risk during an electrical storm, and this fact should never be underestimated when you are riding. A storm can seem a long distance away, but often the lightning will precede it; you and your horse can be struck by lightning at the forefront of a moving storm well before it starts to rain.

A strike close by can also be dangerous, since wet earth may carry electricity a long ways. Lightning can affect you or your horse if it hits a nearby object, traveling through the ground and entering your horse's body through his feet. A horse and rider can also be injured when too close to an object that is directly hit, such as a tree, rock or fence. The electricity may splash onto you from the struck object. During a lightning storm, stay away from tall trees and wire fences, which can carry a charge a long way on the wires, especially with wooden posts. Steel posts draw the charge into the ground and dissipate it. Get away from rocky ridges. Lightning often hits high spots (ridge tops, trees, buildings), but not always. Canyon rims and high ridges usually draw more strikes than the canyon bottoms. If you are in timber, stay in a low spot and away from the taller trees.

Out in the open, avoid flat meadows or beaches. Stay away from anything that stands higher than the surrounding terrain. Get off your horse; you don't want to be the tallest object around. When caught in a lightning storm, crouch on the ground in a low spot, keeping your feet close together and your hands off the ground; keep as little of your body grounded as possible. Pay attention to weather patterns and predictions; if there will be storm activity, try to ride in the early morning. Most lightning storms build up in the heat of afternoon.

If lightning is a common summer occurrence where you live, take precautions to protect your horses at home also. Horses at pasture often bunch together for protection during a storm; if they seek shelter under a tree, they may all be killed if the tree is struck. Metal horseshoes on wet ground put a horse at risk even when lighting hits some distance away; the current goes into the ground, spreading through wet ground or standing water. Lightning can travel along power lines if it hits the line, and the current may come down poles or brace wires. If possible, avoid using pastures containing power line towers or poles.

Probably the safest place for a horse during an electrical storm is in a well-grounded building so that a lightning strike will be directed into the ground. A wooden barn is best, since it does not conduct electricity, but a metal barn can be made safe if equipped with proper lightning rods. All metal conduit and water pipes should be well grounded. Metal fencing (pipe corrals, steel posts, wire fences) can pose a danger in pastures, pens, and paddocks. Wooden or vinyl fencing will not conduct electricity nor carry the charge to a nearby horse if struck. When constructing or repairing horse facilities, consider its safety from electrical charge during lightning storms.

Summer Pasture Heaves

Heaves (chronic obstructive pulmonary disease—or COPD) is a common problem in horses that are stabled or fed dusty hay but practically unknown in pastured horses in northern climates. The best prevention or treatment for horses with COPD is to turn them out on pasture as much as possible so they avoid the dust and molds associated with bedding and hay.

A similar respiratory condition, however, can occur in horses grazing summer pastures in southeastern regions of the United States. Many horses on pasture in Alabama, Florida, Georgia, Texas, Louisiana, Mississippi, and neighboring states develop an obstructive pulmonary disease. Because this condition is not seen in pastured horses during winter, it has been called summer pasture-associated obstructive pulmonary disease (SPAOPD).

The seasonal onset of this respiratory problem varies from year to year. In some years horses may develop problems by late May, but not until late July or early August in other years. Environmental factors that seem to facilitate this condition are heat, humidity, and high moisture content in the soil. Affected animals are usually at least three years old; most horses are about seven to ten years old when they first experience this problem. A horse that develops SPAOPD usually improves during the cooler winter months only to show signs again the next summer.

Diet and allergy may be causative factors. Inhaled mold and pollens are possible allergens; the horse may breathe in some type of toxin while grazing. The lungs suffer from a con-

Listening for wheezing.

striction of the small airways and produce too much mucus (symptoms indica-
tive of allergy). Lush grasses may contain compounds that if eaten in sufficient
quantities could produce airway constriction.

Horses with SPAOPD show varying degrees of exercise intolerance — breathing heavily, becoming short of wind, and coughing frequently. The horse has difficulty exhaling, making an increased effort to push the air out through obstructed air passages, and may have a nasal discharge. In severe cases, even a short walk
in the pasture can exhaust the horse. Severely affected horses show a pronounced
abdominal lift at the end of exhalation, just like a horse with heaves that must
force the air out of his lungs, and they develop the characteristic heave line of
enlarged muscle along the lower abdomen. These horses eat less and lose weight.
If you listen to the horse's chest with a stethoscope, you can hear wheezing
sounds. Your veterinarian can diagnose SPAOPD with tests.

The best treatment is to remove the horse from the offending pasture and use
medication to dilate the airways so he can breathe better. He should be put in a
dust-free stall on a diet of hay or pelleted feeds. This can resolve the problem
within seven to ten days if the horse is treated when symptoms first appear.
Horses that don't respond to the environment change may have more severe airway inflammation or an accompanying infection that requires treatment with
appropriate antibiotics after culture.

To prevent SPAOPD, keep close track of horses at pasture and remove a horse
from the pasture as soon as the first signs appear. If a horse is kept off pasture
long enough to alleviate the condition, he may be able to be put back on pasture
again until signs recur. This type of alternating program can often control the
problem early in summer, but as the season progresses he may have to be
removed from pasture completely until the onset of cooler weather.

Flies and Mosquitoes

Flies and mosquitoes are the most common external parasites of horses during
summer. They cause irritation and spread diseases. Large numbers of insects on
a horse can result in excessive blood loss. Fly bites also can cause skin allergies
due to hypersensitivity reactions (allergic response). The annoyance from flies
can disrupt grazing; horses may run to get away from biting flies or seek shady
areas to cluster together and swish and stomp.

Stable Flies

The stable fly is similar to the housefly in size and appearance. Adult stable
flies often rest on vertical surfaces such as walls, trees, or fences and go to horses
only long enough to get a blood meal. They feed primarily in early morning or
late evening, biting the lower legs, flank, or belly.

Bites are painful, and a stable fly can take from five to ten minutes to drink its fill. It may puncture the skin several times and the bites may bleed freely. Both the male and female take a blood meal two or three times a day. In large numbers, these flies cause significant blood loss and severe irritation.

The female lays eggs in rotting hay and straw (especially if it contains urine) and horse manure. Several generations can develop through the summer. Occasionally a large population of these flies can kill a horse. In a stable or pasture with many flies, more than twenty-five flies may be on a horse at once, but that number represents only 2 to 3 percent of the total flies feeding on that horse daily.

Stable flies spread several diseases, including anthrax and equine infectious anemia (EIA), and act as a mechanical vector for strangles, pigeon fever, and other diseases by carrying pathogens from a sick horse to a healthy one. This fly also acts as an intermediate host for a stomach worm, *Habronema microstoma*, which causes summer sores (habronemiasis).

Control involves removal of breeding places such as rotting organic matter, manure and soiled bedding, piles of grass clippings, or wet hay. Covering compost piles with black plastic can slow the multiplication of flies. Spraying the areas where the flies rest will reduce their numbers, and use of repellents can help protect horses.

Horse Flies and Deer Flies (Tabanids)

Tabanids (horse flies and deer flies) are the worst biting flies in most regions. They may be black, brown, yellow, or gray, varying in size from three-eighths of an inch to more than an inch in length. Their broad bladelike mouth parts cut a deep and painful wound. Blood flows from the bite and the fly laps it up.

Tabanids are found primarily where there are large areas of permanently wet ground. Pastures located far from wet areas have fewer flies. Females lay masses

Flies aggravating a horse.

of eggs on foliage growing near water and the larvae drop into the mud to feed on juices of other insect larvae or earthworms. They stay in the larval stage during summer, fall, and winter, then migrate to drier areas of soil in the spring to pupate. The adult flies emerge when weather gets hot and the females seek a host, pestering horses until a blood meal has been obtained. Some horses develop lumps on the chest, flanks, and upper legs in reaction to the bites.

Tabanids, like stable flies, are often mechanical vectors of diseases, carrying pathogens from one horse to another. Eliminating swampy areas best controls horse flies and deer flies. Sprays or wipe-on repellents may temporarily protect horses. If horses can go into a shed during the heat of the day when flies are active, they may get some relief since most tabanids prefer sunlight. They are most active on hot, sunny days and less active in cool weather or when the day is cloudy.

Horn Flies

Horn flies are primarily parasites of cattle but can also be a nuisance to humans and horses. Horn flies spend most of their time on the host animal, taking twenty to thirty blood meals per day. They may cluster on the withers, topline, and underline of a horse. The constant irritation from their bites may cause sores around the eyes and under the belly, leaving the skin raw and crusted. It can be hard to tell the difference between horn fly skin irritation and cutaneous onchocerciasis (swelling and hair loss due to tiny worms spread by biting midges). Hypersensitivity reactions to the fly and midge bites also may cause hair loss and thickening of the skin along the underside of the belly.

Horn flies are bloodsuckers and cause irritation but usually do not transmit disease. Adult horn flies are only half the size of a housefly. Horses are very sensitive to their bites, and as few as twenty horn flies may seriously annoy a horse. The adults leave the host only to lay eggs in fresh cattle manure. Insecticide wipes or sprays applied to the horse's legs, belly, and flanks can be effective in getting rid of these flies.

Black Flies, Sand Flies, Buffalo Gnats

These are very small gray to black flies, often plentiful in areas with streams or after flooding. The flies attack in swarms and cause great irritation; horses may run frantically to escape them. Some horses develop hypersensitivity reactions to the bites.

Black flies feed inside the horse's ears, on the chest, udder, scrotum, inside the thighs, and under the belly. The bites itch, ooze blood, and create swelling and bloody crusts. Horses can be put in a barn or shed mornings and evenings when flies are most active, since these flies don't go indoors. Fly repellents, sprays, and wipe-on products can help if applied two or three times a day. To protect the ears, use an ear net or apply petroleum jelly inside the ears. The flies will not bite through the jelly.

Midges

Biting midges, also called gnats or no-see-ums, may attack in swarms, feeding on the horse at night. Their bites often cause hypersensitivity reactions; the horse may damage his skin with constant rubbing. Putting horses indoors at night provides best relief from midges. If this is not an option, use repellent sprays or wipe-ons in the late afternoon to help protect horses. If a horse develops an allergic reaction to the bites, consult your veterinarian.

Face Flies

Similar to house flies in size and color, face flies are common pests of cattle; if horses are pastured near cattle, the flies also bother horses, feeding on secretions from the eyes and nostrils and

blood from bites of other flies. Face flies do not bite but use sponge-like mouth parts to feed. They congregate around the horse's eyes, nostrils, or any open wound and can spread bacterial infections. Controlling face flies can be difficult because they stay on the horse only a short time. Insecticides applied to horses' heads and necks can help keep these flies away, as can fly masks or face screens attached to a halter.

Face flies congregate around eyes.

Bot Flies

Bot flies do not bite but often drive horses into a frenzy when laying eggs on the horse's hairs. One species lays eggs on the hairs of the legs, chest, and flanks, another lays eggs on the hairs under the jaw, and a third cements its eggs to the long hairs of the muzzle. The eggs on the body hatch when a horse licks himself, transferring the tiny larvae into the mouth; the eggs under the jaw become larvae that migrate into the mouth. The larvae eventually end up in the stomach lining to spend the winter, passing out with manure in the spring. They burrow into the ground and pupate before becoming adult flies to begin the cycle again.

Bot flies can be a hazard to anyone working around horses, as they can cause horses to run frantically, strike out with a front foot, or itch their chins over each other's backs. When a bot fly attacks a horse, a person nearby may be in danger of being struck or run over. The best control for bots is to eliminate them before they become adults, removing any eggs laid on the horses' hair and deworming in late summer, fall, and again in the spring to kill the larvae within the horse. If your neighbors do not control bots in their horses, however, you may still be plagued with flies that come visiting.

Mosquitoes

Mosquitoes play a major role in spreading diseases and some types of tiny filarid worms. Eliminating breeding sites (standing water) or treating breeding sites with proper insecticides can control mosquitoes. No insecticide applications on horses give long-lasting relief, but some products will give partial relief if applied frequently.

Summer Sores

Habronemiasis is a skin condition caused by the larva of a stomach worm when it tries to develop in the skin instead of the stomach. These tiny worms are brought to the skin by flies. Any cut, open wound, or break in the skin can give access to this parasitic infection and in some geographic regions the resulting summer sores are a serious problem.

The culprit is a small white worm that usually lives in the horse's stomach. The worm eggs pass out with the manure and the larval stage is eaten by larvae of stable flies and house flies; the worm larvae mature inside the flies. When infected flies feed on skin wounds or eye secretions (or other moist places on the horse such as the sheath), the worms leave the flies and enter the horse's skin, creating sores.

The larvae cannot complete their life cycle in these locations but can live up to two years in the skin, causing a non-healing sore. Even a small scratch in the skin can become a serious ulceration if it becomes infested with worm larvae. The immature worms cause severe irritation while migrating through skin and flesh, causing inflammation, swelling, itchy bumps, and often a raw spot that may ooze pus. This attracts more flies; a vicious cycle is created as more larvae are deposited. The irritated tissue cannot heal because of the constant disruption by the worm larvae, and it becomes a larger and larger swollen mass. Some horses develop a hypersensitivity reaction.

If left untreated, the wound may not heal until cold weather. It may seem to heal when flies are inactive (there are less larvae deposited and migrating around in the wound), but warm weather brings it back again. The only way to get rid of the problem is to kill larvae that are migrating in the tissues and keep new larvae from being deposited. For many years the only treatment for summer sores was diligent fly control, surgical removal of lesions, and use of organophosphate (insecticide) medications along with powerful deworming drugs given intravenously to kill larvae within the lesions. Topical treatments don't kill migrating larvae and merely irritate and damage traumatized tissue.

Ivermectin is an easier, more effective treatment. This dewormer works throughout the horse's body to kill a wide variety of parasites, both internal and external. An oral dose of ivermectin kills the larvae within the wound lesion so the sore can heal. Two doses three to six weeks apart may be needed. Sometimes antibiotics are also needed to combat infection caused by the worms' irritation. Wounds should be protected so flies can't get to the exposed tissue. If flies are controlled to prevent reinfestation, the sore can heal within a few weeks unless there is extensive tissue damage, which may require additional treatment.

Ivermectin used regularly for deworming can prevent summer sores. This dewormer kills the mature worms in the stomach also. Elimination of the stomach worm breaks the life cycle so no larvae will be passed in the manure to infest the flies.

Filarid Worms

Another worm that sometimes creates a problem in horses' skin is *Onchocerca cervicalis*, a tiny filarid worm that causes an itchy dermatitis. Originally a problem in the tropics, this parasite is now fairly common in the southern United States. The larvae live in the skin's tiny blood vessels, where they can be picked up by blood-sucking insects and biting flies (especially midges) and carried to other animals. The larvae eventually mature and migrate to connective tissue where they form a small nodule. In horses, these nodules containing adult worms are often found around the fetlock or lodged in a broad ligament in the topline of the neck.

Adult worms live about six to ten years in the nodules and the females shed larvae (called microfilaria) into the bloodstream. They are carried to the skin, picked up by biting insects, and taken to other animals to start the cycle again. While in the skin, the tiny larvae create sores (a reaction to the tiny larvae) along the midline of the abdomen (ventral midline dermatitis) and on the chest, shoulders, withers, and upper insides of the thighs.

The sores often look like fungal growths because hair falls out and underlying skin becomes hard, thick, and sometimes oozing. Unlike fungal growths, however, the spots itch intensely. The sores appear in the spring and tend to go away during winter. A fungus, by contrast, recedes during summer months (longer hours of sunlight tend to kill it) and becomes more active in winter. Like hebronema larvae, this parasite can be controlled by fly reduction and ivermectin (given twice at three- to six-week intervals).

Sweet Itch

Sweet itch (also called summer itch, Queensland itch, muck itch, summer seasonal dermatitis, and summer eczema) is a skin allergy triggered by the saliva of biting insects such as gnats and sometimes by tiny worm larvae in the skin. If a horse is already sensitive, just one or two bites can reactivate an allergic response. Once a horse is sensitized to a particular insect's bite, he becomes even more sensitive every summer.

The most common offender is the tiny *Culicoides* gnat. These gnats are also called no-see-ums, biting midges, sand flies, or punkies. They are active in warm weather when there is no breeze. Some feed on horses at night; others, at twilight; and a few, during the day. In warm regions a horse may suffer year-round.

It seems to take several years of cumulative exposure to gnat saliva to sensitize the immune system. Once the horse becomes hypersensitive, his skin may overreact to bites of other insects as well, such as stable flies and mosquitoes. Horses may rub until the skin is raw and bleeding. Lumps and intense itching often start along the mane, tail, head, belly, or topline. Eventually the horse loses patches of hair, especially in the mane and tail, and the skin becomes thick and scarred from rubbing. The bite areas are warm, red, and oozing serum.

A horse suffering from hives.

If gnats bother a horse, start preventative measures early in the season before his skin becomes seriously affected. Gnats can be somewhat controlled by eliminating the standing water where they breed, and a horse can be protected in a stall with fine gnat-proof screening and use of a fan; air movement tends to discourage gnats since they are not strong fliers. Fly repellents, fly sheets, and fly bonnets (covering ears as well as face) with mesh fine enough to keep gnats out can help as can keeping a horse indoors during the insects' active hours.

Treatment for the allergy may include antihistamines and anti-inflammatory drugs, primarily steroids. Antihistamines must be given several times a day to be effective and are impractical for long-term use. An antibiotic ointment containing a corticosteroid can be applied to the raw sores to help them heal faster and quit itching.

Controlling Flies

Flies that annoy horses can be controlled by diligent management. Your first line of defense is to keep flies from reproducing by eliminating breeding sites. Your second defense is to keep larvae from hatching. Some horsemen give an oral larvicide, putting about an ounce per feeding in a horse's grain. The tiny, tasteless pellets pass through the digestive tract without affecting the horse and end up in manure. The chemical kills the larvae of any flies that lay eggs in the manure.

Another way to break the flies' life cycle is with fly predator wasps. These tiny nocturnal wasps are almost too small to see with the naked eye and spend their entire lives on or near manure. The females search through the manure and lay eggs in the pupae of flies that breed in manure. The wasp eggs quickly hatch and feed on the dormant fly pupae, killing the fly before it can fully develop. The tiny stingless wasps are harmless to people and animals. They are generally present

Eliminate breeding sites.

wherever there are flies, but not in large enough numbers to control the fly population. You can purchase these wasps, which you release early in the fly season, then periodically throughout the summer, to help control fly populations.

Suppliers of predator wasps recommend spreading them directly on and around the manure in corrals, paddocks, and barns in early spring before flies are numerous, and putting more out every thirty days. A female fly can lay three times the number of eggs laid by a wasp, so you need plenty of wasps. The number needed depends on the number of horses on your place. With one or two horses you would need five thousand predator wasps each month; a facility with three to five horses would need ten thousand wasps per month, and a facility with a larger herd should put out one thousand to two thousand predator wasps per horse per month. If you use this type of fly control, you must be careful using insecticides or they will kill the wasp population along with the flies.

Other methods that can help reduce the fly population include flytraps, fly paper, or electronic fly zappers. The latter attract flies to their light and kill them on contact. Fly-killing strips can be used in enclosed areas such as feed rooms or tack rooms. Some types of sticky tapes are designed for location on barn ceilings, where flies like to rest. As tape gets filled with flies that stick to it, it can be rolled onto its empty spool, exposing fresh tape as needed.

Another method for killing flies is a latex paint containing a crystallized insecticide that kills flies within twenty-four hours of contact. It can be painted on surfaces where flies congregate, retaining its effectiveness for about a year. The paint can be used indoors or out, making a clear, odorless surface that is not damaged by rain, sun, or extreme temperatures. The insecticide kills flies, spiders, ticks, wasps, and any other insect that touches it, but it is not toxic to horses that might chew it.

Protecting the Horse

Before the days of insecticides, repellents, and other ways to control flies, horsemen added fringe to halters, bridles, and harness, so the horse could jiggle and brush flies off more easily. The harness net could dislodge flies with the motion of the horse as he walked. Tail extenders were also used if a horse's tail was too short.

Today some of these protections are still available, including improved fly masks and bonnets, fly shakers and nets, and body sheets. Fly masks come in several styles; some protect just the eyes while others cover the ears and cheeks. The mesh screen allows the horse to see while keeping flies out. Some have fleece-lined ear openings and edges (across the face) to keep flies from crawling in under the mesh. The mask or bonnet can be fitted to the horse's head (snug but not tight) with Velcro strips. Fly bonnets for just the ears are also available.

Nylon fly shaker strips can be added to halter or bridle to brush flies off the face whenever the horse shakes his head. Fly nets with longer strips can be buckled onto a harness. Fly boots can be used for horses that stomp a lot to dislodge flies from their legs (an alternative to using fly spray on the legs). Fly sheets are blankets made of cool, open-weave mesh that covers the horse's body to keep flies from biting without making the horse too warm. The open weave allows air flow and sweat evaporation.

Fly masks can protect the head.

A number of insecticides (for killing flies) and repellents (that discourage flies from landing, or keep them from biting if they do land on the horse) are made for horses. Some products contain both; they keep most flies away and kill the ones that do land on the horse. Most products must be used frequently. If the horse sweats on a hot day, the effects won't last long.

Some horsemen repel flies by adding apple cider vinegar to the horses' feed during fly season. The vinegar is mixed with grain, using two tablespoons vinegar to a quarter cup grain. Vinegar seems to make the horse smell different to the flies; they still land on the horse, but rarely bite. To start this program, add a few drops of vinegar to your horse's grain, gradually increasing it over several days until you reach the amount that seems to work. Most horses don't mind the vinegar flavor but you can add molasses to disguise it if needed. Use only pure apple cider vinegar. It takes several weeks for the vinegar to build up to repellent effect in the horse's body, so it's best to start adding it to feed before fly season.

Vinegar also can be used externally, rubbed over the horse's coat. A homemade fly spray with vinegar is used by some horsemen, mixing one ounce of citronella oil, two ounces of Avon Skin So Soft® lotion, one cup vinegar, and one cup water to put in a spray bottle. It must be shaken well before each use; the contents separate.

Using fly repellent.

Some commercial sprays contain ingredients that repel insects. Most of these use a combination of eucalyptus, cedarwood, or tea tree oils with citronella, aloe vera, or lanolin added for coat conditioners. Citronella is a lemon-smelling extract from a species of Asian grass. Aromatic tree oils also have repellent qualities. These natural repellents discourage flies but do not kill them. They can help if a horse (or person) is sensitive to chemical insecticides.

Some insecticides are more toxic than others and also more long-lasting. Least toxic (and also least long-lasting) are the natural pyrethrins. Next are permethrins (synthetic pyrethrins), followed by the carbamates, and then the more toxic and longer-lasting organophosphates. Each type is available in several forms for use on horses.

Topical spray repellents usually contain a small amount of insecticide (usually pyrethrins or permethrins) along with a substance that is irritating to the flies to discourage them from landing or biting. Repellents also may contain sunscreens, coat conditioners, or ingredients to help keep the repellent on the hair longer. Read labels to see if the product is to be used full strength or diluted.

Repellents can be water, oil, or alcohol-based. Oil-based products usually remain on the hair longer but also attract dirt and dust. Some products are claimed to last several days, but their actual length of effectiveness depends on weather, how much the horse sweats, whether he is regularly groomed and blanketed, and whether he rolls. For best results make sure the horse is clean before you apply the spray or wipe.

Wipe-ons are usually oil-based and last longer than water-based sprays. Spraying is convenient but can be wasteful or ineffective unless done properly. Using a cloth or mit to apply a liquid can result in uneven application and wet spots that soak through to the skin (which can be harmful if a horse is sensitive to the product). The thicker creams and lotions are usually water based but stay in place due to consistency. They are impractical to apply to the whole horse and are best suited for around the face and areas that are difficult to spray.

If you haven't used a certain type of product on the horse before, apply it lightly to a small area of the body first to make sure the horse won't have an allergic skin reaction. This is rare, but signs of reaction include hives and swelling. If a horse reacts to a product, scrub him with shampoo and rinse thoroughly to remove as much of the repellent as possible. If the allergy is severe, contact your veterinarian. Equine skin is more sensitive than human skin so always patch test a product before you give a horse a full application. Avoid applying a heavy concentration of insecticide on the sheath or udder; the skin there has little or no protective hair coat and may be sensitive to the chemicals in some sprays. To avoid getting the chemical into his eyes, never spray the horse's head or face.

One insecticide paste is a roll-on that can be applied on a few locations to give total body protection. The manufacturers recommend a smear under each eye, one down each leg (below knee or hock), on the back, and the belly. Certain chemical ingredients enable the permethrin insecticide to bond with natural oils in the horse's hair coat and migrate down each individual hair shaft. It takes about twenty-four hours for it to spread all over the body, but then its time-release action lasts for up to three weeks.

Another way to apply repellent is with towelettes, which are handy to take on a ride or in your pocket. They come individually packaged, don't leak, and are easy to carry or store. One towelette holds enough repellent to protect the face, ears, neck, chest, and legs of a horse (and are nice for horses that don't like the sound and feel of a spray), but is good for only one application. Towelettes and roll-ons are a good way to apply protection around a horse's ears and eyes. Repellent ointments can protect open wounds and abrasions that attract flies.

Strips impregnated with repellents or insecticides can be attached to a halter. These often last several months and are very effective for deterring face flies. Fly masks and light sheet blankets also can come impregnated with fly repellent, remaining effective for two years or longer. These usually contain a permethrin found in many wipes and sprays. The specially treated fabrics are effective for killing and repelling most flies, as well as ticks, spiders, and mosquitoes. Permethrin is highly toxic to insects and other arthropods but relatively non-toxic to mammals.

Stable Sprays

Insecticides can be used in barns and buildings to reduce the fly population. Some types are unsafe to use on horses or bedding and should only be used when there are no animals in the barn. Some forms of insecticide, designed for application on fly resting areas such as bushes or barn rafters, can last up to six weeks,. Fogs and mists that expel into the barn air can be used daily.

An inexpensive stable mister dispenses insecticide from an aerosol bottle with a timing device powered by flashlight batteries. It puts out a spray every fifteen minutes, twenty-four hours a day, for six to twelve months before the batteries need changing. Misters can control flying insects in an area of about six thousand cubic feet (twenty feet wide by thirty feet long, by ten feet high, effectively protecting two or three stalls when properly located). Each can of aerosol spray lasts about thirty days. A more expensive electric mister has a reservoir you fill with insecticide whenever it runs low. Automatic mist systems can be helpful in barns, especially if strategically located where flies tend to congregate during certain times of day. The misters can be aimed at these resting places.

Bees, Hornets, and Wasps

Stinging insects can be a problem for horses, sometimes causing accidents if a horse is stung while being ridden or handled. The situation can become a serious emergency if the horse gets multiple stings around the nose; the subsequent swelling can shut off the air passages and cause suffocation.

When riding, do not use perfumes, scented lotions, perfumed shampoos, or fly sprays with a citrus scent. These smells attract bees. Be alert for places wild bees might nest, such as hollow logs, old tires, and holes in the ground. Watch for bees entering or leaving such an opening or crevice. The ground vibrations of your horse's feet may be enough to alarm the bees and they may attack you and your horse; their instinct is to protect their nest from predators. Before you load a horse into a trailer, check it for wasps and bees that might be living inside. A horse being stung while in an enclosed trailer can cause an accident.

Eliminate any bee or wasp nests around the barnyard and paddocks, especially those of African bees (which are spreading northward from Texas, Arizona, New Mexico, and southern California). These bees are very aggressive and often attack anything that comes near. Horses in a corral, barn stall, or tied up can be very vulnerable because they cannot get away.

You should hire a professional to remove African bee nests, but you can safely remove wasp and hornet nests after killing the occupants with pyrethroid sprays. Use a spray designed for wasps and hornets (sending out a concentrated stream fifteen to twenty feet long). Spray the nest just before dark when the insects are all inside it. Don't use a light or flashlight because it will attract them. If you are spraying in a barn or paddock, remove the horses first to make sure they won't be stung and wear long sleeves and long pants for your own protection. Spray a long, steady stream into the nest opening and be ready to move away quickly if some of the occupants come out fast before dying.

Fall Care

Some aspects of horse care may change in the fall, especially if you live in a northern region with extreme weather changes from summer to winter. During the fall, you may be taking shoes off some of the horses, deworming for bots, and getting your horses ready for winter.

A common problem for horses in the fall is skin ailments. Various types of dermatitis and skin diseases are due to wetter weather or changes in the weather, fewer hours of sunshine each day, or horses being confined in stalls rather than out at pasture.

Rainrot

Rainrot (rain scald) is a skin problem that often appears during wet weather. Typical signs include very sensitive skin, clumps of hair coming off, and raw spots or crusty patches on the horse's back. After a rain you may see the horse's hair standing up in an odd pattern on portions of the body that got wet and where water ran down off the horse's sides. As you run your hand over the horse, you might feel heat and his back may be sore. By the next day he may have tight scabs on the sensitive areas. The scabbing may be a light peppering of small bumps, or the whole area may be a painful sheet of crusty, scabby skin.

The scabby bumps and crusts tend to be located in the runoff patterns on the horse's back and body, such as down the flanks and over the shoulders, back, rump, and neck. A heavy rain that wets the whole horse may cause bumpy crusts over most of the body, while a light rain causes only scattered patches. You may first notice the problem when brushing the horse. In early stages it is easier to feel the emerging bumps than to see them, and the bumps may come loose as you rub. They may be hot and tender and the horse may be sensitive when you brush him. As the disease progresses, the bumps become more raised and tufts of hair stand erect.

Rainrot is caused by the bacterium, *Dermatophilis congolensis*, which seems to have characteristics of both fungi and bacteria. It normally lives in the soil (dirt and mud of a pen or pasture) and is present in dust particles. The combination of water and dirt, such as when a dusty horse gets wet, makes an ideal environment for this opportunistic invader. This microbe can live in a dormant state within the skin for long periods. If the skin is compromised in some way, such as prolonged wetting by rain or high humidity, moisture enables dormant microbes from earlier lesions to establish new infection sites.

Rainrot is rarely a problem in dry weather. Best prevention is to keep horses clean and dry. If rainrot is a recurring problem, regular grooming, with periodic vacuuming to get as much dust and dirt as possible out of the hair, and a bath twice a month with a medicated shampoo can prevent this skin problem.

A common scenario for rainrot development is a period of rain following a dry, dusty spell. The dusty conditions fill the horse's coat with dirt (especially if he rolls), covering the skin with the microbe-laden particles.

A horse with rainrot.

275

The rain then provides moisture for the organism to multiply. The problem often continues into winter if weather stays wet. A long, thick winter coat provides ideal conditions for the organism to keep multiplying.

Rainrot does not occur as much in stabled horses as in outdoor horses because they don't get the chance to roll in the dirt and pick up the microbe. The disease also occurs less frequently in horses that are regularly brushed, keeping the skin free of dust and dirt that might harbor the microbe. Sweat, skin secretions, dirt, and manure in the hair of an unbrushed horse can combine with moisture to get the organism started. Some horses seem more susceptible to rainrot infection. If kept on pasture or in a dusty paddock, they tend to develop the problem every year.

Rainrot is not contagious; it is spread by organisms in dirt and dust rather than by direct contact with an infected horse. It may appear in several horses at the same time, however, if they are kept in the same environment. Rainrot can be spread from one horse to another by dust and dirt on grooming tools and saddle pads. Don't use the same brushes or tack on more than one horse. You may want to disinfect grooming tools occasionally with a mixture of one part bleach and three parts water.

Treatment of rainrot consists of cleaning skin and hair with an iodine shampoo (or human dandruff shampoo or an antiseptic pet shampoo). You may have to shampoo the horse daily for seven to ten days (then several times a week) to get rid of bacteria-laden dirt in the hair coat. Massage the skin as you wash it, gently working loose the scabs and crusts. Leave the shampoo on for five to ten minutes before rinsing it off so the iodine has time to do some good. You can follow the shampoo and rinsing with a diluted iodine solution (one part povidone iodine to ten parts water) and leave it on the horse to dry.

After the horse is clean and dry, apply a mixture of equal parts tamed iodine (povidone iodine, such as Betadine®, which is not as harsh as tincture of iodine) and mineral oil to affected areas (or an ichthammol salve — ointment made from a coal-tar base). The tamed iodine kills bacteria, and the mineral oil soothes raw spots and softens crusts, making removal of scabs easier next time. Never use iodine undiluted on the horse's skin or it may cause burning and irritation. Most horses tolerate diluted iodine with mineral oil, however. The oil leaves a coating on the hair that lasts several days (until next bathing), keeping the iodine in contact with the affected area longer.

Some veterinarians recommend a course of antibiotics, starting at the beginning of symptoms, to halt the infection before it gets well started. Often this halts the problem before it progresses to hair loss. Some cases of rainrot run their course and heal without treatment, but it takes longer. Serious infections should always be treated to prevent complications and scarring.

Unhealthy Edibles

Fall brings ripe seeds and fruits and after frosts some wilted leaves. Some of these can harm or kill if eaten by horses. Horses pastured near apple trees may overeat apples if some fall into the pasture or paddock. Under normal conditions a horse may not suffer adversely except for loose bowel movements, but if he is ridden, the combination of apples and exercise stress may cause colic. This is especially true with crab apples. A horse can develop very painful colic soon after he starts working if he has eaten many crab apples. It's much safer to make sure your horse does not have access to these.

Even more dangerous are acorns. Horses usually won't eat them unless pastures get dry in late summer or forage is short. A horse can die within twenty-four hours after eating a large quantity of acorns. An affected horse becomes depressed and weak, goes off feed, and colics. Horses should be removed in late summer or early fall from pastures containing oak trees, or fed hay if pasture is dry or short. Hungry horses should not be put into pastures with oak trees. If a horse

Chokecherry leaves.

recovers from acorn poisoning, putting him in such a pasture again is not safe because he may be addicted to acorns and seek them out.

Another danger is wilted leaves from certain trees. Red maple and wild cherry (chokecherry) are two of the most deadly; chemicals in their wilted leaves adversely affect oxygen-carrying capacity of the blood. Wilted red maple leaves can be toxic for at least thirty days. About eighteen to twenty-four hours after a horse eats the leaves, he may become depressed, the mucous membranes (gums and eyelids) become pale yellow or brown, and urine becomes dark or red.

After a frost, wilted chokecherry leaves contain cyanide. Death from eating these can occur within minutes or hours. The horse has rapid, labored breathing, red to blue mucous membranes, weakness and muscle tremors, and goes into convulsions. A mild case may recover; a more serious case can be treated, but the horse may die before your veterinarian arrives. It's best to make sure your pastures and paddocks contain no red maple or chokecherry trees within reach of horses. When riding or camping with horse in the fall, keep in mind that wilted fallen leaves of these trees can be deadly. Don't let a horse browse on trees or downed branches, nor graze underneath the trees where he might nibble fallen leaves.

Routine Fall Care

If a horse will not be ridden in winter, his shoes should be removed and his feet trimmed appropriately. Instead of taking the hoof wall down to the sole, leave a fraction of an inch of wall so the horse will not be walking on his soles and become tender. The outer edge of the wall should be well smoothed and beveled — a rounded edge is less apt to chip, crack, or break. If a horse is bare-foot on winter pasture, feet should be routinely cleaned, checked (to prevent thrush and other wet-weather problems), and retrimmed as needed. All too often feet get neglected when unshod. Hoof walls keep growing, however, and must be kept trimmed to proper length to prevent damage.

Fall deworming is important.

Fall deworming is important; winter is usually when internal parasites do the most damage and rob the horse of vital nutrients. By fall the worm eggs and larvae eaten during spring and summer have matured and are living in the digestive tract unless you have been monitoring the horses for worms (checking fecal samples) and deworming the ones that needed it and were shedding the most worm eggs.

If you get cold weather during winter, make sure one of your fall dewormings is targeted for bots. In warm climates bot flies are active through winter, and control of these parasites must be constant and on going. In cold climates, however, there are no more flies after killing frosts. The eggs laid on the horse's hair can continue to infest him after cold temperatures have killed off the adult flies, however, so any bot eggs found on the horse in the fall should be removed. Deworm the horse for bots to eliminate all the immature forms in his mouth and digestive tract.

Fall is also a good time to check a horse's teeth, especially older horses that may have trouble chewing their food adequately. Correcting dental problems in the fall (such as sharp hooks on teeth, making chewing painful) will ensure that a horse gets the most good from his winter feed and will be less likely to lose weight.

Winter Care

Winter care may be easy if your climate is mild or more involved if you must deal with sub-zero temperatures or wet freezing rain. Complexity of your winter horse chores also will depend on whether your horse is indoors or outside. Even if your horse is on vacation, some aspects of caring for him become more important during cold weather.

During winter the horse needs additional forage to create more body heat; clean unfrozen water; and some kind of shelter or windbreak. In some climates he may need blanketing if his winter hair coat is inadequate. Cold weather is not a problem if he's had a chance to grow a good winter coat; it's the wind and wet weather that can chill him.

Horses handle cold weather much better than humans do. Their natural comfort zone (energy-neutral, in which they don't need to expend extra energy to maintain normal body tem-

Horses have natural insulation.

perature) is from about fifteen to sixty degrees Fahrenheit if weather is not wet or windy. The horse's body is better adapted for creating and conserving heat than dissipating it.

Coping With Cold

As fall weather changes to winter, the horse's body undergoes a series of physiological changes, some of which began long before the first frosts. As soon as the days begin to shorten in midsummer, the horse begins to grow a new coat, denser than his summer hair. When brushed in late summer he'll shed some of his short summer hair. His metabolism begins to change, enabling him to store more fat for insulation and energy reserves. A layer of fat under the skin makes it more difficult for heat to escape from the body and protects against cold weather.

As soon as nights start getting cold, his body begins to change, even if days are still quite warm. He grows thicker hair as protection against winter cold, but if he is blanketed to prevent this extra hair growth or clipped, he won't do well outside during winter storms. Clipping makes it easier to cool out and groom a horse being ridden in winter, but don't clip a horse that must spend time outdoors. If he does have a good winter coat, don't blanket him or bring him into the barn just because of bad weather. Horses prefer being outdoors even in the coldest weather and do fine if they have some kind of windbreak or a run-in shed to get out of driving snow or rain. A horse in good condition with a good hair coat is usually better off outdoors.

Long hair traps a layer of warm body heat between skin and cold air. Tiny muscles in the skin make the hair stand erect for more insulation. Blood vessels near the skin constrict, conserving body heat by keeping the blood closer to the warm interior of the body, not allowing heat to escape from the body surface.

A normal winter hair coat is more insulating than most horse blankets. A blanket can make the horse colder because it flattens his hair coat, destroying its insulating effect. Blanketing may be necessary however, for a clipped horse, one moved north during winter without a chance to grow a heavy coat, or a horse that must stand outside in a storm without a windbreak. If a horse becomes so wet and cold he must shiver to maintain body temperature, he'll burn more calories and need extra feed or he'll lose weight. Under those conditions, he'd be better off indoors or blanketed.

A well-fed horse can manage fine at temperatures down to thirty or forty below zero Fahrenheit if there's no wind to ruffle the hair and destroy its insulating quality. The downward direction in which the hair grows — along with the oil glands that waterproof the hair and make it a bit greasy — helps keep a horse dry. The hair coat's density makes such a good overcoat that snow can form ice on the coat's outer surface without the skin becoming chilled.

A lot of moisture is needed to soak through to the skin since most of the water runs off, but once a horse does get wet, he can become chilled. A wet horse loses body heat up to twenty times faster than a dry horse because moisture flattens out the hair and eliminates the air spaces between them. Even a warm winter storm (such as rain instead of snow) can be hard on a horse if he gets soaked and then is chilled by dropping temperatures before he has a chance to dry off. If a horse gets muddy, groom him to keep the coat from becoming matted down.

Make sure horses have adequate flesh. Horses should not be too fat but need enough for an insulating layer. Most wild animals go into winter fatter than they are at other times of year; this is nature's way to protect them against the cold and to give them some reserves for energy and body heat. A layer of fat under the skin needs little energy to maintain and has few blood vessels to lose heat. Humans may frostbite toes and nose in cold weather, but horses rarely do. A horse's blunt muzzle is so richly supplied with blood that it can withstand extreme cold without freezing. Long nasal passages with bone spirals and air pouches help warm the cold air before it gets to a horse's lungs. Feet and legs withstand extreme cold and standing in snow without discomfort or damage. A horse's legs are just bone and tendons below the knees and hocks, requiring less circulation than muscles, making them less vulnerable to frostbite. The cells in bones and tendons need less blood for maintenance and also lose less heat. The horse is able to shunt most of the blood away from his feet and still have a functional foot. When the feet start to get cold, shunts open up so that the blood flows from the smallest arteries directly into the veins without having to pass through the smaller capillaries.

If he gets cold, he starts to shiver, his muscles rapidly contracting and relaxing, which quickly raises his metabolism and rate of fuel burning in the muscles. With large blocks of muscle, the horse can shiver more readily and more comfortably than a human. Most of this muscle action converts to heat, making this a very effective way to warm himself. It takes a great deal of energy, however, to shiver for a prolonged period.

Winter Riding

Give your horse longer warm-up and cooling-out time in cold weather to prevent tendon injury. Frozen ground, cold temperatures, and stiff tendons (not warmed up) can result in damage or even a bowed tendon. Remember that he must work harder traveling through snow than on bare ground. Don't work him really hard in temperatures below twenty degrees Fahrenheit. You may want to do more walking and less work at fast gaits to keep a horse from getting too hot and sweaty (which makes for longer cool-out time) and to cope with bad footing. Frozen ground increases the concussion on feet and legs, and fast work will accentuate it.

Pay attention to footing. Frozen ground can be treacherous, especially on a hillside. Ice or packed snow can be just as slippery. Some horsemen use shoes with spots of borium (tungsten carbide) welded on for more traction on ice or frozen ground. Be careful when using any type of traction device (calks, studs, borium, etc.) as these can cause extra stress to feet and legs by grabbing too well.

A barefoot horse often has better traction than one shod with regular shoes. The bare foot's sharp edges cut into the snow or slick ground a little better than a shod foot (unless shod with calks or studs) and snow doesn't ball up so badly in a bare foot. However, if snow is wet and packing, it can build up quickly in the foot and the horse is soon walking on four balls of ice, which not only is extremely slippery, but also puts great strain on the feet and legs. To prevent this condition, you may want to use snowball pads with domed centers that prevent snow buildup and ice balls. Another option is to grease the bottom of feet with butter, margarine, or petroleum jelly to create a non-stick surface on the soles.

When preparing for a ride, make sure the horse's back is clean and dry before saddling. A wet back will gall more readily than dry skin. An outdoor horse may be woolly and have mud in his coat. Make sure there is no mud or matted hair under a saddle pad. When **Packed snow can be dangerous.**

Do more walking.

bridling, an icy-cold metal bit can be unpleasant. Keep bridles in the house rather than in an unheated tack room. You can warm a cold bit by wrapping a hot, wet washcloth around it, then wrapping a hand towel on top of the washcloth to help hold in the heat and keep it dry until you bridle him.

Plan your rides early enough in the day to finish and get the horse cooled out and dry before sundown. Winter days are short and temperatures can drop quickly. If a horse is wet from sweat, he will take longer to dry than in summer. Make sure his body temperature is back to normal and his hair fluffed up and drying. If you put him away wet, with hair plastered down, he may become chilled.

Daily grooming is sometimes neglected in winter if you are not riding a horse and he is out on pasture. Keeping his coat free of mud and matted hair and cleaning his feet once a day can be very beneficial, however, and gives you a good feel of what's happening with his body condition, and skin and hoof health.

Feeding in Winter

A horse's nutrient requirements increase with cold weather; he needs more calories to generate heat to keep warm. Mature horses in good condition usually don't need grain, however, if they have good winter pasture or grass hay. A little alfalfa hay can be added during cold weather since digestion of protein creates more heat. Young horses and broodmares may need grain and/or alfalfa hay along with their pasture or grass hay to provide the extra nutrition they need. A horse being ridden in winter also will have higher requirements than the idle horse.

You want your horse carrying adequate flesh through winter without losing or gaining weight. If he gets too fat by spring, it will be harder to get him back into top shape and he will be more prone to saddle sores, cinch sores, and other rub spots under tack. Soft, movable skin over the fat is tender and more easily injured, taking longer to toughen up. A horse that loses too much weight can be equally hard to get into good summer condition because he has to gain weight as well as fitness.

A horse with a thick hair coat may look plump; you can't always tell by looking at him how fat he actually is. You should check his body condition periodically, using your fingers along his neck, withers, ribs, and hips to determine how much flesh is under all that hair. Stand beside his midsection and run your fingers under the hair against his rib cage. Doing it both directions gives a clue about how much fat covering he has. If he has a thick hair coat, face his head and push your fingers against the lay of the hair until you can easily feel the skin over his ribs, rubbing firmly back and forth over several ribs.

If you can't feel each rib individually, he may be too fat. If you feel a layer of soft tissue between the ribs and skin but can still feel each rib, he has the right amount of fat covering. If his ribs are quite prominent and there is no soft layer of tissue over them, he is too

Feel the ribs to check condition.

thin. Check him often enough that you could increase his feed before he loses this much weight.

You also can check his backbone and hips with your fingertip test. If no extra flesh exists between the skin and the bones, he is too thin. Another place to check is along the top of his neck at the base of his mane. This will be quite thick and fleshy on a fat horse. Some horses develop bulges of fat alongside the tail head when they become overweight.

In cold weather, feed more hay, not more grain. A horse can maintain heat better if you increase his hay, giving him all the hay he can eat rather than increasing his grain. Corn is not necessarily a good winter feed. It is high in energy but not very useful for heat production. Oats have more fiber and produce more body heat during digestion than an equal weight of corn.

Feed at least twice a day and make sure the larger feeding is given in the evening. Nights are colder and longer. Horses need plenty of roughage at night or they'll start chewing on fences or bedding. You can increase the hay ration another 10 percent for every ten degrees below freezing.

If a horse is cleaning up all his good hay, still looking around for more to nibble on, and is an easy keeper (one you don't want gaining extra weight), you can feed him a few pounds of a

Feed more hay in winter.

more mature grass hay in addition to his regular hay to keep him busier at night and provide the extra heat he needs in cold weather or during a wet spell. Horses are always hungrier when they are wet and cold than when weather is mild or dry.

Check all hay for moldy spots. Bales on the top layer of an uncovered stack can become moldy, as can bottom bales that draw moisture from the ground. Since winter days are short, it may be dark at feeding time and difficult to tell whether the hay is moldy. Always open your bales in the daylight to know exactly what you are feeding and sort your hay when you can see it. If you must feed hay after dark, sort it ahead of time.

Winter Water

Make sure horses have good access to water and are drinking. They drink less during cold or wet weather, but still need an adequate supply or they may become impacted. If water is quite cold or freezes and the horse isn't drinking enough, he'll eat less feed and may lose weight or be less able to keep warm. Horses will eat snow, nibbling a few bites of snow periodically while eating or grazing. A horse at pasture may get along fine if snow conditions are right for eating it easily (not hard and crusted), but there's always some risk for impaction.

If his manure becomes firm and dry instead of soft and moist, the horse is not getting adequate water. He won't eat all of his hay, though this clue may escape your notice if he's in a group and the other horses eat the hay he leaves. If he is dehydrated and not eating enough, his flanks and abdomen will draw up and he'll look gaunt.

Check the water twice daily to break ice if necessary. If horses are using a stream or pond they may be hesitant to step on ice to reach a water hole you've chopped. You may have to spread sand on the ice to give them safer footing. Water in a bucket can be warmed with a submersible bucket heater, but these are risky and can shock a horse if they don't work properly or if a horse plays with the cord. Some buckets have built-in heating elements.

Horses drink more if the water is not ice-cold. Make sure a horse has an adequate amount in the mornings, since he will drink more during the warmer daylight hours. Many horses drink less at night if the weather is cold. Horses drink most of their daily water within three hours after being fed. If you supply them with hot tap water at night (not burning hot, but fairly warm) at feeding time, it won't freeze before they drink it. In some situations, providing hot tap water twice a day is more convenient and safer than using an electrical heater in a water bucket.

Blankets and Blanketing

Most outdoor horses are better off without blankets, but a blanket can help keep a horse comfortable when trailering, during a severe winter storm, or when

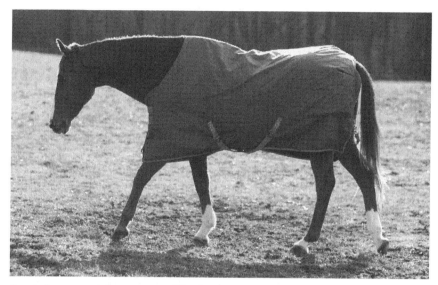

Some horses need to wear a blanket.

a horse is sick and having trouble staying warm. A clipped horse will need a blanket in cold weather.

Some synthetic blanket materials are warmer and more weather resistant than wool. Some have lightweight insulating filler material between an inner and outer shell. The outer shell is usually waterproof and windproof. Some synthetic blankets are more durable than cotton or wool and light enough to not press down on the horse's hair, enabling it to keep its insulating quality.

It can be tricky keeping a horse at the right temperature when using blankets, especially if weather is erratic. If he sweats and gets wet, he may chill later when night temperature drops and he is still wet under the blanket. Don't blanket him for turnout in the cold early morning and leave the blanket on all day if it gets warm in the afternoon. You might want a heavy blanket for cold nights and a light one for daytime.

Whatever blanket you use, make sure it fits. A blanket too large or loose may slip under his belly; a blanket too small or tight will rub. A high-withered horse may develop skin irritation or an infected sore where it rubs his withers. Sewing a band of soft cotton around the shoulder edge of the blanket reduces the rubbing. When putting on a blanket, put it well forward and slide it back into place so it won't ruffle the hair the wrong way.

Try not to use the same blanket on more than one horse; there's less risk of spreading skin problems. If your horse constantly gets his blanket muddy or dirty, use one that can be washed easily. Most blankets can be washed in cold water with soap and disinfectant, then thoroughly rinsed so there's no soap left in them.

Winter Respiratory Health

If a horse is confined in a barn during winter, he is at risk for respiratory problems. Heaves is the most common respiratory ailment in horses that are confined indoors or fed dusty hay. Heaves is characterized by chronic cough, lack of stamina, labored breathing, weight loss, lack of response to antibiotics, and sometimes a watery discharge from the nostrils. It is most common in adult horses since prolonged exposure to respiratory irritants brings on the reaction. The breathing difficulty is due to inflammation and swelling that narrow the air passages.

The main symptom, from which the term heaves is derived, is a forced effort to exhale, sometimes described as double expiration. Air is drawn in easily, but the horse has trouble pushing it out. Forcing it out requires two movements of the abdominal wall (double expiratory lift). The horse has to tense his abdominal muscles to force the air out, giving an exaggerated lift of the flank. Many horses develop an enlarged ridge of muscle along the lower edge of the abdomen from overworking these muscles.

Decreased speed and stamina may be the only symptoms of early heaves, but as the problem progresses the horse has more trouble breathing, eventually developing a large chest and potbelly because diaphragm muscles enlarge. If he has to breathe deeply, as when exercising, he coughs. The coughing spells are also brought on when eating dusty hay.

Whenever a susceptible horse is in an enclosed barn where there is dust or mold spores, his airways become hyper-reactive. The airway walls thicken (reducing their diameter), they produce excess mucus, which tends to block them, and the muscles in the airway walls contract, further constricting the airways.

Even if a horse with heaves is turned out into a non-dusty environment it may take weeks for the inflammation to disappear. If put back into the barn, even for a short time, he will relapse. A horse with this problem must be protected from dust as much as possible and fed dust-free hay or pelleted feed. Pasture is best. A horse with a respiratory problem should not be kept indoors.

Once a horse develops heaves, the only solution is a dust-free environment. For winter, an open three-sided shed with no bedding and a diet of dust-free pellets or water-soaked hay can often keep the horse from relapsing. Even a few minutes' exposure to dust in an indoor stall can start a chain of events that will cause several days of breathing difficulty. Each time the horse experiences an episode of difficult breathing he becomes a little worse. Even if a horse is kept outdoors, he may relapse if brought into the barn for just one night or even just for grooming or saddling.

If you must use hay for a dust-sensitive horse, moisten each flake completely, then drain it well before giving it to the horse. If grain is fed, give it as a mash or with molasses added to reduce dustiness. None of these efforts, however, will help if the horse is indoors and exposed to dusty straw bedding.

Winter Skin Problems

Some of the skin problems that can plague a horse in winter are ringworm, lice, and mites.

Ringworm is a skin disease caused by a fungus, and many kinds are contagious to other animals and to humans. The fungus sends out spores, which start new infections when rubbed into the skin. Brushes, tack, and other equipment used on more than one animal can spread ringworm.

After spores enter the skin, the fungal infection begins in a growing hair, causing it to break off just above the skin surface or in the outer layer of skin. Lesions appear within a week to a month as circular areas in which the hair falls out or breaks off. Sometimes thick crusts form. One type of ringworm produces small round lesions a quarter inch to an inch in diameter, eventually forming blisters that break and leave scabs. This form of ringworm causes intense itching and can be transmitted to humans.

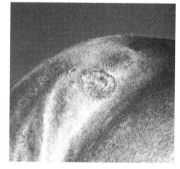

Ringworm.

Another type of ringworm (which can be spread by rats and mice as well as horses) creates lesions that appear on the forehead, face, or neck and sometimes at the root of the tail, but can spread to other parts of the body as well. The fungal growth expands from the center of each lesion outward, spreading from the edges. The lesions are gray and form crusts on their surfaces; broken off hair may protrude from the crusts. Another form of ringworm (which also affects dogs as well as horses and humans) produces small round lesions covered with tiny scales.

Incubation time for the various types of ringworm fungi can vary from as little as four days to as long as a month. If one horse in a group becomes infected, the fungus can spread to the rest, so take precautions to keep the other horses from getting it. Isolate an affected horse. Treat and disinfect saddle pads, grooming tools, and anything else that might be used on more than one horse. Treat the affected horse. Many topical medications (fungicides such as povidone iodine, chlorhexadine solution or ointment, or Captan) can be effective.

Some individuals seem more susceptible and get ringworm readily, while other individuals never do. Ringworm is most likely to appear in winter. Sunlight and heat inhibit the fungus.

Lice are also mainly a winter problem. Warmth and sunshine slow them down, and short hair does not provide a good environment for reproduction. They thrive in cold weather when hair is long.

Lice are tiny insects that spend their entire life cycle on the host. The eggs, called nits, are laid on the hairs next to the skin. Then there are three nymphal stages before the mature lice emerge to feed on the horse's skin. Lice are transferred from one horse to another by direct contact or by harness, grooming tools, blankets, saddle pads, etc. Horse lice are not the same as cattle or human lice. Lice from other animals such as cattle will not infest a horse, nor is there any danger of humans getting lice from horses. A horse can get lice only from another horse or occasionally from chickens.

There are two basic kinds that infest horses: *Hematopinus asini* (sucking lice) and *Damalinia* (Bovicola) *equi* (biting lice). Sucking lice feed on the horse's blood and in severe infestations can cause anemia due to extensive blood loss. Biting lice cause more skin irritation and itching as they feed on skin cells and secretions from oil glands in the skin. The horse may rub and bite at the affected areas, which may become hairless or raw.

You can usually see the lice if you raise the horse's mane and part the hair underneath it with your fingers. The lice will be down on the skin between the hairs. A magnifying glass makes them easy to see. The hair comes out easily where lice have been feeding. Those areas often have greasy skin and heavy dandruff.

Horses rarely suffer lice infestations at pasture during summer; lice are mainly a problem in confined horses during the short, cold days of winter. Several sprays and dusts can help eliminate lice. If weather is cold, use a dust rather than a spray so the horse won't become chilled. Follow label directions and treat the horse in an area where there's no risk for contaminating feed or feeding areas. A second treatment two weeks later is needed to kill lice that hatch after the first treatment (the eggs may not have been killed). Brushes, blankets, or tack used on the infested horse also should be treated before being used again.

Mites are tiny parasites that sometimes bother horses, causing skin inflammation (dermatitis), dandruff and hair loss, tiny pustules, or bloody crusts. One type of harvest mite or grain mite infests horses accidentally but can transmit diseases. The natural hosts for these mites are small rodents. The larvae live in grain and hay, but cause dermatitis in animals grazing infested pastures or eating newly harvested grain. The horse's face and lips can become itchy and scaly.

Another type of mite infests hair follicles, causing mange. Invasion of hair follicles and oil glands leads to chronic inflammation, loss of hair, and sometimes pustules. Some mange mites live deep in the skin, creating nodules that feel like birdshot. Another mite causes a severe, itching dermatitis called sarcoptic mange, barn itch, or red mange. Affected areas of skin (usually on the neck) develop red elevated areas and may be injured by the horse's constant rubbing and biting. Thick brown scabs form over the raw surfaces. These mites are active during cold, wet weather. The adults lay eggs in tunnels they've made in the skin, then the hatching nymphs burrow into the skin. Mites can be spread from horse to horse by direct contact or by bedding, saddle pads, grooming tools, etc.

Other kinds of mites puncture the skin to feed on lymph fluid. The skin weeps and forms crusts that tend to spread, as the mites are most active around the edges. The large thick crusts are found at the base of the mane and root of the tail, and on hairless areas such as the udder. Leg mange is caused by a mite that lives in the long hair on the lower legs in winter, causing severe irritation and itchiness. The horse stomps his feet and rubs the backs of his hind pasterns on anything available and may resent having his feet handled. Eventually the skin may become swollen, scabby, cracked, and greasy.

Your veterinarian should examine any itchy rashes on a horse and take skin scrapings to observe under a microscope for diagnosis. Mites can be eliminated with several types of sprays and insecticides. The affected horses should be isolated so the problem won't spread.

Seasonal Control of Internal Parasites

All horses harbor internal parasites; there is still no practical way to eliminate every type of parasite completely and permanently or keep a horse from becoming reinfested. The conscientious horse owner tries to control parasites to keep them down to a level where they can't interfere with health or proper nutrition.

Horses and parasites evolved together; the parasite can't complete its life cycle without the horse. Early on, these tiny organisms were free-living creatures, finding their own food, but somewhere along the way they found that another animal could do this for them. The tapeworm, for instance, became so good at parasitism that it no longer has a digestive system of its own. The various types of parasites adapted to the internal environment of the host animal. Most are species specific; horse parasites can only survive in horses, cattle parasites in cattle, and so on. If a cow eats the larvae of a horse parasite or a horse eats a cow parasite, the life cycle is broken; the parasite cannot mature.

Horses have also adapted to living with parasites. The young horse builds immunity to some types of worms after repeated infestations. If he did not develop this resistance, he would not be able to handle the stress of heavy infestations; the worms would kill him. The immune system, which fights bacterial and viral infections, can produce a specific immune response against some parasites; the worms release antigens in the bloodstream and body tissues. These antigens trigger the horse's body to produce immunity against the

Know which dewormers to use.

289

invader. Later, when more of those worms come along, the horse's immune system recognizes the intruders and launches a counterattack, reducing both the egg-laying capacity of the female worms and the fertility of the males.

Young horses build this type of resistance to ascarids (roundworms) to keep the larvae from maturing. Thus as the older ascarids die and fewer larvae are produced, the ascarid population in the horse is reduced to a less harmful level. This is why adult horses rarely carry large infestations of ascarids; roundworms are usually a problem only in young horses that have not yet developed resistance. Bloodworms can be a serious problem, however, since horses don't seem to be able to build an effective defense against them.

The domestic horse in confinement is continually exposed to his own manure. In stalls or small pastures horses pick up worm eggs from manure or larvae that have hatched and crawled onto plants. Horses graze the same places and become heavily infested unless they are continually dewormed or manure is picked up daily. In confinement, the parasite population quickly builds to such high levels that no horse can escape infestation without control measures.

Most parasites thrive in a warm, moist environment; spring is the season when horses are likely to become infested. The larvae swarm over green plants, waiting to be eaten. Sunlight, heat, and severe cold can destroy larvae, but the eggs are quite hardy. Any pastures that have been grazed by horses can be a source of infestation, but proper pasture management and a good parasite control program can minimize risk.

Manure control is also important in stalls and paddocks, so horses are not constantly exposed to parasite eggs if they eat hay on the ground or nibble manure (as many horses do). Deworming the horses at appropriate intervals to eliminate egg-laying adult worms or to kill the larvae before they mature can prevent a build-up of worm eggs or larvae in the horse's environment. Deworming with drugs like ivermectin and moxidectin can help protect a horse from damage; they kill the parasites wherever they are in the body. Many of the other deworming drugs primarily kill parasites in the gut and have no effect on the immature stages migrating through other tissues.

Knowing each parasite's life cycle and when to hit it when it is most vulnerable can control these pests, along with monitoring parasite levels with fecal samples.

Deworming Drugs

Some of the drugs that are effective against bloodworms and roundworms invite worm resistance if used a lot, especially if doses are not quite adequate to kill all the worms in the digestive tract. The worms that survive are the most resistant and their offspring are not as susceptible to that drug in the future. The benzimidazole dewormers are safe and effective drugs but promote worm resistance after a time. Cambendazole, oxibendazole, fenbendazole, mebendazole, and thiabendazole can be used in a parasite control program if the worms on your farm have not yet developed resistance to them. These drugs are effective against bloodworms, roundworms, and pinworms but not bots. When treating for bots, use dichlorvos (or some other organophosphate) or ivermectin.

The best control for bots is simply to remove the eggs and treat the horses with an appropriate deworming drug at the times of year—in your region and seasons—to kill the larvae. Consult your veterinarian to help you make the right decisions for treatment and use of the proper drugs. Even though there haven't been any drug resistance issues with bots yet, we commonly see resistance problems with other internal parasites. So even if you are using a product that hasn't had any resistance problems in bots, it may promote resistance in other parasites. Work with your veterinarian to make sure you are using the appropriate products for your region, your horse, and the parasites you are targeting. Control of parasites is a broad issue; don't just look at one species and ignore the others.

To prevent worm resistance, make sure dewormers are given in adequate dosage. This is one reason paste applications are better than putting dewormer in feed. Unless a horse eats the medication readily with his grain, he may only get a partial dose, especially if he tends to sort out the dewormer and just eat the grain. Using molasses to mix a dewormer with grain can help solve this problem (it helps stick the medication to the grain and also tends to disguise any strange taste). But some horses refuse medicated grain even when it is disguised. When using a paste you have a better idea if the horse is actually getting the whole dose.

When estimating dosage for each horse, always try to overdose slightly rather than underdose. Dewormers are safe even in very large overdoses (except for the new dewormer Quest®, which is more dose-sensitive). A partial dose will do more harm than good, since it won't kill as many worms and more will survive to become resistant.

To combat drug resistance, most horsemen rotate classes of drugs in their deworming program. If the benzimidazole drugs are alternated with an unrelated drug such as febantel, pyrantel, or ivermectin, worm resistance won't become a problem as quickly.

Ivermectin is one of the most effective deworming drugs because it kills bots as well as bloodworms, roundworms, and pinworms. It is not harmful to horses and humans and is an excellent drug to use in rotation. It belongs to the avermectin family of dewormers (which includes its newer cousins moxidectin and doramectin). These dewormers have the advantage of killing most parasites in the larval stage anywhere in the body as well as the adults in the digestive tract. Ivermectin also kills any skin parasites that suck blood, such as ticks, lice, and mites. Ivermectin permeates the horse's tissues, eventually reaching the skin cells, where in sufficient concentration it is toxic to adult forms of most external parasites that feed there.

Another option for control of roundworms and bloodworms is pyrantel tartrate given daily in the horse's grain. For best results, a horse should first be dewormed with ivermectin to clean out all stages of the worms. Then the horse can receive a daily dose of pyrantel tartrate to keep him free of them. This drug is not effective against bots, however, and seasonal treatment with ivermectin or another boticide will still be needed.

Parasite control is a continual battle; you need to know which worms to target and when. Your best defense against these robbers is a well-planned strategy developed with advice from your equine veterinarian. If treatments are needed, they should be timed to hit each species at the most vulnerable stage in its life cycle. This can vary depending on climate and geographic region. Strategic deworming, coupled with good pasture management, can keep parasites to a harmless low level. Usually only 1 to 5 percent of the actual worm population (of most species) is inside the horse; most of the eggs and larvae are in the pasture, and many of them can live a long time. Where horses are closely confined, picking up manure twice a week can greatly reduce the level of reinfestation. Your veterinarian can help you plan a deworming program to follow through the year.

Index

Page numbers in italics refer to photos.

oats, 176, 177–78, *178*
oils. *See* fats
oilseed meals, 179
older horses, 109; catching, 74; Cushing's syndrome in, 243; skin cancer in, 261; supplements for, 154, 183, 184–85, *185*; teeth health in, 156, 181, 184, 278; vitamin C for, 154; young horses learning from, 77
Onchocerca cervicalis, 268

paddocks: access to, 126; feeders, 99–100, *100*; fencing, 88; manure management in, 136; pasture purpose compared with, 91; summer care and, 253; unhealthy edibles during fall in, 277, *277*
pain relievers, 236
parasites: bot, 266, 291, 292; fall care of, 278, *278*; filarid worm, 268; internal, control of, 289–92; lice, 287–88; manure management and, 96, 133–34, 135, 290, 292; mites, 288–89; pasture management and, 95, 96; skin sores due to, 267–68; spring care and, 241–42; summer external, 263–67; sunlight and, 107
pasture: fencing, 88, 132–33; foot health and, 227; forages and dietary needs, 166–67; grass, 91–94, 227, *245*, 245–46; harrowing, 95, 96, *96*; heaves and, 262–63; legumes, 92, 93–94, 167; management, *91*, 91–97, *92*, *94*, *96*; manure management in, 95–96, *96*; paddock purpose compared with, 91; parasites in, 292; rotating, 95; safety, 96–97; soil, *92*, 92–93, 245; spring grasses in, *245*, 245–46; summer care and, 253; unhealthy edibles during fall in, 277, *277*; waterers, *98*, 98–99; weeds, 94, *94*
pawing habit, 40–41
pelleted feeds, *180*, 180–82; monensin poisoning and, 192

personal space, protecting, 50, 61–62, *74*, 75–76
pests: control of animal, 127–30; insect, and treatments, 263–68; rodent control and, 127–30, *128*, *129*
pheromones, 17
phone, in barn, 105, 126
physical evolution, 9–13
plants: controlling pasture weeds, 94, *94*; fall, causing issues, 277, *277*; fire prevention and, 124; poisoning from, 18, 79, 171, 174, 277, *277*
pneumonia: fire-related lung damage and, 127; lying down excessively and, 17
poisons/poisoning, 37, 97, 158, 245; acorn, 277; blister beetle, 170; cheap hay and, 170–71; food, 174, 190–92; from forage plants, 18, 79, 171, 174, 277, *277*; monensin, 192; nitrate, 174; rodents and, 129–30; selenium, 162, 225; zinc, 163
potassium, 159
pregnancy: grains for, 178; protein and, 146, *147*, 147–48; supplements during, 184–85
pressure points, 70–71
prey animal instincts, 19–21, *20*
probiotics, 186
problem behaviors, handling, 72–78
protein, 137; amino acids and, 145–46; caution with, 146; in corn, 178; hoof health and, 228; pregnant and lactating mares needs for, 146, *147*, 147–48; requirements, 144–46; supplements, 182, 185; weanlings needs for, 148
psychology and emotions: body language of horse relation to, *54*, 54–56, *55*; confinement impacts on, 28–48; endorphins role in, 29, 38–39, 42, 67, 70–71; evolution of, 19–22; excessive thirst and urination relation to, 43; expectations and familiarity

Acknowledgments

I OWE A LARGE DEBT of gratitude to a great number of people for helping make this book possible — especially my family, who often helped "fill in" for me on some of my other duties as I wrote it. I also want to thank the many horse people I've know during my lifetime, who helped expand my knowledge and understanding of horses. I must also thank the various editors of numerous horse magazines who published my articles during the past sixty years and the publishers of some of my earlier books, including *A Horse in Your Life: A Guide for the New Owner, Your Horse and You; Horses: Their Breeding, Care and Training; The Wild Horse Controversy; Storey's Guide to Raising Horses, 3rd Edition; Storey's Guide to Training Horses, 3rd Edition; The Horse Conformation Handbook; Stable Smarts; Understanding Equine Hoof Care; Good Horse, Bad Habits; Horse Tales: True Stories from an Idaho Ranch*; and several books on cattle care. Some of the information in those books and articles reappears here.

I also gleaned additional information for this book from a number of good writers whose work appeared in such publications as *Anvil, Chronicle of the Horse, Equine Athlete, Equus, Farm & Ranch, Flying Changes, Hoofbeats, Horse Illustrated, Horseplay, Horse & Rider, Journal of the American Veterinary Medical Association, Mid-Atlantic Thoroughbred, Southern Horseman, Thoroughbred Times,* and *Western Horseman.*

I also thank the many professors, researchers, veterinarians, and other professionals that I have interviewed over the past forty years to glean information for the many articles I have written.

Photo Credits

Chapter 1
Paula da Silva: p. 15; Anne M. Eberhardt: 14, 16, 17, 19; Heather Smith Thomas: 11, 20.

Chapter 2
Anne M. Eberhardt: 23, 24, 30, 35, 44, 47; Heather Smith Thomas: 25, 26, 28, 31, 32, 35, 36, 38, 39.

Chapter 3
Anne M. Eberhardt: 58; Dan Johnson, 69; Heather Smith Thomas: 51, 54, 55, 56, 61, 64, 68, 71, 73, 74, 76, 78; Cheryl Manista: 55; *The Horse* magazine: 49, 59.

Chapter 4
Stephanie Church/*The Horse*: 106, 109, 125; Anne M. Eberhardt: 80, 83, 90, 92, 94, 96, 98, 100, 101, 113, 114, 117, 120, 124, 131, 132, 134; Heather Smith Thomas: 80, 81, 82, 84, 86, 87, 88, 89, 91, 99, 106, 107, 120, 128, 129.

Chapter 5
Stephanie Church/*The Horse*:, 180; Anne M. Eberhardt: 165, 169, 173, 175, 178, 179, 182, 183; Heather Smith Thomas: 137, 147, 157, 170, 172, 185, 188, 189.

Chapter 6
Anne M. Eberhardt: 198, 199, 200, 201, 205, 206, 214, 215, 218, 222, 224, 227, 232, 239; Heather Smith Thomas: 201, 208, 222, 225; *The Horse*: 203.

Chapter 7
Anne M. Eberhardt: 245 (bottom), 246, 249, 255, 256, 259 (top), 266, 269, 278, 279, 281, 282, 283, 285, 289; Heather Smith Thomas: 243, 244, 245 (top), 248, 253, 259 (bottom), 262, 264, 270, 272, 275, 277, 281, 287.

About the Author

HEATHER SMITH THOMAS grew up on a cattle ranch near Salmon, Idaho, and while still in high school started writing about horses and cattle. She wrote articles to help pay her way through college at the University of Puget Sound. She has raised and trained horses for sixty years and has been writing about them nearly that long, selling more than 14,000 stories and articles to horse and livestock publications. Most of her magazine articles deal with health care, breeding, training, horse behavior/handling, or veterinary topics (horses and cattle).

Thomas writes regularly for more than thirty farm and livestock publications and about twenty-five horse publications, including *EQUUS*, *The Horse*, *Stable Management*, *Equine Chronicle*, *California Thoroughbred*, *Working Horse*, *Saddle & Bridle*, *Eclectic Horseman*, *Louisiana Horse*, *Florida Horse*, *New Mexico Horse Breeder*, *Polo*, *Central States Horseman*, *USDF Connection*, and others.

She has published twenty-three books, including *A Horse in Your Life: A Guide for the New Owner*; *Your Horse and You*; *Horses: Their Breeding, Care and Training*; *The Wild Horse Controversy*; *Storey's Guide to Raising Horses*; *Storey's Guide to Training Horses*; *The Horse Conformation Handbook*; *Stable Smarts*; *Understanding Equine Hoof Care*; *Good Horse, Bad Habits*; and *Horse Tales: True Stories from an Idaho Ranch*.

Thomas also wrote *Beyond the Flames: A Family Touched by Fire* about her daughter's severe burn injury, sustained fighting a range fire, and valiant fight for life; the long road to recovery; and the effect the experience has had on their family.

Thomas and her husband continue to raise beef cattle and use horses on their Sky Range Ranch in the mountains of eastern Idaho. Their daughter Andrea Daine lives nearby on the ranch and helps with the cattle care, horses, haying, irrigating, etc., and their son Michael and his wife, Carolyn, own and operate the upper part of the ranch.